Anonymous

Chicago's First Half Century

1833-1883

Anonymous

Chicago's First Half Century
1833-1883

ISBN/EAN: 9783744724043

Printed in Europe, USA, Canada, Australia, Japan

Cover: Foto ©ninafisch / pixelio.de

More available books at **www.hansebooks.com**

1833. 1883.

CHICAGO'S

FIRST HALF CENTURY.

THE CITY AS IT WAS FIFTY YEARS AGO, AND AS IT IS TO-DAY.

HE TRADE, COMMERCE, MANUFACTORIES, RAILROADS, BANKS, WHOLESALE AND RETAIL HOUSES, THEATERS, HOTELS, CHURCHES, AND SCHOOLS.

CHICAGO:
THE INTER OCEAN PUBLISHING COMPANY.

W. P. DUNN & CO., PRINTERS.
1883.

CONTENTS.

DISPLAY ADVERTISEMENTS.

A CITY OF SURPRISES.

Chicago has ever been filled with surprises. Discovered by a Roman Catholic priest, settled by a San Domingo negro, sold to a Frenchman and for years with no other hope than that of a French settlement; afterward becoming subject to the Old Dominion and part of a slave State, and then a frontier post in Hoosierdom, what was to be expected of the place? Certainly not that it should be satisfied with the hum-drum, easy-going existence of the towns which had only ordinary causes for existence.

It was a hybrid of the worst order, in which the crosses were so complicated as to baffle all attempts of the genealogist to figure out a future.

There was in her coming into existence nothing but surprising paradoxes, and these gave reason to look for surprises all through her life. So far the promise has been fulfilled and the man who would attempt to picture the future of this Garden City, the metropolis of the Northwest, must have a graphic as well as a prophetic pen and indulge in even wilder speculations than the scribbler who lately sought to show that New York must eventually become the metropolis of the world.

What would be the wildest exaggeration in outlining a future for other cities is but a mild form of prophecy concerning this city of surprises. But it is not the purpose here to make an attempt at such prophecy and fail. Rather is it the aim to record a few of the surprises of the past and show wherein she has achieved distinction.

Not a generation of her sons and daughters but have had some distinguishing event which stands out as a bold landmark indicating the line of march through trials to success.

NOT A PROMISING FOUNDATION.

Though but a marshy and dreary slough in which it seemed all attempts at building a city would sink out of sight, Chicago has been an important point from time immemorial. It is not the new place that some of its historians would make it. It has a history that ante-dates that of older cities in the East.

The Indian trails that centered here long before the white man came to the shores of Lake Michigan are evidence that Chicago the Divine City and home of the Thunder God, was a Mecca for the wandering tribes of the West, just as it now is for all the nations of the civilized world.

How far back this history reaches, it would be idle to conjecture, but Father Jacques Marquette found an Indian village at the mouth of the Chicago River when he returned this way from a visit to the Illinois Indians along the Mississippi River in December, 1674, and was only prevented saying the first mass on the Feast of the Conception because of the bad weather encountered.

Father Marquette was the first white man to visit the place and leave a written account as proof of his enterprise. He claimed the

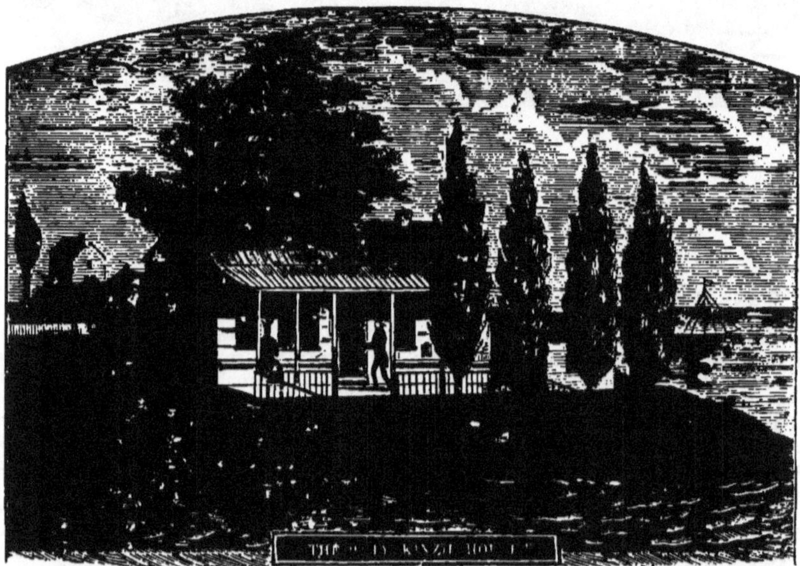

place for the Catholic Church and then returned to Mackinaw and passed to the eternal shores beyond.

THE FIRST SURPRISE.

The first surprise in the history of Chicago was in its settlement. It has been said that the first white settler was a negro. This was Jean Baptise Point au Sable, who came from San Domingo in 1796, and staked his claim on the site of the present business center, rearing his rude hut in the neighborhood of Dearborn and Water streets. This first "white settler" was, however, ambitious to become an Indian chief, notwithstanding his negro blood, and tried to ingratiate himself into the affections of the Indians; but, meeting with poor success, he removed to Peoria, where he died, and with him the hope of planting a San Domingo colony on the banks of the Chicago River.

Then came a Frenchman, Le Mai, a trader, who "jumped" the negro settler's claim, and took possession of his cabin, and, after several years' residence, sold his interest in Chicago to John Kinzie, who was then the agent of Astor's American Fur Company. The cabin was enlarged and improved, and in 1804 became the home of Mr. Kinzie and the first house in Chicago.

The cut given on this page represents the old Kinzie house as it looked in the early days.

From the time of Marquette's visit until 1804 Chicago was essentially French, and had France succeeded in holding the western territory this would have been the Paris of America, with the General Assembly here, composed of delegates from Halifax, Quebec, Montreal, St. Louis, New Orleans, and the Pacific States.

By the treaty between Great Britain and France in 1763, the Canadas were ceded to the former power, and our relations to the two countries were reversed.

THE FIRST REAL ESTATE TRANSFER.

And by the treaty of General Anthony Wayne with the Indians in 1795 the Indians ceded to the United States: "One piece of land six miles square at the mouth of the Chicago River, emptying into the southwest end of Lake Michigan where a fort formerly stood." It is supposed that an old French fort had been built here soon after Marquette's first visit by early French explorers. This transaction between General Wayne and the Indians was the first real estate transfer on record in Chicago. Under the conquest of General George Rogers Clark in the West the whole Chicago country was claimed by Virginia, and in 1788 was created the county of Illinois, embracing the territory of the whole State. Then it was that Chicago belonged to the Old Dominion, and had there been no more surprises in after years there probably would never have been an Emancipation proclamation issued by the rail-splitter President from the prairies of Illinois; and the city which sent so many brave men and gave so much money to put down the rebellion might have been raising slaves instead of helping along to the Canadian shores, by means of the underground railroad, those poor blacks who had escaped from their masters in the South.

IN HOOSIERDOM.

In 1800 the Territory of Indiana was organized, and Illinois was a county of that Territory, placing Chicago in Hoosierdom, but the General Government kindly rescued us from that perilous situation in 1809 by creating Illinois County into a Territory, and then in 1818 into a State. It was, however, under the Hoosier administration in 1804, that Fort Chicago was built, on the south branch of the river, near where Rush street bridge now crosses.

Mr. Kinzie came with the soldiers and began trading with the Indians for furs. Chicago was then a trading post, and was prosperous for eight years. But when the war with Great Britain broke out English emissaries used their influence with the Indians to make them hostile to the American trading posts, and Aug. 15 occurred the great massacre in which fifty-five of the seventy persons at the post were foully murdered by the Pottawatomies after the fort had been evacuated.

In 1817 the fort was rebuilt, and took the name of Fort Dearborn, after General Henry Dearborn, a conspicuous officer in the American Revolution and afterward Secretary of War. The fort was built by the United States Government, and garrisoned with about fifty men. Its location was that occupied by the well-known wholesale grocery house of W. M. Hoyt & Co., at the corner of Michigan avenue and River street.

A FITTING MEMORIAL.

Mr. Hoyt two years ago placed a marble tablet in the wall of his building as a fitting memorial of old Fort Dearborn, which had stood so long in the self-same place. For twenty years the fort was occupied by United States troops, and abandoned in 1837, when most of the Indians had left the country. It stood, however, until 1856, when it gave place to business houses. From the time of the rebuilding of the fort to 1832 Chicago was but a small village, containing only a few huts and not more than one hundred inhabitants. The people on the frontier lived in daily fear of their lives and were ever ready to rush to the fort for protection.

The first point chosen as adapted for a village when settlers began to arrive from the East was at the junction of the north and south branches of the river, on the West Side, and this was called Wolf's Point. There were but few buildings between the point and the garrison on the South Side. The Miller House stood on the point of land between the North Branch and the main channel. It was built of logs, partly sided, and was built by Samuel Miller, who lived there

THE OLD BLOCK-HOUSE.

with his family and his brother, John Miller. A little above its mouth, on the North Branch, was a log bridge, which gave access from that quarter to the business of the agency, but the center of attraction was at Wolf's Point, opposite the Miller House. Here was another tavern, the public house par excellence of Chicago, which served the purpose of all other public buildings combined. This was the tavern kept by Elijah Wentworth. The building was partly log and partly frame, and stood just north of Lake street bridge. North of this tavern was Father Walker's Methodist School-House. It was a log hut, and was used for a school-house. It was the meeting-house of the town. Mr. Wentworth's tavern was the house where distinguished visitors stopped, and was the headquarters of General Scott when he came to Chicago with the troops for the Black Hawk war in 1832.

RAT CASTLE.

It is said by some historians that it was known as "Rat Castle," in contrast with its rival on the North Side, "Cobweb Castle." Over on the North Side were also the log cabins of James Kinzie, Alexander Robinson, and Billy Caldwell, principal chief of the Pottawatomie Indians; the storehouse of Robert A. Kinzie, son of John Kinzie, who had succeeded his father in the Indian trade. Across the South Branch, on the east side, resided Mark Beaubien, the old fiddler, who died two years ago, who also kept a tavern, which in 1831 had risen to a two-story dwelling, with green painted blinds to the windows, and it went by the name of the Sauganash Hotel—the Indian name of Billy Caldwell—and so called in honor of that distinguished chief, because he was one of the prominent residents of Chicago. This house stood at the southeast corner of Lake and Market streets.

During the winter of 1831-32 the inhabitants mostly occupied the garrison. There were no mail routes, post routes, nor post-offices in this part of the country and the only means the inhabitants had of knowing anything of the world was by sending a half-breed Indian once in two weeks to Niles, in Michigan, to procure papers.

Among the new settlers in this year of 1831 were George W. Dole, R. A. Kinzie, F. W. Peck, Dr. Harmon, Mark Beaubien, and Russell E. Heacock. During the season, besides the vessel which carried away the soldiers of the garrison, there were two regular arrivals, the "Telegraph," from Ashtabula, Ohio, and the "Marengo," from Detroit, Mich.

FIDDLER AND FERRYMAN.

Mark Beaubien is not only credited with being a first-class landlord and a jolly fiddler, who played for all the dances gotten up in the frontier town, but he is also spoken of as the first ferryman in Chicago. In the year 1831 travel through Chicago became so great that Mark saw that it would pay to have a ferry for this class of travelers. He therefore obtained permission to establish a ferry at the forks, or rather two ferries, one to cross each branch of the river. For the privilege of controlling this piece of public works, he agreed to transport all citizens of Cook County free, if allowed to charge non-residents. He did a good work for the public and at the same time earned a good many honest dollars from those who were going through from the East to points farther West. The first ferryboat was a scow, which cost $46. The bridge spoken of above must have been a very rude structure, if it existed at all. Early settlers are not agreed upon this.

Clark street was the principal highway from north to south. During excessive rains it was impassable in low places, but the County Board had no money for repairs. The first public money was devoted to building a pound for stray cattle, hogs, and horses. This pound cost $12, and was simply a strong pen. But the roads needed to be improved, and Mr. Williams, President of the Board, negotiated a loan of $60, himself becoming personally responsible for the payment of the debt. This was applied to the improvement of Clark street, and thus the public credit and improvement in Chicago began.

CHICAGO VILLAGE.

HOW IT WAS INCORPORATED.

But as yet Chicago was only a settlement with only the county organization for a government. In1833 the village was incorporated and there were many improvements. It became a place of considerable importance and attracted the great body of immigrants who came West in that year. The Indian lands were to be sold and Chicago started ont with a boom. The inns were crowded, and if the traveler could but secure a place on the floor to sleep, he considered himself fortunate. During the summer 160 houses were built and the number of stores was increased from five or six to twenty-five. Among the new buildings was the Green Tree Tavern, the first structure ever built in the place, especially as a public house. While the old Kinzie house and several other houses had been open to travelers, there had never been a building put up for that purpose until the Green Tree, in 1833.

The United States Government began to pay some attention to the growing town on the lake shore and the harbor was improved at an expense of $25,000. The channel of the river was straightened, widened, and deepened. The sand-bar which was at the mouth and turned the river down the shore from Water street to Madison before emptying into the lake was cut through, and vessels were able to enter and pass up to the forks. The mail arrived semi-weekly and departed for Galena, Springfield, Alton, and St. Louis.

INCORPORATED CHICAGO.

But of all the events of that year the chief was the incorporation of the town of Chicago. A public meeting was called at the Sauganash Hotel Aug. 5, 1833, to take steps toward incorporating a town. There were thirteen citizens present, and those voting for the incorporation were John S. C. Hogan, C. A. Ballard, G. W. Snow, R. J. Hamilton, J. T. Temple, John Wright, G. W. Dole, Hiram Pearsons, Alanson Sweet, E. S. Kimberly, T. I. V. Owen, and Mark Beaubien. Russell E. Heacock, whose residence was out of all probable corporate limits, was the only one to vote against it. The first election for Town Trustees was held Aug. 10 from 11 o'clock until 1. The voters on this occasion were: E. S. Kimberly, I. B. Beaubien, Mark Beaubien, T. I. V. Owen,

Wm. Ninson, Hiram Pearsons, Philo Carpenter, George Chapman, John Wright, John T. Temple, Mathias Smith, David Carrar, James Kinzie, Charles Taylor, John S. C. Hogan, Eli A. Rider, Dexter I. Hapgood, Geo. W. Snow, Medore B. Beaubien, Gholson Kercheval, Geo. W. Dole, R. J. Hamilton, Stephen F. Gale, Enoch Darling, W. H. Adams, C. A. Ballard, John Watkins, James Gilbert—28.

Of those who participated in the proceedings of this meeting only the following are alive to-day: Medore Beaubien, who now resides at Silver Lake, Kan.; Philo Carpenter, who resides on West Washington street; Stephen F. Gale, who resides at 45 South Peoria street, and John Watkins, who resides at Joliet.

The following were elected Trustees: T. I. V. Owen, George W. Dole, M. D. Beaubien, John Miller, and E. S. Kimberly.

THE FIRST CITY LIMITS.

The first meeting was held Aug. 12, and Colonel Owen chosen President. The boundaries of the village were: Commencing at the intersection of Jackson and Jefferson streets, thence north on Jefferson to Ohio street, thence east on Ohio street to the lake, thence south along the lake to the middle of the river, thence up to State street, thence South along State to Jackson street, thence west to the place of beginning, comprising about seven-eighths of a mile square. The jog made from the mouth of the river to State street was because of the military reservation there. This was the incorporated village of Chicago.

But during this time the village of Chicago was fast growing in population, importance and fame, and when in 1837 we find it with a population of over 4,000 people, the citizens thought it time they should keep pace with the surprising growth and have the city chartered. In 1833 the population had been 200, and in 1836 it had increased to 3,820 The harbor was in process of improvement, the Illinois and Michigan Canal had been begun, land speculators were buying up the land, and there was plenty of capital in Chicago.

On Oct. 26, 1836, the Town Board took the necessary steps to secure a charter for the city of Chicago. A public meeting was held Nov. 25, and E. B. Williams, as President, appointed J. D. Caton, Ebenezer Peck, T. W. Smith, W. B. Ogden and Nathan Bolles delegates to draw up a charter for presentation. This charter was presented to the board Dec. 9, was finally adopted, and, March 4, 1837, the Legislature passed the bill approving of the charter.

FIRST ELECTION.

The first election held under the charter was May 2, 1837, and two tickets were in the field. The Whig ticket, anti-caucus candidates, was headed by John H. Kinzie for Mayor, Alvin Calhoun for High Constable, and for Aldermen Charles L. Harmon and Giles Spring from the First Ward; George W. Dole and Thomas Brock from the Second Ward; Alex. Logan and John C. Hugunin from the Fourth Ward, and John B. F. Russell and Nelson R. Norton from the Sixth Ward. The Democratic ticket was headed by William B. Ogden for Mayor; John Shrigley, High Constable; and for Aldermen, J. C. Goodhue and F. C. Sherman, First Ward; Peter Bolles and John S. C. Hogan, Second Ward; John Dean Caton, Third Ward; Asahel Pierce and Frank H. Taylor, Fourth Ward; Bernard Ward, Fifth Ward; Samuel Jackson and Hiram Pearsons, Sixth Ward.

The polling places were: First Ward, "Eagle," No. 10 Dearborn street; Second Ward, Lincoln Coffee House; Third Ward, Charles Taylor's house on Canal street; Fourth Ward, Chicago Hotel, northeast corner of Canal and Lake streets; Fifth Ward, canal office, North Water street; Sixth Ward, Franklin House, on North Water street.

The judges of this first election were: First Ward, Wilson McClintock, E. H. Hadduch,

THE GREEN TREE TAVERN.

and F. C. Sherman; Second, Alex Loyd, P. F. W. Peck, and George Dole; Third, Ashbel Steele, Charles Taylor, and George Vardon; Fourth, David Cox, J. C. Hugunin, and F. A. Howe; Fifth, Joel Manning, Patrick Murphy, and Bernsley Huntoon; Sixth, Gholson Kercheval, J. H. Kinzie, and E. S. Kimberley.

The total vote was 709, with 408 on the South Side, 97 on the West, and 204 on the North.

DEMOCRATIC RULE.

The Democratic ticket was elected, and W. B. Ogden became the first Mayor of Chicago. Mr. Ogden was born in Walton, N. Y., in 1805, and in 1834 was a member of the New York Legislature. In June, 1835, he came to Chicago. In the election Mr. Ogden received 469 votes, and Mr. Kinzie 237.

It will be noticed here that Chicago, in becoming a city, started out under Democratic management, and its politics have been uncertain ever since, except when the Republicans were sure they were to be beaten. The First and Second Wards were in the South Division, the Third and Fourth in the West Division, and the Fifth and Sixth in the North Division.

Francis H. Taylor, who was elected Alderman from the Fourth Ward, is still living in Chicago, and says of his election that it was by voting for himself. His opponent, Logan, was a man who was not very popular in the ward, and the vote was a tie. Logan gallantly voted for Taylor, but the latter gentleman says he considered it better to forget courtesy than to lose the election, and at the urgent solicitation of his friends he voted for himself, thus carrying the election.

The Hon. John Wentworth was in Chicago at that first election and has been a voter in the First Ward ever since. Few elections have passed without him at the polls. In those early days Long John was a Democrat and editor of the Democratic paper.

At this time he had succeeded Mr. Calhoun as editor of the Chicago *Democrat*, and after the election he was appointed Corporation Printer, a position which he held for nearly twenty-five years. He made speeches at that election and worked just as hard for Mr. Ogden and the Democrats as he has in late years worked for the Republicans.

THE PANIC.

Chicago had now become so important a place that speculators were busy building it up to great dimensions on paper, and town lots were staked off all over the prairies. The prices were high and everything was going off with a boom, but in 1837 came another surprise that taught Chicago people that speculation could not be depended upon altogether. The rapid rise in the value of real estate had crazed everybody and few could resist the temptation to dabble in real estate. All classes of people abandoned their usual avocations to devote their time and energy and capital to speculation. This wild spirit found its way into the halls of legislation and controlled the policy of States as it had done that of individuals. It was under the influence of this spirit that those stupendous schemes of internal improvement originated in many new States which led to evils of debt, taxation, and disgrace. Confidence and credit, too long abused, refused longer to lend their aid. The unfortunate victims of the delusion were suddenly awakened from their dream of wealth to the certainty of almost universal bankruptcy and ruin. Thousands, suddenly called upon to investigate the condition of their affairs, found themselves hopelessly involved, and their real estate depreciated in value until it would not sell at any price.

CHICAGO'S FIRST CALAMITY.

To Chicago was this especially calamitous. It was a season of mourning and desolation, and the city with its new charter starting under such fair promises was doomed to disappointment at the beginning. There had been uninterrupted prosperity until now, and this seemed ruin. This was the period in her annals known and remembered as that of protested notes. But in this first calamity Chicago men showed of what metal they were made, and gave an exhibition of that pluck and energy which carried them through the greatest calamity that ever befell a city, in later years.

They returned to their old avocations and began life anew. The consequence was that things began to brighten until 1840, when all was clear again, and Chicago in smooth sailing waters.

THE GREAT FLOOD OF '49.

Another surprise to Chicago was a flood. That the Chicago River, or either of its branches, should get up a current sufficient to cause any alarm to the citizens was a surprise to the people then as it would be to-day. It was never expected, but it came one morning in March, 1849. There had been two or three days' heavy rain following the heavy snowstorms, and one morning the citizens were aroused from their slumbers by reports that the ice in the Desplaines River had broken up and dammed up the waters so as to turn them into Mud Lake, and from thence into the South Branch. This pressure of water broke up the ice in the South Branch, and floating down it became gorged in the main channel. Shipping in the river was in great peril. Then came the flood. The breaking up of the ice was like the booming of artillery, the waters came sweeping down with the power of a mountain torrent, vessels broke from their moorings and went with the flood, and a number were precipitated against Randolph street bridge with such force as to carry it away and send it down the river. On went the great mass of ice and vessels against the iron bridge at Clark street, and that too was carried down stream. All Chicago attended this wild scene, and such excitement had not been since the city began its eventful career.

IN ASHES,

BUT RAISED AGAIN BY PLUCK.

In 1871, when Chicago had become a rival of St. Louis and Cincinnati for first position in the West, and when her growth was the one great surprise to the whole country, there came another surprise, the like of which had never been known. On the night of Oct. 7, 1871, a fire broke out near the corner of Clinton and Van Buren streets, and all the territory between that and the river and Adams street was burned over.

It was the greatest fire that had ever visited Chicago, but it was soon forgotten in what followed. On Sunday night, Oct. 8, the great fire, originating, it is said, from the lamp kicked over by Mrs. O'Leary's cow, began on DeKoven street, a little east of Jefferson, and for two days Chicago was a sea of flame and then a blackened waste. To undertake to give any description of that fire and the scenes which accompanied it would be idle.

THE CITY DOOMED.

It was beyond all human control, and as well might the inhabitants of Sodom and Gomorrah have fought against their fate, as for the people of Chicago to try to stem that fiery tide which rolled over their beautiful Garden City. Before the strong southwesterly wind the fire traveled with marvelous rapidity, taking everything in its course.

Block after block of buildings melted in a moment, and when the river was reached the flames leaped to the shipping and to the buildings on the South Side as though they were but a few feet distant, and built of tinder-wood soaked with oil ready for the lighting. Then it mowed a clean swath down through the business center, taking in its path the solid blocks of stone and iron which were supposed to be fireproof, but melted like wax in the intense heat. Down went the great hotels, fine stores, and other immense buildings, and the old bell in the Court House tower sounded the knell of that beautiful building as it disappeared in smoke and flame.

THE NORTH SIDE.

On to the main channel of the river and then to the North Side, where the finest residence portion of the city lay, when such scenes as attended its course were beyond the power of the most graphic pens of correspondents of renown who visited the city. Whole blocks were blown up, to check the fire, but without avail; and when the people saw that it was useless to try to save homes and tried to escape with valuables or mementoes, they were overtaken and found it difficult to escape with only their lives.

It was a doomed city, and to many it looked as though all must be sacrificed, not even life excepted. There was fire on all sides and there seemed no way of escape, and for many there was not. When this great devourer of a city and its wealth had taken everything in its path from DeKoven street on the West Side to Lincoln Park and the city limits on the North Side, there being nothing more to prey upon, it died away and Chicago was in sackcloth and ashes, particularly the latter.

MILES OF ASHES.

A district more than four miles long with an average width of two-thirds of a mile, and containing more than 1,700 acres, with 17,450 buildings, and property valued at $190,000,000, had in two days been laid waste and 98,000 people were homeless. Such was the history of the great surprise of 1871 called the Chicago fire. And so great had this been that it seemed the end of Chicago. The homeless people gathered in squads in the park and the cemetery, or out on the prairies, and then followed the anxiety over friends. Families had been separated, and none knew what had become of the others. Then came the joyful reunions, but there were many among the missing. It is estimated by those who have made careful investigations that over 300 people lost their lives in that fire.

CHICAGO REBUILT.

But the fire was not to go on record as the greatest surprise in Chicago history.

It had been beyond what the world had ever known, but Chicago pluck soon showed a greater surprise in the rebuilding. The work and the wealth of years had disappeared in a few hours, but not so Chicago—Chicago did not consist in real estate, houses, money, nor wealth of any kind, but in that peculiar quality of her citizens called pluck, which had lifted a metropolis out of the lake, and set it upon a foundation of granite, and this same Chicago pluck, before the stones had cooled and the coals died out, began the building of the second Chicago, lifting from the ashes of millions of wealth the grandest and most beautiful city in the world. This was the climax of all Chicago surprises, and that it will ever be equaled in any other city is doubted, while to surpass it is among the impossibilities.

A YEAR'S WORK.

In one year after the fire the 80,000 feet frontage which had been burned in the South Division was more than half rebuilt with substantial stone and brick buildings, valued at $32,154,700, and to include buildings in course of erection the value would be increased to $45,500,000. And now, when twelve years have passed, there is not a mark of the great conflagration left upon the city except in its new magnificence, which stands out as a monument of the courage and pluck of the men and women who saw it all disappear in smoke and flame only to resolve to more than reclaim it. The inspiration of hope has been the salvation of Chicago. Her citizens have always had good faith in her, and this faith has encouraged them to dare and do, and in that they have won. And to-day it is a city of mammoth business houses and palatial residences covering an area of thirty-six square miles or 23,040 acres, with 651 miles of streets, 50 miles of boulevards and pleasure drives, and more than 100 miles of street railways.

THE SMITHS AND BROWNS.

The people by the name of Miller living here now would double the population of 1833 and be 200 more than the number of votes polled in all Cook County in 1835. The Smiths, the Johnsons, and the Browns who now get mixed up in our city directory more than equal the entire population in 1835, when the town had 3,265 inhabitants, and the Andersons would equal the emigration of six months.

In numbers the city directory of 1883 shows that Chicago has a population of 1,239 Smiths, 1,433 Johnsons, 955 Browns, 875 Andersons, and 795 Millers.

Or to make another comparison, the lawyers in Chicago now would almost three times outnumber the entire voting population of Cook County in 1835, and the doctors are five times the number of all the inhabitants, including women and children, in 1833. The directory presents to the man who would go to law a list of 1,469 who are legalized to act as his counsel, and the man who needs a family physician is perplexed when he finds 1,010 men thrusting their sheepskins under his nose for examination.

RATE OF INCREASE.

In its first decade, from 1833 to 1843, Chicago increased thirty-seven times its population, and in its second decade gained more than 800 per cent. In the third decade the population increased over 200 per cent, and in the ten years from 1863 to 1873 more than doubled itself. In the last decade the increase has been almost 100 per cent. When Chicago was a village just incorporated as a town of 200 inhabitants, New York was a city of 250,000, and

Philadelphia and Boston each had 100,000 people. Even St. Louis claimed to have 8,000 people on the banks of the Mississippi, and Cincinnati boasted of 30,000 as the metropolis of the West.

But see how the Garden City has outstripped all these in half a century's growth. While in that fifty years New York quadrupled her population, Philadelphia increased eight times, Boston nearly four times, Cincinnati eight times, and St. Louis forty times, Chicago has increased in the ratio of 3,000.

In the last decade, from 1870 to 1880, New York's gain in population was 28 per cent, Philadelphia's 25½ per cent, Boston's 44 per cent, Cincinnati's 87 per cent, and St. Louis' not quite 10 per cent. Chicago's gain was 277 per cent.

Such is the record of the most wonderful city in the world, and it has been a glorious surprise to all her people.

THE BRIDGES AND TUNNELS.

AN EARLY PROBLEM EASILY SOLVED.

The first bridge troubles in Chicago were just the opposite of what we have now. Then the three divisions, were jealous of each other, all wanting to be the Chicago of the future, and none dreaming that it would be large enough to include them all. They did not want bridges, because these might be the means of letting some of the business of one division escape to the others.

It is said that in 1840 the North Side wanted a bridge at Clark street, and the West and South Sides both opposed it for fear of losing some of their business. The North Side had the warehouses, and most of the grain came from the West and South. If there was no bridge this grain would have to be sold in one of the other divisions, and it would be the means of bringing the warehouses from the North Side. The Council was evenly divided, but Messrs. Newberry and Ogden made the Catholic ecclesiastical authorities a present of two blocks now occupied by the cathedral on North State street, and in this way influenced legislation and secured the bridge for the North Side.

THAT FLOATING BRIDGE.

The first bridge was a ferry, it is said, and Mark Beaubien was ordered to keep his ferry running "from daylight until dark without stopping." This was probably the "floating bridge" some of the early settlers speak of. It is claimed, however, that Samuel Miller, who lived at the forks, built a wooden bridge over the North Branch in 1832 which could be used by foot passengers. But the bridge over the South Branch, built in 1832, has been called the first one. It was of wood, and its location was between Lake and Randolph streets.

OLD DEARBORN STREET (GLI POINT) BRIDGE

In 1834 the first draw bridge was built across the main river, at Dearborn street. It was completed about the 1st of June, 1834, and the first steamboat that passed through it was the old Michigan, with a double engine, commanded by Captain C. Blake, and owned by Oliver Newberry, of Detroit. The bitter feeling between the North and South Divisions was so great during the time this bridge remained there, that the Council at length ordered it removed. Then came the trouble over securing the Clark street bridge.

RIVER SMELLS.

A good story is told of old Martin Casey, who has been a bridge-tender for over thirty years. A gentleman of the North Side, crossing State street bridge, thought he could never wait on the bank while a boat passed and tried to cross, but was late, and had to remain on the bridge while turned. He remarked to Casey that the smell was bad that day, and that it must be unhealthy. The old bridge-tender said yes, it was unhealthy until one got used to it. He had in a quarter of a century got used to it, and was all right. So we may conclude that however disagreeable these river smells are they cannot be very dangerous to the health of the citizens.

But from the "floating bridge" of Mark Beaubien and the old foot bridge which was used at Wolf Point, there has been a great change. Instead of fighting over the bridges we are now fighting over the lack of bridges. There are now no jealousies and no fear that one division will get more than its share of the trade. All have enough, and the thirty-six bridges at every other street reaching to the river are kept alternately swinging for the great commerce which comes up the river and the masses of people who are every minute crossing them. The want of the hour is more bridges to accommodate the people, or some means of getting from one division to the other without having to wait for the swinging of a bridge.

THE TUNNELS.

When the city began to spread out so that it was impossible to keep it in bounds, and the great shipping interests began to interfere with the travel across the bridges, Chicago enterprise began to talk of tunneling, and to talk is to do with Chicago people. So in 1853 a company was formed, at the head of which was Wm. B. Ogden, with the object in view of constructing a tunnel under the river. Messrs. Wm. Gooding, E. F. Tracy, and Thomas Clarke, proposed plans for the work. Mr. Clarke's was for a structure principally of iron, which the company regarded most favorably, but no decided steps were taken then to carry out any plan. The elevation of the bridges helped the land-travel materially and it was doubted if a tunnel would be a paying investment. From 1864 to 1866 various projects were presented to the City Council and the Washington street tunnel was begun upon a plan prepared by J. J. Gindele. The contract was let to J. K. Lake, Charles B. Farwell, and J. Clark, and the work begun July 25, 1867. A formal opening of the tunnel by Mayor J. B. Rice took place Jan. 1, 1869. The entire cost of the work to the city, including all preliminary expenses up to Oct. 31, 1869, was $512,707.57.

Notwithstanding the great need for more and better means of travel between the South and West Divisions, this tunnel has not settled the problem, for it has been much out of repair, so as to make the travel anything but pleasant, and the grade is too much for heavily loaded teams.

The LaSalle street tunnel was afterward built on a similar plan and cost the city $566,276.48.

CHURCH HISTORY.

THE FIRST WHITE MEN MISSIONARIES.

In her surprising success in business Chicago has not forgotten that the church and school must have front rank in the ideal city. The churches and schools have been kept to the front, and even before we had a community of whites here on the shores of Lake Michigan we find the missionary and the teacher at work in the Indian settlement. Fathers Marquette and Joliet of the Roman Catholic Church were the first white men on this soil, and there was a mass said before anything else was done. The place was claimed for the church, and to see the spires which rise from all over the great city now, pointing out where may be found that restful place of communion with the Father of all, one would not doubt that the church still held possession, even though some have given Chicago the name of the wickedest place in the world.

CLAIMED FOR CHRISTIANITY.

Other missionaries from the Catholic Church followed Marquette, and there also came those other pioneers in Christian work, the Methodists, and before there was yet a village we hear of Father Jesse Walker and his school-house, where he lived in one end, and taught school, preached, and held class meetings in the other. And with the garrison troops that came to old Fort Dearborn in 1833 came also the Rev. Jeremiah Porter, who opened the carpenter shop of the fort as a place for religious services, and, on June 26, organized a church, and began a little building, which was dedicated the next winter.

Father St. Cyr came from St. Louis in May, 1833, and founded a Catholic church, and began the building of a little house of worship at the corner of Madison street and Wabash avenue. This was St. Mary's Church, which last May celebrated its semi-centennial. Then came the Rev. A. B. Freeman for the Baptists, who organized the first church of that denomination Oct. 19, 1833.

These were the pioneers in religious work in Chicago, and their work was well begun, for a great record has been left behind.

THE FIRST CHURCH.

Dr. John T. Temple built the first meeting house for religious worship.

Dr. Temple came from Washington in the summer of 1833, and, upon his arrival here, built, first, a house for his family, and then a small wooden meeting house for the Baptist preacher, who was to follow him from the East, to hold services in. This house stood at the corner of Franklin and Water streets, and is, with the exception of Father Walker's log school-house, the first building put up for such a purpose. For a time all the Protestant people worshiped in this house, the Rev. Jeremiah Porter and Mr. Freeman preaching on alternate Sundays, and occasionally Father Jessie Walker preached there. The Catholic church was not dedicated until late in the fall, and the Presbyterian church the first of January following.

The Hon. John Wentworth says of his early church-going in Chicago, that he was not able to sustain the expense of a whole pew, and, in partnership with S. B. Cobb, another honored citizen of Chicago to this day, rented a first-class one, paying $12.50 a year.

THE PRESBYTERIAN GROWTH.

From this small beginning has been a marvelous growth. The little First Presbyterian Church established its missions, and after a time these became strong, self-sustaining churches, and when it celebrated its fiftieth birthday last June the Rev. Jeremiah Porter, the pioneer pastor, was there, and had the satisfaction of seeing that instead of one little organization with a dozen members there were more than a score of churches and six missions, with about 13,000 members.

The denomination also has a theological seminary, which is one of the best equipped in the country. This institution was founded in 1830 in connection with Hanover College at Hanover, Ind., and in 1859 was removed to Chicago. The first faculty was composed of Drs. N. L. Rice, Willis Lord, L. J. Halsey and W. M. Scott. The institution at first had its home in the basement of the old North Star Church, but was finally located on a twenty-five-acre tract of land just within the city limits, and a building put up at the corner of Fullerton avenue and Halsted street. Other buildings have been added, and to-day the school has a faculty of renowned professors, including Drs. Skinner, Johnson, Marquis, Craig, and Halsey, all men who stand as recognized authority in Biblical teaching. There are now about fifty students in the institution preparing for the work of the ministry.

The church has also seen fit in the last year to locate in Chicago the general committee of the Assembly for the aid of Christian colleges throughout the Northwest, with Dr. Gause as Secretary, having his permanent headquarters here.

THE BAPTISTS.

The Baptists have now twenty-six strong churches and five missions in place of the little wooden meeting-house built by Dr. John T. Temple at the corner of Franklin and Water streets fifty years ago. These churches have an aggregate membership of about 12,000.

To this denomination belongs the credit of founding the Chicago University, in connection with which the denomination had a theological school for many years, but this was removed to Morgan Park a few years ago, where there is a well equipped institution of theology, well patronized.

THE METHODISTS.

The Methodists have increased their churches to twenty, with twenty-four missions and the membership will aggregate 10,000. They have property valued at about $1,000,000 outside of the University and Biblical Institute, located at Evanston. The Northwestern University was organized by charter in the year 1851, and in 1855 the Garrett Biblical Institute was founded. Both are prosperous institutions, and every year turn out large classes.

CONGREGATIONALISTS.

Then in later years came the other denominations, which have added greatly to the Christian army of Chicago. The Congregationalists did not come until 1851, when an offshoot from the Third Presbyterian Church formed the First Congregational. The next year the denomination had two churches, and now it has nineteen and three missions, with a total membership of about 11,000. It also has one of the finest equipped theological schools in the West, located at the corner of Ashland and Warren avenues. The Chicago Theological Seminary was founded in 1854, and to-day the estimated value of its property is about $400,000. A large faculty of able scholars give character to the seminary, and it is justly very popular.

THE FIRST CHURCH IN CHICAGO.

EPISCOPAL AND CATHOLIC.

The Protestant Episcopal Church organized its first parish in Chicago in 1834. This was St. James' Parish, on the North Side, which built the first brick church in Chicago.

Now the church has seventeen parishes, all strong and self-supporting. This church has done more in the way of Good Samaritan work in the city than in building up its own institutions. St. Luke's Hospital owes its existence to the Episcopal church.

The little St. Mary's Roman Catholic Church prospered, and to-day that denomination has forty-five churches in the city, and the diocese has been made an archdiocese, with Archbishop Feehan at the head. The Chicago churches have sent out some of the ablest men to other Sees, and in the last year one of the most popular pastors was appointed Archbishop coadjutor of San Francisco. The church has several schools, all strongly equipped and well supported.

OTHER CHURCHES.

Of other churches the Reformed Episcopal has 10, the Lutherans 32, the Jews 14, the Christians 3, the Evangelical 7, the Evangelical Reformed 2, the Evangelical United 5, the Free Methodists 2, the Dutch Reformed 2, the Unitarians, 4; the Universalists, 5; the Swedenborgians, 4; and there are four independent churches and thirteen not classified.

This shows a strong army for the cause of church in Chicago. In 1840 there were six churches in Chicago for the 4,479 people who lived here; in 1851 there were twenty-eight churches for 28,269 people; in 1862, eighty-four churches for 109,260 people; in 1870, 187 churches for 298,977 people; and in 1880, 243 churches for 503,501 people, or one church for every 2,081 inhabitants.

PUBLIC INSTITUTIONS.

OUR EARLIEST OFFICIALS.

THE FIRST PUBLIC BUILDING.

Public life in Chicago had a very small beginning, but, like everything else planted in the soil on the lake shore, it grew rapidly, and it will not be disputed that this branch of Chicago has kept pace with all the rest.

We are told that the first public officer in Chicago was John Kinzie, whose commission as Justice of the Peace bore date of Dec. 2, 1823; the first "bench" was no doubt in the old Kinzie House, on the North Side.

But the first public building erected and paid for with the people's money in Cook County was an "estray pen," which was built in 1832 by Samuel Miller, who appears as the first contractor. Mr. Miller was a County Commissioner, one of the first board, but it seems that his official position did not prevent his making a bid and being awarded the contract for this first public building. The contract price was $20, but because the structure was not completed according to the plans and specifications the contract price was cut down and only $12 paid. Cook County has not followed the example of the first board and cut down the contract prices, but there has been a pull in the other direction, and all the trouble has been over the extras to be paid when contractors did not follow the original plans.

FIRST OFFICIALS.

Mr. Jonathan Bailey was the first Postmaster, and John C. Hogan seems to have been the first Postoffice clerk. John R. Clark is mentioned as the first Coroner, and his first sitting was on the body of a dead Indian.

The Hon. Isaac N. Arnold was the first City Clerk. The first jail was of logs and stood on the northwest corner of the square where now stands the Court House and City Hall. It was built in 1832. The first man hung in Cook County was John Stone, executed July 10, 1840, for the murder of Mrs. Thompson, and his scaffold stood back of Myrick's tavern, on the lake shore. Such was the beginning of public life in this city.

To-day the county has a granite Court House which cost $2,248,307, and furnished at an expense of over $100,000. Now the public officers and employes of the county in the courts and various institutions number 677, and they cost the people about $650,000.

Uncle Sam has a goodly number of men here now in the Custom House, Collector's office, revenue office, Sub-Treasury, and Postoffice, who add to the public life. Counting the Postmaster and all the men employed in the office, the collectors of customs and internal revenue and all their employes, the men connected with the courts, the pension office, the treasury, and the Marshal's office, there are 950 men, and they cost Uncle Sam nearly $900,000. The cost of the new government building where all these officials are engaged was about $4,000,000.

CHICAGO'S EXECUTIVES.

William B. Ogden was followed in the Mayor's chair by Buckner S. Morris, Benjamin W. Raymond, Alexander Lloyd, Francis C. Sherman, Augustus Garrett, Alanson S. Sherman, John P. Chapin, James Curtiss, James H. Woodworth, Walter S. Gurnee, Charles M. Gray, Isaac L. Milliken, Levi D. Boone, John Wentworth, John C. Haines, Julian S. Rumsey, John B. Rice, Roswell B. Mason, Joseph Medill, Harvey D. Colvin, Monroe Heath, and Carter H. Harrison.

A long list of city officials would follow these to show the number of men who live at the city crib. In the City Council we now have thirty-six men instead of twelve as in the first council. Counting the Mayor, Aldermen, heads of departments, clerks, police, and firemen, there are in the city employ 1,405 men, and if the laboring men employed in the streets and other departments of Public Works were counted, it would increase the number to about 4,000 or more, and the money appropriated by the city last year to run the city government for twelve months was $4,450,506.13.

This will give one some idea of the patronage Mayor Harrison has, and may explain how he succeeds in being re-elected, when we understand that he has between 4,000 and 5,000 men electioneering for him who are in his own employ, besides the friends on the outside.

STARTLING FIGURES.

The figures are rather startling when we come to get them together, showing that outside of the street laborers and school teachers there are 3,032 people in Chicago connected with the Federal, county, and city governments, and that the cost of government was this last year $6,000,506. But this is Chicago, and nothing startles her people.

Chicago has been the scene of some of the most remarkable political struggles this country has ever known. It was the place selected for the National Republican Convention of 1860, when Abraham Lincoln was nominated, which was the first note of alarm to the South. Then in 1864 there was another memorable meeting here when the Democratic party gathered in National convention and nominated as their candidate for President General McClellan. In 1868 the Republicans came to Chicago again on May 20 to nominate a candidate for President, and General Grant was made the standard bearer. Then in 1880 came that memorable struggle where the third term idea was the bone of contention, and after six days' struggle General Garfield was nominated on the thirty-sixth ballot. Each of these conventions has been followed by the most important events in the history of the country.

THE POSTOFFICE THEN AND NOW.

A FRONTIER POSTMASTER.

The first record of a postmaster's appointment at Chicago is March 31, 1831, and Jonathan N. Bailey, an Indian trader, opened his office on the east bank of the river, in the store of John S. C. Hogan, at the corner of Lake and South Water streets. Mr. Hogan was practically the Postmaster, and kept the office; and at the breaking out of the Black Hawk war, in 1832, Mr. Bailey left and Mr. Hogan became his successor. John Bates, still a jovial old settler of Chicago, who celebrated his golden wedding but a few weeks ago, was a clerk in this store, and says he kept the postoffice in a candle-box. The letters were thrown into this box loose, and whenever any one came for a letter they were allowed to look them over to see if the one wanted was in the bunch.

The mail arrived at first twice a month, and sometimes oftener and did not contain more than a dozen letters at any one time. The time of the arrival of the stage-coach was not always known, but the driver's horn announced his approach and the people gathered at the store to give him a welcome. The Postmaster would often satisfy the whole town and distribute all the mail then and there by calling out the names as he went over the letters. When a New York paper came it was handed over to some one with a good voice who would read aloud to all others. After Long John Wentworth came to Chicago he was by common consent chosen reader, and perched upon a dry goods box in the Postoffice, which was then on Franklin street, at the corner of Water, he read to those who gathered around him, and they then discussed politics or whatever happened to be uppermost in the minds of the people It was here Long John had his first lessons in public speaking.

FRANKING LOVE-LETTERS.

In those days the postage had not been reduced to 2 cents, and every missive sent through the mails cost the sender 25 cents.

Long John tells a story of how he franked letters for a Chicago lover to his sweetheart in New Jersey, while a Congressman. The young man would write to Mr. Wentworth, and of course the letters went free to the Congressman, who then wrote to the young lady, franking his letters, of course. In this way the correspondence was carried on for one winter, until his friends at Washington began to wonder when Mr. Wentworth was to be married to the New Jersey girl. Then he advised the young man to get married, as he could not frank any more letters in that way.

THE MODERN POSTOFFICE.

This was the postoffice of Chicago fifty years ago. The candle box of that time has several thousand as commodious private boxes in the first floor of the new Government Building to take its place, and instead of the citizens assembling at the office to greet the carrier, the carrier now comes to their doors, bringing their letters from friends and their papers ready for breakfast. And the office, which cost Uncle Sam $300 when Chicago was incorporated a city in 1837, last year required $613,552 to pay its running expenses, but its earnings were nearly three times this amount, or $1,959,902 for the fiscal year ending June 30, 1883. The balance of $1,-343,350 was turned over to the department. And instead of one man looking after the mail, tending store, and running a harness shop, as old John Bates said was the case in 1833, there are now 723 men besides the Postmaster looking after the letters and other mail matter which comes to Chicago. Of this number 432 are clerks, 252 are carriers, and twenty-eight are in the money order department. There are made 751 delivery trips daily and 580 collection trips.

THE LETTERS WE WRITE.

And what is more, these men are all kept busy. On an average the Chicago Postoffice sends out 3,200 pounds of first-class mail matter, or 192,000 letters every day in the week except Sunday, or one letter for about every other man, woman, and child in the city. That shows that the people are intelligent and know how to read and write.

In a year the Chicago people use up over 500 tons, or 1,001,600 pounds, of letter paper, and send out to their friends in other parts of the world 70,096,000 letters, which require $1,401,820 worth of 2-cent stamps to carry them.

But this is not all. Chicago people also send out 1,300 pounds, or 65,000 circulars every day, or 20,345,000 every year, which cost them $650 a day, or $203,450 a year for stamps.

Then of second-class matter as newspapers there are sent out every year 7,090,389 pounds or 3,545 tons, or, to be more explicit, 21,271,167 papers every year. And of third and fourth-class matter there was mailed in Chicago last year 3,867,282 pounds, or 19,-336,410 pieces. This included articles of merchandise, such as silks and laces bought for country cousins, watches for the boys on the farm, and jewelry for sweethearts at home.

AHEAD OF BOSTON.

It should be mentioned here that last year, according to the report of the Postmaster General, Chicago ranked second in the amount of second-class matter sent out through the mails, and that only New York is ahead in the number of newspapers and periodicals mailed. We stand far ahead of that city of culture, Boston, where it is supposed by many all the literature of this country is produced. We also outrank Philadelphia and all other cities of the country, with the exception of New York.

Chicago receives mail also, about 115,000 letters every day, and about 10,000 circulars. This would make 35,995,000 letters and 3,130,000 circulars received by Chicago people in one year. As for newspapers and parcels, we don't receive so much as we send out, for what could the outside world send to Chicago that would be new and interesting? But we do not object to exchange with our friends on the outside, and as a result we get about five tons or 10,000 pounds or 60,000 pieces every day, or 18,780,000 a year.

In addition to this the Postoffice in one month issued $118,455.55 in domestic money orders and $39,337 in foreign orders, and paid $650,748 domestic orders and

$10,125 foreign. The sale of stamps for a month amounted to $183,646.82, and the first month of the postal notes $1,977 was issued and $82,496 paid.

In this great change in the condition of affairs in fifty years the Chicago Postoffice has not always had clear sailing. The great fire of 1871 drove them out of their home, but at the risk of life the men saved the mail, and again in 1879, when the fire drove them from the Honore Building, they again risked life to save the missives intrusted to their care.

THE WATERWORKS.

HOW AND BY WHOM THEY WERE BUILT.

The first waterworks in Chicago were as near like those of to-day as Mark Beaubien's "floating bridge" was like the great iron swinging bridges that cross the Chicago River at every important street. The primitive ferry answered the purpose of getting the people across the river, and so did the water carts in early days supply the people with water. The carts were driven into the lake and filled. Then the water was peddled to the towns-people.

In 1836 the "Chicago Hydraulic Company" was incorporated by the State Legislature, with a capital stock of $250,000. Owing to the financial difficulties of the succeeding year the company was not formed until 1839, and work was not begun until 1840. A reservoir was built at the corner of Lake street and Michigan avenue, about twenty-five feet square and eight feet deep, elevated about eighty feet above the ground. A pump was also erected, connecting by an iron pipe with the lake. This pump was worked by a steam engine of twenty-five-horse power. The water was distributed to the citizens through logs bored five inches for the main lines and three inches for the subordinate ones.

FIRST CITY WORKS.

Feb. 15, 1851, the Chicago City Hydraulic Company was approved by act of the Legislature, and John B. Turner, A. S. Sherman, and H. G. Loomis were appointed to constitute the first Board of Water Commissioners. William McAlpine was employed as engineer, and submitted plans by which works were constructed on the lake shore near Chicago avenue. A well on the shore was connected with the lake by a supply pipe and from this the engines pumped the water, forcing it into the reservoir in the South Division.

In February, 1854, water was first introduced into the houses. The reservoir was at the corner of Adams and Clark streets and was calculated to hold 500,000 gallons of water.

Two other reservoirs were afterward built in the North and West Divisions. But the first man to conceive and perfect the plan by which Chicago obtains the finest water of any city in the world was E. S Chesbrough.

THE OLD WATERWORKS.

TUNNELING THE LAKE.

As City Engineer, in 1863, he suggested the plan to take the water from about two miles east of the pumping works, where the lake is supposed never to be affected by impurities from the river, and bring it in a brick tunnel to the works, where it might be distributed to the city. Notwithstanding the fact that this was looked upon as visionary and impossible, the necessary legislation was secured in September, 1863, and the contract for building the great tunnel let for $315,-139. The work was begun March 17, 1864, and the last brick laid Dec. 6, 1866. This tunnel is five feet in diameter, two miles long, and will deliver 37,000,000 gallons of water daily.

A similar tunnel was afterward made to

the West Side pumping works at the corner of Blue Island and Ashland avenues.

It is six miles long, and passes under and across the entire city.

THE CRIB.

July 25, 1865, the giant crib for the east end of the tunnel was launched, and, after being towed out to its destination, was sunk.

It is forty feet high and ninety-eight feet in diameter. It is built of logs one foot square, and consists of three walls eleven feet apart, leaving a central space twenty-five feet in diameter, within which is fixed the iron cylinder running from the water line of the crib to the mouth of the tunnel, sixty-four feet below. This crib contains 750,000 feet of lumber, 150 tons of iron bolts, and is filled with 4,500 tons of stone.

In 1869 a new lake tunnel was built, and the capacity of the two is 150,000,000 gallons daily.

The largest engine in the world is one of the four that pumps this water from the tunnel and distributes it to the city. This was built at an expense of $200,000, and at each stroke it pumps 2,750 gallons of water. It is of 1,200 horse power, with a fly-wheel twenty-six feet in diameter. The four engines combined are equal to 3,000 horse power.

When the fire of 1871 swept away the works the water supply was cut off, but almost before the stones were cold the pumps were put in motion again, and Chicago was spared the misery of a water famine.

Last year the city used 24,150,943,884 gallons of water as against 15,346,922,158 gallons in 1876, which shows an increase of 8,804,021,727 gallons in six years.

The expense of running the pumping works last year was $162,483, and the average amount of water pumped daily was 66,166,-969 gallons. During the year over thirty miles of water pipe were laid, making a total of 525 miles of pipe in the city. The receipts of the water office for the year were nearly $1,500,000, and the total revenue since 1861 is about $15,000,000, while the expenditures in the same time amounted to nearly $12,000,000.

THE CANAL.

COMMUNICATION WITH THE INTERIOR.

In 1836 there were two important events in Chicago. One was the location of a branch of the State bank here, and the other the ceremony of breaking the first ground for the Illinois and Michigan Canal.

The latter event was of vital importance to Chicago, and may be looked upon as one of the principal agents in pushing the city into prominent notice before the world. The railroads had not yet been thought of in this country, and the proposition to build a water way from Lake Michigan to the Mississippi was a grand scheme which attracted attention everywhere. This would enable the pioneers of the West to pour their wealth into the lap of the East, and would establish easy communication between the two sections of the country. It was a grand undertaking, and the original plan has not yet been fully carried out, and will not be until the Hennepin Ship Canal is constructed, and the Illinois and Michigan Canal widened and deepened so as to permit large vessels from the lakes to pass through to the Mississippi River. This was proposed nearly a century ago, when emigrants began to "go West" on the Ohio River.

THE RIGHT OF WAY.

In 1822 Congress granted to Illinois the right of way across the public lands from Chicago to LaSalle for canal purposes, having before obtained a strip of land for that purpose by treaty. A belt of land ninety feet wide on each side of the canal for its use was at the same time donated by Congress to the State of Illinois. In 1827 Congress donated alternate sections of land five miles wide on each side of the canal, the proceeds of the sale of which were to be applied to the construction of the canal.

William F. Thornton, Gurdon S. Hubbard, and W. B. Archer were appointed Canal Commissioners, with power to locate a route and proceed with the work. William Gooding was chief engineer. In May, 1836, Mr. Hubbard was able to present two plans for the work to Governor Duncan. One of these was for a ship canal and the other of less dimensions. The former was adopted, and in June the bids for the work were advertised for. July 4, 1836, the first ground was broken for the work at Lockport and Bridgeport, as now called. It was a great day for Chicago, and was so celebrated. All Chicago went to Bridgeport to see the first sod turned in this work.

WORK BEGUN.

The work on the canal was commenced immediately, and up to January, 1839, over $1,400,000 was expended. In 1841 the work was stopped, and in 1842 Arthur Bronson, of New York, W. B. Ogden, Justin Butterfield, and Isaac N. Arnold held a council, and made a proposition to turn over the canal to the stockholders until they were paid. A bill adopting this plan passed the Legislature, and the canal was finished in 1848, and the last of the debts paid May 1, 1871. In 1865 the City Council of Chicago, wishing to get rid of sewage by means of the canal, donated $2,500,000 to deepen the canal so that the waters of Lake Michigan would flow continuously up the South Branch from the mouth, and through the canal to the Illinois River. This work was finished in July, 1871. After the great fire the State Legislature refunded to Chicago the money she had donated for this public work.

STREET RAILWAYS.

EARLY MODES OF LOCOMOTION.

It is said that Chicago turned out in procession when Colonel J. B. Beaubien brought the first two-wheeled pleasure carriage to the town, and when Philo Carpenter and his bride drove down Lake street one day in the summer of 1834, it was an event not second in importance to the coming of the first locomotive fifteen years later, or the advent of street cars in 1859. The "one-hoss shay" and the two-wheeled pleasure carriage of Colonel Beaubien have long since gone, and to-day all Chicago, without regard to condition in life or purpose in view, goes by street car. The millionaire and the boot-black have like opportunities for hanging on by the eyebrows, and the society belle and the scrub-woman are crushed together in a heap in these most democratic of institutions.

Chicago goes to business and to the theater and rides more than twice around the globe every twenty-four hours. The witch that Mother Goose sent on a journey to the moon, and the man that Jules Vernes sent to the same place in a bomb fired from a mortar, could go by quicker time in a Chicago street car, if all in use were used as relays and stationed so as to get the aggregate miles traveled, in a direct line.

IF ST. LOUIS WERE A SUBURB.

And the number of passengers these cars carry every day would be equal to the entire population of St. Louis, so that it would not be difficult to make that town a suburb to Chicago, carrying every man, woman, and child into town every day. The cars in a blockade would extend from State street to Oak Park.

But Chicago people did not always have street cars to depend upon. In 1833 they walked, and had no difficulty in going from the business quarter to the residence part of the town, except to get over some of the sloughs.

It is just a quarter of a century since the first street-car track was laid on State street from Lake to Madison. That was the beginning made by the Chicago City Railway Company in the fall of 1858. There were no cars run, and the short track was but a promise of what would be. The next spring a single track was completed to Twelfth street, and on May day the first car was run over this. It was an important event even at that time in Chicago's history. The company had five cars built at Detroit, four of them for two horses, and one for one horse. The schedule running time was twelve minutes. In July, 1859, the company completed its track to Nineteenth street, and a few weeks later to Twenty-second street, and along that street to Cottage Grove avenue, and on that to Thirty-first street.

THE UNITED STATES FAIR.

In 1860 the United States Fair was held in Chicago, and from Adams street to Cottage Grove avenue the line was made double track. The line on Cottage Grove avenue and that on State, north of Adams street, were left single track. In 1859 the lines reaching to the West Side were begun and a track laid on Madison street to Bull's Head, where the Washingtonian Home now stands. In 1860 a double track was laid on Randolph street west as far as Ann, and from there to the stables, at the corner of Madison street and Ogden avenue, a single track was laid.

The car stables were first at the corner of Randolph and State streets, where the Central Music Hall now stands. In 1861 the car stables were burned, and nine horses and eight cars were destroyed by the fire. This was the first street-car history in Chicago. It was then in the hands of one company.

In 1860 the North Chicago line was built by another company, and opened Aug. 26 the same year. There was a double track on Clark street from Kinzie street to Division, and a single track to the city limits at Fullerton avenue.

The company had six cars and forty horses, and ran the cars every twelve minutes. In that first year the company carried 727,476 passengers. Now they carry 48,000 passengers every day, or 15,000,000 last year.

ON THE WEST SIDE.

In 1863 the West Division Company was organized and purchased from the City Railway Company its interests on the West Side, and also certain franchises in the South Division. When the company started it had eleven cars; six on Randolph street, running every twelve minutes to Ann street and every twenty-four minutes through to Bull's Head. There were five cars on Madison street, running to Bull's Head every fifteen minutes, and through to Western avenue, where the beer gardens were then located, every half hour. The track from Bull's Head to Western avenue was a single one.

The beginning was not very great, but like everything else in Chicago it has had a surprising growth. Chicago has become a city of street cars, and there is no city in the world where they are so much depended upon. Everybody rides in these cars, and better humored crowds could not be found anywhere than are packed together in them.

The crowds carried down town every morning and all through the day are one of the best indications of the growth of Chicago. There are now on every down-town street where car lines can be laid to advantage as many cars as can be handled, and yet not enough to carry the people who want to ride.

HOW THE CARS ARE HANDLED.

With all the lines centering within a radius of four blocks it gives little space for the handling of 1,414 cars. For the West Division alone there must be 226 cars switched and sent out every hour, which is one car starting to the West Side every quarter second. To the South Side the time is almost as quick, and but little slower for the North Side.

A conductor on a box-car says "a load" is about eighty-five people. In that case at the busy time of the day, when people are going home in the evening, the West Side cars would carry nearly 20,000 people in an hour.

As to the miles of track in Chicago, there are fifty-seven miles in the South Division, thirty-five miles double track in the West Division, and fifteen miles double track and two miles single track in the North Division. Over these tracks the South Division run 300 cars, and send them out every two minutes on the State street and Cottage Grove avenue lines. There are 100 grip cars and 200 passenger cars, and they make an average of eight trips every day. The cable system is equal to 2,070 horses, and there are 1,000 horses used on the extensions.

In the West Division there are lines of double track on Madison, Randolph, Lake, Van Buren, Halsted, Canal, Indiana, Clinton, Jefferson, and Twelfth streets, and California, North, Milwaukee, Chicago, Ogden, Western, and Canalport avenues, and over these run 563 cars, with 3,038 horses. They make 2,738 round trips and travel 20,500 miles every day.

THE TIME SCHEDULE.

On Madison street the cars run every minute and a half, on Van Buren every two and a half minutes; on Milwaukee avenue Indiana street, Blue Island, and South Hal.

sted streets, every three minutes; on Lake and Randolph streets and Ogden avenue, every four minutes, and on Chicago avenue, Twelfth, and Canal streets, every five minutes.

The lowest estimate the conductors give for a round trip is sixty passengers, and at this rate they would carry every day 170,280 passengers.

The North Division have 251 cars, of which 100 are summer or open cars, and 1,375 horses. The cars travel about 10,000 miles a day and carry about 48,000 passengers. That was the average for ten months of the last year. In October the line reported 39,103 trips, of which 38,124 were in the city limits and the others on the single track to Graceland.

In the South Division the cars travel 20,000 miles a day. This gives an aggregate of 50,000 miles traveled by the Chicago street cars every day, a distance equal to twice the circumference of the globe.

As to the number of people who ride it might be said that all Chicago goes by this means of travel. Not all the citizens go down town every day, but a careful estimate makes the cars in the three divisions carry not less than 318,000 passengers every day.

THE CABLE SYSTEM.

In the South Division the cars in solid trains move through the streets without visible power of locomotion, the wonder of all visitors and many residents. The motor is hid from view, and even when it is explained that under the ground are miles of endless iron cables which propel the cars, one cannot believe it until he visits the shops and sees the cables coming in from their underground passageways and encircling the great drive wheels put in motion by the ponderous engines.

This cable system was an experiment in Chicago, although it had been proven a success in California before undertaken here. It was an experiment here for the reason that it had never been operated where there were severe winters and much snow and ice. The experiment was tried, however, and cost over $3,000,000, but it has been demonstrated a complete success. To explain the system in detail would be useless without a demonstration at the shops. It may be said, simply, that this system consists in moving cars by means of an underground endless cable. This cable passes over iron pulleys in an arched trench under the track, and at each termination of the line passes round a large pulley which carries it from one track to the other. At the shops, located at Twentieth street, all the cables pass in and around the drive wheels which give them their motion. These cables travel continuously at a rate of eight miles an hour, and furnish the locomotive power for the cars by means of a grip. The grip-car has a lever reaching from the center down through the bottom and the slot or small opening of the track that contains the cable. On the end of the lever is a grip or lever slide which can be made to take hold of the cable by means of a smaller lever attached. When the driver gets his signal to start he moves his lever so that the jaws of the grip come together on the cable and he is carried forward. When he receives the signal to stop he moves the lever so as to loosen the grip and applies the brake. The cable moves through the loose grip and the car stops.

The cable system has been put in the State and Wabash and Cottage Grove lines, and is a great success. It saves time and horseflesh, is a smaller roadbed, and any number of cars desired can be carried in solid trains.

THE CHICAGO CITY RAILROAD CO.

THE CABLE SYSTEM.

New enterprises which are predicated upon new ideas with which the general public is not familiar, are almost always destined to receive more or less unfriendly criticism. The critics are almost invariably ignorant of the subject concerning which they are so free to pass opinions, and it not unfrequently happens that the theory or project which was assailed the most remorselessly in its inception, in the end attains a high degree of popularity and its most violent enemies finally become its warmest and most outspoken friends.

The foregoing general statement is especially applicable to all railroad enterprises which contemplated any departure from some old humdrum notion, from the date of George Stevenson's first experiments with the locomotive engine to the present day. Railroads in the abstract were severely frowned upon by the wise men (?) in silver-bowed spectacles of fifty years ago, and after the irresistible logic of events had demonstrated that the locomotive was superior to the gentle mule as a moving power, and a Pullman palace car was, all things considsidered, a preferable conveyance to the old Concord stage coach or the lumber wagon of the rural districts, every attempted advance in the methods of railroading has had to encounter a certain amount of stupid opposition, and too frequently also from sources whence stupidity was unexpected and inexcusable. The "cable road," as it is popularly known in Chicago, has had its unpleasant experiences in the direction above indicated, but, like all really meritorious enterprises, it has survived malicious slander, ignorant censure, and spiteful innuendo, and is to-day one of the acknowledged great successes of this city of successes. Many of the property-owners along the great thoroughfares through which this system of passenger transportation runs, were almost laughably apprehensive three years ago that these streetcars moved by an unseen power—which was apparently under perfect control, nevertheless—were rather "spookish" in their nature, and were destined in some occult, unexplained, and unexplainable way to destroy or seriously impair the value of their real possessions; but these same men are now ready to admit, with the frankness of true Chicagoans—who are never afraid to say that they were wrong when fairly convinced of the fact—that this same system of street railroads has advanced the value of their property from 100 to 200 per cent. This sounds like an exaggerated statement, but the writer is satisfied that it is substantially true. A sound reason for this is not hard to find by any thinker. A city of the territorial extent of Chicago—inhabited by people whose distinctive characteristic is impatience over the loss of time—required not only safe and comfortable, but rapid transit from the suburbs to the center of business. All these accommodations the cable road managers promised to give the public, and it is no more than just to add that the promise has been fulfilled honorably. As might have been expected, there were more or less accidents when the system first went into operation; the public had to become familiar with the rapidly moving trains and learn to keep out of the way, while the company had to acquire experience in the management of powerful, extraordinary machinery and to organize from the raw material a force of experts to do expert work. All this has been accomplished, and it is no longer a matter of doubt that the cable road—which transports passengers at nearly double the rate of speed attempted by the old-fashioned mule lines—is the safest and most comfortable street railroad in the city.

The cable road now operates twenty miles of line extending out into the best residence districts. It runs 100 grip and 300 box cars, and employs about fifteen hundred men.

The day is not far distant when this system of street railroads will supersede all others in the enlightened West.

CEMETERIES OF CHICAGO.

ROSE HILL A BEAUTIFUL RESTING PLACE FOR THE DEAD.

As in almost every feature that is of importance to the establishmment of a large and crowded city, Chicago is peculiarly fortunate in at least one of it rural cemeteries. The projectors of Rose Hill have wisely selected grounds far enough from the city proper to insure no molestation of the ashes of the dead in the future, and have chosen grounds high enough for the purposes intended, and also those susceptible of improvement at a slight expense. They are of easy access both by rail and drives, which is certainly a desirable feature. A representative of THE INTER OCEAN was detailed to make a tour of inspection of the different cemeteries, and for his pains was rewarded with a sight at Rose Hill that, barring the knowledge of being in the presence of the dead, was as pleasing and interesting as any that Chicago or surroundings can afford.

HOW TO REACH ROSE HILL.

The grounds embrace a scope of 500 acres, and are from thirty to forty feet above Lake Michigan, and mostly covered with native timber. The distance from the city is only six and one-half miles, and is accessible by the Chicago and Northwestern, the Lake Shore drive and Green Bay Roads—all these lines starting from the heart of the city. The character of the soil is such as to forever preclude the possibility of dampness—the cemetery, as a matter of fact, being located on a gravel ridge, and having an elevation above the surrounding country of an average of fifteen feet. The undulation of the surface as well as its elevation above the lake, referred to elsewhere, are perhaps the two great natural advantages that have made this cemetery so acceptable. What may be said of the buildings can be regarded as truthful when the statement is made that they are in perfect keeping with everything else connected with the institution. The receiving vault alone is a marvel in its way, possessing capacity for holding 250, and so arranged as to permit of the handling of coffins without the possibility of the slightest damage.

OTHER ADVANTAGES OF AN ARTIFICIAL CHARACTER.

An artesian well, sunk to a depth of 2,278 feet, furnishes an inexhaustible supply of water, that is conveyed to all parts of the cemetery by a complete system of water pipes, laid below the frost line, and all the modern sprinkling apparatus attached thereto. The sewer system is also perfect in all respects, and everything of an unpleasant nature that may collect is carried off at once.

The artificial lakes add greatly to the beauty of the grounds. The avenues, drives, and walks have been made with a view both to symmetry and permanency, while the large and handsome green-houses and conservatories are constantly filled with the choicest of plants, vines, and flowers to supply the demand for these ornaments. The fact is, there is no cemetery in this country upon which has been spent more money, time, and study than Rose Hill, and the result has been both profitable to the proprietors and pleasing to the patrons. The public will be surprised to learn that the uniform price in all parts of the cemetery is only 50 cents per square foot, which affords those desirous of selecting family lots an opportunity of making their own choice without any additional charge. Lots can be obtained from the small 10x15, in regular gradation, up to 100x100 feet. Parenthetically it may be of interest to state that the board of managers of Rose Hill are now discussing the advisability of advancing prices at least 100 per cent, as they are of the opinion that they should not dispose of their property at less figures than other cemeteries.

A CONTEMPLATED RAISE IN PRICES.

This being a matter of interest to the residents of Chicage desiring to purchase family burial plats (as all must sooner or later), the officers of the Rose Hill Company were called upon to learn at what time the proposed advance in prices would be made. They informed the writer that, while it was true that such an advance was contemplated in the near future, the public would be duly notified of it through the press and otherwise before going into effect, that they knew of no good reason why they should continue to sell the finest and most desirable grounds for cemetery purposes that could be found anywhere near or of easy access from Chicago for 100 per cent less than many citizens pay elsewhere for low, wet prairie; that the great expense of labor and permanent improvements made in Rose Hill during the past four years was the result of a firm determination on the part of its managers to make it not only a beautiful cemetery, but *the* rural cemetery of Chicago, and that the improvements would go steadily and rapidly on until this object was accomplished; that the location, extent—500 acres

ENTRANCE TO ROSE HILL CEMETERY.

—and natural advantages of the grounds warranted them in this determination to give to the citizens of Chicago a rural cemetery that would compare favorably with any in the land. While it is agreeable to know that they are so determined, and that such information is a matter of public interest, yet the intention of this article was to give more the impression created by investigation. All who visit Rose Hill confess that in point of location and natural advantages, as well as in its improvements, it must be accorded the first place in the list of rural cemeteries near or adjacent to Chicago.

AN IMPORTANT FEATURE.

From a very interesting and important pamphlet issued by the Rose Hill Company, the information is gleaned that an important feature has recently been introduced at the request of a number of the most prominent and wealthy citizens of Chicago who desired to secure large and handsome lots for themselves and heirs. Several sections in the finest part of the cemetery have been laid out on the lawn plan, to be disposed of for all time to come. Special covenants were incorporated and given in the warranty deeds, covenanting not only as to the lots conveyed, but also that no lots in said section or sections shall be subdivided or sold in fractional parts.

This portion of the cemetery bids fair to become the handsomest and most desirable of any within its borders. A large number of prominent citizens already own lots in this locality, but space will not admit the long list of familiar names found inscribed on the handsome family monuments in this part of the grounds—and in deference to the many all are omitted.

A PERPETUAL CARE FUND.

Like all cemeteries of a responsible character, this one has a fund created under the provisions of its charter, for the perpetual care of the cemetery grounds after all lots therein shall have been sold. This fund already amounts to more than $35,000 of principal alone, and is rapidly on the increase; so that the completion of the principal amount of $100,000 required by its charter is fully assured. That the readers of this issue may glean some idea of the solidity of the fund, it is only necessary to mention that the Hon. Charles B. Farwell, Orrington Lunt, banker, and Henry F. Lewis constitute the committee which have control of all moneys belonging thereto, which is invested in interest-bearing bonds, as required and particularly designated by the charter, which bonds are incontrovertible for any other purpose whatsoever.

ROSE HILL'S FUTURE.

To all who are interested in Rose Hill, and to those who are undecided as to where and in what cemetery they should secure a family lot, THE INTER OCEAN would suggest:

That the future of Rose Hill, as a large, permanent, and beautiful rural cemetery, free from molestation, is assured. Its superior advantages of location and adaptability for cemetery purposes, over any other ground near or conveniently accessible from the city, have been enumerated and need no further mention. A visit to the grounds will convince the most skeptical of the correctness of the statements in regard thereto. Chicago may grow and become a city of one, two, or even three millions of people—a continuous city, north along Lake Michigan to Evanston, and yet Rose Hill, a city in extent within its own borders, is away from the line of growth of the city along the lake. It is a city set apart by itself; a resting place for the dead, where they will not be disturbed or molested by the encroachments of the living; and still it is within a convenient distance, and of easy access from the great city of Chicago.

The exceedingly low price of lots, as compared with other cemeteries, where ground is sold for double the price asked for the finest lots in Rose Hill, may be an inducement for some to purchase in this cemetery. It is true that those who purchase now get the benefit of the present low prices, yet we do not hold this out as an inducement to the public. There are other and greater advantages possessed by Rose Hill, advantages that are far above and beyond any mere money considerations; advantages that elsewhere money cannot buy.

GRACELAND CEMETERY.

THE BURIAL GROUND OF NOTABLE MEN.

This beautiful city of the dead is situated near Lake Michigan, north of the city. It is formed by a series of ridges left by Lake Michigan as it receded from the shore and of little valleys between them.

Within the last three years large additions have been made to Graceland, doubling the area available for burial purposes and providing lots to supply the demands of the next twenty years at least. This new part has been laid out on the landscape lawn plan and improved at great expense, and it is now by far the most attractive portion of the grounds. It rivals the public parks in beauty, and is worthy to rank with the famous cemeteries of America. Thousands of people from far and near visit Graceland, drawn by its growing reputation for scenic beauty. There is an almost endless variety of foliage and a diversity of surface which is a surprise to those who think of the surroundings of Chicago as a monotonous prairie. The pieces of ornamental water have been managed with great skill, and when the trees and shrubbery around them are fully grown they will be very unusually picturesque.

A BIT OF HISTORY.

Graceland was founded in 1861 by the Hon. Thomas B. Bryan. The first Board of Managers contained the names of some of the men who have been largely instrumental in making Chicago what it is—among them William B. Ogden, Sidney Sawyer, and Edwin H. Sheldon. Most of the historic names of Chicago are to be found in the list of lot-owners, or on the tombs of Graceland, such as William B. Ogden, Judge Manierre, Mahlon D. Ogden, Jonathan Burr, the philanthropist; John H. Kinzie, N. B. Judd, Justin Butterfield, H. H. Magie, Alexander Fullerton, Walter L. Newberry, W. F. Coolbaugh, Eli B. Williams, Dr. Brainard, E. G. Hall, John C. Calhoun. Mr. Calhoun is the gentleman who established the first newspaper in Chicago, and whose biography appears elsewhere. Among the lot-owners, the names of men who control the vast industries of Chicago, or represent its interests to-day, are found: Mayor Harrison, Judge Drummond, E. W. Blatchford, J. V. Farwell, N. K. Fairbank, Wirt Dexter, Joseph Medill, Keith Brothers, L. C. Huck, Jerome Beecher, L. J. McCormick, Albert Keep, T. W.

SCENE IN THE CEMETERY.

Harvey, John De Koven, Henry W. King, Lorenz Brentano, Volney C. Turner, Daniel A. Jones, Edwin H. Sheldon.

SOME OF THE MONUMENTS.

Great sums have been expended on the monuments in Graceland, and they compare favorably with those of any cemetery in the country. Conspicuous among these are the costly gothic mausoleum of H. H. Taylor, the fine obelisk of Washington Smith, the stately Egyptian column of T. M. Avery's, surmounted by a noble figure; the Corinthian column, with its statue, of D. B. Shipman; the fine monuments of E. H. Haddock, C. B. Blair, William Blair, Henry Whitbeck, W. D. Fuller, with its background of dense foliage, and the massive tomb of William J. Wilson, of original and striking design. There are many others perhaps equally striking and important, among the number being a mausoleum built at a cost of $15,000. It is an interesting fact that the interments in Graceland exceed those in any other cemetery in America, except Greenwood, near New York—the number of silent residents of Graceland being more than 37,000.

THE ROUTES TO GRACELAND.

Graceland is reached by a drive along the lake shore through Lincoln Park, and thence by North Clark street; or by horse-cars on Clark or State street, which run to the cemetery every half hour. The Chicago and Evanston Railway will be in operation in a short time, and will carry passengers from the Union Depot on Canal street or from the Kinzie street bridge to the new cemetery entrance.

The intention of the management of Graceland is to preserve the wide and beautiful sweep of the lawns by excluding, as far as possible, stone and marble from the new grounds, the monuments being restricted in number, and the headstones being kept low and unobtrusive, while all the old-fashioned and repulsive stone edges, fences, posts, chains, and all other unsightly lot-enclosures once in vogue have been forbidden. In dry seasons, when the grass even in Lincoln Park turns brown, the turf in the new grounds in Graceland is kept as green as in June by plentiful sprinkling by means of a steam-pump, the water being supplied from living springs which feed the artificial lakes.

PERPETUAL FUND.

A large and constantly growing fund, known as the Graceland Improvement Fund, in the hands of a Board of Trustees consisting of Edwin H. Sheldon, George C. Walker, Jerome Beecher, A. J. Averill, Hiram Wheeler, John De Koven, E. S. Williams, M. C. Stearns, E. W. Blatchford, J. W. McGinness, Daniel Thompson, and William Blair, guarantees the perpetual preservation and maintenance of Graceland Cemetery.

PARKS AND BOULEVARDS.

A MAGNIFICENT SYSTEM.

Nothing in this great city better shows the spirit of Chicago people than the magnificent park system, which is the wonder of the age, attracting the admiration of visitors from all over the world, and it is generally conceded that no other city on the continent has so elaborate a park and boulevard system as the Garden City of the West.

In this, as in everything else where Chicago saw her need, she went to work on a scale that would have satisfied even Ponce de Leon, in his visionary schemes, and she had the energy to push all she undertook to successful endings. The early Chicago had the lake shore for a breathing place, the boundless prairies for a ramble, and the little public square, with its rustic town pump, for a mall, and with these they were satisfied, until one day in 1853 Mrs. Carpenter put it into the head of her husband and Reuben Taylor to have a park on the West Side.

THE FIRST PARK.

The surveyors were stopped in their work of laying out town lots where Union Park now lies, and the tract of twenty-three acres was purchased by the city for a public park. And such it has ever since been, though it must be admitted that in later years it has been much neglected, and is of little use to the people who live in its vicinity.

Then other portions of the city became envious, and little parks were laid out, some of them no more than small squares, but they served their purpose, and to-day are delightful play-grounds for the neighborhood children. These small parks which now are under the control of the city are: Union, 23 acres; Jefferson, 5 3-5 acres; Vernon, 3 acres; Ellis, 2 acres; Lake, 40 acres; Wicker, 5 acres; and Washington Square, 2½ acres, making a total of 81 acres devoted to parks in the city limits.

But Chicago's pride is her grand park system outside the limits, where the dry prairies and bottomless bogs have been converted into the most beautiful pleasure grounds—veritable places of enchantment. These with the little city parks make up a grand total of 2,353 acres of pleasure grounds in Chicago, and the money expended could only be counted by the million.

LINCOLN PARK.

Lincoln Park was cut off from the lands of the Chicago Cemetery by city ordinance in 1864, and for several years bore the name of Lake Park, but the name was changed by common consent without official action. It then contained sixty acres and was under the control of the city government, but in 1869 the Legislature provided for its improvement and appointed E. B. McCagg, Andrew Nelson, John B. Turner, Joseph Stockton, and Jacob Rehm as the first Board of Commissioners. It is supported by taxation of the North Division. It now has a total of 310 acres and is said to be the prettiest park in this country.

It was in 1866 that the people first began to agitate the question of laying out parks of this kind and George M. Kimbark, Paul Cornell, Chauncey T. Bowen, George R. Clarke, Obadiah Jackson, J. Young Scammon, and J. Irving Pearce should have the credit of the first move. These gentlemen proposed two South Park bills to be presented to the Legislature, one providing that the whole city should be taxed and the other that only the South Division and Hyde Park. This passed, but when the people were asked to indorse the action at the spring election it failed.

ENACTED BY THE LEGISLATURE.

A second bill was passed fixing the location where it now is, and this passed the Legislature and was indorsed by the people. The first Commissioners were John M. Wilson, L.

B Sidway, Paul Cornell, G. W. Gage, and C. T. Bowen.

The South Parks contain 1,100 acres, and the land alone cost $1,700,000. The Drexel, Oakwood, and Grand boulevards are built in connection with this, and several millions of money have been spent in improving the grounds.

The West Parks system was established in the same manner. This has three large parks —Douglas on the south, Central or Garfield in the center, and Humboldt on the north. Douglas has 180 acres, Garfield 185, and Humboldt 225. All are connected by boulevards, and soon other boulevards will be completed connecting them with the parks in the other divisions.

With over 2,000 acres of pleasure grounds and fifty miles of boulevards, Chicago stands without a rival in the extent of her park privileges for her citizens.

THE WASHINGTON PARK CLUB.

THE HOME OF THE TURFMEN.

One of the most important and certainly the most aristocratic club in the city is the new Washington Park Club. Not only in the turf world, but in the social as well, this institution takes precedence. The Jockey Club in London embodies the highest aristocracy in England, and to be a member of that association is considered one of the leading honors of the country. Several crowned heads are numbered on its roll of memberhip. Many of the nobility are also members, but the mere fact of their being noblemen is not a qualification for admission to the club. The Committee on Membership scrutinize the application in the most rigorous manner, and the fact of a gentleman's election to the London Jockey Club is heralded as a distinction as notable as a gazette in the army.

THE FRENCH JOCKEY CLUB.

France has its national jockey club, located in Paris. Its exclusiveness is noted the world over. Many Americans of fabulous wealth, resident in Paris, have tried with unavailing effect to gain an election in that organization, but no influence could be brought to bear that would overcome the exclusiveness of the by-laws. New York has in the American Jockey Club an institution comparing favorably with these two clubs in Europe. It is composed of the best men in the aristocratic social circles of New York: August Belmont, Leonard Jerome, James Gordon Bennett, D. D. Withers, Charles Constable, Henry Hilton, Augustus Schell, Whitelaw Reid, Russell Sage, Pierre Lorillard, William A. Travers, Judge James Munson, and others of equal wealth and celebrity in New York City. This club is fully as exclusive as either of the European clubs. It is a power in the world of fashion, and its indorsement stamps the thing as being proper.

CHICAGO'S NEW JOCKEY CLUB.

That Chicago was ready for such an institution is shown in the altogether splendid response which has come to the call of the directors of the Washington Park Club. The first thought of this club originated in the brain of Albert S. Gage, Esq., who has never faltered for a moment in his efforts to make this club a grand success. Through his instrumentality a stock company was formed with a capital stock of $150,000. With this start the club has to-day one of the finest courses in the country, if not in the world. They own eighty acres of land just south of South Park, lying between Sixty-first and Sixty-third streets, Cottage Grove avenue, and the Grand boulevard.

A SPLENDID BUILDING.

Upon this has been erected a club-house which cost upward of $50,000, and which far surpasses anything of its character in the world. Of course the London Jockey Club has extremely valuable property in its town house, not to speak of the various courses and other houses it owns at Epsom and elsewhere. But there is nothing in America that can compare with the Washington Park Club. When the gates are opened next June Chicagoans will see the handsomest club-house in the United States. In the laying out of the grounds the club has had the good fortune to have the combined talents of Mr. S. S. Beman, who built Pullman, and Mr. N. F. Barrett, well known in the East and West as a landscape engineer. These gentlemen have worked together with a view of making the buildings and landscape harmonize, and the entire plat as picturesque as possible. There will be ample drives for the club members, and a perfect track for public meetings and members' speed trials. The grand stand will be the finest in the world, being 500 feet long, two stories high, fitted with refreshment rooms, parlors, and reception rooms. the whole costing upward of $40,000, and capable of seating 10,000 people. Stables are now completed to accommodate 280 horses, and as many more will be erected in the spring.

AN ARTISTIC INTERIOR.

The club-house, which will occupy a position twelve feet above the track, with a lawn sloping from it, will be completed by May 1. It will be 136 feet long by 97 wide, and two stories, basement, and attic in height. In the basement will be the kitchen, store-rooms, heating apparatus, cellar, etc., and the attic will contain the servant and lumber rooms. On the main floor will be a spacious entrance-hall, club office, cafe (with serving and wine rooms off), billiard-room, a ladies' waiting-room, a parlor for the directors, a lavatory, and five private dining-rooms. Extending around the entire building on this floor is a veranda 16 feet wide, which will be provided with chairs and other conveniences for witnessing races. The second floor contains a grand dining-hall, seven private dining-rooms, wine and serving rooms, a grand hall, ladies' parlor, ladies' toilet and private room, and cloak-room. A covered balcony, 16 feet wide, also runs around the entire building of this story. All of the rooms and halls have fire-places specially designed for each by Mr. Beman. Upon the third floor are also some sleeping-rooms and bath-rooms, and upon the roof of the building are two open observatories, from which every part of the park and surrounding country can be seen. The grand dining-hall referred to will have an elaborate timbered ceiling, and all of the private dining-rooms will have sliding-doors, so if desired they may be thrown together. The main entrance halls and staircases will be finished in white ash, and the rest of the structure will be treated in white pine. The main staircase will be an elaborate affair, and will be a very attractive feature of the large hall. The families of members are expected to visit the club, consequently the necessity of the strict scrutiny spoken of previously. At the present moment there are 300 members admitted to this club.

A LARGE MEMBERSHIP.

The initiation fee is $150, and the applications for membership are quite numerous. Before the gates open it is expected that there will be 500 members. There is not a name on the rolls but what has passed the most rigid scrutiny, and a membership in the Jockey Club is virtually a guarantee of the owner's standing in society. The club have opened stakes for the various ages of thoroughbreds, and will give their inaugural meeting beginning June 28, closing July 12. Racing on alternate days. In the young classes the stakes closed Oct. 15, with 375 nominations. The entries for the general meeting close Jan. 15, at which time fully as many more entries will probably be made. This new club will offer an opportunity to those who enjoy the better qualities of the turf sports. The thousands who have each summer gone to Saratoga and other Eastern resorts to enjoy racing will now make this city the terminus of their summer tours. To the residents of Chicago who have long desired an objective point for their drives will find in this club the fulfillment of these desires. It will elevate the taste and benefit the turf. Fine turnouts will be numerous, and the sport will be dignified. Mr. J. E. Bewster, the efficient Secretary, has done much to further the success of the club, he being a member of the American Jockey Club of New York.

THE SPORTING CAPITAL.

THE TURF, BASE BALL, THE WHEEL, AND BILLIARDS.

The advance that Chicago has made in the matter of sporting affairs in the past twenty-five years has become a question of wondering surprise, not only throughout our own country but on the other side of the Atlantic. The early days of Chicago saw little or no sport save in its primitive character. There were no remarkable characters in the sporting world. Who ever heard of Chicago, much less come to visit the city?

John C. Heenan came here but it was only en route St. Louis. It has been since 1860 that Chicago has achieved her present position in the sporting world. The era of sensation, or, better, originality, began with that year, and the eyes of all lovers of sports have been turned toward Chicago ever since.

IN TURF MATTERS

there have been more and greater remarkable events here than in any city in the world. Dexter, Goldsmith Maid, Rarus, Hopeful, St. Julien, Maud S., and Jay-eye-see all found their laurels in Chicago, and the list of great performances is large and varied.

In base ball affairs this city occupies the parental position, professional playing having been originated here. The Chicagos have always been at the top or close to it ever since the game has been a reality. Starting with the best amateur club in America, the old Excelsiors, and going from better to best in the way of professional players, Chicago stands pre-eminent among all cities where the game is known. The sport has been fostered and upheld here to such an extent that there is no other city which patronizes the games as does Chicago. In fact, the city is looked upon as the center from which emanate many of the decrees and other details of the sport.

Cricket also finds a foothold in Chicago, having two full-grown clubs in existence, one of those possessing two or three players on the international team.

IN BOATING MATTERS

This city has to labor under the disadvantage of rough water most of the time, and so in the years gone by the many clubs that have been formed have tossed along on the rough lake and but little success has been achieved. But to-day there are three or four good clubs. Two of these are equal to anything anywhere in point of strength and financial standing. The Farraguts head the list, and the Pullmans are second. The latter has done much to overcome the rough water by the construction of their course at Pullman.

The bicycle is of such a recent invention that Chicago has hardly had time to win the first place in that matter. It was only a few years ago when the old velocipede was introduced in this city by the opening of a school in the old skating rink at the corner of Wabash avenue and Jackson street, where the Matteson House now stands. This was in 1867. The sport did not seem to take a strong position at that time. Later, when the bicycle came into existence, it proved an attractive sport, and it gradually grew, and to-day the riders are numbered by the hundreds in this city. Schools have been opened, and the traffic in this expensive sport has become a thing of wonder.

The billiard world has also found a Mecca in Chicago. Some of the greatest experts in the world first came to the surface in this city. The perfection in the manufacture of implements of the game has been achieved here, and the greatest tournaments find their field within Chicago's walls. Thus it is that this city has reached a very pinnacle, indeed, in the world of sports, such as no city ever held in this country before, and which no other city is ever liable to win. There have been established rolling-skating rinks which find patrons in the best ranks of society, and the public parks afford ample scope for the regular ice skating.

Chicago, with her two turf clubs and two professional base ball clubs, is fast becoming the home of champions. The bicycle has several world beaters residing here. Base ball has a champion club here. Billiards will have one or more of the big stars in this city. Chicago stands

IN FRONT IN THE SPORTING WORLD

at least in two departments, namely, the turf and base ball. In all other matters of sport she has a place near the top, and is always looked upon as a prime factor in any gathering of sportsmen. The gun has no city in which there is a greater following than here in Chicago. There are more gun clubs and wealthier ones than in any other city. The best marksmen and trap shots are here, and the last convention showed a better average than any of those held in the East. Thus in this Western metropolis, not only in business, but in sports, does the great energy and progress of Chicago manifest itself. It was here that many now world renowned names were first crowned with victory in the world of sports, and it is here that thousands have yet to achieve celebrity and fame.

A. G. SPALDING & BROTHERS.

THE SPORTING HEADQUARTERS.

No man has done so much to encourage and stimulate out-door sports in Chicago and the West as Mr. A. G. Spalding, the President and Manager of the Chicago Base Ball Club. To him that club owes its organization and success, and he is the patron saint of the base ball fraternity in the West. To him more than to any other man Chicago owes the reputation of its club and the honor of the championship it has carried for so many years. After retiring from the diamond Mr Spalding opened a store for the sale of base ball supplies and other sporting goods, and his emporium at No. 103 Madison street is now the rendezvous and headquarters of the sportsmen of Chicago and the Northwest.

Here is sold at wholesale or retail every appliance or essential known to the sporting world. Here can be found the largest stock of guns in the West, at the lowest prices, and every article that goes to make up the outfit of a well-equipped huntsman or fisherman. The wheelman can find the most complete stock of bicycles and tricycles, and those who cultivate "the poetry of motion" will be charmed by the assortment of skates for parlor, rink, or pond. In base ball goods the Spaldings are the leaders and recognized authority from Maine to California, and they provide the necesaries for every other sort of out-door game or sport.

For business men, clerks, and others whose occupations prevent them from securing a proper amount of healthful exercise they provide "the Home Gymnasium," which can be set up in a parlor, a library, a bed-room, or an office.

Sleds and printing presses, magic lanterns, toy telephones and steam engines, dog collars, whips and blankets, carving-knives, penknives and scissors, dumb-bells and Indian clubs, fencing sticks, boxing gloves, and every invention for the health, pleasure, and profit of mankind can be had at the lowest prices.

EDUCATIONAL INSTITUTIONS

THE OLD PEDAGOGUE.

HIS FIRST SCHOOL.

In education John Watkins claimed to have taken the lead. He claimed that he was the first school-teacher in Chicago. He came West in May, 1832, and in the fall, after the close of the Black Hawk war, opened his first school. His school-house was on the North Side, about half way between the lake and the forks of the river. The building was owned by Colonel Richard J. Hamilton, and was erected for a horse stable, and, in fact, had been used as such. It was twelve feet square. The benches and desks were made of old store-boxes. The school was started by private subscription with thirty scholarships. But, as there were not that many children in town then, it was a free school for all who would attend. The first quarter Watkins had twelve scholars, and only four of them white. The others were quarter, half, and three-quarter Indian. After the first term Mr. Watkins said he moved his school into a double log house on the West Side. This was Father Jesse Walker's Methodist school-house.

WOULDN'T BE CIVILIZED.

In the winter of 1882-3 Billy Caldwell, Chief of the Pottawattomies, offered to pay the tuition and buy books for all Indian children who would attend school, and if they would dress like Americans he would buy their clothes. But there was not one that would accept the last proposition. Among those who attended this first school in Chicago were Thomas, William, and George Owen, Richard Hamilton, Alexander, Philip, and Henry Beaubien, and Isaac N. Harmon.

The first Sunday school was organized by Philo Carpenter, who is still living on the West Side. This was also held in Father Walker's school-house, at the Point, and was first opened Aug. 19, 1832. There were fifteen scholars, mostly children of the French and half-breed residents. The teachers then not only had to instruct the little urchins, but go about from house to house and gather them up and bring them to school every Sunday morning. Mr. Carpenter was Superintendent of this school for several years. John Wright was the Secretary and Librarian, using a silk handerchief to carry the "library" to and from the place of meeting.

FIRST SCHOOL-HOUSE.

But in November, 1840, may be dated the earliest fair footing of education in Chicago. The Board of Education then consisted of Wm. Jones, John Young Scammon, Isaac N. Arnold, Nathan H. Balles, John Gray, J. H. Scott, and Hiram Hugunin. Teachers were paid $100 for a quarter, consisting of three months. There were but four: A. G. Rumsey, H. D. Perkins, A. D. Sturtevant, and A. C. Dunbar.

The first public school building worth mention was erected in 1843, and stood where THE INTER OCEAN office now stands. It was built at the urgent instance of Alderman Miltimore, and was for years known as "Miltimore's Folly," it being very generally assumed that there would never be children enough in Chicago to fill so large a building. The Mayor in an official message to the Council recommended that it be converted into an Insane Asylum or sold, and the proceeds used to erect smaller buildings "suitable to the present and future requirements of the city."

This was afterward known as the Dearborn School. In a single year there was need for more room and the Jones School was built at the corner of Clark street and Harmon court. In 1845 the Kinzie School was built on Ohio street, near LaSalle, and in 1846 the Scammon School, on West Madison street, near Halsted.

In the year 1883 there was an average enrollment of 60,251 children in the schools and an average daily attendance of 55,991. There were in November 704 children who

CLUB-HOUSE AT WASHINGTON PARK.

had sought admission to the schools but could not be accommodated for want of room. The number of teachers employed was 1,150 and the number of schools 60, with 911 rooms and 56,790 sittings. The value of the ground on which the schools of Chicago stand alone is worth $1,200,000 and the buildings about $1,260,000, while the furniture cost $110,000, and the heating apparatus $240,000, making a grand total of $3,800,000 invested in school property in the city.

There are also 118 private schools and 29 academics, seminaries, and colleges, embracing all departments of education.

FIRST SCHOOL OF MEDICINE.

The first man to think of a medical college at Chicago was Dr. Daniel Brainard. As early as 1836 he had conceived the idea of establishing such a school. He called in the assistance of Dr. G. C. Goodhue, and the two secured the passage of an act of incorporation by the Legislature at Vandalia, which was approved by the Governor in March, 1837. This was the first instrument of the kind issued to any educational institution in the State of Illinois, and Rush College was the first medical college in the Northwest.

UNIVERSITY OF CHICAGO.

Although the charter was obtained in 1837, no lectures were given until 1843. In that year two small rooms were fitted up on Clark street, and Dec. 4, 1843, a course of lectures was begun, the faculty consisting of Drs. Brainard, Blaney, McLean, and Knapp. There were twenty-two students, and at the close of a sixteen-weeks session William Butterfield received the only degree conferred, and was the first doctor graduated in the Northwest. In 1844 several liberal citizens gave the institution a building on the North Side, which was used until 1855, when a larger building was built in the same place. The fire swept away everything in 1871, and in 1872 the spring course was begun in the amphitheater of the old County Hospital. In 1875 the present college building, at the corner of Harrison and Wood streets, was begun, and it was opened Oct. 4, 1876.

The Central Free Dispensary is located in the college building, and nearly 10,000 patients are treated here every year.

HOMEOPATHY.

Hahnemann Medical College was chartered in January, 1855, and the first course of lectures was given at No. 168 Clark street in the winter of 1859-60, when twenty-five students attended, and eleven were graduated Feb. 14, 1860. A new college building was erected on Cottage Grove avenue in 1870.

ECLECTICS.

In the spring of 1868 arrangements were completed for the establishment of an eclectic medical college in Chicago, and on Nov. 2, 1868, was inaugurated Bennett College of Eclectic Medicine and Surgery. It first occupied rooms on Kinzie street, between La Salle and Fifth avenues, and thirty students were in attendance at the first session, ten of whom graduated. The second home of the institution was at No. 180 East Washington street and then 461 South Clark street was used until 1875, when the new college building was built at 511 and 513 State street.

CHICAGO MEDICAL COLLEGE.

The Chicago Medical College, at the corner of Prairie avenue and Twenty-sixth street, was organized in March, 1859, and first known as the Medical Department of Lind University. It continued under this title until 1864, when the name was changed to that which it now bears. In 1869 it was adopted by the Trustees of the Northwestern University as the medical department of that institution. The real founders were Dr. H. A. Johnson, N. S. Davis, W. H. Byford, E. Andrews, R. N. Isham, and David Rutter. The first course of instruction was commenced in October, 1859, with a class of thirty students. The present college building was erected in 1870. This institution was for ten years the sole representative of a systematic and graded course of medical instruction in this country.

FOR WOMEN.

In 1852 Emily Blackwell attended the first course at Rush Medical College, but was denied a second, and graduated at a Cleveland college. In 1866 and in 1868 women

CHICAGO HOMEOPATHIC COLLEGE.

knocked at the doors of Rush College, but were denied admission. In 1869 four ladies were admitted to the Chicago Medical College and a little later on, Oct. 3, 1871, the Woman's Medical College was organized, the first regular course of lectures being delivered at No. 402 North State street. The fire destroyed the home of the institution, but Oct. 10, before the fires were all out, it was decided to go on with the enterprise.

The students were collected at No. 341 West Adams street, but the hospital in connection with it was located at No. 508 Adams, and the college went there too. All this within one year. In the winter of 1872 the Chicago Relief and Aid Society donated the Hospital for Women and Children $25,000, and a hospital was built at the corner of Adams and Paulina streets. On the rear of the lot was a small barn, which was used by the college. A new college building was erected in 1877, and in 1879 seventy students were graduated.

EDUCATING LAWYERS.

Chicago is also largely engaged in the business of making lawyers for all the Northwest. In addition to the number of young men who study with the older law firms of the city, there is the Chicago Law School, which was founded in 1859, and the graduates from this are admitted to practice by the Supreme Court from their certificates and not by examination by the Appellate Court, as are the others. This school since its beginning has graduated twenty-four classes and about 700 lawyers, who have gone out to practice in all parts of the country. A great many remain in the city to swell the large number of 1,400 who are already engaged in practice here.

CHICAGO HOMEOPATHIC COLLEGE.

ITS FACULTY.

The Chicago Homeopathic Medical College, situated on the corner of Wood and York streets, directly opposite the great Cook County Hospital, is one of the most elegant and commodious educational edifices in the city. It is generally conceded to be the largest and best equipped homeopathic building in this country. It was incorporated by the authority of the State of Illinois, in 1876, for the purpose of establishing and maintaining a high grade of medical education; and its history has been one of continued and almost phenomenal prosperity.

The course of instruction in this institution is graded, scientific, and eminently practical, and every facility is afforded for acquiring a thorough medical education. The daily clinics held in the college building, lying-in and general hospitals, give special advantages unsurpassed by any other homeopathic school.

The regular faculty consists of the following well-known gentlemen: Drs. J. S. Mitchell, A. G. Beebe, J. W. Streeter, G. F. Roberts, R. N. Foster, J. H. Buffum, E. H. Pratt, A. W. Woodward, J. R. Kippax, R. N. Tooker, N. B. Delamater, Clifford Mitchell, H. M. Hobart, W. F. Knoll, L. C. Grosvenor, and Curtis Beebe.

The officers of the college are: R. N. Foster, A. M., M. D., President; R. N. Tooker, M. D., Vice President; J. R. Kippax, M. D., LL. B., Secretary; A. W. Woodward, M. D., Treasurer; and A. G. Beebe, A. M., M. D., Manager.

As will be seen from the above list, the gentlemen of the faculty are the leading physicians of the new school in Chicago, and their personal character and professional reputation are a sufficient guarantee of the standing of the institution and its thorough and complete system of instruction. Its object is not to graduate as many students as possible, but to provide those who do graduate with a thorough knowledge of medical and surgical science and see that they are well equipped for the practice of their profession. A diploma from the Chicago Homeopathic College is a passport that the medical profession throughout the world receives and recognizes as an evidence of ability and learning.

Students from outside the city can find pleasant and comfortable boarding-places near the college building.

H. B. BRYANT'S CHICAGO BUSINESS COLLEGE.

H. B. Bryant's Chicago Business College, Phonographic Institute, and English Training School is of too great importance to be omitted from the annual review of the leading interests in Chicago. This great institution wields a powerful influence in forming the character of the younger element that is annually added to the ranks of the business community. Hundreds of well-trained young men and women pass from this institution into the various business activities of the city and country every year. When it is remembered that this has been going on uninterruptedly for twenty-five years, some idea may be formed of the immense influence for good thus exerted by this institution through the systematic arrangement of business records and the intelligent management of business affairs.

There are at the present time over five hundred students in attendance, and this number will be largely increased during the season.

It would be difficult to find any business house in Chicago in which Mr. Bryant's college is not represented by its graduates. The sons and daughters of the best business men of the city are to be found in the classes of this establishment enjoying the advantages to be derived from a faculty of twenty first-class instructors and the sixty or seventy class recitations that are conducted daily, together with the large amount of individual instruction given.

The apartments are ample for the accommodation of 1,000 students, there being more than 25,000 square feet of floorage.

The highest standard of excellence can be seen in each and every department of this institution.

An office force of from seven to ten persons is busily engaged from morning till night in transacting and recording the large and increasing business of the establishment.

Nothing like it can be seen in any other business college of the country. It is perhaps as fair a representative as we have of business force and activity in Chicago.

THE CHICAGO VETERINARY COLLEGE, situated at 79 to 83 Twelfth street, chartered under the laws of Illinois, first opened its doors to students Oct. 15 last, seven entering upon a full course at that time, a larger number than ever commenced the initial course of any similar institution. The faculty is composed of gentlemen holding the highest rank in their profession, and are well known throughout the great Northwest. There is a grand field for such an institution in this city, and we predict for it a brilliant and successful future. For prospectus and full particulars apply to R. J. Withers, M. D., V. S., Registrar.

OUR MUSICAL HISTORY.

ITS BEGINNING AND ITS PROGRESS.

The musical history of Chicago may be said to have commenced in 1860, when the first opera was given in this city under the management of Strakosch, Patti and Brignoli being the leading stars. They sung at McVicker's Theater, and gave scenes from the operas without the aid of a chorus. In 1862 Grau brought out a full company and gave a three-weeks season at the same house. In 1865 Crosby's Opera House was completed and then the annual visits of opera companies became regular. The Chicago Musical College was founded in 1866, and in 1867 gave the first grand concert by home talent. In 1869 Theodore Thomas came with his famous orchestra for the first time, and thereafter was a regular visitor.

The fire swept away the musical centers and demoralized the organizations. For a time afterward North Side Turner Hall was the only public place in which concerts could be given, but in the winter of 1872 Carpenter and Sheldon gave a series of concerts with Thomas' Orchestra at the Michigan Avenue Baptist Church on the South Side and the Union Park Congregational Church on the West Side. These concerts were repeated the next year at the same places, and in 1873 Strakosch brought Lucca and Kellogg for a season of opera at McVicker's Theater.

Then the Kingsbury Music Hall (now the Olympic Theater) was built, and in 1874 McCormick Hall, on the North Side, was completed. In 1877 the summer night concerts at the Exposition Building were inaugurated, and have been repeated nearly every year since. In 1880 Central Music Hall was built, and now Chicago only needs a grand opera house to be a well equipped city for musical entertainments.

CENTRAL MUSIC HALL.

The Apollo Club was organized in 1873, with Mr. Dohn as conductor, who was succeeded by Mr. Tomlins, who came to Chicago at the head of the Richings-Bernard Old Folks Concert Company. Then the Beethoven Society was organized by Carl Wolfsohn. and others have since followed, until Chicago can now produce as fine choral music as can be heard anywhere in the land. The National Sangerfest was held here in 1881, and a grand musical festival in 1882, both doing much to stimulate musical culture. The city owes much to Theodore Thomas, William L. Tomlins, Florence Ziegfeld, George B. Carpenter, Hans Balatka, and other leaders in musical affairs, for they have been at the head of its progress.

WEBER MUSIC HALL.

THE CENTER OF THE MUSICAL SYSTEM.

Weber Music Hall has become one of the established constituents of our growing musical system in Chicago, and it is within the limits of probability to say that in no other audience-room in the city is so much music heard in the season, and perhaps so good music of that kind which is best understood by the phrase, "chamber music." The house of Weber—long known for the superb quality of the pianos it produces—has always found its interests closely identified with the cause of music, and if Weber Music Hall serves a business end as well, it will not detract from the sagacity of the management that they have been able to find their interest in ministering to the needs of musical art. Certainly nothing has ever been provided in Chicago that is so near to the wants of professional musicians and has so powerfully forwarded the cause of musical education in our midst, as may be instanced by the uses to which it has been put. On every Monday evening the Mozart Society are wont to hold their rehearsal within these walls, sacred to divine melody, and on certain afternoons the ladies of the St. Cecilia Society, under the direction of Mr. Tomlins, of festival fame, lift their less strident and equally tuneful voices in preparation for more formal occasions, while regular events of the musical season here are the concerts and reunions of the pupils of Mr. Liebling, Mr. Ledochowski, Mme. Rice, Mrs. Cole, Mr. Pratt, Miss Fay, Mr. Mathews, et omnes. The building itself, which is shown on this page, is a sightly structure of quiet but impressive style, and elegantly and suitably furnished and decorated throughout, both in the warerooms and hall, where the superlative merits of the Weber pianos are shown before audiences whose critical acumen is a crucial test from which instruments of less noble quality might well shrink. In the warerooms may be seen samples of the work of the house in all styles of grand, upright, and square pianofortes, elegant in design and superb in case-work and the interior musical merits. The house makes a specialty of unique designs in cases made to order and suited to the particular nook they are to occupy in the home of the purchaser, having a number of such under way for wealthy residents who are able to appreciate the outline of beauty as well as the limpid purity of tone characteristic of the Weber pianos.

WEBER MUSIC HALL.

THE CHICAGO MUSICAL COLLEGE:

IN ITS SEVENTEENTH YEAR.

This college, which is now in its seventeenth year, has done more than all other institutions to educate the people and stimulate musical culture in Chicago. It stands without a rival in the West, and by the side of similar institutions in Cincinnati and New York. The taste for music was never absent from our people; it was only held in abeyance in the eager pursuit for wealth, and needed only to be developed. Much, and it may be said most, of the development is due to the efforts of Dr. Ziegfeld, the President and founder of the Chicago Musical College. It occupies a large portion of Central Music Hall building, and has branches in the South and West Divisions of the city, and in several of the larger cities of the Northwest.

Under the able and efficient management of Dr. F. Ziegfeld, President, it has steadily and continuously progressed, until it now ranks second to no musical school in this country, and probably in the world. The faculty in the different branches of instruction is as follows, namely: Piano—Dr. F. Ziegfeld, Louis Falk, J. J. Hattstaedt, W. E. Louis, Miss Zula Goodman, Miss Hattie Cronkhite, Mrs. Dr. A. H. Hull, Miss Lizzie M. Campbell, and Miss L. Clara Osborne. Vocal Music—M. L. Bartlett. Organ—Louis Falk. For the Violin—Edouard Heimendahl and Oswald Cohen. Violoncello—Emil Winkler. In Harmony, Counterpoint, Canon and Fugue—Dr. F. Ziegfeld, Louis Falk, and Albert Ruff. Free Composition—W. C. E. Seeboeck. History of Music—J. J. Hattstaedt. Elocution—Mrs. Anna Cowell-Hobkirk. Physiology of Vocal Organs—Dr. Roswell Park. The German, French, and Italian languages, the flute, harp, guitar, and other branches of music are also taught by competent professors. The aim of the college is to furnish a symmetrical and thorough musical education, equal to any to be had in the world. Although careful and competent instruction is given in every department of music, the specialties of the college will remain as they have been, the piano, organ, singing, violin, harmony, composition, and elocution. Surely a proficiency in all or any number of these might be called a good musical education. Dr. Ziegfeld, the founder of the college in 1867, is entitled to the credit of its success. He has done more than any other man to advance the art and science of music in the West. He is now in the prime of his life and usefulness, and it is the hope of his many friends that he will yet live many years in the enjoyment of health and vigor and to continue his work as a true educator of the people. The good which he has conferred upon his adopted country is incalculable, and although no person now living will witness its entirety, he has the proud satisfaction of having left the impress of his labors, his talents, and his genius upon the culture and progress of a whole people.

MUSICAL INSTRUMENTS.

THE CONN MANUFACTORY AT ELKHART.

The success which has attended the efforts of Mr. C. G. Conn, of Elkhart, Ind., in the manufacture of band instruments reads almost like fiction, so remarkable has been his experience as an inventor and so rapid has been the growth of his business. Less than seven years ago he placed in the hands of the musical fraternity an invention known as the Elastic Face Mouthpiece, which immediately met with a great demand, and was pronounced by all who used it as a decided improvement over the metal face mouthpiece then in general use. With a sagacity characteristic of the American people he foresaw that there was an opportunity for improving band instruments, and in a small shop, employing only three men, he began a series of experiments with a determination to persevere until he could manufacture the best band instruments in the world. The first year his efforts met with no favorable results except to convince him that the system of manufacture then employed was not calculated to produce a good instrument. With this knowledge he invented what is known as the Four-in-one cornet. His next improvement was the patent clear-bore valve. Both of these inventions met with ready sale, and were considered great improvements. Not yet satisfied Mr. Conn next patented the conic clear-bore valve instrument, which the band fraternity demanded in so large a number as to compel him to erect a large factory and increase his facilities for their production. With a desire to improve he continued his experiments, and the next invention in band instruments with which he favored the musical world was the celebrated Ultimatum valve cornet,

THIS IMPROVEMENT

is acknowledged as the only perfect instrument ever manufactured, and is used by all of the celebrated artists, including Jules Levy, the world's favorite; Walter Emerson, the great American soloist; Signor A. Liberati, the phenomenal Italian virtuoso; Henry C. Brown, Boston's favorite; H. N. Hutchins, the popular artist of Chicago; H. Schultz, the great Philadelphia artist; H. Billstedt, the soloist of Cincinnati; Louis F. Boos, the celebrated prize-winner of Michigan, and in fact all the prominent musicians of the world, to which Mr. Conn furnishes ample testimony in the publication of a book containing over 3,000 testimonials.

BURNED OUT.

On Jan. 31, 1883, his large factory, which employed about one hundred and twenty-five men, was entirely consumed by fire, destroying his entire stock, tools, patterns, and machinery, which had taken him years to perfect and complete. To many this loss would have been irreparable, but to Mr. Conn it signified only a reverse with which fortune had stricken him, and with characteristic energy he immediately began the rebuilding of his factory, and in less than sixty days was again employing over a hundred men in the construction of band instruments. While the loss of his tools and machinery was serious, and financially considered was a great misfortune to him, he deems that his loss has been a benefit to his patrons, for the reason that in replacing his tools he has made many improvements which would have never been otherwise introduced. The new factory now occupied by Mr. Coun is the largest in the world for the manufacture of *first-class band instruments*, and is situated upon the Elkhart Hydraulics. The machinery is run by 90-horse water power, and the different floors of the building cover an area space of over 12,000 square feet, and he employs over 130 skilled workmen, many of whom have been brought from the celebrated workshops of Europe. Each instrument he manufactures is constructed upon the *Conic* principle and none but the best material employed. Each separate part is drawn by the aid of powerful machinery to a perfect mathematical proportion upon steel mandrils, so as to insure

AS NEAR PERFECTION AS POSSIBLE.

and after each separate part has been fashioned to the desired shape and proportions it is carried to the testing-room, where it is subjected to a practical test in the following manner by a skillful and experienced musician: First, a perfect set of valves are chosen, and from the different branches and bells are selected the parts that compose the instrument and the parts that blow the freest, easiest, and best in tune are adopted for that particular set of valves. The instrument is then soldered together, and subjected to a hydraulic test by means of a powerful pump, after which the different intervals are compared with the tones of a large organ, and it is then ready for the finishers' department.

Among the many ingenious machines used by Mr. Conn is one with which the holes in the valve cases and the valve pistons are drilled, and so accurately is the work done that each part can be duplicated or replaced at any future time. The process of manufacturing the small bends and crooks is also original.

HOW THE INSTRUMENTS ARE POLISHED.

After the tubing has been bent to the desired shape it is placed in a steel mold, and by a powerful process a steel ball is driven through it so that the inside of the crook is perfectly polished and free from imperfections. By this new process the entire instrument also receives a perfect polish on the inside of the different crooks and bends so that the vibratory current of air will pass through it without restriction. The principal excellence of Mr. Conn's instruments may be attributed, without doubt, to his invention of the conic clear-bore valves which permits a perfect and even temperament of tone throughout the entire register of the instrument, each valve tone being precisely similar in quality and volume of tone to the open tones, and as there is positively no stricture in the wind passage, the instrument must blow easier than when the old system of valves is employed, for it is an incontrovertible fact that when an instrument has not a free open wind passage through the valves it cannot blow easily, and there will always be a brassy flare in the tone which is destructive to the production of pleasing music. The voicing of band instruments in sets is a feature to which Mr. Conn has given a large amount of study and attention, and bands who desire to provide themselves with instruments with which to produce the best musical effects should apply to him for information. Each set of instruments sent out from his factory is thoroughly tested and

TUNED BY TRUMPET NOTES,

so that the ensemble may be perfect in all keys. Nearly all of Mr. Conn's instruments are manufactured for artists and military bands, both in America and Europe, and so general has become their use in both countries that scarcely a soloist of any consequence will be found without one of them. To all who may request, Mr. Conn will send his instruments for comparison and trial with any others made in the world, paying all charges for transportation himself should they not be found superior in workmanship, durability, ease of blowing, and all points of excellence. Among the important inventions of Mr. Conn, which he manufactures for sale, are the ultimatum solo cornet, the vocal cornet, the combined slide and valve trombone, the melophone or melody horn, the four-in-one cornet, the perfection cornet, a new invention not yet introduced; the elastic face mouthpiece, the electric face mouthpiece, the adjustable mouthpiece, which can be used for E flat or B flat cornet; the harmonia mute and the combination music stand. Mr. Conn has also a large music publishing establishment, and he has just completed a new process for printing music, which will undoubtedly, because of its cheapness, revolutionize the publishing of music.

ARTISTIC DECORATION.

J. B. SULLIVAN & BRO., 266 AND 268 NORTH CLARK STREET.

No city in the Union can boast of greater progress in the matter of house decoration than Chicago, and nowhere else can be found more artistic work than that which adorns the palatial homes of this city. The oldest and most famous firm in this line is that of J. B. Sullivan & Brother, 266 and 268 North Clark street, who opened their establishment in 1855, and have been at their present location ever since. They have always taken the lead in decorative art matters, paper-hanging and painting, and their reputation is such that they are called to do the most expensive and elaborate work all over the West. What Tiffany is to New York, the Sullivans are to Chicago. Their designers and decorators are the most celebrated in the West, and their work is famous for its originality and artistic merit. The Tabor Opera House, of Denver, known the world over as the finest in America, was decorated by them, as was also the Grand Opera House at Chicago, the Grand Opera House at Colorado Springs, and other theaters in the West.

The contract for decorating the New Orleans Cotton Exchange, one of the most magnificent trade palaces in the world, was awarded to them, and they have been called to Minneapolis to beautify the new million-dollar hotel there. They decorated the Windsor Hotel at Denver, "The Antlers" at Colorado Springs, and the Palmer House of Chicago. Illustrations of their church work can be found in the Episcopal Cathedral at Omaha, the Catholic Church at Danville, Ill., the Methodist Church at Ottawa, the Congregational Church at Watertown, Wis., the Unity, New England, and other churches in Chicago. The Chicago Club, the Illinois Club, and the new First National Bank Building were decorated by them, and the residences of Samuel W. Allerton, Marvin Hughitt, H. H. Porter, S. M. Nickerson, Perry H. Smith, Henry W. King, Julian S. Rumsey, Henry Strong, W. E. Strong, and those of many other gentlemen of wealth and artistic taste.

CHAPTER II

THE ART PRESERVATIVE.

NEWSPAPER HISTORY.

FROM THE DEMOCRAT TO THE INTER OCEAN.

It would take up too much space to give the history in detail of the time when the great city was a village, or to tell even a small part of the incidents illustrative of early life in Chicago. But it was no doubt a happy, contented life the early settlers led, if it was at times filled with hardships. They were a free and easy people, and were all on a level, without caste in society. When there was a wedding everybody went, and when there was a dance all the boys were there. It would form an interesting group to see these men—all of them since prominent in local, State, or National affairs—assembled on the floor of the dining-room at the old Sauganash, the Green Tree, or the Western Hotels, marching through the Virginia reel, or whirling through a waltz. There would be the stalwart form of Long John Wentworth, Judge Caton, the Hon. Isaac N. Arnold, and a score of others as well known.

There was no daily paper then to chronicle the events of the day, and we have left no reports of the political meetings at which speeches were made by Long John Wentworth, Judge Caton, J. Y. Scammon, and others, and a great loss to the history of Chicago it is that these are missing.

THE FIRST NEWSPAPER.

Neither were there any reports made of the parties, and we don't know what the belles of Chicago wore in 1833. There was not a newspaper of any kind published here when the village was incorporated, and it was not until Nov. 26, 1833, three months after the incorporation of Chicago village, that the people had a newspaper of their own. This was a six-column four-page sheet called the Chicago *Democrat*, and published by John Calhoun, who had just arrived from Sackett's Harbor a few weeks before.

It was about the middle of September, 1833, that Mr. Calhoun shipped his printing-press, type, and other material, including a small quantity of paper, from Sackett's Harbor in charge of two apprentices. A three-weeks' voyage brought them to Chicago early in October. When Mr. Calhoun arrived he found his apprentices at the Wolf Tavern, then kept by Chester Ingersoll. He secured an office in the second story of a building which was then being erected at the southwest corner of South Water and Clark streets. By helping on with the work, holding a candle while Ashbel Steele plastered the room at night, it was soon ready for occupancy.

WHAT SHOULD IT BE.

Then the editor stopped to consider what should be the politics of his paper. He did not know whether to take a neutral stand or one side of the political question.

Being an ardent admirer of President Andrew Jackson he concluded to be a Democrat, and therefore the name of his paper.

The Chicago *Democrat* was published every Tuesday and the terms of subscription were $2.50 in advance. The paper received a liberal patronage, many of the citizens subscribing for three and four copies each to have sent to their friends in the East. This little weekly was the beginning of journalism in Chicago and its first numbers outlined the policy of Chicago papers ever since—making local improvements of more importance than outside affairs. The *Democrat* advocated the completing of a railroad to Chicago, which was already moving Westward, and it urged the building of the canal. In the winter of 1834 the editor ran out of paper, and had to suspend his publication until the following spring.

The subscription list of the *Democrat* in its first years contains the names of 147 people, so we can see that Chicago journalism, like all great things, had a small beginning. But Mr. Calhoun also ran a job-printing office in connection with his paper, and his account book shows that printing ball tickets was no inconsiderable item. He also printed the government blanks for the land office, and for want of a lever press his wife ironed out the sheets with a flat-iron.

The last issue of the paper by Mr. Calhoun bears date Nov. 16, 1836. Then it was sold to Isaac Hill, and immediately transferred to John Wentworth.

FIRST DAILY PAPER.

The *American* was the first daily paper in Chicago and in the State of Illinois. It was started by William Stewart April 9, 1839. It was discontinued for want of support Oct. 17, 1842, and on the last day of the same month W. W. Brackett, who had been one of its editors, started the *Express* as its successor. In 1844 the political friends of Henry Clay bought out the *Express*, and started the *Journal* as a Whig paper, the first number being issued April 22, 1844. The stockholders appointed an editorial committee, consisting of T. J. Lisle Smith, W. H. Brown, George W. Meeker, J. Y. Scammon, and Grant

Goodrich, with R. L. Wilson and J. W. Norris as office editors and business managers.

This was the small beginning of journalism in Chicago, and it has branched out until it would be almost impossible to give its history. The little beginning made by Mr. Calhoun would now cover one of the largest industries in the city. The man who then wrote leaders, reported balls and dog fights, and edited all the copy, besides setting the type and running the presses, and his little weekly paper would find that fifty years had put a great difference between the paper of 1833 and that of 1883, and that his work was now done by not less than 10,000 people.

It would be a great surprise to the editor of the *Democrat* to see so many men taking care of his work in so short a time as fifty years.

SOME FIGURES.

There are now in Chicago more than 2,000 printers—men who do nothing but set the type for the volumes of matter prepared for them in book or newspaper articles, bills, or other forms of advertisements. There are 250 printing establishments outside the newspaper offices, and there are over 300 publishers who employ from half a dozen to a hundred men. The great dailies have from 100 to 200 men at work on them in various capacities, and truly the little printing office started in 1833 has grown into a great surprise.

The list of newspapers and periodicals and other publications issued regularly includes 275, and they run from the daily paper to the advertising sheet sent out by large industries. Not a branch of trade is without its organ.

A STRIKING COMPARISON.

There can be no better illustration of the growth of Chicago than is furnished by a comparison of THE INTER OCEAN of 1883 with the *Democrat* of 1833.

In place of the 147 subscribers who read the *Democrat* fifty years ago, THE INTER OCEAN now sends out every week more than 300,000 copies, reaching 150,000 families.

Instead of one man as editor, printer, and mail clerk, occupying a single room in the second story of a little frame building, THE INTER OCEAN now has a great block, in which 200 men are employed, with a weekly payroll that would be sufficient to equip more than fifty printing offices such as that which Mr. Calhoun established in 1883.

Instead of having the papers printed by the wife of the editor passing her flat-iron over the type, THE INTER OCEAN is produced upon three of the finest presses in the world, with a capacity of 50,000 an hour, and by which the papers are printed, folded, cut, and pasted by a single process.

THE INTER OCEAN prints as many papers each week as would have supplied the subscribers of the *Democrat* for twenty years. And instead of receiving its news by a half-breed Indian on a pony, once a week, or by a vessel around the lakes, semi-occasionally, it has private telegraphic wires to New York and Washington, and correspondents in every part of the globe. It receives seven cablegrams from London, where the editor of the *Democrat* received a letter once; and pays pays each month for news an amount that, in his time, would have been considered a princely fortune.

The postage account of the paper—the money it expends to prepay the postage upon its mail edition—reached over $20,000 last year; proving, by the official records, that it had the largest circulation of any weekly paper in the United States.

CHICAGO NEWSPAPER UNION.

REPRESENTING 550 PUBLISHERS.

The metropolitan proportions assumed by successful business ventures and corporations in Chicago has no more striking illustration than is presented by the growth and present extended operations of the Chicago Newspaper Union. Established in October, 1870, it was left by the great fire, one of the largest printing houses in the city. Steady growth compelled removal to 114 Monroe street, and from there to the present and permanent location at 271 and 273 Franklin street, where substantially the entire large building is occupied. This success, like all permanent business success, rests upon the supply of something needed and demanded by the people. In most instances the publisher of the country journal, although encouraged by good words and the moral support of the community, is not blessed with such substantial income as will warrant heavy expenditure on general editorial work. If he gives due attention to local news and interests it is about all he can do, with profit. Here the Chicago Newspaper Union steps in, to the relief of the overworked editor and the tangible benefit of his subscribers. It furnishes him with an important portion of his paper, ready printed. Upon this part of his journal he has the help of trained journalists, who provide his readers with matter fresh, readable, condensed, and carefully edited. He knows, and his patrons know, that no matter of any importance will escape the notice of these associates or fail of due attention at their hands. Thus relieved, he has time to make for his readers a better local paper than he otherwise could, and he gives them a better general newspaper than could be provided on any other plan at ten times the expense. The Chicago Newspaper Union now supplies partially printed sheets to over 550 publishers. It reserves a limited space for advertising in each paper, and as these are the home papers, read and reread through the week, no better advertising medium can be found. The present officers are: President, John F. Cramer, and Manager C. E. Strong. Fifty skilled employes are kept busy and eight modern presses. The Union also publishes the Chicago *Ledger*, a weekly literary journal, circulating from ten to fifteen thousand copies. The establishment also deals in printers' supplies, carrying in stock all material for newspaper or job printing outfits, together with a complete stock of papers and envelopes.

THE PUBLISHING TRADE.

ITS RAPID GROWTH.

For many years Chicago was content to leave the book publishing business to Eastern cities, but since 1860 this line of trade has developed to a surprising extent, so that now Chicago ranks fourth among American cities in this industry. In 1882 over 3,000,000 books were turned out by Chicago publishers. Its total publishing business in 1880, including printing, binding, lithographing, newspapers, etc., engaged

226 establishments, $2,610,000 capital, 4,740 employes, and turned off products of the value of $9,075,000.

A feature of the publishing business which has developed of late years to a marvelous degree is the production and sale of books to be sold by subscription This is manifested by the statistics of the subscription book agencies. It is reported that one Eastern firm has through such agencies taken orders for more than 250,000 copies of a single work since the first day of last August. Chicago is following close after its Eastern competitors in this trade, and many of the most successful publications of this nature are issued here.

☞As one method of ascertaining what

THE BOOK APPETITE

of the toiling, reading and thinking American masses calls for, it is worth while to note the contents of one of this class of works. On the shelf behind us stands a work entitled "The Secrets of Success in Business Life," a late addition to the text-books of the people's home college. It is the result of years of study and experience by men whose business it has been to master the problems of commercial and manufacturing transactions and transportation and teach them to others—Messrs. G. L. Howe and O. M. Powers, conjoint principals of the Metropolitan Business College of this city. Now, a work of this nature, admirably adapted to school young men and women in the lessons of practical life, in the art of getting on in the world, touches the whole race of bread-winners on a subject in which they are all interested, and it is not surprising that shrewd subscription agents, versed in the wants of the people, are eagerly engaged in pushing the sale of it.

The following are a few of the chapter heads: Business Writing, Business Forms, Political History of the United States, Book-keeping, Elements of Success in Business, The Bank Clearing House, Wholesale and Retail Business, Railroading and Express Business, The Chicago Board of Trade, The Union Stock Yards, Mining, Wall Street and the New York Stock Exchange. That such books sell far more rapidly than romances is an indication that the American mind prefers fact to fiction, substance to fancy.

DIAGRAMS AND PICTORIAL ILLUSTRATIONS

are employed in teaching nowadays much more than ever before. They are absolutely requisite to the clear understanding of most subjects, and the people know it. The book above mentioned answers to this popular requirement, for it contains about 200 diagrams and engravings, some of which are said to have cost several hundred dollars each. The one above illustrates the operation of the Chicago Bank Clearing-house, an institution through which the banks of this great city make daily settlements, aggregating millions on millions of dollars. The engraving is accompanied with others on the same subject, and several quarto pages of explanation, prepared with the assistance of the Manager of the Clearing-house, William Henry Smith, Esq. Similarly lucid explanations follow all the 200 illustrations.

CHICAGO CLEARING HOUSE.

Add to such a work a good dictionary of the English language, a good cyclopedia, a standard history of the United States and a wisely compiled synopsis of universal history, and a first-class newspaper, and the possessor's home college may produce self-taught men and women ready to achieve greater success in life than the average college graduate.

interesting weekly periodical in the United States. Its success, though phenomenal, is deserved. It has been wholly the result of years of thorough preparatory work. Its subscription list is already as large as most of the old-established periodicals and it covers every State and Territory in the Union, as well as an important foreign constituency. The *Current* gives, each week—not once a month in the dreary, half-forgotten fashion of the monthlies—brief, terse, and intelligent discussion of all matters of real human interest; and, besides this, furnish the largest number of brief, valuable, and fascinating literary articles, including poems, short stories, serials, sketches, essays, papers, and political and scientific discussions, of any weekly publication in the world. It has already engaged and has first manuscripts from upward of 100 of the best known writers of America and Europe. The *Current* is clean, noble, and elevating, and deserves a place, as it will surely have, in the home of every intelligent family in America. The subscription price is only $4 per year. Send for it. Address simply the *Current*, Chicago.

AMERICAN PRESS ASSOCIATION.

TWO HUNDRED DAILY PAPERS.

This association, established in Chicago Aug. 1, 1882, and later in New York, Cincinnati, and St. Louis, serve over 200 daily papers with 8,000 words of the latest news, stereotyped and expressed night and morning. This service is supplemented by a wire report. They also supply several hundred papers with fresh miscellany, short and continued stories. Their latest feature is the furnishing of original matter, obtained at great expense from the most popular writers.

THE REMINGTON TYPE-WRITER is unqualifiedly superior to all other type-writing machines in principle, in construction, in material used, in workmanship, and in speed. It is also more durable, easier to separate, and in every way more desirable than any invention of the kind which has been offered to the public. Merchants, lawyers, and journalists now use the Remington Type-writer, and are largely dispensing with the services of pen-copyists at a vast saving of time and money. It is sold by Wyckoff, Seaman & Bendict, No. 38 Madison street.

PAPER AND STATIONERY.

BRADNER SMITH & CO.

MANUFACTURERS AND DEALERS IN PAPER.

The firm of Bradner Smith & Co., manufacturers and dealers in paper, is just twenty years younger than the city of Chicago, having been established in 1853 at No. 12 La Salle street in a little store 20x60 feet in size. It was a small beginning, but the firm has kept even pace with the development of Chicago, and has kept growing each year as the city has grown until it is now the largest in Chicago, and one of the largest in the world, doing a business of $2,000,000 a year. The firm has now three establishments in the city of Chicago, branch houses at Kansas City, Minneapolis, and St. Paul, and operates six paper mills, manufacturing and selling every sort and size of news, book, wrapping, writing, blotting, and other papers, card board, envelopes, twines, wood pulp, and paper manufacturers' supplies.

There was very little paper manufactured in the West when Bradner Smith & Co. commenced business, and most of their stock was brought from Eastern mills, but now they not only make their own stock, but supply hundreds of other houses with their manufactures, shipping paper by the train load from their several mills.

Bradner Smith & Co. commenced manufacturing in 1854 at Rockton, Ill., having that year purchased the Winnebago mill, which now makes ten tons per day of express, manilla, rag, and straw wrapping paper. They continue to operate this mill, and their other manufactories are the Ledyard Pulp Mill, at Ledyard, Wis., which makes four tons of dry pulp per day; the Rozet Mill, at Three Rivers, which produces four tons per day of print and book paper; the Tippecanoe Paper Mill, at Monticello, Ind., which makes two tons of print paper daily. The Marinette Mill, at the place of the same name in Wisconsin, manufactures five tons of print paper, and the mill at Menominee, Mich., produces four tons of manilla paper and six tons of wood pulp daily.

Besides their own manufactories, Bradner Smith & Co. carry all varieties of fancy goods, wedding and other stationery, imported and domestic, the Hurlbut plate paper, Crane's pure linen flats, the Germanic flat and ledger papers, and all other classes of goods used by stationers, printers, book-binders, and publication houses. Regular sizes and standard weights are always in stock, but special sizes and weights can be made to order and furnished promptly at mill prices, the facilities of the firm for supplying the trade being unequaled by any house in the West. A full stock of colored papers is always on hand, and fancy papers for special purposes will be made to order in quantities to suit. They are also manufacturers of the very best map paper, and will furnish any weight or size desired at short notice. In cover papers Bradner Smith & Co. have the largest and best-assorted stock in the country, East or West.

The firm are sole agents for the sale of Weston's pure linen ledger and record papers, which were awarded the gold medal at the Paris Exposition and the highest award at the Centennial Exposition for a combination of all the desirable qualities. They are also sole agents for the celebrated "commercial safety paper," for checks, notes, bills of exchange, bonds, letters of credit, etc., which has been officially indorsed and recommended by the clearing-house authorities of the principal cities of the country. This is really a safety paper, combining positive security from fraudulent alterations, either by the use of chemical agents or mechanical means. This paper is made from the very best materials, treated chemically in its manufacture with agents which give positive results. Any attempt at alteration by chemical means immediately destroys the color in the body of the paper, also the surface tinting or lining, which, being once destroyed, cannot be restored.

Bradner Smith & Co. make a specialty of fancy ruling, using only the very best inks, which, for brilliancy of color and durability, are not excelled. They also carry a full line of all colors, sizes, and styles of envelopes, and will make odd sizes to order. All kinds of fancy stationery and stationers' sundries are kept in stock, and also a full line of illustrated advertising cards, manufactured by Marques, Gair & Bailey, of Paris, London, and New York.

The reputation of the firm and the character of their goods needs no indorsement. A record of thirty years of active business places them at the head of the trade in the West, and their references are their customers.

THE J. M. W. JONES
STATIONERY AND PRINTING COMPANY

is the oldest and most extensive establishment of the kind in Chicago, and has no rival in this country. The house was established thirty-five years ago and has been under the general management of Mr. J. M. W. Jones, the veteran stationer of Chicago and a leading business man for a period of twenty-six years. No mercantile house could enjoy a higher reptuation than this one in the estimation of Chicagoans, and no concern is more entirely deserving of popularity. The house possesses every facility for conducting a first-class business, and now offer to the public as fine a stock at as low prices as was ever exhibited in this city.

THE J. W. BUTLER PAPER COMPANY.
A WELL-KNOWN LANDMARK.

Any list of prominent business concerns of the city would be incomplete indeed without reference to the well-known landmark in Chicago business circles, the name of which heads this paragraph. The J. W. Butler Paper Company is the direct successor of the firm of Butler and Hunt, which commenced the paper business at 48 State street in 1844, the senior member of the firm being Mr. Owen Butler. From the first the policy of the house has been a safe enterprise, controlled by such conservatism as sought legitimate growth, rather than any brilliant venture. Under this policy the business has grown to be unsurpassed in the magnitude of its trade and the amount and variety of paper carried. In no other house can be found so large a variety of stock, the J. W. Butler Paper Company handling the production of fifteen paper mills. The mammoth proportions the business has assumed fully occupy 51,300 square feet of flooring, and the books show average sales amounting to twenty tons of paper per day.

THE SKEEN & STUART STATIONERY COMPANY

was established within the present year, succeeding the old and popular house of Skeen & Stuart, which was organized in 1873. The new company commenced business with a capital of $100,000, and with Mr. J. C. Skeen as President, E. C. Stuart Vice President, H. E. Thayer Secretary, and Dwight Jackson Treasurer. The company do a large and rapidly extending business as wholesale and retail stationers, printers, blank-book manufacturers, and lithographers. Their establishment, No. 77 Madison street, is one of the largest of the kind in the city, and supplied with every appliance which such a business could by any possibility require. Their stock is complete in every detail, their prices cannot be discounted, and their work is perfect. Messrs. Skeen & Stuart have a multitude of friends in Chicago—friends who have been made in the best of all ways, in the course of business, and who have been retained because they find it for their business interests to continue old relations. The specialty of this company is commercial stationery, printing, and blank books. In these departments of their great business it is safe to say that they cannot be excelled.

PRINTERS AND ENGRAVERS.

W. P. DUNN & CO.
ARTISTIC PRINTING.

When anybody in Chicago who is really posted wishes something elaborately nice in the way of artistic printing they go instinctively to W. P. Dunn & Co.'s, No. 57 Washington street. The head of this concern, which is now so well known in Chicago, is an old INTER OCEAN employe, and while in that employ made it so constantly manifest that he was a first-class man, that it was no matter of surprise when he suddenly struck out on his own account, and made just such a pronounced success as such a man in any department of life invariably achieves when he determines to take the chances which are inevitable in every business career. Mr. Dunn understood the printers' art in every particular before he attempted to establish a printing house in this city of printers, and he has so constantly given his attention to the minor details of his business, and has so persistently secured, regardless of expense, the best workmen to be had, that he has secured for his establishment a reputation which it is safe to say is second to that of no printing house west of the Atlantic seaboard. It is not with the miscellaneous public alone that Messrs. Dunn & Co. have succeeded in securing customers, but these gentlemen have so emphatically made their mark in their own peculiar avocation that the daily newspaper offices of Chicago have fallen into a way of looking to them for assistance in any emergency that arises.

THE INTER OCEAN Company is pleased to acknowledge that Messrs. W. P. Dunn & Co. have printed the musical supplement, which has been such an attractive feature of their Wednesday issue for a long time, in a manner which has redounded not only to their credit, but which has been entirely satisfactory to the patrons of this journal.

Messrs. Dunn & Co. are prepared, at their elaborately furnished and provided headquarters, to do anything and everything in the way of job, book, circular, or catalogue printing. The firm has every modern appliance in the shape of presses and material. They employ about fifty workmen—all experts

—and do not permit any other printing house in Chicago to underbid them in price, or to do more thoroughly artistic work.

CRUMP LABEL COMPANY.

A SINGULAR INDUSTRY.

Among the interesting and singular industries of the age may be classed label printing. The demand for labels has reached astonishing proportions in the last few years; nearly every package, box, can, and bottle bears its distinctive label in every conceivable shape and style of ornamentation. Production of these goods requires long experience, rare designing powers, inventive genius, and intricate machinery.

The officers of the Crump Label Company are Samuel Crump, President; R. S. Dickie, Vice President; Joseph Crump, Director; George W. Averell, Secretary; N. S. Colman, Treasurer.

The works are the largest of their kind in the world, located at Montclair, N. J. With a floor surface of 82,770 square feet, or an area of $2\frac{1}{3}$ acres of land, special and valuable machinery, unequaled facilities, and skilled labor enable them to produce 1,000,000 finished labels daily, upward of 350,000,000 having been manufactured in 1883.

They make all styles of work, from the most simple, for can or package, to the very largest, most expensive, and artistic showcard and chromo work by either letter-press or lithography; all being handled with ease and skill so pre-eminently the attribute of this house. They have branches in five different cities, each doing a large business.

The Chicago department, at 60 and 62 Wabash avenue, was established in 1873, and is under the capable management of Mr. R. S. Dickie, the Vice President of the company. Any information desired by merchants, manufacturers, producers, and other consumers of labels in regard to their goods will receive immediate and courteous attention by addressing the Chicago house.

J. W. MIDDLETON,

Blank book manufacturer, printer, and stationer, 55 State street. This house was established at 196 Lake street in 1863, and for the past twenty-one years has been justly celebrated for the excellent quality of its blank books, printed work of every description, and stationery for office use. Bankers, manufacturers, and the mercantile public in all Western States and Territories here purchase their supplies in small or large quantities, and are happy because they get their moneys' worth in good goods, so says THE INTER OCEAN, and from experience it procures its blank books of Middleton, and has found his goods entirely satisfactory in price and quality. Mr. Middleton always carries a full line of whatever goods one would expect to find in a first-class Chicago stationery house. He does not allow himself to be undersold.

A. ZEESE & CO., 155 AND 157 DEARBORN STREET.

ELECTROTYPING, MAP, RELIEF-LINE, AND WOOD ENGRAVING.

The above establishment is the oldest and most extensive of its kind in Chicago, established by A. Zeese in connection with S. P. Rounds in 1856. The first electrotypes ever made in Chicago were made by this firm. In 1861 the firm of A. Zeese & Co. was formed, and their business soon became the leading one of its kind in Chicago. Like many others, the establishment was totally destroyed in the great fire, but was the first one in the field again.

The business has since grown into large proportions, and every description of electrotyping and stereotyping, from the smallest label to the largest volume, is turned out with unexcelled rapidity and in first-class style. All kinds of map and relief-line work are executed by this firm, and largely patronized by railroads, publishers, and others. Maps made by this firm have frequently been printed in THE INTER OCEAN.

A. Zeese & Co. are also publishers of the *Electrotype Journal* and the *Specimens of Electrotypes*, in which are shown the latest designs of ornaments, borders, cuts, etc. Their stock in this line is the largest and most select in the country, and has a very extensive sale, not only on this but also on the other side of the Atlantic, as well as in Australia.

WOOD ENGRAVING.

LARGEST AND OLDEST.

The largest and oldest wood-engraving establishment in the West is that of Baker & Co., corner of Clark and Monroe streets, Chicago. They were established in 1857. A quarter of a century of prosperous business attests the excellence of their work. They are a live house, and keep up with the times.

PHOTO-ENGRAVING IN THE WEST.

LEVYTYPE COMPANY.

It has only been within the past two years that the art of engraving on type metal by photo-chemical means has reached that degree of artistic and mechanical excellence which places it on an equality with the work of Eastern establishments. The levytype process of photo-engraving, as operated by the Levytype Company, 159 LaSalle street, Chicago, gives the highest artistic results. For many purposes it surpasses the slower and more costly method of engraving on wood, producing more natural and finer artistic effects, as in the landscape, architectural, portrait, and figure work. By the levytype process wood engravings, steel engravings, lithographs, and other engraved work in lines and crayon can be reproduced at small cost.

TYPE FOUNDERS.

A PLACE WORTH VISITING.

BLOMGREN BROS. & CO.

People who come to Chicago with an intention of seeing what is really worth looking at, and of gaining valuable information, should make a point of visiting the electrotype and stereotype foundry of Messrs. Blomgren Brothers & Co., at No. 162 South Clark street. The brothers are natives of Sweden, and brought with them to the new world the energy and frugality which are essentials to existence in the mother country and which produce such splendid results in substantial prosperity when exercised in the broader and more productive American field. Messrs. Blomgren Brothers & Co. are not only mechanics of the highest grade, but they are, strictly speaking, artists also, and the industry in which they hold an acknowledged leading position is so essentially scientific in its multifarious details that only strictly first-class men can engage in it successfully.

THE INTER OCEAN has for a long time employed this house to do its fine electrotype and stereotype work, and when it is stated further, that such work has been entirely satisfactory, the readers of this journal will be disposed to think that the house is fully competent to compete with any establishment of the kind west of the Atlantic seaboard.

The Blomgren brothers are genial gentlemen, thoroughly interested in their calling, and always ready to show visitors through their great foundry, where an enormous capital has been employed in the purchase of the most expensive and elaborate machinery, and in the employ of the best experts, whose exclusive time and talents can only be commanded by a large compensation. In the business to which these enterprising Scandinavians have devoted themselves absolute accuracy of detail is necessary, and that accuracy characterizes all their operations is abundantly demonstrated by the big reputation they have gained throughout the Northwest. The firm has been nine years in business, and is now in the weekly receipt of orders from all parts of the United States. All work done by this house is thoroughly done and will give perfect satisfaction.

CHICAGO TYPE FOUNDRY.

MARDER, LUSE & CO.

The Chicago Type Foundry, which is the synonym of this well-known firm, was established in 1855. Although the city since then has quintupled in growth, the business of this house has surpassed even this wonderful development. It not only has kept up to the demands of the near trade, but has established successful branch houses at San Francisco for the Pacific trade, and at Minneapolis for the convenience of the Northwest.

Aside from correct principles of trade, which are interwoven with all the transactions of this firm, much of its success may be attributed to the fact that it has brought its productions to an exact science. Instead of casting the various types at hap-hazard, as has been and still is the custom of many other founders, every font produced in this house bears its precise mathematical proportion to its standard. Practical printers appreciate this advantage to such an extent that other foundries are beginning to yield to the inevitable by conforming to "the American system of interchangeable type bodies," which is the standard adopted by this house.

The rapid growth of Chicago business has forced many firms into prominence, but it is a matter of local pride to instance Marder, Luse & Co., who have not only responded promptly to the demand made upon their facilities, but have added laurels to the Western metropolis by establishing a standard which is rapidly being followed by the older cities of the East.

It is not too much to say of this house that it can thoroughly equip a printing establishment of any magnitude, and that no office can be entirely complete without drawing to some extent upon its resources.

In addition to a comprehensive price list and catalogue, which leaves nothing to be guessed at, they also issue a quarterly specimen showing their latest productions.

THE ILLINOIS TYPE FOUNDING CO.

LOCATED AT 265 FRANKLIN STREET,

was incorporated in 1872, and commenced business the same year at 61 and 63 West Lake street. They were afterward at 106 South Clark street, then at 177 Fifth avenue, and in 1882 movedto their present commodious quarters. They manufacture type, brass rule, leads, slugs, etc., and are general dealers in printing presses, paper-cutters, and all articles used by printers. Entire offices fitted out with all that may be required. This foundry aims particularly to supply Western and Northwertern offices with goods suitable to their requirements. Some of the largest offices in this section have been furnished by them, including THE INTER OCEAN, and the universal satisfaction their goods are giving is sufficient evidence that their type is of the best character. Specimen books and special estimates are cheerfully furnished to all who contemplate purchasing printers' material.

CHAPTER III

THE CHICAGO THEATERS.

HISTORICAL.

EARLY DAYS ON THE CHICAGO STAGE..

Among the evidences that best determine the substantial growth of a community are the increase and prosperity of its theaters. The desire for amusement is so great in human nature that it finds expression in the coarsest forms and commonest surroundings, and the class or quality of the entertainment progresses toward a higher tone and more elevated plane as the variety of taste enlarges and improves with the development of population. A retrospect of fifty years is too great in the art view of Chicago life. At that time the actual events of a day were sufficiently dramatic and exciting, and the wild sounds of the prairie had enough of weird music in them to quite shut out thought of the mimicry of dangers, emotions, and suffering. But presently there grew into favor a number of athletic games that evinced the craving for the stir of the fancies, and the masquerading of the young people as Indians foreshadowed a time when the play should be the thing.

It was not, however, until 1846 that anything deserving the name of theatric enterprise was projected in Chicago. Some few entertainments had been given in halls and chance places, quite vagrant in character, though there is a tradition that these pioneer mountebanks were immensely

AMUSING AMONG OUR EARLY SETTLERS

There was some local talent, besides, that played the fiddles, sang songs, took off persons, and cleared some of the obstacles from the way of the coming drama. In the winter of 1846-7 there was an attempt at regular theatrical entertainments, performances being given in the second story of a building on Dearborn street, near South Water.

About that time John B. Rice came from Buffalo to Chicago, perceived the excellent chance for a theater, and enterprisingly set to work to take advantage of the growing demand. He built a small frame theater on Randolph street, east of Dearborn, and kept it open during the spring, summer, and fall seasons. The winter season, now the best, was then quite dull, so Mr. Rice used to run his company, a very good stock organization, up to Milwaukee for the winter period. The plays were generally classic or at least of standard worth, a taste for trash and absurdity not having prevalence then. But it was the fashion, in order to relieve any undue strain upon the patience or sensibilities of an audience, to give variety to the performance. So it was the custom, when the curtain had descended on an act of a play, Shakespearean perhaps, to send some one before the curtain to sing or dance. A sailor's hornpipe or a Highland fling was often the prelude to

A SOUL-STIRRING TRAGIC EPISODE,

and in some cases one of the actors of the drama did the entre act diversion. There was generally a farcical afterpiece to send the audiences away in good spirits. The variety show of to-day was then unknown. The stars who traveled in annual tour of the country used to play at this house, so that the public got the best fruits of the American stage, save in exceptional instances. This theater, the progenitor, so to speak, of the magnificent structure of theaters now our pride, was burned in 1850, and J. H. McVicker and Sam Myers, members of the company, took the troupe on the road, playing on their own account, while Rice devoted himself to the building of a new theater, this time of brick and on Dearborn street, between Randolph and Washington. This was then regarded as a very imposing edifice, and was opened in the spring of 1851.

McVicker built a theater in 1857, and opened it with "Money." From that time began the real theater life of Chicago, and about that period hovered what many now believe to have been the spirit of the best days of the drama. There were memorable times, to be sure, between that date and the fire of 1871, which, practically, began a new era for Chicago, and it would be a pleasant task to here set down the things that are chiefly worth remembering were space available. There are recollections of great actors gone, of others in the decline of power, still others grown since then into the flower of greatness, and many who, then obscure, are now prominent in place and favored by popularity. Fifty years is but a miracle of time in a city's life, but it is very long for the contemplation of panoramic events, most of them ripening before the birth of that which makes the Chicago of to-day.

THE FIRST OF ANY OPERA

heard in Chicago was in 1860. Strakosch then brought out a concert company, at the head of which were Patti and Brignoli, and they sang parts of opera at McVicker's. This experiment was so very well received that Grau came out next year with a thoroughly equipped opera company, numbering seventy people, and gave three weeks of opera. It was a sensation. The musical sense of Chicago was vindicated, and the taste of the people highly extolled. There is no fear that we do not get credit for equally nice discrimination to-day.

The theater tone, however, is much purer, and it is only that melancholy devotion to things forever gone out of reach that permits any one to contrast the condition of thirty years ago to the disadvantage of the present state of affairs. We are much better off in many respects than we were when the stock companies of McVicker's, the Museum, the Adelphi, Hooley's, or the permanent minstrel companies gave the entertainments, varied by the occasional coming of a star like Cushman, Forrest, Booth, Barrett, Ristori, Edwin Adams, Owens, Lucca, Parepa Rosa, or any of those, who came with more eclat than do corresponding players now, when we are used to a constant round of greatness in rivalry. There were but three or four theaters then, and events were rarer; enthusiasm was greater, because patronage was more special to the theater. In the past ten years the theatric growth of Chicago has been larger and of vaster importance to the city than during the thirty years preceding them, and we get more in one year than the people of a quarter of a century ago obtained in ten years. We have now

SIXTEEN PERMANENT PLACES OF AMUSEMENT

and five or six halls where there are occasional entertainments, exclusive of private institutions that continually appeal to the public with one or another form of diversion. The recognized theaters are McVicker's, Haverly's, the Grand Opera House, Hooley's, the Olympic, the Academy of Music, the Criterion, the Lyceum, the National, the Chicago Museum Theater, the Halsted Street Opera House, the New Metropolitan, and the West and South Side Museums. In Central Music Hall, Farwell Hall, Weber Hall, Hershey Hall, the West End Opera House, there is oftener something doing than not. The theaters named are capable of accommodating 25,000 people nightly, and it is a small computation to say our theaters entertain 100,000 people every week, on an average, throughout the year. The value of Chicago as an amusement center can be very clearly perceived. On this basis —which is very just when we remember that it covers no other patronage than that set down to the regular theaters and takes the middle range of prices—the people of Chicago spend more than $5,200,000 for their amusement each year. Not one of the Chicago theaters but is a largely profitable enterprise, and yet there is only one manager who owns his own theater. His income per annum is, therefore, some $20,000 greater than any of the others, though he plays to no larger business, theaters of his class considered. The rent of Chicago theaters ranges from $5,000 to $30,000 a year. The total value of theater property in Chicago is about $3,000,000. The contrast between this prosperous condition and the wooden theater of 1846 demonstrates what Chicago has done in less than forty years, for the enterprise of which this is an illustration has been universal in corresponding effects, since the theaters follow commercial growth and prosperity, and are never found successful in laggard communities.

M'VICKER'S THEATER,

AND ITS VETERAN PROPRIETOR.

To write the history of McVicker's Theater would be to review the dramatic record of Chicago, for it is the oldest house in the West, and has always been at the head and front of theatrical affairs. Science and art have suggested no practical improvement it has not been the first to adopt, and for a play to have been presented or an actor to have appeared before its footlights has been a certificate of merit to the public and to the profession. It has always been recognized and respected the world over as a perfectly successful theater, conducted solely in the interest of the truest and best types of the drama, and the motive of its proprietor during the third of a century he has spent in Chicago, has ever been to elevate the taste of the people, to encourage that which is good, and to condemn that which is bad in the art of which he is so noble a representative.

Mr. McVicker was born in New York in 1822, and in his early youth developed a fondness for the drama, which naturally led him "behind the scenes." He made his first appearance in amateur entertainments, but entered the profession at the bottom of the ladder as a call boy at the St. Charles Theater of New Orleans, then under the management of

THE FAMOUS SOL SMITH.

Here he educated himself by observation and by the study of the famous actors whom it was his duty to call upon the stage. After three years of this sort of service, at the age of 20, he was given minor parts in the plays, his debut being a speech ten lines in length.

Having shed his swaddling clothes, he went to Nashville in the company of Mr. Neafie, where he appeared in heavy tragedy with considerable success; but his first adventure in the higher role of the drama was at the National Theater of Cincinnati, being there given the proud position of "first walking gentleman" of a stock company that was quite celebrated in its day.

A few years after he returned to New Orleans and played comedy parts at the American Theater, making his first great hit as "the grave-digger" to Edwin Forrest's Hamlet in 1847, being then 25 years of age. He accompanied Forrest on his tour, and finally landed in Chicago, where he joined John B. Rice's company at the old theater on Dearborn street, and remained here four years.

While here he purchased the comedy pieces of Dan Marble, and in 1852 started out as a star, meeting with wonderful success and becoming recognized as the leading comedian of that day. In 1855 he made a tour of Europe, and played "Sam Patch" for twelve consecutive weeks in London.

THE FIRST "M'VICKER'S THEATER."

Returning to America in 1856, he assumed the management of Wood's Theater in St. Louis, but remained there only one season, returning to Chicago in 1857 to stay. He built a theater on the site he occupies today, and on the 5th of November, 1857, opened it with the following bill, the original copy of which hangs in his office:

M'VICKER'S NEW CHICAGO THEATER.
Madison, between State and Dearborn, Chicago.

Proprietor and Manager..............J. H. McVICKER
Assistant Manager.....................F. HARRINGTON

This new and beautiful Temple of the Drama, erected at a cost of Eighty-five Thousand Dollars, and in every particular the Most Elegant Theater in the West, and capable of seating comfortably Two Thousand Five Hundred Persons, will be open to the public

THURSDAY EVENING, NOV. 5, 1857.

The Manager, believing he has succeeded in giving to the public of Chicago a Theater worthy of their liberal patronage, assures them that his endeavors will be to place before them attractions which Cannot Fail to Please. He has also made arrangements with all the

First - Class Legitimate Stars

IN THE COUNTRY.

Miss Charlotte Cushman, Mr. Chas. Matthews.
Miss Eliza Logan, Mr. Jas. E. Murdoch,
Miss J. M. Davenport, Mr. Edwin Booth,
Mr. A. J. Neafie, Mr. Jas. Proctor,
Mr. and Mrs. John Drew, Mr. Henry Placide,
Mr. and Mrs. Florence, And Mr. H. A. Perry,

Who will appear in rapid succession.

He will also introduce a

STOCK COMPANY,

Whose talents alone will be a guarantee of Superior Entertainments, among whom may be enumerated

Mr. David Hanchett,	Miss Alice Mann,
Mr. F. A. Monroe,	Mrs. Lottie Hough,
Mr. F. S. Buxton,	Miss Eliza Mann,
Mr. W. C. Forrester,	Miss Fanny Rich,
Mr. A. J. Grover,	Mrs. R. J. Allen,
Mr. J. B. Uhl,	Mrs. W. C. Forrester,
Mr. R. J. Allen,	Miss Fanny Price,
Mr. W. Gay,	Miss Julia Florence,
Mr. Havelock,	Mrs. W. Gay,
Mr. H. B. Jones,	Miss Emma Logan,
Mr. J. Taylor,	Miss Nellie Gray,
Mr. W. S. Higgins,	Miss Jennie Seacore,
Mr. F. Harrington,	Miss Julia DeLancey,
Mr. J. H. McVicker,	Miss Mary Wright,
	Miss J. Martin,
	Mrs. E. DeLancey,
	Mrs. Anna Martin.

THE ORCHESTRA

Will be Composed of Twelve Solo Performers, selected with great care.

Musical Director.................Mons. LOUIS CHATEL
Scenic Artists } .... { J. R. SMITH / R. S. SMITH
Machinist........................ Mr. WALLACE HUME
Decorator.............................Mr. A. J. MARTIN
Costumer............................ Mrs. A. J. GROVER
Assistant Manager.......................F. HARRINGTON

THE OPENING ADDRESS

(From the pen of B. F. Taylor, Esq.), will be spoken by

MISS ALICE MANN.

The Glorious National Anthem,

THE STAR SPANGLED BANNER

Will be Sung by the Entire Company.

The old favorite and much-admired actor,

H. A. PERRY

Who, having returned, after an absence of four years, will make his first appearance as the

DUKE ARANZA.

Tobin's Comedy of the

HONEYMOON!

And Buckstone's Farce of the

ROUGH DIAMOND

Will introduce the candidates for public favor.

The entertainments will commence with a National Overture by the Orchestra; Leader, Mons. L. Chatel.
After which the Opening Address will be spoken by Miss Alice Mann.
The entire company will then be introduced and sing "The Star Spangled Banner."

GRAND OVERTURE.........................ORCHESTRA

After which, Tobin's comedy of the

HONEYMOON!

DUKE ARANZA..............................H. A. PERRY
Rolondo...................................Mr. F. A. Monroe
Balthazar..................................W. C. Forrester
Count Montalbin...............................Walter Gay
Jaques...F. S. Buxton
Lopez..A. J. Grover
Compillo.......................................W. Higgins
Pedro..J. H. Jones
Juliana....................................Miss Alice Mann
Volante...................................Mrs. Lotty Hough
Zonora....................................Miss Fanny Rich

OVERTURE.................................ORCHESTRA

To conclude with Buckstone's farce of the

ROUGH DIAMOND!

Cousin Joe...................................J. H. McVicker
Margery......................................Lotty Hough

HE SUCCUMBS TO A PANIC.

The financial panic which overturned business in 1857 brought McVicker down with the rest, and he was compelled to sell his pet and pride, but not without a mental reservation that he would buy it back again, which he did a few years after, having in the meantime returned to the stage. Having recovered his house, he resumed the work he had begun, of giving Chicago a theater that equaled any in the land, and through his enterprise the people of Chicago were enabled to witness the performance of every dramatic celebrity that has ever appeared in America.

He often took comedy parts with the famous stars that visited Chicago in the days before the fire, and the old residents remember when a play was not complete without McVicker in the cast. To give a list of those who have trod his boards would be to furnish a catalogue of all the dramatic planets that have illuminated the last half century. His favorite characters were Sam Patch, Nick Bottom, the weaver, in a "Midsummer Night's Dream," and Dogberry in "As You Like It."

IN PRIVATE LIFE

and in business affairs Mr. McVicker has been an influential and esteemed citizen. Although always charitable and generous, he has never hesitated to fight when he found a foe, and to whisper a word against his profession has always been to tread on the tail of McVicker's coat. On the platform and in the press he has been an able and eloquent defender of the stage against its assailants, and he writes and speaks as well as he acts.

He has been an energetic and successful manager, in business affairs as well as in the line of his profession, and his influence and standing in commercial circle-is equal to that he has always exercised in dramatic affairs. Several times has he been suggested as a candidate for Mayor of Chicago, and he might have adorned that and other official positions but for a horror of politics and political intrigue.

The beautiful dramatic temple McVicker now owns and occupies, and which is as dear to him as the blood that throbs in his veins, is the third theater that has borne his name. That which was erected in 1857 was enlarged and remodeled in 1869, and was superb in all its appointments. This was destroyed two years afterward in the great fire, but the work of re-erection was commenced as soon as the bricks were cold.

THE PRESENT M'VICKER'S THEATER

stands as a model in all of its appointments, one of the most beautiful, comfortable, and convenient houses in the world, and is surpassed in no way. If any one can suggest an improvement that will bring McVicker's Theater nearer perfection the owner will adopt it before sundown; but that would be impossible to do, for no one is more familiar with the science of theater construction and arrangement than he, and in all the details his house stands as near the ideal as human ingenuity can make it.

McVicker always has the best; the finest scenery, the most luxurious equipments, the best orchestra, the most artistic displays are a matter of study and pride with him, and he has the admirable faculty of inspiring the same feeling and ambition he himself possesses in every one of his employes. None of the faults that plague other managers, none of the annoyances that are endured by the public at other play-houses are tolerated here, and, although his patrons are the most fastidious in the country, there never is made a complaint. One may heap abuse upon Mr. McVicker and he will smile like a philosopher, but to cast a reflection upon his theater is an insult he will never forget or forgive.

FOR PUBLIC PROTECTION.

His hobby is the protection of the public against panics and fire, and he has made it the study of his life. There is no theater in the world so amply provided with safety appliances, or so well arranged for exits. The house stands alone, with a broad street in front and a broad alley upon each of the other three sides. It can be entered and left from any of the four points of the compass, and the largest crowd that ever occupied the building could be discharged into the street in two minutes. There are forty exits, one at the end of every aisle in every part of the house.

Although he had adopted every fire-proof appliance he wasn't satisfied with them, but has erected on each side of his house iron balconies and iron stairways, which lead from the galleries to the streets. These are reached by doors which can be instantly opened and afford the safest means of escape that can be provided.

HOOLEY'S THEATER.

THE PARLOR HOME OF COMEDY.

There is no more familiar face in the city of Chicago, and no man better known, than Mr. R. M. Hooley, or "Uncle Dick," as he is called by the dramatic profession of which he has been so honorable a representative, and to which he has been so devoted a patron. He has built or remodeled more theaters than any man living, and his experience as a successful manager is almost without a parallel. With his benignant eye and patriarchal beard, he looks what he is—the patron saint of the drama, and one to whom every member of the profession appeals in distress. His relations with the public have always been such as to command the greatest confidence and the highest esteem, and among his associates he is regarded with an affection that is akin to reverence. In his business and social intercourse Mr. Hooley has been considerate, honorable, and upright, and it is not from any act of his own that he has an enemy in the world.

Although born in Ireland (in 1822), his parents removed to Manchester, England, when he was a mere child, and it was there that he received the education and training which fitted him for a long and honorable career of usefulness.

HIS FATHER WAS A PROSPEROUS MERCHANT,

and intended that the son should enter the medical profession, and he was started upon a course of academic study to that end. But in his 18th year he developed such a passion for music that the idea of medicine was abandoned, and young Hooley diligently applied himself to perfecting the artistic taste. Science lost what art gained, for Mr. Hooley possessed that peculiar force of character and power of mind that compel success in whatever direction they are employed. Having acquired a knowledge of music, Mr. Hooley naturally turned toward the theater for its expression.

He began humbly, but he was not of the sort to remain in a subordinate position, and as he gained favor he reached hopefully to higher things. He had the qualities of management, and he, in due course of time, convinced others that his business in life was to govern not be governed in his relations with the theater.

It is impossible in a brief sketch to follow a man of such wide experience along the successful progress of his career, comprising as it does, nearly forty years of managerial enterprise. His personal resources were wonderful, and his execution was never less than his aim, his acts being always to improve. He has controlled theaters in London, New York, Brooklyn, Williamsburg, San Francisco, Madison, Philadelphia, and Chicago, besides having theatric interests that were without a local habitation. Though he has encountered many of the vicissitudes from which no manager has ever been free,

HIS INDOMITABLE SPIRIT AND TIRELESS ENERGY

have led him to triumph over misfortune and secure victory, where others less capable would have accepted defeat. He has invariably kept pace with the spirit of the times, changing base with altered conditions of public taste and education, holding himself abreast of progressive movements in any other direction of social or artistic impulse. He is, therefore, to-day, what he was in his prime, a representative manager.

Mr. Hooley did not permanently settle in Chicago until 1869, twenty-four years after his first visit here. He then devoted his attention wholly to maintaining a theater here. As his greatest delight is found in making others happy, he naturally sought to amuse by an appeal to the joyous in human nature, preferring to excite laughter to playing upon the graver emotions. He was then possessed of a handsome fortune made from his phenomenally prosperous management of his Brooklyn theater.

He purchased the Bryan Hall property, occupying the site of the present Grand Opera House, and converted it into an exquisite beautiful theater, superior in elegance to any of the smaller opera houses of the country. It immediately became a popular and highly favored resort.

MINSTRELSY WAS THEN THE INSTITUTION.

Mr. Hooley was one ot the pioneers in the elevation of this style of entertainment from the crude Ethiopianism of its infancy to the refined and musical delight it afterward became. He was, indeed, for a time associated with the memorable George Christy, who is set down as the father of negro minstrelsy.

Mr. Hooley opened his charming little opera house and for a year maintained it as a minstrel resort. In the summer of 1870, however, the interior was remodeled, made even more pleasing than before, and converted into a comedy house, Frank Aiken and a well-selected company giving the entertainments, that were the boast of the community.

The great fire destroyed this place, and Mr. Hooley suffered a loss of something more than $150,000. Such was his established prestige as a manager he had no difficulty in keeping the people with him in new ventures; and when he became manager of the theater that now bears his name, he found the old patronage ready to hail him as he rose from the ashes of his first fame, and

HOOLEY'S PARLOR HOME OF COMEDY

secured a popularity that made it distinguished throughout the country. There flourished the most numerous and most admirable body of comedians that ever graced a Chicago theater as a home organization.

Men and women who have since become celebrated in independent lines of work co-operated in the production of well chosen plays, gaining for the theater a pre-eminence in general regard that continued uninterrupted until Mr. Hooley sent the company on its memorable excursion to San Francisco, and the combination system set in with all its destroying forces leveled against art and the best interests of the theater. Since that time Mr. Hooley has, somewhat mournfully we imagine, seen the reins of management pass out of the hands of theater proprietors, who have become servants in their own establishments to the speculative ventures of the combination directors. Yet for all that Mr. Hooley exercises a vigorous inspectorship of all attractions that desire to secure dates at his theater, and he takes every possible precaution against the admission of organizations that he thinks are below the standard of excellence he is desirous to maintain for his theater.

Though one of the kindliest and most generous of men, he is admittedly "cranky" when he finds that he has unwittingly imposed upon his patrons something that does not meet his expectation. The condemnation of critics is mild compared with his vehement protests on such occasions. He has the amplest charity, on the other hand, for deserving but unfortunate enterprises. The instances are many where he has turned his theater over to such concerns for their entire advantage, uncomplainingly submitting to the loss of his usual percentage of receipts. He

PREFERS DOING OTHERS A GOOD TURN

to receiving a benefit himself. He rejoices in making people happy, and in his whole life probably never did another an injury that he did not make good a hundred-fold of his own volition.

The standard of Hooley's Theater to-day is nearer that of the old Parlor Home than at any time since the fire, which proves that Mr. Hooley does not run behind in the race. The interior structure of the house is admirable in architectural arrangement and beautiful in decorative effects.

A short time ago the auditorium was subjected to a complete transformation, embodying many novel designs in adornment, and presenting the most unique idea in boxes anywhere to be seen. There are two tiers of boxes on each side of the proscenium, twelve in number, made of iron in the most artistic pattern of light open-work effects, so arranged that they nowhere obstruct the view of occupants of seats in other parts of the house, commanding a full view of the stage, and being richly gilded in gold, they lend a a charming effect to the picturesque study in gold, brass, tinting, and paper designs throughout the house. The arch and its double-point projection and girder are other evidences of the architect's skill and taste, the casts giving a mediæval tone to the more modern accompaniments that make up the harmony of visionary pleasure.

MAKING THE THEATER SAFE.

Though much has been done in the way of making the theater attractive, quite as much more has been done toward rendering it safe. The stage is supplied with a patent contrivance by which that entire end of the theater can be at once converted into a flue with terrific draft, so that a fire could, by the mere force of suction, be prevented from spreading into the auditorium. In addition to this there are all the regulation fire precautions required by the authorities or suggested by the thoughtfulness of the management. The exits are numerous and easily accessible, so that for beauty, comfort, and safety Hooley's should be more than ever regarded as the Parlor Home of Comedy.

GRAND OPERA HOUSE.

THE HOUSE OF LIGHT OPERA.

In considering the experience of Mr. John A. Hamlin as a theatrical manager, there is presented before the immediate view three years of extraordinary and uninterrupted success. While it is true that Mr. Hamlin was for a long time previous to the opening of the Grand Opera House connected with one or another form of amusement enterprise, in every undertaking demonstrating his shrewdness and ability as a financier, it is perhaps quite as true his great pride grows out of his prosperous relation to the beautiful house he now controls. And he has admirable reasons for making the distinction, inasmuch as his present position is evidence of his capability for coping with unfortuitous circumstances, and proves the determination and spirit of a man who could surmount obstacles that would have dismayed many another, and could convert apparent disaster into substantial profit.

Though he is now past the middle period of his years and can look back upon a busy life of mercantile care that began in his youth, he is yet young in management, and it is the highest gratification to him to know that he has not only kept pace with the older managers but has succeeded in very nearly taking

THE LEAD IN LOCAL ENTERPRISES.

Mr. Hamlin is peculiarly constituted, being at once a companionable, free-hearted, and rather jovial gentleman, and an exacting scrupulous man of business, and although the two qualities are often seen together in his intercourse with men they never conflict—one never getting into the proper place of the other.

JOHN A. HAMLIN, Manager.

Those who have known him longest remember these were always marked characteristics with him, and through their exercise he gained friends wherever he desired without ever losing the respect of men with whom he had business transactions. A notable trait of moral nature with Mr. Hamlin is the high estimate he places on his pledges. He believes in the old virtue that a man's word should bind him no less than his written obligation, and when Mr. Hamlin gives his assurance of an act or office, in friendship or in business, he will make good the promise even at the sacrifice of his own personal interests.

His career has been a varied one, for he began his encounter with the world at an early age, and his sanguine, nervous temperament led him into adventures for financial gain that early taught him the principles since so successfully applied in all his undertakings. He began in Cincinnati, quitting college to enter the great school of practical things, and at the age of 21 had already acquired a substantial footing and gained a valuable business acquaintance. In a few years he got together a comfortable capital for more extensive operations. He believed that large success could only come of large undertakings, and he inaugurated a scheme wholly new then that soon made

HIS NAME KNOWN THROUGHOUT THE COUNTRY.

This was the manufacture and sale of a medicine to which he shrewdly gave the brand "Wizard Oil," because of its remarkable properties as a curative. Instead of settling down to the conservative methods of local trade to wait for slow-coming fortune, Mr. Hamlin built a number of elegant wagons of an elaborate and unique design, drawn by four and six splendid horses, furnished them with cabinet organs and sent them into all parts of the country accompanied by a regular concert company. The effect of this Napoleonic move was magical. Crowds thronged about these wagons in city or in town to enjoy the very excellent entertainment given and to purchase the wonderful fluid, the merits of which were expounded by expert lecturers, and Mr. Hamlin made an immense fortune in very short order.

He had a clear perception of the advantages afforded by Chicago for the investment and accumulation of money, and bought property here very extensively. His business had grown so large that he took his brother into an interest with him and began to realize what it is to be a rich man.

After the great fire of 1871 Mr. Hamlin bought the famous site of the Bryan Hall, that had been converted into Hooley's Theater, and erected what was then considered one of the most magnificent buildings in the city, and which is now one of the most desirable pieces of property in the commercial center. The principal floor was fitted up as a superb billiard hall, and was leased and run by the well-known Tom Foley, and became perhaps

THE MOST POPULAR RESORT IN CHICAGO.

Mr. Hamlin, like many another rich man, felt the evil force of the panic of 1873, and was seriously crippled in his business concerns, and for the first time in his life saw his plans go amiss. He was a man of too prolific resources to be dismayed by his losses, and immediately set about restoring his impaired fortune. He began by converting the billiard hall into a place of resort known as the Coliseum, which at once became popular, and proved a money-making enterprise.

But, after running the Coliseum for a time, Mr. Hamlin become dissatisfied with the sort of patronage the place attracted, and, though his income was very great and his expenses quite low, resolved to convert the building into a theater for a more respectable public. He instituted Hamlin's Theater, a cozy little house where dramatic spectacular, and vaudeville entertaniments were given.

In the management of this house Mr. Hamlin got the idea that he could establish a very different theater, and determined upon making a bold play for the lead in Chicago theater enterprises. He therfore announced the entire demolition of Hamlin's Theater, to make way for an opera house that should be the realization of artistic loveliness. Many discouragements were thrown in Mr. Hamlin's way, and there were numerous croakers ready to predict the folly and certain failure of the project. But Mr. Hamlin feels a confidence in the success of any undertaking to which he gives his personal endeavor, and he went resolutely ahead with his plans, until in good season he opened to the public the most charming, beautiful, and exquisitely arranged theater then existing in the city. It was as bright and attractive as the others were gloomy and old-fashioned, so that it not only became the talk of professional people, but secured the immediate indorsement of the public and became the

FAVORITE RESORT OF FASHIONABLE PATRONAGE.

The house has continued for three years without any interruption of its enviable success, and Mr. Hamlin has had the extreme satisfaction of demonstrating his entire capacity for first-class theatric managment and of triumphing over the opposition he encountered on entering the field of his present labors.

The Grand Opera House has been made as nearly perfect in respect to convenience and public safety as it is possible to have such a building. One cannot conceive a catastrophe possible to this house, fortified as it is with a multiplicity of exits and armed underneath with a fire-wall that would absolutely prevent the spread of a fire from the stage to the auditorium. Every precaution against danger is observed, and in some instances there have been wholly unnecessary steps taken to insure the welfare of an audience

Though the theater is one of the prettiest and most enjoyable in the country, Mr. Hamlin intends to further beautify and embellish it during the present year, so that by the opening of the next winter season it will be as new and beautiful to the eye as the night three years ago when it was so auspiciously inaugurated by the Emma Abbott Opera Company. As its name implies, music is the specialty of the house, all the important light opera companies of the country having bookings here, for one reason, because Manager Hamlin cultivates that sort of attraction, and for another reason, that the people prefer to sing in that house. But the attractions are by no means confined to opera, it being the aim to have the best standard attractions, be their line what it may, and the house is known for its choice.

HAVERLY'S THEATER.

IMPROVEMENTS FOR THE NEW YEAR.

Not only because that house is of most recent date, but because its story already reaches out toward the future in a fashion at once distinct and interesting, an account of Haverly's Theater will serve most fittingly to close this article. It will not be necessary in this relation to more than refer to the old Adelphi and to Mr. Haverly's reign there as lessee. He gave his own name to the old house as long as the old house was there to be called by any name. When the shadows of destruction had foregathered about it, and the stately outlines of the now First National Bank Building began to erect themselves into a solid intention, Mr. Haverly carried his name across Monroe street and bestowed it upon the structure which bears it now.

The theater was a surprise to every one, even in Chicago, where celerity is a prevailing habit and Time has in most things been knocked out of time. The first stone was turned upon the ground on the 12th of June, 1881. Ninety days later—on the 12th of September—the new theater, completed at every point, was thrown open to the public. If the world can offer another case in which a permanent edifice of equal size, beauty, and solidity was so well and so rapidly put together, this writer has yet to learn of it.

THE HOUSE AND THE MEN.

The house was built by General John B. Carson, of Quincy, Ill., the General Manager of the Hannibal and St. Joseph Railway. Immediate supervision of the work in all its details was confided to Mr. James D. Carson, his son. Mr. Oscar Cobb was the supervising architect.

The first artists to appear upon the stage of the new theater were the comedians Robson and Crane, who played Sir Andrew and Sir Toby in "The Twelfth Night." The vast auditorium was crowded to the very doors, and the success of the enterprise was assured from the moment of its submission to the public. There was but one opinion expressed, and that one was favorable if not enthusiastic.

The business of the theater has never been less than prosperous in even the dullest months of the year; and it is to be questioned whether an equal aggregate of receipts in the average of all months during the last two years could be shown by any theater in the world, saving the principal of those which are devoted exclusively to grand opera at high prices.

The theater is admittedly the most popular in the city, and its conveniences include everything that up to the time of its erection was known to modern stage mechanism. It is the only theater in the city which has the Edison incandescent electric light in every department. This light is used on the entire stage, in the dressing-rooms, auditorium, private boxes, foyer, vestibule, and offices, while the facade of the house is brilliantly illuminated by Edison arc lights. The theater is thus rendered perfectly free from the noxious odors of coal gas, and by an improved system of ventilation the atmos-

HAVERLY'S THEATRE.

phere of the auditorium is kept perfectly pure, and therefore healthful.

In addition to the largest and most comfortable seating capacity, Haverly's Theater has twenty-one private boxes, all luxuriously furnished and commanding a full view of the stage. Retiring-rooms and cloak-rooms for both ladies and gentlemen are connected with the foyer, and during the winter the house is thoroughly warmed by steam radiator. The main floor is on a level with Monroe street, and unlike any other South Side theater, occupants of the parquette and parquette circle and the private boxes have not a single step to climb.

THE POLICY OF THE THEATER

having been a very liberal one, the best attractions before the public have sought it; and thus such great dramatic lights as Edwin Booth, Lester Wallack, John McCullough, T. W. Keene, and Mme. Janauschek, such distinguished organizations as the Union Square Company and the Brooks and Dickson Companies, and such operatic attractions as Mme. Adelina Patti, the McCaull, Duff, and Grau comic opera companies, have all chosen to appear within its walls. The sensation caused by Mrs. Langtry, in social as well as theatrical circles, demanded a theater equal to the occasion, and Haverly's Theater was chosen for her Chicago engagement. So in the case of Mr. Henry Irving and the Metropolitan Grand Opera Company, both under the management of Mr. Abbey, and both to appear at this house during the coming month.

Enough has been said to indicate how greatly superior in every respect this theater is to any similar edifice in Chicago, and how carefully and energetically the management of the house strives to live up to and by continued effort continuously to deserve the popularity so quickly and so completely won. The public having shown so responsive an appreciation of all that has been done for their amusement and comfort in the construction and conduct of the house, the present lessee, in the feeling that the effort will be understood and approved, has determined to widen its province so as to include all arts and all appliances that conduce to the best and most æsthetic tastes and pleasures. This intention involves a very distinct, even a bold departure from precedent; but it has been formed after sufficient consideration and in the full belief that a temple of dramatic art is of all places the most fit and deserving to be adorned with all that is beautiful in other arts; since to dramatic art itself all others are contributive, and by dramatic art all others are heightened and in turn adorned. His theater will therefore be in as strong a way as possible a grouping point for all the rest.

NEW IMPROVEMENTS PLANNED.

To this end, with the close of the present season, the whole interior of the house will be changed to conform to new and practical ideas in theatrical architecture, which have been suggested and applied only within the last year. These improvements will extend not only to the stage, but to the auditorium, and while the interest of the public will be enlisted by charming innovations in the presentation of dramatic works, in so far as the stage dressing is concerned, it will also be directed to the contemplation of the most luxurious and beautiful auditorium in America. The metamorphosis will be very thorough in every department. The walls will be treated by a new process of construction and decoration. The private boxes will be reconstructed on a more pleasing and artistic plan and furnished still more luxuriously. The seats will be changed for seats of a pattern much superior. The foyer will be enlarged and two spacious

RICE'S DEARBORN STREET THEATER.

reception rooms will be added, each of which will be elaborately furnished and adorned with bric-a-brac, paintings, statuary, and rare books and prints. These innovations should, and in every likelihood will, mark a point of new departure in the history of Chicago theaters. That they will be greeted with pleasure and rewarded with substantial approval by citizens of all sorts and conditions may at even this distance of time be taken as a conclusion well foregone.

The work of beautifying the place will be made equally apparent in every tier, so that the patron of the top floor, as well as the patron of the higher-priced places, will find much that is entertaining, amusing, or instructive to contemplate.

The plans for this great change are nearly perfected. The work will commence about the 1st of June, and in the early autumn the doors of the theater will open to reveal a splendor as well as a comfort that will amaze and delight those who are familiar with the present interior. The class of attractions to be presented during the next season will excel as a line anything known to even this most successful and prosperous of theaters.

The present lessee of the building and proprietor of the theater, Mr. C. H. McConnell, President of the National Printing Company, is the gentleman to whom Chicago will be indebted for this elegant temple of art. No person who has visited the elegant offices of the National Printing Company will need any assurance of the refined taste which will characterize the theater in its new habiliment. The management of the house devolves upon Mr. William J Davis. Mr. John S. McConnell is the Treasurer, and Mr. George S. Bowron musical director.

THE ACADEMY OF MUSIC.

DAN SHELBY'S SUCCESS.

When Mr. Daniel Shelby came here from Buffalo and took the lease of the Academy of Music, there were few who thought he could make a great success of the undertaking, because of his announced determination to lift that theater into competition with those of the South Side. There were free predictions that he would very soon be glad to return to the smaller city and content himself with a more restricted field of management.

Mr. Shelby is, however, one of those serenely decisive men who are rarely turned aside from their course by the ready evil auguries of others, and he set quietly about carrying his plans to a successful issue, the more resolved on triumphing for the opposition he encountered. He received the Academy as a variety theater with a fixed patronage of people whose tastes were on a level with the character of the entertainments. He was told that he must keep this clientelage or lose the money he adventured. He answered: "I intend to have a theater that the best people in town can feel safe in visiting." It required less time than two years to make this prophecy good.

Mr. Shelby proved to be a shrewd, enterprising, and conscientious manager. He first gained the respect and then the confidence of the community, and being already in possession of the good will and regard of professional people, managers, and actors throughout the country, he had scarcely any difficulty in prosperously establishing the house on the basis of a new policy. He began bidding for the leading attractions among the combinations, and soon had a large number of first-class attractions booked for his house, and when it was found how thoroughly in earnest he was in an endeavor to elevate the tone of his theater, the public came admiringly to his support. Mr. Shelby is to-day one of the most positively representative managers of Chicago, as he has fallen fully into the active, pushing spirit of the community, is liberal-hearted and open-handed in his business as he is in private, and never hesitates to make expenditures, where he believes he is likely to please his patrons. He has beautified the theater until it is a fit shrine for the noblest forms of dramatic art and delightful to the most refined taste. He has given the surroundings an inviting atmosphere, and can well claim to have as popular a theater and as genteel a class of patrons as any theater in the city. Mr. Shelby really is entitled to the gratitude of the people residing on the West Side for having been the leader in establishing in that part of the city a first-class theater, and for having inspired others to emulate his example. Though his success has brought about some rivalry, prompting others to follow where he led, there is no fear that such a wide-awake, progressive and strategic manager will be seriously affected by any sort of honest competition.

CHAPTER IV

HOTELS TO BE PROUD OF.

OUR HOTELS.

THE OLD TIME TAVERNS.

In no one feature is progressive Chicago better or more forcibly illustrated than in her hotels. Over on Milwaukee avenue, near Fulton street, stands a two-story frame building, not prepossessing in appearance either from the outside or within, and the saloon which takes up most of the ground floor is of such character to warn one fond of a social drink that he should go farther and fare better. There is nothing inviting about the place, and yet fifty years ago the people of Chicago were very proud of the building, and there was much talk about the new Green Tree Tavern about to be opened. S. B. Cobb, one of Chicago's millionaires to-day, came tramping into the city about that time, and, not finding an opening in his own line of business, engaged himself to the boss carpenter and helped nail the shingles on the roof of the new tavern, the first building put up in Chicago designed for a public house.

POLITICS AT THE GREEN TREE.

The Hon. John Wentworth was in the habit of strolling over the old flat bridge to spend an evening in the bar-room of the Green Tree with the genial proprietor, Chester Ingersoll, and some of the "boys," who came in to talk politics, tell adventures, or read the papers from the East, which were perhaps a week or two old, but filled with news for the people of the frontier settlement. John Gray, of Grayland, a beautiful Chicago suburb, was at one time the jolly landlord at the Green Tree House, and when not kept busy with his guests sat in the door and shot wolves that came to carry away his young pigs at the barn across the street.

The house when built stood at the corner of Lake and Canal streets, on the site now occupied by the building of the American Iron Works. Now it is in decay, but fifty years ago it was the new palace hotel of Chicago, and far outshone the taverns which had taken care of the visitors to Chicago.

The old Kinzie House, even when it was the only white man's dwelling here, had its latch-string always hanging out for strangers, and others who followed were just as hospitable in offering entertainment. When the settlement became larger the little log hut on Wolf Point, at the intersection of the two branches of the river, was opened as a tavern.

FIRST LICENSED HOTEL.

The County Commissioners of Peoria County granted Archibald Caldwell a license to keep a tavern there Dec. 8, 1829, and he was assessed to pay a tax of $8, and give a bond with security for $100. By this license he was allowed to charge the following rates:

	Cents.
Each half-pint of wine, rum, or brandy	25¼
Each pint of wine, rum, or brandy	37¼
Each half-pint gin	18½
Each pint gin	31¾
Each gill of whisky	6½
Each half-pint whisky	12½
Each pint whisky	18¾
Each breakfast, dinner, or supper	25
Each night's lodging	12½
Keeping horse over night on grain and hay	25
The same as above, 24 hours	37¼
Horse feed	12

In front of the door stood a tall pole, from which swung a sign and on this was painted a rude picture of a wolf, but the house received its name from the point of land on which it stood. It was at this house that General Scott made his headquarters when he came to Chicago in 1832 to put down the Blackhawk disturbance. Elijah Wentworth had an inn on the West Side in 1830, which was probably the Wolf Point House.

HUNG UP FOR THE NIGHT.

The Miller House, which stood on the other side of the North Branch, and was partly of logs and partly frame, was also opened as a tavern. Then came Mark Beaubien, in 1831, who opened a tavern in a small log house on the South Side, which he called the Sauganash, in honor of Billy Caldwell, chief of the Pottawatomies. It was in this little house where the jolly fiddler said he first filled his beds, then the floors, and afterward hung up his guests on nails and hooks on the walls.

These were the hotels before 1833, when the Green Tree House was built. This supplied the want for a while, and then late in 1833 was commenced, on the northwest corner of Lake and Dearborn streets, the first Tremont House. It was a small wooden building, and could easily be placed in the reception room of the present Tremont House, and it would take two or three like it to fill the dining room. In 1836 this house was enlarged so as to accommodate fifty people, and in 1839 it was burned. John Wentworth made this his home until it was burned.

The old Sauganash kept by Mark Beaubien afterward took on another story and then changed its name to the City Hotel.

MRS. MURPHY'S "BOYS."

In 1836 John Murphy and his wife came to Chicago and opened the United States Sauganash. Mrs. Murphy is still living on the West Side, and is one of the sprightliest old ladies in Chicago. She speaks of the Hon. John Wentworth, S. B. Cobb, and a dozen other old citizens as "her boys." They boarded with her in these early days, and were always coming in late at night, getting into her pantry, which was next morning usually found to be empty, especially of pumpkin pies and cakes.

In 1837 Mr. and Mrs. Murphy went to the West Side and opened the United States Hotel, which they kept for several years.

Other early hotels were the Eagle House, at the corner of Canal and Madison streets, built in 1836; the Mansion House, on Lake street, opposite where the Tremont now stands, built in 1835, and kept by Abram A. Markle; the Steamboat House, on North Water street, near Kinzie, kept in 1835 by John Davis; the Lake House, on the North Side, near the river, on Michigan street, finished in 1836.

A MARVELOUS HOTEL.

The opening of this house was another event in the early history of Chicago. The village had by this time outgrown the Green Tree House, and John H. Kinzie, Gurdon S. Hubbard, Captain David Hunter, and Major James B. Campbell built the Lake House, at an expense of over $90,000. It was opened in 1837, and was the marvel of the day.

It was built of brick, and when finished there was nothing between it and the lake. The main entrance was on Michigan street, and nearly the whole of the first floor on the left was given to the reception parlor. The dining-room and bar-room, sixty feet long, was a wonderful room to the people, who had been living in hotels where the whole house was not so large as this room.

Jacob Russell came from Middletown, Conn., to take charge of the house, and it was opened with great promise. But it was not in the line of the city's growth, and in a few years was a complete failure.

The City Hotel was built on the northwest corner of Clark and Randolph streets in 1836 and 1837, and in 1844 became the Sherman House.

The Western Hotel, built on West Randolph street in 1834, it is claimed, was the first entire frame building put up in Chicago. It was built and kept by W. H. Stowe, and a part of the old house still stands at the corner of Randolph and Canal streets.

THEN AND NOW.

These were the hotels in Chicago before 1840.

But since then there has been a change. The great need of the city in late years has been hotel accommodations for the great crowds of people who came here either for business or pleasure. The great fire swept the down town district clean, and when the hotels were to be rebuilt there was nothing of the old to be worked into the new.

THE WESTERN HOTEL.

Thinking of the future, and calculating for the rapid growth of the city, the hotels were built on a grand scale that surprised the world, and called out criticism and predictions of utter failure. Millions of money was put into mammoth piles of iron and stone, and in a year or two after the fire the grandest and most magnificent hotels in the world were thrown open to the public.

All the hotels of Chicago in 1840 piled together could be stowed away like so many trunks in any one of five large hotels now open, and the whole population of the city at that time could now be easily taken care of in these houses. The Wolf Point Tavern, the Miller House, and the Sauganash Hotel of 1832 could be set up in the news exchange of the Grand Pacific like so many relics, and the Green Tree and Western Hotels might each occupy an end of the grand dining-room and leave as much space of marble flooring between as there then existed of prairie grass. The Palmer House could have housed and fed General Scott's army, that came to fight Blackhawk and his Indians in 1832, and here also gathered in all the settlers of Northern Illinois, and protected them from the scalping-knife.

HOTEL ACCOMMODATIONS FOR A CITY.

In this house, which cost more than $2,-000,000, and contains more than 17,000,000 bricks, and covering an area of 72,500 square feet, one of the early settlers would get lost as easily as in a city.

The hotels of Chicago to-day number 160, with an aggregate accommodation for 25,000 people. This is in addition to the large number of large boarding-houses scattered throughout the residence portions of the city. And these hotels are always full of guests, having often to resort to cots to give accommodation. The city is acknowledged everywhere to be better able to take care of great crowds of people than any other on the continent—with the exception of New York. At the time of the Republican National Convention, and again at the Knights Templar Triennial Conclave in 1880, there were 50,-000 strangers in the city, and all were taken care of without trouble. During the Conclave the Palmer House and Grand Pacific each had over 1,000 guests, and the Palmer one day dined 2,500 people. The Sherman, Tremont, and Leland were only a little way behind these.

There has not only been a change in the size but in the appointment of the hotels in Chicago. The men who allowed Mark Beaubien to hang them up for the night on hooks and nails, and those who slept on the floor of the bar-room and dining-room at the Green Tree, or went to the haymow if all other places were full, now want the very best of everything, and in Chicago they get it.

They are not satisfied with a room, but must have a suite, with everything as complete as if they had spent a fortune in building and furnishing a home of their own.

THE PALMER HOUSE.

ONLY FIRE-PROOF HOTEL IN THE COUNTRY.

Chicago is famous for its public-spirited citizens, but there is no man who has done more to build up the city, and give it a reputation for push and enterprise, than Potter Palmer. Monuments of his energy and public-spiritedness can be seen in every direction, and any one of them would satisfy most ambitious men, but the Palmer House is the greatest of them all. Wherever Chicago is known—and where is it not—wherever newspapers and travelers go to tell of the grandeur of the city that has been raised from a swamp once, and then from the ashes, to be the finest in the world, the Palmer House is told of as one of its greatest ornaments and most attractive institutions.

It was only two months ago that the tenth anniversary of the completion and opening of this monstrous inn was fittingly commemorated. Then gathered, as the guests of the Palmer House, the principal citizens of Chicago, the Mayor, the Collector of Customs, the Postmaster, the judges, and other prominent officials, State, Federal, and municipal, and several hundred private citizens, the leaders of commerce and trade, the bright lights of the bar, the pulpit, and other professions, to celebrate an

EVENT OF WHICH THEY WERE PROUD.

It was then that they realized more plainly than ever before the fact that Potter Palmer was wiser and farther-sighted than most of his contemporaries, and that in the construction of a hotel, which at the date it was erected was far ahead of its time, he builded better than they knew.

Mr. Palmer had erected two hotels before, but both were destroyed by fire, and he determined this time to erect a building which "moth and rust could not corrupt" and which the hottest flames could not consume. The ashes of the great fire of 1871 had scarcely gotten cold before Mr. Palmer, with that energy for which he is famous, selected the finest location in Chicago, and commenced the erection of a building which every one said would make him a bankrupt. An income of $200,000 a year had been swept away by the fire, and he had little but pluck and land left. It was then that the reputation he had been acquiring in Chicago for twenty-five years became his capital, and while other rich men were sitting disconsolate in the ashes Mr. Palmer borrowed $1,-500,000 and commenced the erection of

THE MODEL HOTEL OF THE WORLD.

With Potter Palmer, to have anything, is to have the best, and although he undertook what most men called a hazardous venture, ten years have justified his faith and vindicated his judgment, for in building his hotel he constructed a mint, which has been pouring dollars into his lap ever since.

While other hotels failed and dragged into bankruptcy the men who managed them, the Palmer House has ever and always been a success. The reason is that Mr. Palmer realized what the people wanted, and gave it to them. The location he selected was the most advantageous for the purpose in Chicago, being convenient to both the wholesale and retail trade, to all of the street car lines, to all of the railroad depots, and to all of the places of amusement. It is at the very focus of business, the heart of the city, and when one wants to describe the distance of any point to be reached he always says, "So many blocks from the Palmer House."

Another reason why the hotel has been so successful and popular is that

IT IS ABSOLUTELY FIRE-PROOF.

Soon after it was built an active discussion was engaged in as to whether it was actually fire-proof. Mr. Palmer said that the underwriters might select any room in his house, build a fire in the center of the floor, of the fiercest combustibles they could find, lock the door, and go down to dinner with him. If the hotel burned or was injured he would stand all the loss, and give $10,000 to any charity that might be named. If the fire burned out without doing any damage except to carpet and furniture, they should give the same amount. The underwriters looked the house over and decided not to accept the test. The writer, who was a reporter for THE INTER OCEAN at that time, well remembers this discussion and the interest it caused.

No other hotel in the world is so safe from

fire as the Palmer House, and the several hotel conflagrations at which so many lives were lost made it the stopping place for all the wise people who came to Chicago.

SOME OTHER ADVANTAGES.

Another, and an equally successful advantage in hotel keeping, which was introduced at the Palmer House, and is still continued there, was the graded system of prices. A man does not have to pay $4.50 per day for the privilege of stopping at a first-class, fire-proof hotel, and then take his chances of getting a poor room. He can select whatever room he likes, and pay for it accordingly, take his meals where he chooses, at the restaurant, or the cafe, or, if he prefers, at the houses of his friends, or eating-places about town; the price he would be charged at a third-class hotel, and have all the advantages enjoyed by one who pays $8 or $10 a day, except in the location of his room. The dining-room and the bill of fare is the same for all guests, but the only difference is in the location of the room. In all the requirements which go to make up a perfect hotel the Palmer House is complete, and there is none more elegantly and luxuriously furnished.

A CITY IN ITSELF.

When the hotel was first erected it contained only 400 rooms, but that number soon proved too few, and had to be increased, first to 500, then to 600, and now it is frequently impossible to accommodate the numerous patrons of the house in the 750 rooms belonging to this great hostelry. The house can accomodate 1,200 people comfortably, and several times as many as 2,500 have taken their meals there in a single day. It is the largest hotel in the country with one exception, and that is the Palace Hotel of San Francisco. Next year Mr. Palmer proposes to add another story, which will increase the number of rooms to 850, and furnish accommodations for 1,500 people.

There are two large passenger elevators, constructed with all the safety appliances, and made perfectly secure, which are kept running all the time, in addition to the usual number of stairways, so that the upper rooms are quite as accessible and convenient as those upon the lower floors.

The Palmer is the only hotel in the city where the guests have a choice of the European or the American plans, and they can take their meals in any one of the three magnificent dining-rooms on the parlor floor or in the Cafe or Restaurant on the office floor. The Restaurant, which is the most elegant in Chicago, and is not surpassed in the country, is an imperial apartment, circular in form, and made of marble and mirrors. It is the favorite resort of the fashionable people of the city for lunches and dinners, and for suppers after the theater or opera.

PALMER HOUSE.

The classes of guests a hotel entertains are the best index of its character, and those who go the Palmer House are men who know where to find the best accommodations. General Grant always makes it his home while in Chicago. The Marquis of Lorne and the Princess Louise stopped here. President Diaz, of Mexico, the Corean embassy, and other distinguished people inscribe their autographs upon its register every day.

It is not necessary to allude to the luxuriance with which it is furnished, for that is a proverb the world over. The attendance is always the best, the bills of fare are the finest offered in the city, and the cooks cannot be surpassed in the country.

Mr. Willis Howe, the managing partner, gives every detail his personal attention, and to his ability and energy the success of the hotel is largely due.

THE GARDEN OF EDEN.

FINEST BATH-ROOMS IN THE WORLD.

Attached to the Palmer House, and connecting with the main office, are the finest barber shop and the finest bath-rooms in the world. They are known as "The Garden of Eden" from the name Mr. W. S. Eden, the proprietor. There is no place of the kind on either continent fitted up with such magnificence. The cost of the fixtures in the barber shop alone was $23,000, and of the bathing department, $30,000. The former, which is 40x100 feet in size, is furnished with mirrors on every side and overhead, in which are reflected many times the burnished brass fixtures, the gilded columns and cornices, the marble walls and floors, the elegant plush and velvet sofas and chairs, the nicely dressed and silent knights of the brush and razor, and the merry whisk of the sable artists who wield the broom. In all, there are 200 square feet of mirrors, one being 100x150 inches, the largest in this country. The washstand, which cost $3,000, is composed of seven different colored costly marbles, and over it is a handsomely designed marble arch in which is a pyramid of elegant French clocks that are set to the time of different cities.

The bathing department is a marvel. Every known bath can be had. Marble floors, marble baths, and marble scrubbing beds are everywhere. In the "Macerecure" room twenty different kinds of baths are furnished. In one room is a diving tank, 15x50, with a depth of 5½ feet. The "needle" shower bath, with its million sprays, cost $1,000. The Russian and Turkish bath-rooms are fitted up in the highest style of perfection, and throughout the whole department nothing is wanting to make it the most consummate triumph of modern art and taste. Nothing like it has ever been attempted before, and it is a crowning triumph for its projectors.

THE TREMONT HOUSE.

THE PALACE HOTEL OF CHICAGO.

The history of Chicago would not be complete without a reference to the Tremont House, the oldest, one of the most popular, and one of the most successful of the great hotels that are the pride of the city to-day. It was first established in 1833, the year that the city was incorporated. In 1840 it was enlarged and rebuilt. In 1849 the foundations were laid for a new house, which was built of brick, and opened in 1850, as the only really first-class hotel in Chicago. In 1861 it was remodeled and stood until the great fire swept everything away. The present magnificent structure, erected on the old site, is in the minds of many the handsomest building in Chicago.

The present building stands at the corner of Lake and Dearborn streets. It is in the central business district, and therefore the most convenient for merchants who come to Chicago to trade. It is six stories high, of beautifully carved Amherst sand stone, and in design and construction has no superior for the purpose for which it was erected in America or in the world. The offices and parlors are finished and furnished in a style that could not be surpassed, and the chambers are as luxurious as can be found in any private palace in the city, each having hot and cold water, marble mantels, grates, etc., all perfectly lighted and ventilated from the street or the central court, furnished with solid black walnut and

TREMONT HOUSE.

velvet, or polished rosewood with satin draperies and carpets matching or contrasting tastefully.

Especial attention has been given to sewer connections and drainage—the arrangement of traps and otherwise perfect plan of plumbing successfully guard the hotel from all noxious gases, giving absolute security against malaria in any form from the usual auses.

A shaft 120 feet high, 4x5 feet area, heated, into which are led ducts, taking the foul air, if any, from every department, out of and above the building, completes the system of ventilation, and as a result the Tremont excels in the purity of its atmosphere, being free from the pernicious odors always found with less considerate construction.

There are four stairways from the basement to the top of the house, and two elevators for the use of guests, affording easy access to all stories, and ample egress in case of alarm from any cause.

The building is practically fire proof, being constructed with all modern means for protection from damage by that element. Standing waterpipes, with thirty openings, having hose attached of sufficient length to flood with water every room and corridor, connected with a stationary steam engine, the floors all laid with cement, the partitions filled in with brick, preventing any possibility of fire spreading in case of accident, and there have been placed in the halls of the house gongs, rung by electricity, as an alarm in case of fire, under control of the office, and will be set going instantly on the slightest alarm, and continue to ring. This ringing, with the system of calling each room by watchmen stationed on the floors, insures the speediest alarm to guests it is possible to give in case of accident.

There are red lanterns in each hall, showing the stairways, and at the end of every corridor outside the building are iron-ladder fire escapes to the ground.

From the roof and the three stores below it there is access to the tops of adjoining buildings, making a way of escape over the roofs, from Dearborn to State street, a full block, giving security to guests no other hotel can offer.

There are ample accommodation for 800 guests in a first-class, unequaled way, and although located so conveniently in the busiest quarter of the city, central to all the great depots, the banks, wholesale stores, and places of elegant shopping and amusements, it is yet most quiet and homelike.

The management of the proprietors, John A. Rice & Co., is liberal, and the scale of rates per diem is lower than ever before made for equal accommodations, on the American plan. The house is regarded as the most pleasant and comfortable hotel home for the tourist and resident guest in Chicago, and no effort of expense or personal attention is spared to maintain the high reputation which has already won for the enterpise the pride and admiration of our citizens and the world of travelers.

The elegant barber-shop connected with the Tremont House is managed by Mr. W. S. Eden, who also has the Garden of Eden at the Palmer.

GRAND PACIFIC HOTEL.

THE HEADQUARTERS OF STATESMEN.

If a newspaper reporter or a citizen wants to find traveling statesmen he goes to the Grand Pacific Hotel, for it is there they always stop. Mine host Drake has entertained more famous men than any landlord of his generation, and within the walls of the great palace over which he presides have been lodged and banqueted all the great men of the generation. It was here that President Arthur stopped during his recent visit to Chicago, and while he was attending the National Convention in 1880. It was here that General Garfield was when nominated for President, and here his first reception was held. All the Senators, Congressmen, Cabinet officers, and other dignitaries make the Grand Pacific Hotel their rendezvous while in Chicago.

It is also the headquarters of the railroad managers, and in one of its club-rooms their frequent gatherings are held. Mr Vanderbilt and Jay Gould always stop here when in Chicago, and all men whose taste leads them to select the best that can be had. Patti, the famous cantatrice; Nilsson, Gerster Kellogg, Albani, and all the famous artistes make it their home during the opera seasons. It is the stopping place of princes and dukes and earls when they visit us, and the list of famous people could be lengthened out to fill columns. Scarcely a day passes but some man or woman of worldwide fame writes his or her name upon the register, which bears the autographs of kings, emperors, and presidents.

The Grand Pacific is not only a great public ornament, and one of the sights rural visitors go to see, but it is kept in a manner that makes the people of Chicago proud of the house and its proprietors. All the great banquets are given here, and they are given on a scale that eclipses anything ever seen in the West. The Bar Association chose it as the proper, and, in fact, the only place at which Lord Coleridge could be entertained in a manner consonant with his dignity and fame.

It was with rare foresight and judgment that the hotel was located, for when its foundations were laid, it stood upon the extreme limit of the business district of the city, and thoughtless people said it was a foolish thing to place so noble a structure so far from the center of trade. But time and the growth of Chicago has demonstrated the wisdom of its projectors, for it is now in the most convenient and accessible locality. The Postoffice and Custom House have since been placed across the street in one direction, and the new Board of Trade, one of the finest buildings in the land, stands opposite in another. It will soon be the center of the new commercial district, for around it are being erected the finest blocks and business houses in Chicago. It is the nearest first-class hotel, to the three great depots of the city.

It is conveniently located to the places of amusement and other attractions for which Chicago is famous. In convenience of location, in the luxuriousness of its apartments, in the elegance of its table, its splendid service, and in all the whys and wherefores that go to make up the attractions and advantages of a hotel, it stands pre-eminent, and there is no place in the world where a traveler can secure such comforts, such style, and such attractions for the prices that are charged.

The senior proprietor, Mr. John B. Drake, who has kept a hotel here ever since Chicago is a city, and whose name is familiar to the traveling public, gives the affairs of the house his personal attention, and is scarcely absent a day during the entire year, but remains in the house looking after the comfort of his guests, greeting them upon their arrival, and bidding them farewell upon their departure, with a cordial courtesy that they always remember. His partners, Mr. Turner and Mr. Parker, are gentlemen well-known to the traveling public, as hosts of the highest order, and the gentlemanly corps of assistants are always attentive and polite.

THE SHERMAN HOUSE.

AN HOTEL WITH A REPUTATION.

The history of Chicago could not be accurately written without a reference to the historical Sherman House and its proprietor, J. Irving Pearce, one of the oldest and best-known hotel men in Chicago, who kept the Adams House, at the corner of Lake street and Michigan avenue, when the place where the new Board of Trade now stands was a cow pasture.

Mr. Pearce was for many years President of the Third National Bank of Chicago, but became proprietor of the Sherman House a little more than a year ago, and is now giving his whole time to the hotel business. Since he became proprietor, he has put entirely new furniture throughout the house, and it is now not surpassed by any hotel in the country for the attractions and advantages it offers to the traveler. Its rooms are larger and more convenient than those of any other hotel in the country and are luxuriously furnished.

The location, at the corner of Clark and Randolph streets, opposite the Court House, is in the exact center of the business district of the city, and within a block of the Board of Trade and telegraph offices. The ticket offices of all the railroads are immediately under or around the Sherman House, and it is within two minutes' walk of the principal theaters.

LELAND HOTEL.

THE BEST LOCATION IN THE CITY.

The Leland Hotel, owned and kept by Warren Leland, a member of that famous family of landlords whose name is a synonym for a well-kept house, is noted and conspicuous for several things. In the first place it occupies the best location of any hotel in the United States, and one that is not surpassed in the world. Just on the edge of the wholesale and retail districts of the city, on the Grand Boulevard of Michigan avenue, across from the Lake Front Park it overlooks the lake, and furnishes a delightful summer resort as well as a cozy and comfortable winter home. The fashionable driveway of Chicago passes its doors, and it is a rare sight to witness from the Leland windows the beautiful equipages and their handsomely dressed occupants who are continually passing and repassing.

In the second place, it is quiet, aristocratic, and luxurious in all its appointments. It caters only to the best classes of people, and the fact that one stops at the Leland is almost a certificate of high character and reputation. The house is sought as a residence by such merchant princes as John V. Farwell, and such lawyers and statesmen as Emery A. Storrs. General Schofield, who has recently succeeded General Sheridan in command of the Department of the Missouri, resides here with his staff, and all the army officers make it their headquarters when in Chicago. It is free from the noise and confusion that make the larger hotels so uncomfortable, and Mr. Leland's guests find as much quiet, as much comfort, and as much luxury as can be had at the mansion of a millionaire on Prairie avenue.

In the third place, it is one of the best-kept houses in the land. The rooms are elegantly furnished, and the dust and smoke that choked the occupants of other houses do not invade its windows. Its caterer seeks the best markets and its cook is famous. The bill of fare is a model, and its dinners are sought by men who wish something better than can be elsewhere obtained. As a family hotel, or a stopping-place for ladies traveling alone, the Leland can be recommended, for there is no hotel in the country so famous for the courtesy and attention paid to its guests.

The reputation of Mr. Leland as a proprietor is enough to make the hotel noted, and it may be said that although it has passed through the hands of several people since it was erected and christened the Gardner House, after the fire, it was never a success until he took hold of it.

THE CLIFTON HOUSE.

A COZY AND COMFORTABLE HOTEL.

For those who want a cozy and comfortable house, without the noise and confusion that cannot be avoided at the larger hotels, we cordially recommend the Clifton House, one of the neatest, nicest, and most luxurious hostelries in the country. Here everything is quiet, genteel, and aristocratic, and the proprietors pride themselves upon the high character of the people who make the Clifton their stopping place. It is situated at the corner of Monroe street and Wabash avenue, just at the edge of the wholesale district, and is surrounded by the finest retail establishments in the city. It was reopened a little more than a year ago by Messrs. Woodcock and Loring, formerly of the Matteson House, and was then newly furnished throughout.

THE ATLANTIC HOTEL,

BY W. P. F. MESERVE,

is a structure of marble, containing 150 rooms, situated on Van Buren street, opposite the Lake Shore and Rock Island Depot, and only half a block from the Postoffice and new Board of Trade Building. It furnishes first-class accommodations for $2 per day. W. P. F. Meserve is the proprietor.

MUNGER'S LAUNDRY.

THE BEST IN THE COUNTRY.

Confessedly at the head of the laundry interests, not only of Chicago but of the entire United States and Canada, stands the firm of G. M. Munger & Co., whose headquarters are established at Nos. 1345 and 1347 Wabash avenue. Within a few years this former unimportant calling has grown to a gigantic industry, in which large capital is invested, and which furnishes profitable employment to thousands of men and women who now look to it for support. Something concerning the acknowledged leaders in this department of business, their methods and establishments, cannot fail to interest such readers of the trade review as hold to the doctrine that "cleanliness is next to godliness" among the Christian virtues.

The brothers who comprise the firm are three in number. Mr. G. M. Munger, the senior member, came to Chicago in 1868, and was subsequently joined by his younger brothers, who are now associated with him. Soon after Mr. Munger's arrival here he purchased a small laundry, which was then established at No. 53 Washington street. The business thus secured increased so rapidly under his skillful management that the confined quarters in which he found himself were soon inadequate to its requirements, and about two years later he moved into a more commodious building in the rear of Nos. 87 and and 89 on the same street, and opened a receiving and delivery office at No. 86 Dearborn street, in the old Postoffice building. The new establishment had just been placed in complete working order, and a season of genuine prosperity appeared to be opening before the young laundryman, when the great fire occurred and swept away in a night all of his tangible assets. But before the smoldering embers were cool Munger had his plans matured for the future, and by the time the burned out Chicagoans had skirmished round and procured something in the shape of garments to wash, he was ready to wash them in a new laundry on Lake avenue, near Thirty-ninth street. In the spring of 1872 the firm had in a measure recovered from its losses, and opened a commodious establishment in the Hemlock block, at the corner of LaSalle and Michigan streets, where it remained until it removed into its present quarters on Wabash avenue. The building now occupied by the brothers at the above location is 50x150 feet, and is wholly devoted to laundry purposes. To describe it, together with the processes and machinery in use, would exceed the prescribed limits of a trade review article. Suffice it to say, that the building is simply complete in all its appointments, and is fully equipped with whatever is latest and most perfect in the way of laundry machinery. In this connection it may be mentioned that Mr. G. M. Munger, while neither a mechanic nor an inventor, has frequently improved upon and perfected the crude ideas of others, and may be fairly considered as the real originator of many of the labor-saving processes which he uses.

In 1881 the brothers started their West End Laundry at No. 523 West Madison street. This proved to be such a pronounced success that two years later they felt justified in purchasing, at an expense of $15,000, the property Nos 518 and 520 on the same busy thoroughfare, and erecting thereon, at a further expense of $25,000, a building to accommodate their West Side business. The West End Laundry, while not the largest, is said to be the most perfectly appointed establishment of the kind in the United States, and is frequently visited by laundry proprietors from other parts of the country in pursuit of "pointers." It is under the personal supervision of Mr. L. I. Blackman, who has abundantly proved by his management of it his business ability. In 1882, G. M. Munger & Co. started a laundry at Des Moines, Iowa, which, like all their other ventures, has proved eminently successful. The latest scheme in which the Messrs. Munger have engaged is marked by the foresight and energy which are characteristic of the men. They have recently purchased a handsome property on Washington avenue, St. Louis, upon which they are now erecting another monster laundry, which will be a credit to that beautiful city and to themselves. It will have as large a business capacity as that on Wabash avenue. The Messrs. Munger have six receiving and delivery offices in this city; their business is enormous and rapidly increasing; their reputation as sagacious, honorable men is without a blot, and the great establishments which they conduct with such ability are among the prominent objects of industrial interest in Chicago.

GURNEY PHAETON AND CAB CO.

CHEAP AND STYLISH LOCOMOTION.

Every citizen of Chicago must necessarily be interested in the company above named. The business in which they are engaged fills a need long felt in Chicago, and this has been signified by the active patronage the company have enjoyed since last spring, when it first commenced business. The company has been incorporated under the laws of the State with a capital of $150,000. Mr. Smith Niles is President, Mr. A. G. Ashley Secretary and Treasurer, and Mr. L. B. Starkweather Superintendent. The business of this company is to carry people from point to point in the city at a very low rate of fare. The vehicles used are neat and tasty and afford a comfortable ride, and are without doubt the most complete and comfortable two-wheeled vehicle in use. The rates are seventy-five cents per hour for one or two persons, and $1 per hour for three or four persons, and twenty-five cents per mile for one person. The popularity of this mode of conveyance will be seen when we state that thirty Gurneys are now in use, and that there is business constantly for many more. Fully 150 will be in use by this company within the next year. The vehicles cost about $500 each, and as yet the company have not been able to get them manufactured as fast as they have been wanted. These Gurneys are manufactured under patents, and the company above named have bought the right to use them in Cook County. It is only within a period of nineteen months that these vehicles have been introduced in this country. This company are about to erect a large barn for the use of their stock, which will be finished in May and will accommodate 300 horses.

CHAPTER V.

THE ROME OF RAILROADS.

THEY ALL LEAD TO CHICAGO.

THE FIRST TRACK LAID.

In this city, where railroads center with enough track to twice belt the globe, it is not only wonderful and instructive but it is also amusing to look back to the time when the people were disposed to look with doubt upon those great agents of civilization, and were afraid they would destroy the trade of Chicago.

It was always a superstition with the people of olden time that every new invention or idea had its origin with the devil, and the people who had the courage to push forward such new ideas and inventions were persecuted as witches, or persons of unclean spirits possessed of devils. This was no more fallacious than the idea that took possession of the retail merchants of Chicago, when they bent their energiet to defeat the first railroad scheme for fear is would destroy their trade.

AFRAID OF THE SPIRITS OF WIND AND WATER.

The old superstition of the Chinese, who were afraid to offend the spirits of wind and water by building a railroad, was not more ridiculous than the fear of early Chicagoans that the building of a railroad from here to Galena would take away their retail trade, which was then the only boast of the town.

Instead of taking from Chicago her retail trade the railroads have made the place the great center of the wholesale trade in the West, and have given her that prominence over all other places, to which she never could have attained without the miles of iron track, reaching out like so many arteries from the heart, over which course the pulses of trade, as measured by the metropolis. With only the marine advantages of the lake it is doubtful if Chicago could have outstripped her rivals—St. Louis and Cincinnati—on their magnificent river routes, but with the railroad systems of the Northwest, all beginning here, and connecting with the trunk lines to the East, there was no longer any question as to where would be located the trade center.

RAILROAD PROPHESY.

It is curious to note that the first prophesy of Chicago as a railroad center was by a young soldier stationed at Fort Dearborn in 1830, and his prophesy was for a road over a line which has become one of the most important in linking the West and the East together.

This railroad prophet was Lieutenant John G. Furman, of the Fifth Infantry, United States army. He was at Fort Dearborn for several years, and enjoyed the hunting on the prairies and the fishing in the lake and river so much that, June 13, 1830, he wrote to a magazine published in Baltimore, urging the editor, who was his friend, to come out and join him. In that year there was only twenty-three miles of railroad in the country, and not a rail laid west of the Alleghany Mountains. The few miles in the East was only an experiment, and yet the young soldier who believed in Chicago spoke of his friend coming West as though the Baltimore and Ohio Road had already been built through to Chicago, and only awaited a formal opening. He said: "When the railroad is finished between Baltimore and the Rock River perhaps you may be induced to come out and take a week's sport with us, or if you cannot spare the time we must try and pack up some of our good things in ice and send on a locomotive steam-propelling car."

IT IS FULFILLED.

Lieutenant Furman's prophecy has long ago been fulfilled, and now there is nothing easier than to pack up good things in ice in Chicago and send them to suffering humanity down in Baltimore.

But one of the most curious things in Chicago's railroad history is that it was a beginning point, rather than a terminal, and yet it was not considered so important as the little mining town way up in the northwestern corner of the State, which was the terminal point. When the charter for the old Galena and Chicago Union Railroad was granted by the Legislature, Jan. 16, 1836—before Chicago was yet incorporated as a city—there was so little thought of Chicago's chances to become a great city that, while backed by Chicago capital and pushed by Chicago men, influence enough could not be brought to bear upon the Legislature to induce it to grant the charter until the name had been switched around with the engine in the rear, and, instead of the Chicago and Galena Road, it had to be called the Galena and Chicago Road.

WISE MEN MADE FOOLS.

The wise men who controlled the destinies of the State of Illinois in those days were so possessed with the Western idea that they went to the furthermost point of their territory to find the railroad Mecca, and believed that Galena was of much more importance than Chicago. It might have been then, with its lead mines and its river route, but the change was but another of the Chicago surprises which have played such an important part in her history.

The primary incentive to the incorporation of this road was the advancement of real estate prices in Chicago. Its capital stock was $100,000, with power to increase it to $1,000,000. It was optional with the company to make portions of it, with branches of the same, a toll-road, to be operated either with horse or steam power. William Bennett, Thomas Drummond (now Judge of the United States Circuit Court), J. C. Goodhue, Peter Semple, J. M. Turner, and J. B. Thompson, Jr., were authorized as commissioners to receive subscriptions to the stock. Their charter allowed three years from its date as the limit of the time in which work on it should be commenced, to comply with which provision the company commenced the questionable enterprise in 1838.

THE FIRST ROAD.

This was a road from the West Side, and, as the whole broad prairie, now occupied by the most populous division of Chicago, was then a great slough, and in the spring of the year a veritable lake, on which one might row from the river to Oak Park—a place better fitted for steamboat travel than for railroading—the first problem was how to get a foundation for a road. There was a popular superstition with the people that this slough had no bottom, or, at least, none that could be reached with any practicable length of support for tressle. Piles were resorted to with longitudinal stringers to secure support from one to another.

In this way the work of building the road was begun along Madison street. It did not progress far, however, and was abandoned, and no more attempts made until 1846, when William B. Ogden, John Turner, and Stephen F. Gale purchased the charter from Messrs. Townsend and Mather, of New York, who, up to this time, held it with the assets of the company. They were to pay $10,000 in stock down, and $10,000 on the completion of the road to the Fox River. A preliminary survey was made, and the work put in charge of Richard P. Morgan. It was at this juncture that the opposition made its appearance, because of the fear that the road would injure the retail trade of Chicago. It was feared that by quick and easy transfers the farmers would find their goods delivered to them nearer home, and Chicago would cease to be a trade center, as it was fast becoming.

NEW LIFE AND THE RESULT.

But through the efforts of Benjamin W. Raymond and John B. Turner in negotiating loans in New York, and the reluctant home subscriptions to the stock, the road was finally completed to Cottage Hill, a distance of sixteen miles, in December, 1849. The road-bed was not good, and the track consisted of wooden stringers faced with strap iron. It was Chicago's first railroad, and its opening was an important event, despite the fact that the company had to bring old and worn-out rolling stock from the East. The engine was one of the first pattern, and the cars were of the most primitive order.

It was not until three years later, May 21, 1852, that Chicago had any Eastern railway connection. The Michigan Southern Road, begun in 1837, and the Michigan Central, begun in 1842, were sharp rivals in the enterprise of reaching Chicago, and work was pushed with all the rapidity possible by both roads. The cars of the Michigan Central ran into Chicago May 21, and those of the Michigan Southern the day following. Both were greeted with shouts of welcome by the people, who had then learned to look upon the railroad in its proper light, as a stimulant of prosperity.

THE ROME OF RAILROADS.

The other railroads now centering in Chicago followed in a few years after these first efforts, and to-day it is appropriately called the Rome of Railroads. In place of the rickety strap-iron Galena and Chicago Road, we have the great Chicago and Northwestern with its nearly 5,000 miles of track threading all parts of the Northwestern States and Territories, and instead of the old wornout rolling-stock brought from the East for the first road, there are mammoth locomotives and solid trains of magnificent parlor, sleeping, and dining cars, while one might as well attempt to number the cattle on the plains as to count the freight cars that carry the great wealth of products from the garden of the Nation to the store-house of the world.

As its great rival for this Northwestern trade comes the Chicago, Milwaukee and St. Paul Road, with 4,400 miles of iron binding the States of Wisconsin, Minnesota, and Dakota to Chicago as their metropolis. To the West reaches the 4,000 miles of the Chicago, Burlington and Quincy, and almost as many miles of the Chicago, Rock Island and Pacific, laying out the States of Illinois, Iowa, Nebraska, and the Territories beyond in garden plats, and the Southwest is held in a firm grasp by the 6,000 miles of the Wabash system, and St. Louis made a suburban station.

SECRET OF NATIONAL RECONSTRUCTION.

The South is more firmly united to the North by the band of steel from Chicago to New Orleans, which forms the Illinois Central system, than by the laws that force her to remain in the Union.

Instead of Chicago belonging to Hoosierdom or the Old Dominion, as was once boasted, these localities now belong to Chicago by the right of her furnishing a market for their hooppoles and rye whisky, as well as all other products, and transportation over the Monon route, the Eastern Illinois, Western Indiana, and Panhandle Roads.

To New York Chicago is a twin sister, as inseparably united by the iron ligament of the eight trunk lines of railroads as were the Siamese twins by their natural bond of conjunction.

Of the total 122,813 miles of railroad in the United States to-day, there are roads representing 40,792 centering in Chicago, fully one-third, and making it the greatest railroad center in the world.

THE ILLINOIS CENTRAL.

TO THE SUNNY SOUTH.

The Illinois Central Railroad has been one of the most important factors in the development of Chicago and the West. It was one of the first roads built, and has been the commercial backbone of Illinois, making its products marketable, and increasing its growth and wealth. It now covers fifteen degrees of latitude, and connects Chicago with the Missouri River and the Gulf of Mexico.

It is the only road that has an unbroken, direct line to the South, and makes a journey to the land of perpetual summer agreeable, safe and speedy. Through cars of the most lüxurious pattern run to all the desirable resorts sought by winter tourists, and the journey offers attractions that cannot be found elsewhere.

The completion of the Pensacola and Atlantic Railway gives a through line from Chicago to Jacksonville, Fla., by way of New Orleans, and permits the tourist to visit all of the popular resorts on the Gulf coast. The advantages of this line to invalids cannot be overestimated. The connections for Texas and California are such as to offer the best winter route, the line being always free from snow and ice and cold, and the fare is as low as by any other road. By going this way the traveler has the opportunity of visiting New Orleans, Galveston, and other Southern cities, and is within easy reach of the charming city of Monterey, the most famous and popular watering place in Old Mexico. When this resort, with its magnificent hotels and medicinal hot springs becomes better known in the North, it will be as fashionable a residence in winter as Saratoga is in summer.

San Antonio, Austin, Galveston, and Houston, Texas, are made the objective points for no less than twelve routes, via New Orleans going, and via either the Missouri Pacific or Iron Mountain routes and St. Louis returning, or vice versa. Havana, Cuba, and Hot Springs and Eureka Springs, Ark., are also excursion points.

Exceedingly low rates are given on round trip tickets to Chicago and all the above points, good to return until June 1.

During 1883 extensive improvements have been made in the Illinois Central plant. The motive power has been substantially increased; the passenger and freight equipments have received handsome additions; new double-track iron bridges have been placed across the Calumet and Chicago Rivers. New passenger and freight depots have been built at South Chicago, Seventy-ninth street, Jeffery avenue, and in Jackson, Winona, and Wesson, Miss. A double-track branch to South Chicago, four and a half miles long, has been completed; the middle division has been extended from Colfax to Bloomington, twenty miles; and spur lines, aggregating 130 miles in length, leading into the timber and farms lands of Mississippi, are rapidly approaching completion, a portion of the distance being already open for traffic.

The Illinois Central was the first railroad to introduce suburban trains, having commenced running them as early as 1856. To its management is due the development and growth of the beautiful suburbs south of the city, as its frequent trains made them even more accessible than some of the resident portions of Chicago that are reached only by the street cars. Upward of three million people are carried annually upon these suburban trains, and the number that go to South Park and Pullman sometimes reaches thousands per day.

THE "MONON ROUTE."

THE LOUISVILLE, NEW ALBANY AND CHICAGO RAILWAY THE GREAT SOUTHERN ROUTE.

Scarcely two years have elapsed since the opening of the Monon Route—officially known as the Louisville, New Albany and Chicago Railway—into Chicago, connecting the great Northwest with Louisville and the South and Southeast. Recalling the exorbitant rates, slow time, vexatious delays, and numerous changes in dingy coaches that attended a trip to Louisville and the South of a few years ago, the business man and tourist alike appreciated the advantages of the Monon Route, with its solid trains and Pullman palace sleepers, its reasonable rates, its fast time, its smooth tracks, and its courteous officials. Being the only line to Louisville from Chicago under one management, it offered to its patrons accomodations that no other line could and gained the good-will of the public at the start by its low and reasonable rates. Gaining friends daily by service and splendid equipment, supplemented by fair dealing, the Monon Route to-day is one of the most popular lines, both with the tourist whose journey South is attended with every pleasure and comfort possible, and the merchant who finds that by this road only can he ship his wares to the Ohio River without change or delay. The traveling man, knowing the

COMFORTS OF A SOLID TRAIN AND PULLMAN BUFFET SLEEPERS—

and the finest only are run via Monon—will take no other line to Louisville. To the Monon Route belongs the credit of introducing the first and only Pullman sleeping-car line through from Chicago to Jacksonville without change, and is still the only route by which Pullman car service is secured via Louisville to Florida. The route is characteristically a tourist line, leading from the South to the cool resorts of the Northwest in summer, and from the chilly blasts of the North to the balmy breezes of a mild South in winter. The time was, and not two years ago, when a trip from Chicago to Florida or the Gulf resorts was a slow and tedious undertaking, attended by so many annoyances that few had the courage to make it. Now, thanks to the Monon Route, a trip to Southern resorts is a pleasure in itself. It is a specialty with the route, whose line of single and round-trip tickets includes every resort in the South or Northwest. Their system of through checking is perfect, the baggage going on the same train with passengers to destination. The main line of the Louisville, New Albany and Chicago Railway extends from Louisville to Michigan City, adistance of 288 miles, passing through some of the oldest settled and

MOST PROSPEROUS PORTIONS OF INDIANA,

among the towns being noted Salem, Orleans, Mitchell, Bedford, Bloomington, Gosport, Greencastle, Crawfordsville, and Lafayette. The scenery along the route is pleasing and interesting, soothing with its constant and easy changes rather than startling with its suddenness and abruptness. In the midst of the hills about Orleans are found several delightful springs, notably West Baden and French Lick Springs, which, on account of the curative waters, picturesque location, and fine hotels, have become popular resorts. The Air Line Division of the road extends from Chicago to Indianapolis, and is eleven miles shorter than any other to the Hoosier capital, the distance from Chicago being 183 miles. The Monon Route proper is via the Air Line to Monon and thence to Louisville, the through trains running that way. Similar trains with

THROUGH COACHES FOR LOUISVILLE

run from Michigan City to Indianapolis via Monon. The Air Line was not formally opened from Chicago to Indianapolis till last October, when two daily trains were put on. Six weeks later an arrangement was made with the Cincinnati, Hamilton and Dayton Railroad and the Air Line trains now run solid to Cincinnati through Indianapolis. Like the Louisville line, parlor cars are attached to the day trains and Pullman palace sleepers to the night trains. Monon, where the main and Air Lines cross, is eighty-five miles from Chicago. The name is derived from "Melamonon," an Indian title of a stream near by, which in olden times was no doubt a swift-running river, as the meaning of the word is "waters running swift." Very properly the word Monon was adopted for the route, and it is a

SWIFT-RUNNING ROUTE.

By the opening of this Cincinnati line, the Monon Route now offers its patrons a choice of routes to Florida and the South via Louisville, Cincinnati, or Indianapolis, direct connections being made with all through routes below the Ohio River. Briefly, there is not a point of interest in the South or Southeast which cannot be reached by the Monon Route, and only by that route can passengers get Pullman car service via Louisville or Cincinnati.

The general offices of the company are at Louisville, the "Capital of Hospitality," as designated by a well-known writer. It is not surprising then that this company should display the same liberal spirit in its management, and that it should win popularity thereby. Colonel E. B. Stahlman, Vice-President of the company, has, by his rare executive ability as Traffic Manger, been a valuable aid to Colonel Bennett H. Young, the President and General Manager. At the head of the passenger department, Mr. Murray Keller has won a national reputation as a successful General Passenger and Ticket Agent. In fact, the

POPULARITY OF THE MONON ROUTE

may, in a large measure, be attributed to him. Colonel Sidney B. Jones, the General Traveling Passenger Agent, whose headquarters are in Chicago, is a thoroughly experienced railroad man and a perfect gentleman. His assistant, Captain J. L. Whelan, is a graduate from THE INTER OCEAN reportorial ranks, and as Northwestern Passenger Agent maintains his reputation. Mr. E. O. McCormick, City Ticket Agent, 122 Randolph street, has the routes and rates at his fingers' ends, and, like the others, has a store of information of the South which he distributes freely. For maps, time-tables, books on Florida and the South call on or address any of the above at 122 Randolph street and receive that prompt attention for which the Monon Route is noted. No other route makes such time, and offers such rates and accommodations as the Monon Route to the South.

CHICAGO, BURLINGTON AND QUINCY.

STRETCHING OVER THE GREAT WEST.

Like all large Western institutions of magnitude, the extensive railroad system known as the Chicago, Burlington and Quincy Road had a small beginning, but grew with, or more properly caused to grow with it, the West. Its origin is found in two roads, now considered small by comparison, but at the time their charters were granted then regarded as vast and important.

On Feb. 12, 1849, a railroad company was organized in Illinois under the name of the Aurora Branch Railway Company. In June, 1852, the Chicago and Aurora Railroad Company obtained its charter and immediately proceeded to lay its track between Chicago and Aurora. The Central Military Tract Railroad Company owned the road between Mendota and Galesburg, and in 1856, just after the Chicago and Aurora Company had completed its line of track, these two roads consolidated. The company thus formed adopted the name of the Chicago, Burlington and Quincy Railroad Company.

From this grew the road which covers so extensive an area. Small at the start, it now runs and controls over 4,000 miles of track distributed throughout Illinois, Iowa, Missouri, Nebraska, Kansas, and Colorado. About one-half of this mileage is in Illinois and Iowa. It is happy in the possession of five routes. The most important is its own through line via Pacific Junction and Plattsmouth to Denver. The other routes are: Through Omaha via Cheyenne, over the Union Pacific; through Quincy, to Kansas City or Atchison, via the Hannibal and St. Joe, thence resuming the Burlington route proper; through Kansas City, via Topeka, over the Union Pacific, and through either Atchison or Kansas City, via the Atchison, Topeka and Santa Fe, whose cars run via Pueblo, and thence over the Denver and Rio Grande.

Passengers have choice of above routes in going to San Francisco, or may go via the Santa Fe and Southern Pacific line, or via El Paso over the Gould roads and the Southern Pacific.

Other favorite lines of the Burlington and connections are as follows: St. Louis, Rock Island, and St. Paul; St. Louis, Burlington, and St. Paul; Chicago, Freeport, Dubuque, and Sioux City; Chicago, Hannibal, and Texas; Chicago and Des Moines.

The completion of the Denver and Rio Grande Road from Denver to Ogden during the past year further extends and makes more complete lines of travel offered by the Burlington. This arrangement gives the Burlington what is practically its own line to Ogden, the road from Denver winding through the finest scenery of the West.

The equipment of the road is elegant, and comfort is combined with safety and rapid travel.

CHICAGO, ROCK ISLAND AND PACIFIC.

THE MODEL LINE.

The Chicago, Rock Island and Pacific Road, which was the first to connect Chicago with the Mississippi River, thus making more accessible the thriving cities along the Father of Waters, was begun in 1852. In 1847 a company was formed under the name of the Rock Island and LaSalle Railroad Company, and procured its charter in the same year. Good management has been characteristic of the road since its opening, and the alert managers have been in continual readiness to make every advantageous extension and acquisition.

In 1851, by an act of the Legislature, the name was changed to the Rock Island Company, and it was under that name that the road was constructed between Chicago and Rock Island. In 1866 the road consolidated with another in Iowa called the Chicago, Rock Island and Pacific Road, and as its termini and connections were such as to warrant the managers in adopting the name of the road with which it consolidated, this was done. It has been known by that name ever since. At the time the charter was granted Illinois was a border State, Iowa being a territory, but since the border line has been moved further West, and the territories are now States whose products find an accessible outlet in Chicago.

The causes which produced the changes of the past thirty years are numerous, but probably none figures more prominently than the railroad in question, one of the pioneer roads of the West. It has contributed vastly to the development of both Illinois and Iowa. Its reward has been a world-wide reputation and bountiful earnings. There is probably no railway in the West which earns a greater revenue in proportion to its mileage. It is the great central line from Chicago to the West, passing through the most fertile portions of Illinois and Iowa, and forming connections which make it a through line to the Pacific coast. It reaches the most thriving of the cities in Iowa and Kansas.

A few years ago the management, not content with business coming over the road extending to the West, opened up what is known as the Albert Lea Route. This route, which is quite a favorite with tourists, and which does an extensive freight business, extends through the great Red River Valley, and the great Northern Pacific country in Minnesota and Dakota. It reaches to Minneapolis and St. Paul, and renders accessible the beautiful scenery of Minnesota and the Upper Mississippi. It is also used as a means of transporting a large percentage of the traffic between the East and Manitoba. The year which closed yesterday has witnessed the beginning of the new Board of Trade Building, just opposite the depot of the road in this city, which, it is claimed, will result in an increase in the already large suburban travel. The road is well equipped throughout, and by means of its coaches, sleeping, and dining cars, supplies all the comforts known to travel.

CHICAGO AND NORTHWESTERN.

FOUR GREAT TRUNK LINES.

The history of the Chicago and Northwestern Road is one of consolidation, and for the most part combined in that of the old Galena and Chicago Union Road, which is the real pioneer line. The old Galena and Chicago Union Road was chartered in 1836. A panic followed in the footsteps of the charter, which delayed further operations until 1847, eleven years later, when the first rail was put down. This was done on what is known as the Galena Division, or the Freeport line. In 1853 the line from Chicago to Freeport, a distance of 121 miles, was completed, and there are many people now residing in Stephenson County who remember with what pleasure the completion of the line was hailed, as previous to that time a trip to Chicago and return, lasting frequently for two weeks, was necessary in order to dispose of products. The Illinois Central Road, which passes through Freeport to Galena, enabled the road to extend its operations to the lead mines at Galena. This road was absorbed by the Chicago and Northwestern Road in 1864.

CHICAGO AND ROCK ISLAND DEPOT.

In 1854, ten years prior to this consolidation, the Chicago and Northwestern Road constructed the line which connects Chicago and Milwaukee. While this road enters Chicago upon three distinct lines of rail, it may be said to have five principal lines all terminating in Chicago, the first of which is the one extending to Milwaukee. This line skirts the lake shore, and now reaches the Michigan peninsula.

The second extends in a northwesterly direction, and touching Beloit, Madison, and Elroy, reaches St. Paul and Minneapolis. The third line extends west from Elroy, crosses the Mississippi at

Winona, Minn., and extends across Minnesota and Dakota on a direct line to the Black Hills. From Tracy the road extends further on to Watertown and Redfield. From Huron, on the main line, a branch extends north up the James River Valley to Columbia, D. T. The fourth line runs from Chicago directly west across Illinois and Iowa, terminating at Council Bluffs. The fifth line begins at Tama, 142 miles west of the Missouri River, and extends in a general northwesterly direction to Hawarden, on the Big Sioux. During the year just ended a bridge has been placed over the river and the road extended into Dakota to a junction with the Dakota Central. In addition to these main lines there are a number of profitable branches. By connection with the Chicago, St. Paul, Minneapolis and Omaha Road it has the advantage of two important lines to Lake Superior ports and tapping the pine region of Upper Wisconsin. The mileage of the Northwestern system, including the Omaha line, aggregates about 5,000 miles.

ATLANTIC AND PACIFIC RAILROAD.

ALL-THE-YEAR-AROUND ROUTE TO CALIFORNIA.

Last September was opened a new line to California, which was dubbed the "All-the-year-around" route, and which, when travelers find out its attractions, will have a popularity that none of the transcontinental roads have ever achieved, and be preferred to any other for many reasons. It is the Atlantic and Pacific Railway, which connects with the Atchison, Topeka and Santa Fe Road at Albuquerque, and is the only line running *Pullman sleeping-cars from St. Louis and Kansas City to San Francisco without change.*

The road is located upon the thirty-fifth parallel of latitude, and passengers thus avoid the snow blockades and alkali plains of the North, and the barren and dusty deserts of the South. It is and always will be the favorite route to the Pacific coast for the invalid, the tourist, the sportsman, and all to whom speed, comfort, safety, delightful climate, and wonderful scenery are attractions. It is the shortest and the best route to San Francisco, Sacramento, Los Angeles, San Diego, and other Pacific coast points. Prescott, and the mining camps of Northern, Central, and Western Arizona are now reached direct by this line without long and tedious staging.

The most remarkable scenery in the world is along the line of the Atlantic and Pacific Railroad. It crosses the Colorado River at the foot of the Grand Canon, which has been the subject of several descriptive letters in THE INTER OCEAN, and is acknowledged to be the grandest and most sublime natural spectacle on the face of the globe. The canon is reached by stage from Leach Springs, after a ride of eighteen miles, and the tourist will find admirable accommodations for his entertainment.

The ancient and curious Indian villages of Zuni, Moquis, Acoma, and Laguna are reached by this road, the trains passing within a stone's throw of the latter place, which is many centuries old, and inhabited by the descendants of the Aztecs. Remarkable ruins of the cave and cliff dwellers are found near Flagstaff Station, and possess a deep interest not only to the scientific world, but to all who visit these abodes of half-civilized nations extinct for centuries. The Atlantic and Pacific is the most attractive route to the Yosemite Valley, and the big trees of Mariposa County, California.

The company has 20,000,000 acres of the finest grazing land in the world for sale, in New Mexico and Arizona. For maps, rates, and other information apply to F. W. Smith, General Superintendent; C. R. Williams, General Freight and Passenger Agent; or J. A. Williamson, Land Commissioner, Albuquerque, New Mexico.

CHAPTER VI

CHAMBER OF COMMERCE.

A HISTORICAL CHAPTER.

THE OLD AND THE NEW BUILDINGS.

The Board of Trade in Chicago has not been a dictator but a leader; the business has always centered around the Chamber of Commerce, and right well has it deserved such a recognition. When, for the first years of its existence, the board had its home down on Water street, near the river, that was the business center of Chicago, but when the First Baptist Church resigned the corner of Washington and LaSalle streets to the Chamber of Commerce, the quiet residence neighborhood there changed to the great trade center, and blocks of fine business houses went up there to accommodate the great army of business men who wanted to be near the heart of trade, that they might ever feel its pulse nearest the life source.

But Chicago did not always have a Chamber of Commerce about which to center her trade. It was not until the spring of 1848 the merchants began to make application of the old adage that "in union there is strength." The city about that time began to be noticed as a commercial center, and the merchants deemed it for their common interest to organize a Board of Trade. What the special object had in view was, or whether there was any special object, does not appear from any of the records left.

FIRST ORGANIZATION.

But it is certain that in April, 1848, there was such a board organized and eighty-two members enrolled. These men represented the commercial interests of a city of 20,000 inhabitants.

It was before the completion of any railroad to Chicago or the construction of the canal, and the only means of communicating with the interior and the West was by the slow stage coach and the slower "prairie schooner," but the location of the city at the head of the great chain of lakes predestined it to be a trade center.

At first the board was a voluntary organization, but in 1850 it became incorporated under a general law of the State, and in 1859 a special act of incorporation was obtained from the Legislature, which has since remained the basis of organization.

Its general object, as expressed in the preamble to its Rules and By-laws, are: "To maintain a commercial exchange; to promote uniformity in the customs and usages of merchants; to inculcate principles of justice and equity in trade; to facilitate the speedy adjustment of business disputes; to acquire and disseminate valuable commercial and economic information; and generally, to secure to its members the benefit of co-operation in the furtherance of their legitimate pursuits."

REVERSES AND STAGNATION.

The enthusiasm which organized the first Board of Trade did not continue long, and in 1851 the membership had dwindled to forty, and there was very little business transacted. Then the merchants began to take fresh interest, and in 1859 there were 520 members. It has continued to increase rapidly ever since, until it has reached nearly 2,000, and is there practically restricted.

The board began with a member's fee of $5, but a membership ticket is now held at $10,000. This is not regarded as the real value, but is the price put upon new memberships as a restriction upon further increase. Membership tickets already held are only valued at about one-third that amount, or $3,500, and are frequently sold for that figure.

In its early days the board was migratory, changing its quarters as the city changed. Its first home was a room in the third story of a building at the foot of LaSalle street. No elevator carried the merchants and commission men up to this room, and they were obliged to climb two narrow and steep stairways. In 1860 a building was erected for the use of the board on Fifth avenue, near the bridge, but the business so rapidly increased that in 1863 the question of enlarged accommodations again began to be discussed, and in February, 1864, a building association was organized, with a capital stock of $500,000, and the Chamber of Commerce chartered.

The Board of Trade contracted to lease the building for a term of ninety-nine years, at a rental of $20,000 per annum, and in less than twenty years they have abandoned the building and site for want of room.

THE BOARD IN THE FIRE.

The new building was first occupied in August, 1865, the membership at that time being over 1,400. At that time the Chamber

THE NEW CHAMBER OF COMMERCE.

of Commerce was by far the largest and finest building in the country used for that purpose.

In 1871 this temple of trade was swept away by the fire, but before the great conflagration had been checked in its course the members who had lost all came together and out of nothing began to do business again. A room on Franklin street was secured and the Board of Trade there opened, not for speculation, but for the noble purpose of aiding those who were only less fortunate than themselves in losing their courage. When the help from all over the country began to come in, the board took possession and distributed these things as they were most needed. Then they turned their attention to business, and from Oct. 9, the day of the fire, to Oct. 31 the receipts of grain aggregated over 3,750,000 bushels, notwithstanding the ability to care for such a business had been greatly impaired.

Among the first official acts of the board was the determination to reoccupy its old quarters, and the Chamber of Commerce was rebuilt, but in more magnificent style, and in just one year, Oct. 9, 1872, was re-opened.

Until now this beautiful and substantial building has served as a home for the organization, and trades aggregating millions have been made there every day.

In Exchange Hall have been witnessed some of the wildest scenes that ever transpired in the commercial world, and fortunes have been made and lost in a few hours.

THE NEW CHAMBER OF COMMERCE.

But for several years there has been a need for more commodious quarters, and another removal was arranged. The corner-stone of the new Chamber of Commerce was laid with appropriate ceremonies Dec. 13, 1882, and since then the walls of the magnificent building have gone up with marvelous rapidity, but this new temple of trade is on such a grand scale that it will be another year before it is brought to completion and ready for the machinery of commerce.

The new building, of which a cut is here given, fronts on Jackson street and extends back to Van Buren, occupying the full width of the block between Sherman street and Pacific avenue. It will have a frontage of 175 feet and 225 feet in depth. It is in the modern Gothic style, built of Fox Island granite. The grand tower is 32 feet front, and is to be 300 feet high, the masonry extending 225 feet and the remaining 75 feet of iron. At the height of 225 feet there will be a clock dial on each of the four sides of the tower, twelve feet in diameter.

A MAGNIFICENT TEMPLE.

All the external entrances to the building will have large prominent doors, finished with polished red granite square columns. The external ornamentation is to be on a scale never before equaled in the city, and this will be one of the finest buildings used for commercial purposes in the world, costng $1,500,000.

One of the brightest pages in the history of the Board of Trade was the unwavering support it gave the country in the hour of its greatest need. The echo of the first gun awoke the loyal sons of the Board of Trade, and they rallied for the defense. Grain and pork and beef and stocks were forgotten for the flag, and the "boys on 'Change" showed that they could fight with the same enthusiasm and with the same recklessness that they could buy on the market.

Three regiments of infantry and a battery of artillery were organized and equipped by the Board of Trade, who kept watch over them during their service of three years. They were allowed to want for nothing that money could buy. The board also raised $150,000 to help on the cause of the Union.

Secretary Randolph, in speaking of the board, with which he has been connected in an official capacity for so many years, says: "That the men composing this body are, in general, possessed of unusual business ability, are remarkable for their quick perception of business possibilities, and are of untiring devotion to business affairs, will perhaps be freely conceded by all acquainted with their habits and modes of conducting those affairs; the best indications of their true manhood, however, are to be found in their generous treatment of the unfortunate, whether of their own numbers or of distressed humanity throughout the world."

TRANSACTIONS IN THE MILLIONS.

As an estimate of the business done on the Board of Trade, it may be noted that the clearings alone amount to more than $2,000,000 a week. As this is but a small per cent of the transactions, the actual business of the board amounts to millions of dollars every day.

Last year there was shipped from Chicago $90,388,000 worth of flour and grain, $100,939,000 worth of live stock, $117,592,000 worth of meats, lard, tallow, and dressed hogs, $11,114,000 worth of butter and cheese, $24,778,000 worth of wool and hides, $9,358,000 worth of seeds and broom corn, $2,451,000 worth of distilled spirits, not including the tax, and $9,924,000 worth of miscellaneous products, making a grand total of $372,544,000 worth of products from this market, and all passed through the hands of these merchants and commission men on the Board of Trade.

But this does not begin to give an estimate of the business transactions which take place there. The wheat, corn, and other products are often sold and resold a dozen times in one day, and not only is business done by the 2,000 men on the floor, but many of them are acting as agents for men throughout the whole country. There is no place in the world where so much of this kind of business is done, and Chicago by right is called the trade center.

L. EVERINGHAM & CO.

COMMISSION MERCHANTS.

There are few commission houses whose business career has been so uniformly successful and who are so well known for their financial strength and reliability as to be representative houses, and among those who take the front rank in this regard is the house of L. Everingham & Co., whose offices, 125 LaSalle street, adjoin the Board of Trade.

This firm point with pride to a record for upright and honorable dealing, from the establishment of the firm in 1865 to the present time, and their fidelity to those who have intrusted business to them has resulted in a constantly increasing volume of business.

From the first they pledged themselves to the prosecution of a strict and legitimate commission business, having no joint accounts, and engaging in no speculations for their own account, hence their judgment has been unbiased by investments of their own, and their large list of successful customers are always sure of their undivided attention and personal interest.

Their facilities for obtaining the latest and most accurate reports of the crops of the country are unequaled, which, together with their special letters indicating the course of the markets, have proved to be correct in numberless cases.

Their order department is complete in all of its details, and is kept separate and distinct from the receiving department.

The execution of orders for the purchase and sale of grain and provisions on the Chicago Board of Trade for future delivery, on margins, is a specialty, and the promptness and faithful manner with which such orders are filled is most gratifying and satisfactory to their customers.

The selling of consignments by sample is also a speciality, and all items of expense in the sale and delivery of shipments and the weight and inspection of grain are carefully supervised, and the interests of the shipper are thus protected in every possible way. Their carefully prepared special letters as to what quality and kind of grain will strike a good market are greatly appreciated, and are highly valued by those who consign their shipments to them.

Their remarkably correct crop reports and their special letters regarding the course of the markets, are freely furnished upon request.

WILLIAM C. DUELL & CO.

YOUNG BUT ENTERPRISING.

While one of the young firms on the Board of Trade Messrs. Duell & Co. have from the commencement of their business career occupied a prominent position among Chicago commission men, and have earned a reputation for enterprise, sound judgment, and financial skill of which many old-established concerns might feel proud.

It is by no means uncommon in this city to find men under 30 successfully managing large and important mercantile or manufacturing interests. The young man who possesses industry, tact, and determination, together with integrity and correct personal habits, may, with a fair show of good luck, pass rapidly to the front in this metrropolis of the Northwest, without as a rule incurring the ill will or envy of less fortunate men who have been longer in gaining the goal of their ambition. But while the truth of the foregoing remarks is frequently proved by the rapid preferment of the young men of exceptionably good ability who naturally gravitate to Chicago, where that class are always in demand, the success of Mr. W. C. Duell has been so pronounced as to be justly regarded as phenomenal since he came here at 18 years of age in 1875 to make his way and acquire a fortune without the accessories of influence or capital to assist him. He had, to be sure, the advantages of a liberal education, and upon arriving in Chicago was so fortunate as to secure a position with one of the largest receiving firms on the Board of Trade. In that employ he mastered the details of the business to which he has subsequently devoted his energies with such flattering results, and when he started on his own account about three years ago, he not only carried with him the good wishes of his whilom employers and other leading commission firms with which he had been brought in contact, but the generous prediction that he was entering upon an eminently successful career. The prediction has been more than verified; the young house not only immediately took a leading place, but has sustained it through all the vicissitudes of temporary business depression "corners," etc. Mr. Duell is now less than 27 years old, and at the head of a firm doing a large and constantly extending business—a firm which from present indications will have few rivals to fear in the future. He is a pleasant, unassuming gentleman in his office, keen, incisive, self-relient, and prompt to act when on 'Change. Mr. Duell is a member of the regular Board of Trade, the Open Board, the Call Board, and of the Stock Exchange, in all of which he is a conspicuous figure, and has abundantly proven his ability to hold his own. His specialty is deals for future delivery, and it is not advidious to say that no member of the Board of Trade more entirely comprehends the market and how to take advantage of it. The firm does business at No. 22 Chamber of Commerce.

A REPRESENTATIVE HOUSE.

CHARLES E. CULVER & CO.

There are connected with the Board of Trade, as with the dry goods, the hardware, and other interests of this city, a few representative firms, which appear to stand as the embodiment of whatever is commercially above reproach, and as so, beyond the shadow ot a doubt, financially, that the most malicious of critics never attempt to advertise their mendacity by attempting to malign them. In the foremost rank of these representative commercial houses of Chicago the commission firm of Culver & Co. is honorably conspicuous. It has for years been known as one of the largest and strongest receiving firms in connection with the Chicago Board of Trade. In all the history of the house there has been neither blot nor blemish to detract from its mercantile fair fame. It is one of the firms of which that great, far-reaching, and powerful corporation above referred to is with reason proud, and it has not been chary of the commercial honors which it has conferred upon it. Mr. Charles E. Culver, the head of the firm, has been twice elected Vice President and once President of the Board of Trade, and has, moreover, been for years in continual service upon some of the leading committees of this the most important commercial combination in the civilized world. After saying so much, it is the next thing to superfluous to add that this model house possesses not only everything which a Board of Trade commission firm should possess in the way of business facilities, but a subtile knowledge of the inner mysteries of the speculative market which could only be born of a long experience and an acknowledged leadership among the wonderful manipulators of prices who congregate at the unpretending granite building at the corner of LaSalle and Washington streets, and determine the price at which the inhabitants of New York, London, Paris, and Berlin shall purchase the material for their dinners. Any business intrusted to Messrs. Culver & Co. will most emphatically be left in safe, competent, and honorable hands. Their place of business is at Nos. 122 and 124 Washington street.

EDWARD. A. DRIVER & CO.

OF HIGH REPUTATION.

Among the Board of Trade firms which have gained an exceptionally high reputation for business sagacity, honorable dealing, and, better than all, success, Messrs. Edward A. Driver & Co. hold a leading and influential position. The house was founded in 1869 by Mr. Spear, the father of its present junior member, and Mr. E. A. Driver, and almost immediately secured in the estimation of commission men and the speculating public in general that high character which usually only comes as the reward of long years of patient toil. This character it has ever since sustained, and is not at all likely to forfeit it hereafter. The firm does an extensive regular commission business in grain and provisions, for the most part for future delivery. Being possessed of ample means, abundant experience, and all the multifarious and far-reaching facilities which are required for the proper conduct of the affairs of a first-class Chicago commission house, it transacts with the precision of clock-work its extensive and rapidly increasing business. Messrs. Driver & Co.'s customers are principally in the representative cities of the country—New York, Philadelphia, Baltimore, Detroit, Toledo, St. Louis, etc. The firm is composed of Mr. E. A. Driver, B. F. Ives, and F. R. Spear. All are natives of Massachusetts, and thorough business men. Their place of business is room 2, No. 157 Washington street.

T. M. BAXTER & CO.

COMMISSIONS.

So great and varied are the commercial interests of a metropolis like Chicago that it would be impossible to classify them all in an annual trade review. Only a few of the representative houses of each particular branch of trade can be mentioned in the space allotted. Ranking first in importance may be considered the grain and provision trade, in which some of Chicago's heaviest capitalists and business men are interested. Among the firms holding a high position in this line is the enterprising commission and provision house of T. M. Baxter & Co., 127 LaSalle street, Room 5. Mr. Baxter, the head of the firm, is well known in commercial circles as the originator of the Open Board of Trade, an institution which is fast becoming a strong competitor of the regular or the "up-stairs board," as it is now termed. In proposing and perfecting the plans for establishing an Open Board, Mr. Baxter met with bitter opposition from a majority of the members of the "big board," of which he is also a member. This, however, did not deter him from carrying out his project, claiming as he did that the outside trade demanded an institution founded upon principles less conservative than those held by the regular board. Some of the members were inclined to look upon Mr. Baxter's proposition as a sort of "Will 'o the Wisp" scheme, as so many futile attempts had been made to organize an Open Board.

Mr. Baxter was not to be discouraged. He knew his own power, and proceeded to utilize his enterprise and energy, and the success which has attended the Open Board is of such a magnitude as he may well feel proud. The growth of the institution is without a parallel in the history of Chicago. The membership has increased so rapidly as to necessitate more commodious quarters than those now occupied by the board. This question has already been acted upon, so that the officers are now erecting a new building, which will, without doubt, be ready for occupancy by the next year. The institution is certainly an honor to both the city and its founder. T. M. Baxter & Co., in addition to their immense trade in futures, deal largely in provisions and breadstuffs. The house, though young in the business, has succeeded in a remarkably short space of time in making for itself an enviable reputation. A few more years of success like that which has marked its efforts in the one just past and the firm will be in a position to cope with the largest grain and commission houses in the West. Although much of this success is due to Mr. Baxter's indomitable will and courage, he has held the position of President of the Open Board for three terms. The pluck, energy, and perseverance, which are the leading characteristics of this house, has given to it the high degree of prominence which it now enjoys. It is a sound house in every respect, and a customer once secured always remains.

There is nothing like success to make a man popular, and since Mr. Baxter has proven that he is able to both originate and and carry out a great scheme, his business has increased tenfold. The public was not slow to discover the fact that the house of T. M. Baxter & C. was a safe one with which to make investments.

J. T. LESTER & CO.,

25 AND 27 CHAMBER OF COMMERCE.

This is the largest and best known stock, bond, and grain commission house in the West. Mr. John T. Lester, the head of the firm, is an old resident of Chicago, and has been actively engaged in the grain trade here for over twenty years. Mr. Samuel W. Allerton, the millionaire farmer, packer, and banker, is a special partner in the house. The firm has always been noted for its great push and enterprise. They secured the first private telegraph wire ever used between New York and Chicago, a piece of business sagacity which brought them an enormous Wall street clientage Other houses afterward followed in Lester & Co.'s footsteps, and secured direct telegraph connection with New York, until now no house of any consequence pretends to do business between the two great speculative centers without the facility of a private wire. Lester & Co. have always kept the lead they first gained, however. Their first wire ran along the Lake Shore and New York Central Roads, but finding that lake storms sometimes interfered with its proper working, the energetic firm promptly leased another private wire to New York from the Baltimore and Ohio Telegraph Company, at the same time retaining the original wire, thereby insuring prompt connection with Wall street at all times. Of course, all this involved a very large expense, yet for every dollar expended ten came in. The house has been correct on the markets during the past year, and gentlemen who have placed their business with them are well pleased. We have no hesitancy whatever in recommending J. T. Lester & Co. to our readers as enterprising, reliable, safe, and conservative brokers. The New York connections of the firm are of the best.

CHANDLER, BROWN CO.,

COMMISSION MERCHANTS,

177 LaSalle street, who are among our largest receivers, and also do an extensive order business in grain, seeds, and provisions, are too well and favorably known to the trade to need any introduction at our hands in this review of the Chicago Board of Trade, having beenestablished in 1863, since which they have continued to do a prosperous business, which is rapidly growing in volume. They still have a house in Milwaukee, where they started in the business.

We desire to say of Mr. J. A. Brown, who is in charge of the business here, and with whom we are personally acquainted, that he is thoroughly a business gentleman, having a high regard for honor, a thorough knowledge of the business, energetic, and reliable—one of those to whom Chicago is indebted for the push and enterprise which has transformed it from a country village into the magnificent metropolis which it is now acknowledged to be.

KEMPER BROS. & ERMELING.

BUTTER, EGGS, VEAL, AND POULTRY.

One of our most successful produce commission houses occupies the store No. 165 South Water street, and are prominent members of the Produce Exchange. During the last year their trade has increased fully 35 per cent and their list of customers in about the same ratio. Their specialties are butter, eggs, veal, and poultry. Under the supervision of the proprietors and aided by experienced and competent salesmen, and honest and square dealing, the firm business has been steadily increasing since its establishment in 1873.

This firm was originally known as Wm. Ermeling, but last May Messrs. Kemper Bros., formerly associated with the house, were admitted as partners, and we cannot but admit that the influence and experience of these parties, coupled with that of Mr. Ermeling's, bespeaks for the house enterprise and success.

RUMSEY & BUELL,

Successors to Rumsey & Buell and Charles Ray & Co., 108 and 110 Fifth avenue, is one of the most thoroughly reliable commission houses in Chicago. It is one of the great surviving houses.

BROSSEAU, BOOTH & CO.

This well known commission firm, consisting of Z. P. Brosseau, and W. S. Booth, is located at No. 116 LaSalle street. It rates first-class in every respect.

SMITH, McCORMICK & CO.,

No. 128 LaSalle street, is one of the best known and strongest commission houses on the Chicago Board of Trade.

CHAPTER VII

THE BANKS OF CHICAGO.

BANKING IN EARLY DAYS.

IT COMMENCED IN 1830.

The banking in Chicago fifty years ago would hardly be recognized as such to-day and it was only the integrity of the men who started the first bank, and their reputation for absolute honesty, that made such an institution possible in those days. The first currency in the Northwest consisted of skins and furs, it is said, and these were exchanged for stores at the trading posts. There was no money, and but little need of it. But in 1830 it is recorded that Chicago had a bank. There came to Chicago two Scotchmen, Patrick Strachan and W. D. Scott, as agents of the Scottish Fur Company. Soon after them came George Smith, another Scotchman, who succeeded to their business, and then started a bank of deposit in a small way, under the firm name of George Smith & Co. The Wisconsin Marine and Fire Insurance Company, at Milwaukee, was succeeded by the Marine Bank, with George Smith and Alexander Mitchell at the head. These gentlemen issued certificates of deposit in the form of bank notes, and these were put in circulation and used as money.

INTEGRITY FOR BACKING.

There was nothing but the integrity of these men to insure the payment of the certificates, but their reputation for that was so good that the notes were never questioned, and there was never a failure on their part to respond to a call for coin. These certificates were in circulation for twenty years, and were considered just as good as National bank notes or greenbacks are now.

But while this bank was established in good faith with the object in view of meeting a great want in the country, it was in a measure responsible for a very dangerous system of banking in the West. The success of Smith and Mitchell encouraged others to embark in like enterprises, and banks were started in great number, which issued certificates of deposit, but failed to redeem them. This wildcat speculation which followed was responsible for the financial embarrassments of 1837.

There were private banks where business was conducted in just as straighforward a manner as by Smith & Mitchell, and among the men whose signatures were good as gold in early Chicago history were Isaac H. Burch, Alexander Bond, F. G. Adams, and James M. Adsit.

SETH GREEN'S CHRISTIAN BANK.

One of the characters of early Chicago was a pseudo banker who united with his business the work of preacher and editor. This was Seth Green, a spiritualist, who issued certificates of deposit and depended upon the spirits to inform him through a long haired medium whether a call for coin should be responded to and the certificate redeemed. The spirits were nearly always averse to paying when these calls were made, unless something more than moral suasion was brought to bear upon the banker; then they permitted him to pay. Seth edited a little paper under the name of the *Christian Banker*, and the editorials and quotations published in this were supposed to be from the spirit world. The *Christian Banker* and the Spiritualist bank of Seth Green were of short duration, and after the "bank" had been mobbed several times, it wound up business, and Seth and his mediums departed for parts unknown.

In 1835 a branch of the State Bank of Illinois was established in Chicago, of which W. H. Brown was the cashier.

THE PRESENT CHICAGO CLEARING HOUSE.

The present membership of the Chicago Clearing House Association consists of eleven National banks, five State, one private banking company, and two large Canadian banks that have branch offices here. The capital and surplus employed by these institutions, as returned to the Clearing House Oct. 2, which was the last date that their reports were made up, aggregated $18,817,000. Their detailed statements returned to the Clearing House on the date mentioned, compared with the same time in 1882, were as follows:

	1883.	1882.
No. banks.	19.	18.
Capital	$13,886,000	$10,886,000
Surplus	4,931,000	3,279,000
Deposits	81,078,000	82,612,012
Loans	61,509,000	48,728,955

Banks outside of the Clearing House are understood to have about $11,000,000 deposits.

The decline in deposits as given above was due to the low average of country deposits. The interior bankers having employment for their funds at home were borrowers instead of creditors of their city correspondents, and the large excess of loans this year was mainly due to heavy rediscounts for intenor bankers. In addition to the capital and surplus given above, six banks outside of the Clearing House report an aggregate capital of $1,735,000. It is also estimated that other private bankers who decline to make returns employ a capital of $1,500,000, making a

TOTAL AGGREGATE BANKING CAPITAL.

$1,000,000 of which has been added by Clearing House banks since their last report —of $23,152,000.

This, however, does not fully represent the capital employed in banking, as the Canadian banks having offices here are at liberty to use ten times the amount of capital they return to the Clearing House, the latter merely being the amount with which they are charged as fixed capital by the banks they represent.

Within the year one National bank has opened with a capital of $2,000,000.

It is creditable to the managers of Chicago banks that no failures have occurred since 1877.

Chicago bankers handle more foreign exchange than all other Western cities combined. Nearly All the foreign bills drawn by millers and provision dealers in the Northwest and West are sold here, and the business of the year just closing shows a very material gain in this department of finance. Chicago banks also supply the bulk of the Eastern exchange made in the West, and in turn supply bankers in all other cities, including Cincinnati, Toledo, and St. Louis, when they are short of Eastern bills. The transactions in this line of banking have been materially in excess of 1882, or any preceding year.

THE PRICE FOR BANKERS' DRAFTS

on New York exchange has also been at or above par for a large portion of the year. During only a few brief periods has the discount been sufficiently large to permit funds to be brought from them by express. This was due, as above stated, to the he heavy demand from other Western cities.

The miscellaneous business of the banks has also been unusually large, their discount lines showing an expansion commensurate with other departments, and no other branch of business has been so uniformily satisfactory to those conducting it. Every bank of consequence has earned dividends, ranging from 10 to 15 per cent, besides adding a liberal balance to their surplus on undivided profits, and every institution of prominence has found it necessary to employ additional clerical force, and a number were compelled to enlarge their offices. The clearings for the year show an increase of $159,086,139 over 1882, being the largest on record, and $800,938,000 over 1880. Manager Smith, of the bankers' Clearing House, estimates that the establishment of a similar institution

BY THE BOARD OF TRADE

for the settlement of balances on transactions on 'Change has lessened the bank clearings at least $$2,500,000 per week, compared with the old system, as one check now settles a large number of trades. Under the old system of settling such trades half a dozen checks, and not unfrequently twice that number, were given for the same property. Hence, the doubling up process largely swelled the clearings at the banks. It will therefore be seen that the present bank clearings more clearly reflect the volume of legitimate business than those of any previous year with which comparisons are made.

The expansion of the city's commercial and financial transactions during the past years is partly reflected by the report of the Chicago Clearing House, furnished by its efficient manager, W. S. Smith, Esq., which is as follows:

COMPARATIVE CLEARINGS.

The following shows the clearings from 1865 to 1883, inclusive:

1865 (nine months)	$319,606,000.00
1866	453,798,648.11
1867	580,727,331.43
1868	723,293,144.91
1869	734.664,949.91
1870	810,676,036.28
1871	868,936,754.20
1872	993,060,503.47
1873	1,047,027,828.33
1874	1,101,347,948.41
1875	1,212,817,207.54
1876	1,010,092,624.37
1877	1,044,678,475.70
1878	967,184,093,07
1879	1,257,756,124.31
1880	1,725,684,894.85
1881	2,229,097,450.60
1882	2,306,536,855.00
1883	2,525,622.944.00

STOCKS AND BONDS.

The business in stocks and bonds for the year was the largest of any previous one in the West and is constantly growing. The sales of railroad and miscellaneous bonds on the Chicago Stock Exchange aggregated $9,100,000, and in railroad and other stocks 57,500 shares. There was also a large amount of bonds handled by the banks, the majority of which were not reported to the Exchange, and were nearly equal to that amount.

THE FIRST NATIONAL BANK.

THE THIRD IN THE COUNTRY.

There are a few Chicago institutions of which all Chicagoans are pardonably proud because they illustrate the marvelous growth of the most wonderful city which marks the culmination of the genius of the nineteenth century. At the present time this city is nothing in the estimation of its citizens unless it is the acknowledged queen of the commercial world, consequently no man or institution is held in much esteem unless he, or it, has established the right to a position in the front rank.

The occasion of the annual review is auspicious to mention the great banking house, which is an honor to this city, which aspires and has secured a cosmopolitan reputation. The banking house is a concomitant of civilization. The savage or the frontiersman has no need of it. When a people have advanced from a barter to a money basis of financial transaction, the banking house becomes not only a convenience, but a necessity, and just in proportion as the hamlet throws off the rural and assumes the city character the bank is transformed from a little broker's shop to the palatial repository of millions. Two hundred years ago Chicago needed no bank, and had none; twenty years ago Chicago was a city, and required good banking facilities. At the latter date the First National Bank was established, with a capital of $300,000, with E. Aiken as President, Samuel Nickerson as Vice President, E. E. Braisted as Cashier. In 1882 Chicago was a metropolis, and the First National Bank was recharted, with a capital of $3,000,000, with Samuel Nickerson President, and Lyman J. Gage as Cashier. The first President of this great financial institution held his office until his death, which occurred in 1867, when he was succeeded by the present incumbent. In 1868 Mr. Gage assumed the duties of Cashier, and has discharged them ever since in a manner which has not only been entirely satisfactory to the giant corporation he serves, but has made him a prominent figure among Chicago financiers, and known by name the world over. This corporation moved into its present magnificent quarters in November, 1882. The banking office proper is said to be the largest and finest in the world. It is at all events as elegant as variegated marble and carved oak can make it, and with its clerical force, ninety-five in number, all in sight and busy over books of accounts, or in counting piles of gold, silver, and currency, it reminds one irresistibly of some wild tale of the Arabian romances. But with all this display everything is severely practical. The First National Bank has reason to feel proud of the officers to whom have been intrusted its interests from first to last. They are gentlemen with whom slander never meddles, and who are never assailed by the tongue of reproach.

PRESTON, KEAN & CO.

LEADING PRIVATE BANKING HOUSE.

This leading private banking-house was established in 1860, and for three and twenty years has been earning a reputation for safely keeping and judiciously investing the money of others which is second to that of no financial concern in the West.

This firm safely survived the great fire and the several panics and periods of business depression which swept away so many concerns; and its record is such as to fully warrant the confidence its clients have always reposed in it, and the belief that it can fully discharge any financial trust placed in it.

In their banking department Messrs. Preston, Kean & Co. offer as liberal terms for the accounts of bankers, merchants, and others as is compatible with business principles.

In their foreign exchange department they issue bills on all the principal European cities, and also letters of credit for the convenience of travelers. The house makes collections in all parts of the world, and is specially peculiar for its promptness in this line of its business.

The firm is probably the oldest one in the West in the line of investment securities. It was connected with the first government loan issued for the prosecution of the recent civil war, and has been largely instrumental in placing every subsequent loan, and it is admirably prepared to serve the interest of investors in this connection.

The firm are also large dealers in bonds issued by States, counties, cities, etc., often buying and selling entire issues of cities for municipal purposes, in some single transactions amounting to several hundreds of thousands of dollars. They also deal in railroad bonds of the leading trunk lines.

It has for some years, made a specialty of Chicagor Car Trusts, which certificates run from thee months to seven years, draw 6 per cent interest, payable quarterly. By some of the best Illinois lawyers they are regarded as being exempt from taxation.

The certificates are not only the direct obligatin of the road issuing, but are also secured by the rolling stock.

The bank does not undertake any speculative business.

The remarkable success with which this banking-house has been attended since its inception can be laid to no other source than the financial skill of its management.

CHARLES HENROTIN.

PRESIDENT OF THE STOCK EXCHANGE.

This gentleman has been so intimately associated with the Chicago Stock Exchange ever since its organization that the mention of one invariably suggests the other. Mr. Henrotin is now serving his second term as President of the Stock Exchange, a position which he has filled with marked ability and to the entire satisfaction of the members of this important corporation. He has been thirty-seven years in Chicago, and has always enjoyed a high reputation and exceptionably for integrity and good business tact. Indeed, Mr. Henrotin is one of our best and shrewdest financiers. He is a leading banker and broker, and as he was for years the cashier of one of the leading banking houses in the West it is almost unnecessary to add that he has had just the experience which fits him for the successful prosecution of the business in which he is engaged—buying and selling of bonds, stocks, commercial paper, and safe-investment securities. He is one of our few financial operators who always has on hand a full line of choice securities from which customers can select, or, if they please to leave the selection to him, they will discover that they have confided their interests to an honorable and competent gentleman. Mr. Henrotin is now, and for years has been, the government representative, as consul, of Belgium and Turkey at this port. He is a ripe scholar as well as an accomplished banker, and is admirably fitted for the important official position he holds.

THE NATIONAL BANK OF ILLINOIS,

GRANNIS BLOCK,

is one of the strongest and soundest financial establishments in the country. It has a paid-up capital of $1,000,000, and is probably doing as safe, and, at the same time, as profitable a business as any bank in Chicago. Its facilities for transacting business, domestic or foreign, are simply perfect, or as nearly so as is compatible with human infirmities. The officers of this excellent concern are George Schneider, President; William H. Bradley, Vice President; William A. Hammond, Cashier. The Board of Directors embrace, besides two of the gentlemen above-named, S. B. Cobb, Frederick Mahla, Henry Corwith, Ernst Prussing, W. L. Peck, H. N. Hibbard, B. H. Campbell, George E. Adams, and A. A. Munger. The above-named gentlemen enjoy a high reputation in business circles east and west. Mr. George Schneider, the President of the Illinois National Bank, is considered one of the ablest financiers in

Chicago, and to his admirable management the bank is largely indebted for its pronounced success.

CONTINENTAL NATIONAL BANK,

NOS. 115 AND 117 DEARBORN STREET,

Chicago, was established on the 5th of March, 1883, with a capital of $2,000,000, and under the most favorable auspices. This financial corporation has been exceptionably fortunate in securing for its officers gentlemen of the highest standing in commercial circles, whose names are a sufficient guarantee as to the unimpeachable character of the institution. The officers are: C. T. Wheeler, President; John C. Black, Cashier; Douglass Hoyt, Assistant Cashier. The Board of Directors embrace such well-known names as P. D. Armour, A. G. Van Schaick, Henry Botsford, M. C. Stearns, etc. This bank will commence foreign exchange business Jan. 1, 1884.

N. W. HARRIS & CO.

THIRTEEN MILLIONS BEHIND THEM.

That the importance of Chicago as a financial center increases steadily is confirmed by the recent establishment here and signal success of these representative investment bankers at No. 176 Dearborn street. At their back, besides personal resources, is the long purse of one of the solidest trust companies of the East, having some $13,000,000 assets, for which company the firm places loans in Indiana and Illinois. A feature with which they are especially identified is dealing in bonds of counties, cities and towns, when once personal visitation and rigid scrutiny have approved the legality of the proceedings issuing them, and certified that they were strictly for municipal purposes. Among these bonds more recently placed by the firm were $100,000 of the Saginaw bonds, $90,000 of South Bend, $60,000 of Sioux City, Iowa, $60,000 of Columbus, Ohio, $50,000 of Moline, Ill., $40,000 of Ringgold County, Iowa, $77,000 of Dakota Territory.

BENNETT'S LAW AND COLLECTING ASSOCIATION,

130 Dearborn street and 99 Madison street, was established in 1872, and has probably a larger clientage than any other law or collecting association in this city. Horace C. Bennett, a lawyer of ability and large practice and experience, is the head of the law department, and THE INTER OCEAN, having had frequent occasion to employ Mr. Bennett, bears cheerful witness to his skill and integrity. He is also the Chicago attorney for the Stationers' Board of Trade, the Hardware Board of Trade, and the Carpet Trade Association, all of New York City.

REXFORD & PRENTICE—LAWYERS.

GENERAL LAW AND COLLECTIONS.

This firm is composed of Henry L. Rexford, a native of this county, and a son of Stephen Rexford, who came to Cook County in 1833, and David K. Prentice, formerly of Genesee County, New York. By great diligence and much hard work they have established a fine general law practice and collection business. They have a large list of good clients both at home and abroad. A distinguishing feature in their collection methods is the constant attention to all claims, whether small or large, believing that the abandonment by attorneys of all small claims after very slight efforts to collect is not as effectual a plan as should be adopted by a well managed collection house. This firm refer by special permission to the Chicago National Bank and Lyon & Healy, of Chicago, and the National Park Bank and Steinway & Sons, New York City. Their offices are located at 89 Madison street, two doors west of THE INTER OCEAN office.

CHAPTER VIII

THE INSURANCE BUSINESS.

SOMETHING OF ITS HISTORY.

THE FIRST AGENT.

No city in the world ever gave to insurance men such a painful surprise as did Chicago in 1871, and never before nor since did the fire insurance companies make so grand a record for honesty and uprightness in business. The total loss by the fire was estimated at $185,510,000, and the fire insurance companies had risks on this amounting to $100,225,780, of which more than one-half, or about $50,178,780, was paid. By this conflagration sixty-eight companies, having assets of $24,807,109, were placed in liquidation. In that year there were sixteen local companies and twenty-eight outside companies doing business in Chicago, with their agencies permanently located here.

The first insurance agent in Chicago was Gurdon S. Hubbard, who received his appointment from the Ætna of Hartford in 1834. In that year he wrote the first policy ever issued in Chicago or Cook County. For over thirty years Mr. Hubbard continued to represent this and other companies in Chicago, and retired from business in 1867.

MARINE INSURANCE.

In 1835 the Alton Marine and Fire Insurance Company of Alton, this State, was chartered, and it is claimed this was the first company chartered by the State.

The second company to establish an agency in Chicago, however, was the Howard of New York, with E. K. Hubbard as agent, early in 1836. In January, 1856, the Chicago Marine and Fire Insurance Company was chartered, and in 1837 the third company to appoint an agent for Chicago was the Hartford, of Hartford, Conn., with Julius Wadsworth as agent.

In 1839 Chicago had its first fire of any importance, when, on Oct. 27, the Tremont House, then standing where the Commercial Hotel now stands, and twelve other buildings on Lake street, burned. This naturally awakened the people to the advantage of insurance, and the business for that year increased very rapidly. Chicago had become a city, where one must be protected from fire if he would feel safe that business of one day could be resumed the next, even if the fire fiend swept away all the property he owned.

BOARD OF UNDERWRITERS.

In 1849 the increase of fires and the competition among insurance companies led to conferences and meetings of those engaged in agency work, and at a meeting in New York such steps were taken relative to the larger cities of the country that organization of local boards began.

The first mention of the local board of underwriters in Chicago is of the date Dec. 3, 1849, with George W. Dale as President.

In 1852 fire and life insurance was so attractive that the Hon. E. C. Larned delivered a lecture on the subject at the Chicago Commercial College, April 9 before a large audience composed of the leading representatives in commerce, banking, and law, and a committee of prominent citizens deemed this lecture of such value to the community that they published it in pamphlet form for distribution.

The Chicago Board of Underwriters was organized in 1856.

The Chicago Fire Insurance Patrol was organized, and made its first appearance Oct. 2, 1871, just seven days before the great fire, with Captain Ben B. Bullwinkle at the head. After the fire the patrol became efficient, and has been of great service in aiding the department and saving insurance.

There are now 262 insurance companies with agencies in Chicago, and the business in fire insurance amounts to about $3,000,000 a year, while the life and marine insurance will add $2,000,000 more.

GENERAL AGENCIES.

PLATE GLASS INSURANCE.

A MATTER THAT BUT FEW ARE CONVERSANT WITH

The business as carried on by the Lloyds Plate Glass Insurance Company, of New York, enables parties having plate glass showcases, or valuable mirrors to protect themselves against all accidents, whether broken by careless servants, the criminally disposed, or the acts of Providence. Very few are aware of the numerous ways in which plate glass is broken. Few tenants are aware that they are liable to the owner of the dwellings or buildings they occupy for all glass broken, and breakages occur in numerous ways, and among those are breakage by burglars, runaway horses, intoxicated persons, mischievous boys, cleaning windows, children playing, stones thrown, pistol balls, hailstorms, windstorms, ladders falling, shutters falling, signs falling, awnings falling, receiving goods, delivering goods, slamming of doors, warping of sashes, settling of buildings, lightning, tornadoes, explosions, snow slides from roof, slipping on sidewalk, carelessness of employes, carlessness of expressmen, expansion by heat, contraction by cold, goods falling, inside or out.

The Lloyds Insurance Company saves the owner of the glass not only money, but trouble and delay, for when a breakage occurs it is only necessary to notify the agents of the company, and they immediately replace the broken glass.

ASSETS.

United States Governmens bonds		$104,000
Cash in bank and other assets		26,000
Total assets		$130,000

LIABILITIES.

Losses in course of adjustment	$1,400	
All other liabilities	5,600	$7,000
Surplus to policy-holders		$123,000

George W. Montgomery and William C. Magill, composing the firm of Geo. W. Montgomery & Co., are agents, 151 LaSalle street, Chicago, Ill.

THE WESTERN MANUFACTURERS

MUTUAL INSURANCE COMPANY, 113, 115, 117 MONROE STREET.

This company under the able and efficient management of Secretary P. A. Montgomery has become one of those which can be relied upon to make substantial progress under all circumstances, and in 1883 has increased its net assets over fifty thousand dollars, besides declaring a 12¾ per cent dividend to policy-holders. This exceptional success is due to the nature of the risks written, which consist entirely of the best manufactories, widely scattered and under the supervision of skilled inspectors, none of whom are paid commissions.

The officers are: President, the Hon. Jesse Spalding; Vice President, William H. Turner, Esq.; Treasurer, the Hon. Clinton Briggs; Secretary, P. A. Montgomery. The business is purely mutual, and the member ship comprises a majority of the large manufacturing firms of the Northwest.

Mr. Montgomery is an underwriter of considerable experience, having been connected with the Millers' National Insurance Company, of this city, in a responsible capacity for several years previous to his appointment as Secretary of the Western Manufacturers' Mutual, and having previous to that a wide experience as special agent and adjuster for several leading stock companies. That the Western Manufacturers' Mutual is well handled may be inferred from the fact that it has returned during the past four years an average of 25 per cent of premiums annually to its policy-holders, or one year's premium out of every four.

THE TRADERS' INSURANCE CO.

This company began business under its reorganization April, 1872, with a cash capital of $500,000. It has uniformly made money every year since, and has returned to its stockholders their entire outlay and considerable besides. Its gross assets now reach $1,150,000, with a surplus as regards policyholders of $860,000. It has entirely outgrown the prejudice against local companies, and, having a firm hold on the public, gained by fair and prompt dealing with all, and an extended agency system, which furnishes a large income, the Traders is justly regarded one of the solid, permanent institutions of this city. Among its officers and directory are found names which are familiar to all as gentlemen of wealth and standing, and being located in the center of the great Northwest, its future is bright and promising. We are glad to know that the company has had a very prosperous year, and makes a splendid showing in its annual statement.

R. J. Smith, the Secretary and manager, is well and favorably known among underwriters everywhere

SUN FIRE OFFICE OF LONDON,

ENGLAND, ESTABLISHED 1710.

Probably the whole history of Insurance contains no name more remarkable than that of the Sun Fire Office, which has just reached the great age of 174 years. It is possessed of large accummulated assets, and is backed by the unlimited liability of its wealthy shareholders, both of which are equally responsible for all losses in the United States as in England. Its advent to this country was cordially received by all classes of insurers, and it has already acquired a leading place among the kindred institutions in this country.

In England we learn that its business is gigantic in its proportions and of the highest order, and that it stands among insurance companies in a similar position to that occupied by the Bank of England among the banks. The Sun has agencies in all the principal cities of the United States, and is represented in Chicago by Messrs. H. J. Straight & Co., at No. 150 LaSalle street.

CREAM OF THE BUSINESS.

LIVERPOOL AND LONDON AND GLOBE

This insurance company is one of the largest and best known in the world. The unlimited liability of the stockholders is a guarantee that has not escaped the attention of any man who has property to insure, and in consequence, like a few other standard companies, this one is able to select the cream of the business and decline that which is not gilt-edge. The amount of losses paid by the Liverpool and London and Globe in the great fires at Chicago and Boston footed up the astonishing sum of four millions and five hundred thousand dollars. Remaining in the field it soon reaped a rich reward, and, as it always has and no doubt always will, continued to grow in the estimation of the public.

No better illustration of the integrity of the company can be offered, in a local sense, than to enumerate the Chicago Board of Directors: John Crerar, of Crerar, Adams & Co.; Levi Z. Leiter, late Field, Leiter & Co.; Ezra J. Warner, of Sprague, Warner & Co. The Chicago office is in the Oriental Building,

No. 124 LaSalle street, and is in charge of Mr. William Warren, Resident Secretary.

THE NEW ORLEANS INSURANCE CO.

OF NEW ORLEAN'S LA.,

was organized in 1805 and has an honorable record of more than three-quarters of a century, paying millions of dollars for fire losses promptly and honestly. At the close of the late civil war it charged off its books as worthless hundreds of thousands of dollars depreciated securities, the result of war, and yet it possesses a half million unimpaired, paid-up capital, with a handsome net surplus in addition and above all liabilities and capital. It can, therefore, properly claim that it is time-tried, war-tested, fire-proof, and deserves the confidence and support of the insuring public.

Colonel W. W. Caldwell is the manager of the company for its Northern department, which embraces the business of all States north of and including Kentucky, with headquarters at Chicago, Ill. Agencies will be maintained in all principal cities.

THE FIRE INSURANCE ASSOCIATION,

LIMITED, OF LONDON, ENGLAND.

This company has only been doing business in this country about three years, but has evidently made rapid strides toward the front, as is manifested by its premium receipts in 1882, which amounted to $950,000. The capital of the company is $5,000,000, and they have about $1,000 000 invested in this country.

The stockholders and officers are among the most prominent men in England, the present Lord Mayor of London being one of its directors.

Messrs. Fred S. James & Co. are the local agents in Chicago, and Mr. Theo. W. Letton, 101 LaSalle street, is the Manager for the Western States and Territories. He now has more than five hundred agents in his field, and the receipts for 1883 show a very handsome increase over those of last year, demonstrating conclusively that the company is popular in his department.

NORTHERN ASSURANCE COMPANY.

ITS CHICAGO AGENCY.

One of the stanchest fire insurance corporations doing business in this country is that popular old Scotch company, the Northern Assurance Company of Aberdeen and London, which commenced business away back in 1836 with a premium income that year of $4,500. Some idea of its success and popularity may be gleaned from its record, which shows a constant and steady increase, until last year its receipts for premiums reached the enormous figure of $2,300,500. It has a paid up cash capital of $1,500,000; net fire assets of over $6,000,000, of which $4,344,002 is a surplus over all liabilities for the security of policyholders. In this country it has assets invested to the extent of $1,221,601, over two-thirds of which is surplus. The company's business in the Western States is managed from Chicago by W. D. Crooke, office 204 LaSalle street. Residents in Chicago can obtain policies of the Resident Agent, Henry H. Brown, No. 185 LaSalle street.

THE NIAGARA FIRE INSURANCE CO.

OF NEW YORK.

The sixty-fifth semi-annual report of this well-known and deservedly popular insurance company furnishes abundant and gratifying evidence of its high financial character, and the admirable manner in which its affairs have been managed by its officers. According to the report above referred to the corporation has assets amounting to $1,-780,490.35, and a net surplus over and above its liabilities of $536,858.52. This is a kind of showing that invariably wins public confidence, and as would naturally be expected, the Niagara has enjoyed during the year just closed a season of prosperity and remains where it has been for years, at the front rank of fist-class fire insurance companies. The Niagara has been fortunate in securing for officers men of ability and integrity. Messrs. Peter Notman and Thomas F. Goodrich, its President and Secretary; O. S. Blackwelder, Chicago Manager, and Morris Franklin, associate. are all conspicuous figures in insurance circles East and West.

THE PHŒNIX FIRE INSURANCE.

R. S. CRITCHELL & CO.

In fire insurance, as in most other things, the best is the cheapest. R. S. Critchell & Co., who for fifteen years past have had the agency of some of the strongest and best managed companies, are agents for the Phœnix Fire Assurance Company of London, the Springfield Fire and Marine Insurance Company of Massachusetts, Niagara of New York, County Fire and Lumbermen's of Philadelphia, and others. These companies possess over $11,000,000 of assets, and have paid $100,000,000 in losses since their organization.

Critchell & Co.'s agency is without a superior in the city in any respect, and no pains are spared to do their business carefully and promptly. Their office is at 141 and 143 LaSalle street.

THE HOME.

"EQUAL TO ANY EMERGENCY."

The Home Insurance Company of New York, one of the largest and most popular fire companies in the world, has an immense ncome and assets equal for any emergency. It insures against fire, lightning, and tornadoes, and has agencies in all the cities, towns, and villages of the United States. Since the organization, in 1853, it has paid over $35,000,000 in losses. The following statement shows its condition on July 1, 1883:

Cash capital	$3,000,000.00
Reserve for unearned premiums	2,212,267.00
Reserve for unpaid losses and claims	209,711.21
Net surplus	1,749,292.61
Total cash assets 1st July, 1883	$7,171,270.82

The managers of its Western department

and local agents for Chicago are Messrs. Ducat & Lyon, No. 155 LaSalle street.

NEW YORK ALLIANCE.

AMONG THE BEST AGENCIES.

This favorite organization is composed of the Pacific and New York Bowery Fire Insurance Companies of New York. E. W. Lyman is General Agent for the Western States, with headquarters at 150 and 152 LaSalle street. These companies stand in the front rank and are justly considered among the strongest and best doing an agency business. With long experience, ample capital, large net surplus, and investments of the most solid character, being mainly in government bonds, their policy is sought by business men who desire the best indemnity. The New York Alliance is represented in all the principal cities and towns of the United States. The Chicago agency of the Alliance is represented by E. W. Lyman & Co., at 153 LaSalle street.

THE LANCASHIRE INSURANCE CO.

OF MANCHESTER, ENGLAND.

This sterling company was incorporated in the year 1852. Commenced business in the United States in 1872. Since its organization it has paid in losses over $13,500,000. It has paid in losses in the United States over $5,000,000. The following statement shows the condition of its United States branch Jan 1, 1883:

Assets (United States bonds).......	$1,447,492.58
Total liabilities......................	719,467.59
Net surplus........................	$728,024.99

Messrs. Fred S. James & Co. are the Chicago agents. Mr. W. G. Ferguson is the manager of its Western Department, No. 161 LaSalle street, Chicago.

CITY OF LONDON FIRE INSURANCE CO.

OF LONDON, ENGLAND.

This company commenced business in the United States with the unusual large initial remittance of $550,000, all invested in United States 4 per cent bonds, held in absolute legal trust for the security of United States policy-holders. The Trustees are Charles F. Choate, President Old Colony Railroad Company; Oliver Ames, of Oliver Ames & Son, and Reuben E. Demmon, President Howard National Bank of Boston, Mass. John C. Paige, of Boston, Mass., is Resident Manager, and Edwin A. Simonds, No. 153 LaSalle street, Chicago, Ill., is General Agent of the Western department of this company.

LOCAL AGENCIES.

E. W. LYMAN & CO.,

152 LASALLE STREET.

The members of this firm, E. W. Lyman and Henry W. Rice, have been for many years leading underwriters in this city.

The companies they represent are the New York Alliance, Rutgers, People's, Merchants, and Franklin and Emporium (all of New York City), and the Citizens', of Pennsylvania. The names of these companies are familiar to the business men of Chicago, and only need to be mentioned by us, when they will be at once recognized as among the very best represented in this city, strong and conservative, and always prompt in settlement and payment of losses.

S. M. MOORE & CO.,

THE WELL-KNOWN INSURANCE FIRM

on the southeast corner of LaSalle and Madison streets, report their business as steadily increasing year by year. They continue to represent the Orient of Hartford, the Lion of London, the Louisville Underwriters, and the London and Provincial of London, all strong companies financially, careful in management, and prompt in settlement of claims, therefore worthy the support of the insuring public.

GRANGER SMITH & CO.

SOME BIG COMPANIES.

The old and favorably known agency of Granger Smith & Co., 158 LaSalle street, represents the following standard companies: Mechanics and Traders', of New York; Manufacturers and Builders', of New York; New York Fire, of New York; Buffalo Insurance Company, of Buffalo, N. Y.; Security Insurance Company, of Cincinnati, Ohio.

DUCAT & LYON.

This well-known firm, 155 LaSalle street, have the local agencies for Chicago of the Home, Howard, Citizens', and National, all of the City of New York, and first-class standard companies.

LIFE INSURANCE.

A BIT OF HISTORY.

Life insurance is a system of charity where every man provides for his own after he is gone. The oldest American life insurance company dates from 1759, and the writings of that old philosopher, Benjamin Franklin, show that he knew much more about this business and of what value it would be to coming generations than do many people to-day. The growth of the business has been like the rising of the sun, so steady that the changes in position could hardly be noticed, but now, when at the zenith, we can look back over the course and see the wonderful progress. Its growth in the last forty years has been one of the wonders of the century. Quietly it has made its way into every city, town, and village, and thrown its protecting arms around millions who would otherwise have no refuge from the cold charity of the world.

FIRST AGENT IN CHICAGO.

In Chicago that old pioneer, Gurdon S. Hubbard, was the first to interest the people in this business. He opened his office as agent of one of the oldest insurance companies in the country in 1834, and did business in both fire and life insurance. This was the beginning.

To speak of the business done in Chicago now would be difficult, for this is the grea center for the business throughout the West. All the companies of any prominence in this country and Europe have their Western agencies here, and to speak of the business in Chicago is to speak of it as a whole.

Not long ago a careful estimate was made, which showed that there were over 5,000,000 people in this country having a direct or property interest in life insurance—that is, more people were looking to the life insurance companies than the combined population of New York, Philadelphia, Boston, Chicago, St. Louis, Cincinnati, St. Paul, San Francisco, New Orleans, Brooklyn, and Minneapolis.

WOULD PAY THE NATIONAL DEBT.

This great army of insured hold policies to the amount of $1,649,484,953.16, which would pay off the National debt. In the past there have been paid $823,897,319.37 to policy-holders, as losses have occurred. The assets of all the life insurance companies last year were $468,541,788.93, or more than all the railroads in New England cost, more than $100,000,000 in excess of the circulation of all the National banks, and almost equal to the capital stock of all the National banks in this country.

As said before, the amount of insurance in force would pay the National debt, and exceed by $108,000,000 the individual deposits in all the National banks. It is generally supposed that the banks of the country control the financial business, but here it will be seen that the life insurance companies owe their patrons $100,000,000 more than do all the banks.

And to go further in comparison, the amounts paid in by the policy-holders in premiums in a year was $60,444,996, and the amount paid to policy-holders in the same time, $58,388,283; so it will be seen that the difference is not so great as some suppose.

Estimating the population of the United States at 50,000,000, it will be seen that those interested in life insurance equal one-tenth of the entire number of people.

ESTATES LEFT BY INSURANCE.

Some of the largest policies ever paid in life insurance are as follows:

Sir Robert Clifton, England, $1,250,000; Abbott Lawrence, Massachusetts, $40,000; W. H. Langley, Galliopolis, Ohio, $300,000; John J. Roe, St. Louis, $200,000; Andrew Johnson, Tennessee, $100,000; Reverdy Johnson, Baltimore, $100,000; C. C. Wait, New York, $100,000; Francis Whittaker, St. Louis, $100,000; W. H. Seward, New York, $100,000; Horace Greeley, New York, $100,000; W. H. Ferry, Lake Forest, Ill., $50,000-Geo. R. Chittenden, Chicago, $76,000; Chas; E. Norwood, Chicago, $75,000; Mahlon D. Ogden, Chicago, $60,000; Wm. F. Coolbaugh, Chicago, $100,000; J. M. Dake, Chicago, $140,000; Sextus N. Wilcox, Chicago, $60,,000; W. W. Switzer, St. Louis, $310,000-Daniel Drew, New York, $150,000; J. M; Beebe, Boston, $100,000; W. H. Ovington, Chicago, $45,000; James A. Garfield, Ohio, $35,000; H. T. Blow, St. Louis, $117,000; J. W. Crafts, Boston, $110,000; Dean Richmond, New York, $106,000; D. S. Voorhes, New York, $50,000.

An idea of who are some of the large policy holders may be had from the following list:

Each man in the appended list carries at least $50,000 life insurance, and most of them considerably more, some of them being insured for over $100,000: S. M. Nickerson, Elisha Eldred, C. I. Peck, N. K. Fairbank, L. J. Gage, Nelson Ludington, William Bross, J. O. Rutter, H. Z. Culver, S. D. Kimbark, Ferd W. Peck, C. M. Henderson, J. H. McVicker, Charles Vergho, J. V. Farwell, J. Sherman Hale, Edson Keith, Ebenezer Buckingham, George M. Pullman, T. W. Harvey, Perry H. Smith, W. C. Grant, A. B. Mecker, L. D. Norton, E. W. Blatchford, Albert A. Munger, Frank D. Gray, S. K. Dow, S. H. Kerfoot, W. H. Chappell, H. D. Colvin, W. B. Phillips, J. L. Norton, Harlow Higgenbotham, Carter H. Harrison, Anson Stager, Erastus N. Bates, A. N. Eddy, Marshall Field, H. A. Rust, William A. Fuller, P. C. Hanford, E. P. Griswold, Frank Parmelee, Ira Holmes, Francis B. Peabody, E. G. Asay, Leander J. McCormick, L. Z. Leiter, Henry Field, Levi L. Atwood, Horace White, David H. Hills, Morris Barbe, A. M. Wright, J. M. Daggett, J. Russell Jones, Robert Law, A. Booth, J. Y. Scammon, H. H. Shufeldt, Lyman Baird, Alfred Cowles, B. Lowenthal, Elbridge G. Keith, Redmond Prindiville, Charles Fargo, Hiram Wheeler, E. G. Mason, Samuel J. Walker, F. A. Bryan, C. F. Gates, David Stettauer, C. B. Nelson, Morris Einstein, Bernhard Roessing, I. H. Burch, H. C. Nutt, Potter Palmer, T. M. Avery, Lewis Morganthau, H. V. Bemis, William H. Bradley, C. J. Hull, L. L. Bond, Charles Gilman Smith, J. Edward Fay, Edward Ely, C. P. Kimball, A. C. Badger, F. A. Stevens, William Sturges, George H. Wheeler, George W. Hart, Charles Schwab, John S. Gould, W. E. Burlock, A. E. Neeley, Robert D. Fowler.

THE MUTUAL RESERVE FUND
LIFE ASSOCIATION

was established in 1881 in New York, in obedience to an imperative demand on the part of the public for a cheap and reliable system of life insurance, which would be within the means of the million, and at the same time prove a perfectly safe way of investing small savings for the benefit of the loved ones. The association is purely mutual in character, but differs from ordinary mutual benefit companies in the possession of a reserve fund, designed to guard against increasing assessments, as its members grow older, and to make the "last man" insured as well as the first, equally secure. It also provides against excessive loss through epidemics, etc. This association does not purpose to accumulate large surpluses in excess of what is required to protect its policy-holders; any surplus is immediately placed to the credit of the insured and is employed to pay assessments. The result is, its policies are nearly or quite self-sustaining after about fifteen years. The cost of insurance in this excellent association, which has received the unqualified indorsement of the best insurance experts and actuaries, is best explained by an illustration. The writer, 50 years old, is insured in it for $10,000 at the following cost: Admission fee, $30; medical examination, $3; annual dues, $20; six possible assessments per year (the average has been less than four), $20 each, $120; total, $173.

Deducting admission and medical examination fees—which are not required a second time—it costs the man of 50 about $140 a year to carry $10,000 insurance in the Mutual Reserve Fund. The same insurance in the high-rate companies would cost about $475 per year, leaving a difference in favor of the Mutual Reserve Fund Association of $335 annually. This is worth considering. The association is entirely reliable, and has promptly paid every loss sustained. The office of its Western Department, at No. 113 Adams street, Chicago, is under the supervision of its Vice-President, Dr. D. M. Caldwell, an accomplished gentleman and physician. Within less than three years this association has placed 17,000 members upon its books, and issued policies covering $75,000,000.

CHAPTER IX

MERCANTILE.

THE WHOLESALE TRADE.

WHEN AND BY WHOM IT WAS BEGUN.

The first wholesale trader in Chicago is hard to locate, since all the retail stores made a point of fitting out inland camps and stores. As early as 1836 Stiles Burton was in the wholesale grocery and liquor business, and was located at the corner of Lake and State streets. He did a large and lucrative business, as he fitted out many of the smacks and luggers that plied the lakes.

L. M. Boyce did a wholesale drug business at No. 121 Lake street, and W. H. & A. F. Clarke did a wholesale drug business at No. 128 Lake street; George Delicker carried on a wholesale grocery at No. 163 Lake street, in 1839, and Harman, Loomis & Co. were also in this line in that year. William Lill was running his brewery on the north lake shore in that year. Nicholson & Co. had a large general wholesale and retail store on North Water street in 1839; G. F. Randolph carried on a wholesale dry goods business at No. 109 Lake street; Robert and James Woodworth were also in the wholesale dry goods business at No. 103 Lake street; George White had a general store and was city crier about this time.

BUSINESS BEGINS.

In 1850 the wholesale trade had become a definite and separate business. In the dry goods line Cooley, Wadsworth & Co. were the leading house and carried on a large business at No. 205 South Water street; Mills, Bowen, Dillenbeck & Co. were the only other large dry goods house here then, and were located at No. 100 Lake street. The business was not remarkable in the light of the present day, and altogether did not reach five million dollars; still it was great for those days. Barrett, King & Co. were a large gents' furnishing house at No. 189 and 191 South Water street. They did a large business from the fact that they had a partial monopoly of their line.

The wholesale grocers were numerous about this date, there being no less than twenty-two firms engaged in that line exclusively. Chicago has always been the second city in the Union, since the war, in the wholesale grocery line, and in 1850 was not far behind Boston or Philadelphia. The leading firms at that time were Gould Brothers, No. 135 South Water street; Flanders & Wadsworth, No. 173 South Water street; J. H. Dunham & Co., Nos. 92, 94, and 96 South Water street; Saterlee, Cook & Co., No. 64 Lake street; Warner & Clark, No. 107 South Water street. The wholesale druggists were Barclay Brothers, No. 218 South Water street; Bay & Baldwin, No. 139 Lake street; Brinkerhoff & Penton, No. 94 Lake street.

AS THE CITY GREW

and the railroad facilities improved, so did the wholesale trade advance. In 1865, after the war, the wholesale houses were more plentiful in Chicago than in any other city except New York. The wholesale grocers were thirty in number, and Day, Allen & Co., J. W. Doane & Co., D. J. Ely & Co., Boynton & Smith, Hinsdale, Sibley & Endicott are some of the prominent firms of that date. They did a business of from $500,000 to $2,000,-000, and were shipping goods all through the Northwest.

The wholesale dry goods trade was represented in those days by what was then considered large concerns, American & Smith, Bowen Brothers, Carson, Pirie & Co., Cooley, Farwell & Co., Field, Palmer & Leiter, Richards, Crumbaugh & Shaw were some of the merchant princes of those busy times. The wholesale drug men were also noticeable then, for the fat contracts for medicines were let in Chicago. J. H. Reed & Co., Fuller, Finch & Fuller, Smith & Dwyer, Burnhams & Van Schaack are some of the leading wholesalers of that date.

The business of the years preceding the fire of 1871 gradually increased. After that date the increase was marvelous, and so great was the expanse of the trade in this city that several smaller cities which had drawn upon

CHICAGO AS A BASE OF SUPPLIES

turned about and took up the wholesale trade, cutting into Chicago's business considerably. But the natural increase of population in the Northwest has more than doubled the wholesale traffic of this city since the fire, and it is admitted on all hands that capital invested in business here pays a better interest than in any other city.

The magnitude of the trade to-day is marvelous, reaching as it does to a business of $30,000,000 for one firm, and overtopping the trade of any other city in the Union in many lines. Chicago to-day stands at the head of certain lines of business, and is second only to New York in any line whatsoever.

The importing of tea is a specialty with this city, and this year the imports promise to be 25 per cent greater than ever before.

Ever since 1881 Chicago has imported more tea than any city in the world.

The first dry goods house in the country is here, the first millinery establishment, and in the wholesale grocery line but one house in the country exceeds some of the Chicago establishments, and that is in New York. The half century sees Chicago next to the head. The century will see her, at the same rate of progress, at the head of every commercial city in the world.

MARSHALL FIELD & CO.

THE LARGEST DRY GOODS HOUSE IN THE WEST.

To thousands of people scattered from Maine to California and from Hong Kong to London, Chicago and Marshall Field & Co. are synonymous terms. They are not the same, as any one living in this city can testify, but there are many people in distant parts of the world who hear of the former only because of something sold to or bought from the latter's great dry goods house that the mistake is not so unnatural as might be supposed, for Marshall Field's store is as distinct in its position as an unrivaled dry goods house as the city is in its as the only Chicago.

HISTORY OF THE ENTERPRISE.

The history of this great commercial enterprise does not date back half a century for its beginning, and it is not a quarter century since the name of Field had any connection with it. Potter Palmer was the founder. He came to Chicago in 1852 and opened a dry goods store in a small, unpretentious store on Lake street, between Clark and Dearborn, which was then in the very heart of trade in the city.

The enterprise was a success, and from that small beginning came the great unrivaled Marshall Field & Co.

In the fall of 1864 Mr. Palmer retired, disposing of his interests to Messrs. Marshall Field, L. Z. Leiter and Milton J. Palmer, and the name was changed to Field, Leiter & Palmer. In 1866 Mr. Milton J. Palmer retired and the firm was Field & Leiter, a name that was familiar all over the country, for under that name was achieved some of the greatest triumphs of the establishment.

THE FIRST FIRE.

In October, 1868, the firm first occupied its present site. The great fire of October 9, 1871, swept away all its wealth of beautiful goods gathered from the four points of the compass, along with the building, but the men at the head were like Chicago and not to be discouraged by a total loss, began at once the rebuilding and in a short time the site of the ruins was reoccupied by a fine building.

Again, in 1877, this beautiful trade palace was visited by fire and all was swept away. But the Exposition Building was rented and Field & Leiter occupied that until 1879 when the new marble palace, the best arranged retail store on the continent, was opened. It has been occupied ever since, and the perfect fire-proof structure bids defiance to any more such disasters as have been experienced in the past.

WHO MARSHALL FIELD IS.

In January, 1881, Mr. Leiter retired from the business, and the firm became "Marshall Field & Company," with Marshall Field at the head. This gentleman is yet in the prime of life, being 48 year old, and a resident of Chicago since 1868. Of few words, quiet demeanor, unblemished moral character and habits, pleasant manner, liberal, thoroughly public-spirited and sympathetic in nature, is this handsome man, who is to be seen at his desk every day in the wholesale department, managing this great enterprise as though it were a machine with his hand on the lever.

The business is dual in its operations—a wholesale house, with its own establishment, management and commercial ramifications, and a retial trade, with its management and special features, each absolutely distinct in every particular.

The managers and superintendents of the various departments in the retail store daily visit the wholesale house and make such purchases as they need in their stock, discounting their bills for the cash down, thus buying their goods precisely as do other customers. The cost for all such purchases are regularly paid over by the retail to the wholesale house each day promptly, before the close of banking hours, and no credit whatever is allowed between the houses.

IN THE RETAIL STORE,

the division is into departments—dress and fancy goods, carpets, upholstery, and two manufacturing departments. The dress and fancy goods department occupying the first floor, is subdivided into thirty-nine divisions, each under the supervision of a competent man who looks after his stock as though he had a store entirely distinct from all the rest.

The whole retail store is under the management of J. M. Flemming, the carpet department is managed by Albert H. Dainty, and the upholstery department by Charles H. Ward. Each of these gentlemen effect their own purchases from all parts of the world.

There are over 1,500 men, women, boys, and girls in this store to look after the welfare of the customers who often number 5,000 at once.

J. V. FARWELL & CO.

THE LARGEST BUILDING IN THE COUNTRY.

Perhaps no firm in the United States is better and more favorably known in this country than J. V. Farwell & Co., importers and jobbers of foreign and domestic dry goods. Within the past year they have moved into their new building, the largest, most extensive, and best arranged for their business in the East or West. It is the general verdict of merchants who have been in every similar institution in the land that this is the case, and the extent and completeness of this house has become so universally known that thousands of people consider their visit to Chicago only half made without going through the Farwell Building.

Regarding the architectural beauty of this building, it can be truthfully said to rival any building in Chicago. It is constructed of Philadelphia pressed brick, with stone trimmings, and the architects and contractors were evidently given all the latitude they desired in planning and construction. Its massiveness makes it, in fact, the most attractive building on Market street, and other buildings that were once considered to be giants of stone and brick now sink into insignificance

FARWELL'S BUILDING.

when compared with the great Farwell Block, that looms above everything, and can be seen at a great distance from almost every direction.

DIMENSIONS OF THE BUILDING.

The dimensions of this building are 280x 400 feet, it is six floors above ground and two below, i. e., a basement and sub-basement, besides immense storage-rooms under Market street. The building itself cost $1,-000,000 and stands on ground worth $500,-000 more. The boiler and engine-rooms front on Adams street and extend across the entire building from east to west. The boiler-room is 70x90 feet, 20 feet high, and is said to be the best boiler-room in Chicago. The engine is an improved Corliss, 250-horse power, with a 20-foot fly wheel; there are eight boilers 84 inches and 16 feet in length; 12 elevators are used in the building; two large-sized Worthington pumps for feeding boilers; one 8-nose pump for fire purposes; one 5-nose pump for pumping water to a tank of 40,-000 tons capacity, located on the roof; 250,-000 feet of steam pipe is employed to heat the building. Electricity is used in lighting the building. The Schroll smokeless furnace has recently been attached to the boilers, and gives perfect satisfaction.

WHAT CLASS OF GOODS ARE CARRIED.

The first floor contains the offices, salesmen's desks, and a general line of prints and other domestic goods. On the second floor is found an immense stock of imported and domestic dress goods, velvets, silks, shawls, etc., and in this specialty Farwell & Co. are second to no firm in the United States. The third floor is devoted to upholstery, woolens, and flannels; the fourth to white and knit goods, hosiery, yarns, gloves, etc. The fifth floor is filled entirely with as complete a line of notions, ribbons, threads, jewelry, clocks, watches, etc., as can be found in this or any other country. Reaching the sixth floor, the largest stock of carpets and oil cloths in the West is displayed. The light throughout the entire building, one of the essentials to the proper display of goods, is so distributed as to be perfect in every respect.

TERRITORY REACHED AND ANNUAL SALES.

In response to the question as to the territory reached by Farwell & Co., they replied that they went east as far as Detroit, south and southeast to Cincinnati, and beyond St. Louis, west to the Pacific coast, and north to the British possessions—embracing a scope of country the extent of which will hardly be recognized by the casual reader at first glance. Within this radius are included seventeen States and every Territory in the Union.

The sales of this house reached the enormous figures of $20,000,000 the past year, an increase of 20 per cent over those for 1882, and 50 per cent over those of a few years ago, a fact that will astonish the commercial world, and cause competitors to be surprised at the marvelous growth of J. V. Farwell & Co.'s business. It is questionable if there is another institution of the kind in this country that can make as good an exhibit or show a healthier growth, and is only one more illustration of the grand possibilities of Chicago's future. The fact that this is an exclusively wholesale establishment must not be excluded from the mind of the reader, the proprietors resisting the temptation of reaping the profits of an extensive retail store in this city, and giving thereby their customers the opportunities that rightfully belong to them, and at the same time being enabled to throw their entire energy and time into the wholesale business.

THE STOCK OF GOODS CARRIED

by this house, amounting to $5,000,-000, is, of course, in accord with its other immense proportions, and the force required to move and control this enormous business is 500 employes. Twice each year a large corps of general salesmen are sent throughout the entire territory controlled by this house to visit the trade and introduce the many novelties they are constantly securing for their customers.

For the past thirty years J. V. Farwell has been actively engaged in mercantile life in Chicago, and otherwise identified with its interest, and the house of which these lines have spoken may very properly be classed as the pioneer. A remarkable fact which, by the way, speaks well for employer and employe, in this connection, is that some of them have been together for the space of a quarter of a century—having grown gray in the service, with the bonds of good fellowship still, doubtless, as lasting as life.

C. M. HENDERSON.

BOOTS AND SHOES.

The annual sales in this line of goods at Chicago have reached such dimensions that this city now ranks first in importance as a producing and distributing point. Everything from the finest ladies' shoe to the stoga of the cattle ranch is manufactured here, and the brands of the Chicago manufacturers have become more widely known and familiar to the country than any other make.

The goods bear a high reputation for style and finish, and the shoe buyer finds that no other market offers such inducements for purchase as this city, not only as regards prices but in the variety of selection and unequalled facilities for shipment. Among the men who have by their persevering efforts given to Chicago this proud position

C. M. HENDERSON & CO. ARE ALWAYS NAMED AS THE LEADERS.

They are the largest and among the oldest boot and shoe manufacturers in the West. Beginning years ago (1851) in a small way, they have reached in 1884 the pinnacle in the boot and shoe trade. This position has been secured in the face of many difficulties. The great boot and shoe manufacturers of the East were a few years ago firmly seated on the throne of trade, but this firm has overcome the competition and the influence of the plutocracy of the seaboard, by persisting in manufacturing superior goods and selling them at small profits.

The manufacture and sale of boots and shoes requires perhaps a greater variety of talents and versatility to win popularity than any other line, and these qualities are evidently possessed by this firm to an unusual degree. They have two immense factories, and their facilities for producing goods cheaply are unsurpassed.

The most popular and durable children's shoe ever made was created not long since by this firm, to meet a special and long-felt want. A stylish, tough, and everlasting piece of pedal architecture, just the thing for boisterous school children. Our readers will recognize the brand under the name of the Henderson "Red School House" shoe, a name-which is becoming a household word throughout the land, and a synonym for durability and strength.

WILLIAM BLAIR & CO.

OVER FORTY YEARS OLD.

This extensive hardware house, established in 1842 under the above name, is located at 172, 174, and 176 Lake street. Mr. Blair, its present senior member, was its senior member then, and very properly Mr. Blair may be designated as the father of the hardware trade of Chicago, if not indeed as a business man of almost any other line of business in this progressive city. The firm has thus been in continuous existence, without change in name or in government, for a period of over forty years. It is also a noteworthy fact that this firm commands a larger amount of actual capital than any other house in this line in the West. The main secret of the great success of Messrs. William Blair & Co.'s house is due to their honorable dealing with their customers, and with the careful study of the demands of the trade and the wants of the community. The firm deals largely in shelf-hardware of all varieties, tin plate, tinners' tools and machines, stamped and japanned tinware, tinners' stock, metals, sheet iron, agricultural implements, plain and barbed wire fence, etc. Their trade now is unlimited, and covers every State and Territory in the West and Northwest, and as it is constantly increasing and assuming proportions second to none in this line, they naturally wield a wide influence and enjoy the rich harvest that is now meted out to them. We can join with their many friends in best wishes for a continuance of their merited success.

MORRISON, PLUMMER & CO.,

WHOLESALE DRUGGISTS,

have steadily increased the range and volume of their wholesale drug trade since the organization of the firm in 1876, until they have become one of the leading houses in this line.

Robert Morrison, Jonathan W. Plummer, and Leonard A. Lange constitute the firm which, in addition to its business as importers and wholesalers of drugs and druggists' stock, does a large and growing trade in manufacturing a general line of pharmaceutical preparations, which, owing to quality and price, are rapidly finding favor with their customers. This firm, like many other of our leading houses in the different trades, have built themselves up on their own merits, integrity, and enterprise being the fundamental principles, and coupled with the most assiduous study of the trade and the wants of the people, have made their goods almost a necessity and very popular. Retail druggists are invited to send for their new pharmaceutical list.

HENRY W. KING & CO.

OLDEST JOBBING CLOTHING HOUSE.

The clothing business has become so important in this day and generation that it must demand particular and careful attention. Years of labor and great capital are invested, and extensive stocks of goods must be carried that the wide field and diversity of tastes, which characterize all communities, may be satisfied. The large capital invested in this commodity, and the great number of men, women and children to whom it furnishes employment would be surprising, if figures were taken into consideration.

The house of Henry W. King & Co. is the oldest jobbing clothing house in our city, Mr. King having began business in January, 1854, and continuing ever since with but two changes in style of firm. Within the past few years this house has established, in addition to its wholesale business, retail stores in several cities outside of Chicago. Among them may be mentioned Milwaukee, Cincinnati and St. Louis, all of which are conducting business under the name of the Golden Eagle Clothing Store, each having an experienced manager in charge. In the different cities where these branch houses are located they are without a single exception, doing the leading business in their line of trade. Therefore, when we state that the house of Henry W. King &Co. is doing a large and prosperous business, and stands high in the commercial world, we simply state facts.

JONES & LAUGHLINS, LIMITED.

IRON MERCHANTS.

Among the changes of the year, we notice that the business so long conducted by the firm of Jones & Laughlins has been incorporated with the above style. There is no change in the interests or management, either at the mills in Pittsburg or at the warehouse and office in Chicago.

They report the business of the year greater in volume than previous years, but prices have been low, and for some articles not remunerative. The quality of the goods manufactured by them, and their reputation for excellence, have given them their full share of trade. In cold rolled shafting and fittings, the sales have been much larger than former years.

Their warehouse in this city contains a complete assortment of American refined, Clair, Norway, and Low Moor bar iron, American, Russia, and planished sheet iron, steel, nails, spikes and chains. Their stock is the most extensive of its kind in the United States, and embracing as it does all the sizes of iron used in the construction of cars and locomotives, is a valuable source of supply for railways.

Their friends will be welcomed on all occasions.

CLAPP & DAVIES.

WHOLESALE JEWELRY.

At Nos. 63 and 65 Washington street is eminently a Chicago firm of old established reputation, well and favorably known throughout the country. The individual members of the firm are Mr. Caleb Clapp and Mr. Thomas Davies. They conduct the wholesale jewelry business in all its branches, at Nos. 63 and 65 Washington street, carrying at all times a large and excellently assorted stock of fine, medium, and fair quality goods, and also affording ample opportunity for the selection of high-priced goods. They also carry a full line of Waltham, Elgin, and other watches. During the last year the firm have enjoyed an excellent trade, and have sold goods in territory which they have not covered heretofore. They attend promptly to all mail orders, and customers have sufficient confidence in the personal ability and judgment of Messrs. Clapp & Davies to entrust them with the selection of goods. Their prices are as low as consistent, when the quality is considered, and they buy for cash, thus giving their customers the benefits that they are often able to obtain by having ample cash assets at their command.

CARSON, PIRIE, SCOTT & CO.

We present our readers on this page with a cut of the large wholesale dry goods house of Carson, Pirie, Scott & Co., Madison and Franklin streets. This firm is well and favorably known throughout the entire West as honorable, reliable, enterprising, and energetic merchants. There are few if any houses in this country or Europe who carry so large and well assorted stocks in every department as they do. In looking through their numerous departments this week we found them quite busy opening new importations in laces, embroideries, hosiery, linens, white goods, etc. As they purchase these goods in large quantities for cash from manufacturers, buyers can rely on getting the best values from them to be had anywhere in this country.

SENECA D. KIMBARK.

IRON, STEEL, AND HARDWARE.

Prominent among the dealers of the hardware trade and in iron and steel supplies in Chicago is the above-named firm, now located corner of Michigan avenue and Lake street, with 132 feet frontage. This house, established in 1853, has built up an immense trade in the specialties of iron, steel, nails, heavy hardware, carriage hardware, trimmings, and wood material. This house also supplies extensively blacksmiths' machines of every description and of the latest improvement in make, and all materials required in the blacksmith trade.

The house employs 100 men in its sales and manufacturing departments, doing considerable manufacturing in Michigan at a factory of its own. Great credit is due Mr. Kimbark for the energy and superior management that has placed his business on the present substantial basis and commanding position in the trade. This characteristic was taxed, and proved its eminent efficiency in the rapid recovery and replacement of the damaged parts of this great establishment by their recent disastrous fire. The wheels were kept in motion and the business carried on with scarcely an hour of detention, and they now announce their full capacity of attending to all orders in their usual prompt manner. Mr. K. reports a satisfactory increase of sales over former years.

THE RETAIL TRADE.

AN HISTORICAL CHAPTER.

THE FIRST MERCHANT IN CHICAGO.

The first half century of Chicago's existence as a place draws to a close with the year 1883. The miraculous growth of the city is hardly apparent to those who have made their home here only since the rebuilding of the city after the great fire of 1871. The contrast of the business to-day and the business of even twenty years ago is remarkable. But as this is a semi-centennial of the city a short retrospect of its early commerce is appropriate.

In 1833 Chicago was nothing but a military

trading post with a block-house located at the point where River street and Michigan avenue unite. There were no streets, just simply two roads; one ran south along the lake shore, which is now Michigan avenue; the other ran southwest a short way and then west, conforming to the stream. This was called Water street later, and it proved the main road upon which all the great trade of this metropolis was built.

THE FIRST STORE.

Philo Carpenter had the first store outside the post in 1833, and later P. F. W. Peck built a store. Both these stores were on Water street. Carpenter's was near Franklin street, or rather where the road turned to go over the river at the point where Lake street bridge is now located.

Peck's store was on the corner of a cross-road known now as LaSalle street. These two were the original retail stores, and wholesale, too, for that matter, upon which the commerce of Chicago was founded. They both handled general goods, and obtained their supplies from Detroit mostly by water, but sometimes by wagons across the country.

They did not find it hard to dispose of their goods since they made large profits, and as this became known new stores were built by traders from the East. In 1834 there were no less than eight stores in Chicago, and the village kept growing. A. G. Burley opened the first crockery store, and he even went so far as to build his store on the new street or road just opened, and called Lake street. Burley's store was up near the point where LaSalle street is now located.

In 1836 the village had grown to the proportions of a town, and there were about fifty stores in the place. There were streets as far south as Madison street, and as far north as Indiana street, with an extension on the West Side of Lake street and Randolph street; and Canal and Clinton streets were blocked out also.

JOHN AND JAMES CARNEY

were the large retail grocers, and were located at No. 133 Lake street. This street had arrived at the dignity of numbers in 1837, and about all the stores were located thereon. In 1839 Chicago was a city of considerable importance, having more than a hundred stores of all sorts on its few streets, Lake street being the main artery of trade. Burley's crockery store was located at 161 Lake street. South Water street was the original street, and the largest houses were located there. B. A. Berry & Co. had the largest dry goods store on that street.

Philo Carpenter kept his drug and stationery store at the old stand on South Water street. Dodge & Tucker had a large ship chandlery on this street. George Chacksfield had a pretentious grocery store on the same thoroughfare. John Fenherty had the first fancy dry goods store on this street, near Clark street ferry. Isaac D. Harmon had a dry goods store on the same street, just opposite Fenherty's. H. O. Stone had a grocery and provision store in this street.

On Lake street, however, the more pretentious stores were to be found. Here were located J. H. Wicker, grocer, No. 87 Lake street; B. W. Raymond, general store, No. 122 Lake street—Mr. Raymond was the Mayor; Hobbie & Clark, dry goods, No. 142 Lake street; J. W. Hooker, grocer, No. 152 Lake street; A. Goodenow, dry goods, No. 184 Lake street; N. Goold, grocery and provisions, No. 155 Lake street; John Wentworth, editor and proprietor of the Chicago *Democrat*, over W. F. Wheeler's dry goods store, No. 107 Lake street; Ira B. Eddy and John Calhoun, ironmongers and stove dealers, No. 105 Lake street; S. W. Goss & Co., dry goods, No. 105 Lake street; S. F. Gale, book store, No. 159 Lake street; S. B. Collins, boot and shoe store, No. 140 Lake street; Thomas Church, grocery, No. 111 Lake street; S. B. Cobb, saddlery and harness-maker, No. 171 Lake street; Ira Couch kept the Tremont Tavern at the corner of Lake and Dearborn streets; T. B. Carter & Co., fancy dry goods, No. 118 Lake street.

ON DEARBORN STREET

were several stores, noticeably A. Follansbee, grocery and provisions; George F. Foster and George A. Robb, grocers and ship chandlers; Charles Follansbee, grocery; Goodsell & Campbell, dry goods and grocery.

These are but a few of the retail stores then located here, and they were supplying not only the 20,000 population of Chicago, but numerous villages and farmers for a circuit of thirty miles around. They each did a business of from $10,000 to $200,000 a year; of course the line of goods handled had much to do with the amount of business. Their goods were still coming across the country by wagon, though not so far as before since the railway extended as far as Niles, Mich. The favorite means of transportation was by water from Detroit and Buffalo. But when navigation closed the wagon train was resorted to.

Ten years later, in 1850, Chicago had reached a position of importance, and the railways opened up a field of commerce for her that afforded an ample opportunity for the establishment of large retail concerns. About this time will be noticed the name of Potter Palmer, dry goods, No. 137 Lake street; Ross & Foster, No. 169 Lake street; J. B. Shay, No. 102 Lake street; Fitch & Hewes, No. 82 Lake street; all of these were

LARGE RETAIL DRY GOODS HOUSES,

each doing more than a million dollars worth of business. The drug trade too had some well-known names in the retail list. O. F. Fuller, No. 195 Lake street; Honore & Co., No. 200 Lake street; F. A. Bryan, No. 2 Tremont House; M. Jerome, corner of Clark and Adams streets, where the Custom House now stands; J. H. Reed & Co., No. 144 Lake street. Among the retail grocers of that time were: Henry Sayrs, Nos. 54 and 56 State street; W. F. McLaughlin, corner of State and Madison streets; Henry Schoelkopf, corner Washington and Wells streets.

The commerce of Chicago gradually increased with each new railroad that connected her with the Northwest. The civil war had much to do with the prosperity of trade in Chicago. Fortunes were made in a short time, and the commerce of the city was something wonderful to the merchants of the East who came here.

In 1865 Chicago's marts of commerce presented as busy an appearance as they do to-day. The war was over, and the city was filled with soldiers who were mustered out and paid off. The retail stores reaped a golden harvest. Lake street, from end to end, was like the State street of to-day. The retail dry goods houses were Putney, Knight & Hamlin, No. 105 Lake street; Ross & Gossage, No. 167 Lake street; J. B. Shay & Co.

No. 163 Lake street; Simpson & Hughes, No. 181 Lake street; A. G. Downs & Co., No. 150 Lake street. There were some large retail grocers, such as Stanton & Co., No. 135 Lake street; H. C. Champlon & Co., No. 9 Clark street; L. D. Boone & Co., No. 164 State street; Taylor, Watson & Co., No. 10 LaSalle street. The leading retail druggists of that date were George Buck, No. 93 Clark street; Bliss & Sharp, No. 144 Lake street; Gale & Blocki, No. 202 Randolph street.

From the localities above named the course of the retail trade of this city may be readily traced. The names of most of the firms are no longer familiar to the public, but from most of these firms do many of the present magnificent establishments date their existence.

THE HOUSE OF A MERCHANT PRINCE

A SKETCH OF S. GUY SEA.

The youngest and in many respects the most remarkable of Chicago's merchant princes is Mr. S. Guy Sea, whose name has not been before the public for many years, but is already a familiar household word, and is known to every lady shopper in the Northwest. To strangers who visit the city Sea's store is as much an object of interest as the waterworks or the parks, and they go there to look and listen if not to buy. During fair times, and when excursions are daily coming into the city from all parts of the Northwest, one can see a constant procession of lion-hunters passing in and out of the wide doors that open into the store from State street. As the poet said of the waves of another sea—

They come and go incessant.

During holiday times, and in the days of heavy fall and spring trading, when Sea gets in new stocks of goods, or when he is offering some famous specialty from his counters, the throng is so great that policemen have to be stationed at the entrance to turn the ebbing and the flowing tide of humanity into the proper channels, or there would be a blockade and a crush of people packed as closely as sardines. But Sea looks out for all this, and the stentorian voice of his usher is heard above the confusion, shouting:

"Keep to the right, ladies, keep to the right."

This is good advice in any place, under all circumstances, and if Mr. Sea would have it painted on a large placard, and placed in a conspicuous position, it might be the means of diverting some poor creature from the wrong way in the outer world as well as in his mammoth store.

But this article did not start out to be a song or a sermon, but was intended to present a few facts relating to the remarkable life and astonishing success of Chicago's youngest merchant. He is the typical Chicago man; very young and very energetic, and the story of his success is simply a parallel to the growth and development of Chicago. No man among the entire 600,000 people who go to make up this city could be selected to better represent the go-ahead-and-get-the-business style of Chicago than S. Guy Sea.

Mr. Sea commenced his business life thirteen years ago, and, though then but 14 years of age, had been well grounded in not only the rudimentary branches, but in the higher mathematics and the languages. At 18 we find him in New York as buyer for Carson, Pirie, Scott & Co., of this city, and was known as the "boy buyer, whom no quantity staggers if the price suits him." Leaving business against the wish and advice of his employers, he spent his 20th year at Racine College, but his was too nervous and active a temperament for a scholastic life, and at the close of that year, original and peculiar advertisements attracted much attention and comment. They were signed "Sea, State Street," and Mr. Sea may be said to have inaugurated that lavish display advertising that has since become a necessity of mercantile success. Meanwhile Sea has become a merchant prince. Like the beanstalk of Jack the Giant Killer, Sea's business grew almost in a single night, and became greater and greater so rapidly that he was an active even competitor with the other merchandising firms before they knew he was in the race. It has required but seven years to build up the great trade he now commands, and to acquire the enormous capital that stands behind his two concerns in this city and the one in Minneapolis. His sales in a single day often reach $30,000, and his business of 1883 was a third greater than that of 1882. His annual holiday bazar is an established feature, and at Fourth of July time the demand for his goods compels him to open branches in all parts of the city.

Sea's Minneapolis store, which he purchased last October, is his latest enterprise, and it occupies an entire block, with a frontage of 272 feet. The moment his name was announced as proprietor, the store at once took the leading position in Minneapolis, its sales being more than double those of any retail house there, and three times greater than Sea himself had expected.

There is a moral to all stories, and there is a very striking and emphatic one to the story of Sea's success. People will ask,

"Upon what meat hath this our Cæsar fed,
That he hath grown so great,"

and the answer is truthful—advertising. Sea knows what the people want, he gets it, tells them that he has it, and sells it to them cheaper than they can get it any where else. The public look for Sea's advertisements in the newspapers each day as they look for the telegraph dispatches, and they find a list of articles for sale with the prices attached. They make a list of such articles as they desire to buy and go to Sea's counter and get the goods, saving time, money, and the wear and tear of mind that they have to endure in other stores. It is this system of advertising that has made Sea successful. He believes in selling a large quantity of goods with small profits, rather than a small quantity at large profits, and using printers' ink to tell people so.

"THE FAIR."

LEHMANN'S IMMENSE "STORE" THE LARGEST IN THIS CITY.

There is but one place of the kind in the world and that is "The Fair," owned, controlled, and managed by Mr. E. J. Lehmann. There is probably not an intelligent man or woman in this city, and but very few who read the papers outside of Chicago, but who know where Mr. Lehmann's immense store is, located—State, Adams, and Dearborn streets. Although covering more ground than any other "store" in this city his quarters are entirely too small for his great business, and Chicago may awaken any morning to learn that Lehmann has let contracts for the construction of the largest business building in the city.

"The Fair" is all that the name implies, for everything from a cambric needle to the largest article of a portable character can be obtained there. In fact, "The Fair" has grown to be the most wonderful enterprise in the Northwest, and no visitor has "gone the rounds" or "done the town" unless having paid his or her respects to Mr. Lehmann. The success of this institution, for it is nothing more nor less, is due to several causes, principally owing to the proprietor's knowledge of the business, his push, and his manner of advertising. With one or two possible exceptions he is said to have the faculty of putting his advertisements in such a shape as to compel even his competitors to read them, and to an extent of forcing them to copy after him. Having secured the crowds by legitimate methods,

HE CARRIES OUT HIS PROMISES

by selling them goods at prices which seem ruinous. He is enabled to do this by purchasing in enormous quantities and turning his money at a rapid rate. Goods that would lie for months in some houses are taken in the back door at "The Fair" in bulk, distributed to their respective departments, and carried out of the front entrances in the arms of customers in the space of a few hours. The system established for the convenience of supplying immense crowds of people is something marvelous. His diminutive city of merchandise is divided into about forty departments, and he employs at least 500 people.

It has only been a few years since Mr. Lehmann launched out so extensively, and yet his success is the most striking that was ever known in this country. To-day he is climbing rapidly to great wealth, and being a young man by a large majority, it would seem that before his hair is strewn with the inevitable silvery threads he will be one of Chicago's wealthiest and most influential citizens.

THE BEE-HIVE.

A PHENOMENAL SUCCESS FROM THE START.

The Bee Hive was started at Nos. 174 and 176 State street last April, and has met with phenomenal success. The firm enlisted in this enterprise includes Maximilian Morgenthau, Gustav Morgenthau, Jacob H Bauland, and Joseph H. Bauland. The store front displays a titanic show of windows, the furnishings of which catch the eye and tickle the fancy, the unique sign surmounting them showing for a center-piece a large golden bee-hive. The interior of the store realizes the claim of the trade-mark, for it is a veritable hive, where the public seek the honey of bargains, and business is brisk from early morning until evening.

This firm believe in quick sales and small profits, and by doing a strictly cash business are enabled to sell goods at bottom prices, in some lines underselling the wholesale trade. Millinery forms a large and lucrative portion of the business, drawing a large out-of-town trade. The firm claim in this stock to compete with wholesale houses.

The basement of the building presents a display of china, glassware, and house-furnishings. The first floor of the store is as well arranged for the comfort of patrons as it is for the display of goods. Its departments comprise dress goods, silks, gloves, hosiery, and fancy goods. By an easy flight of stairs or capacious elevator one may ascend to the second floor, where there is a large display of millinery, cloaks, suits, corsets, and underwear. The third floor is devoted to carpets, upholstery, shoes, and boys' clothing. The upper floor is devoted to the wholesale department and offices.

The store is supplied with a corps of competent and agreeable lady clerks, and the excellent facilities of the establishment please patrons as well as the goods they receive for value received. The Bee Hive promises to be busy both winter and summer, and make progressive growth in accord with its patronage.

F. SIEGEL & BROTHERS.

This well known and enterprising firm are engaged in the manufacture, importation, and sale of cloaks and suits. They are located in the new Robert Law Building, at numbers 126, 128, 130, and 132 Market street. The above cut represents the beautiful building they occupy, the interior of which is finished in light woods, which gives it a fine appearance. In this building are employed by this firm from 400 to 500 hands, whose pay roll amounts to from $150,000 to $200,000 per annum. Over 40,000 square feet of floor room is occupied by this firm. Their machinery is all run by steam, thus relieving their operatives of much fatiguing and hurtful labor. This house manufacture all classes of goods in this line, from the cheapest to the most expensive. They are said to be the heaviest importers of this class of goods in the West. Ten traveling salesmen are employed, who travel from Pennsylvania to California. Large sales are made by them on the Pacific coast. This firm commenced business here eight years ago, and since that time it has been constantly increasing and expanding year by year, until the business of 1883 will not fall far short of $1,000,000. Every article purchased from which their goods are manufactured is bought at the lowest possible price, and their business is managed in a careful and judicious manner, so that the goods when placed upon the market are offered at the lowest possible price, while the class of goods are said to be unexcelled for the price charged for them. During the years they have been engaged in business, they have given their customers splendid satisfaction, and the consequence is they seldom loose a customer when his trade has once been secured. In the commercial fields the firm of F. Siegel & Brothers stand high, and have the confidence of all. The gentlemen comprising this firm are all young men, the oldest member being less than 36 years of age. They have all had a thorough experience in the business, and, therefore, rank among the successful merchants of Chicago.

PARDRIDGE'S EMPORIUM.

THE GREAT CASH RETAIL STORE OF STATE STREET.

When the writer approached Mr. M. J. McClellan, one of the managers for C. W. & E. Pardridge, he found that gentleman full of business, but ready to give THE INTER OCEAN readers some account of the trade for 1883. This house, as is well-known, is among the survivors of the great fire—organizing immediately after that event, and proceeding at once to business. Pardridge Brothers, possessing unlimited financial resources, have adopted, and strictly adhere to, the cash system—both respecting purchases and sales. They own the property, a handsome five-story building, covering the three numbers, 112, 114, and 116 State street—an advantage enjoyed by but few houses in this city. Doing business on a cash basis and having no exorbitant rents to pay, it is plain to be seen that they are in a position, if they so desire, to take advantage of competitors, and put goods upon the market at prices that would be ruinous to some. They are very liberal with their trade, accommodating customers by cheerfully exchanging goods, and are studiously careful that no attache of the place is allowed to make misrepresentations in order to complete a sale.

WHAT LINE OF GOODS THEY HANDLE.

The Pardridges are importers and dealers in dry goods, fancy goods, carpets, millinery, etc., and carry a stock running up into the hundreds of thousands. They make a specialty of promptly executing orders for samples, and people a thousand miles from Chicago can purchase goods to as great an advantage as those who walk in and trade over the counter. Their magnificent display in their front windows, in the minds of the best judges, has been, for the past six months, the finest in the city.

Regarding the sales, considering the various drawbacks in the way of bad weather, etc., they correspond favorably with 1882, while the aggregate profits, under a change of management, are above those of any previous year, which, after all, is the key note to absolute success. Altogether, there is not a house in this city that can show a better record, or one which has brighter prospects for 1884.

GILES BROTHERS & CO.,

the well-known jewelers, are still increasing their business in both the wholesale and retail departments, and supply the jewelry trade from the Alleghanies to the Pacific. The three medals for superiority in watches, awarded by the greatest exposition for railway appliances ever held anywhere, were won by Giles, Bro. & Co., and it is an indisputable fact that no house in the world surpasses theirs in this respect. These three medals are represented here, and they constitute, without a doubt, the highest honors that a watchmaker can obtain. They have added

A NEW INDUSTRY

to the manufacturing interests of Chicago in the shape of a diamond-cutting department.

They certainly deserve great credit for their enterprise. This is the only establishment of

the kind in the West, and has been seldom attempted outside of the old hereditary diamond-cutting establishments of Amsterdam. They import their rough diamonds free of duty, and by using the best labor-saving machinery, are able to offer their patrons the benefit of first cost prices. Giles Brothers & Co. employ over 100 hands, and their stock runs up into the millions.

WM. M. DALE,

THE POPULAR DRUGGIST.

Corner Clark and Madison streets, and 75 State street. This gentleman occupies such a commanding place in the retail drug trade of Chicago as few merchants achieve in a city of such size and so cosmopolitan in character. His motto, "In Medicia Puritas, in Compositione Veritas," a very free translation of which would be, "Pure Drugs Compounded with Fidelity," has been so consistently carried out in his business that when a difficult prescription or rare drug is demanded every one sends to Dale. For something over twenty years Mr. Dale has been engaged in the retail drug business in this city, and the popularity which he enjoys is well and honorably earned. The new store which Mr. D. has recently opened at No. 75 State street is an ornament to that thoroughfare, and will be quite a convenience to his lady patrons, who can thus avoid the crowded corner of Clark and Madison streets.

It is an item of vital importance that too many ignore, in having their prescriptions in thoroughly competent hands, and for the indorsement, of this house in their accuracy and reliance their growing and extensive patronage but bespeaks.

E. BURNHAM,

THE HAIR DEALER.

71 State street. The gentleman whose name appears in the above heading, although young in years, has shown an aptness for business which has placed him in the front in the line of hair goods and all the novelties, tools, etc., which come under the head of this business. He imports all his own goods and does an extensive wholesale business. He established himself in this city in 1871, and by his enterprise has built up a trade of which he can justly feel proud. His customers are from among the best ladies in the city. In addition to his retail business he has a wholesale department and factory at No. 6 East Washington street, occupying two large floors, where he employs about eighty hands.

M. THOME.

Will supply the hair trade at his wholesale Hair Depot at 148 State street. Send for price list.

J. W. GRISWOLD & CO.,

244 AND 246 MONROE STREET.

This firm are manufacturers and importers of cloaks, suits, cloakings and trimmings. They have been engaged in the business for over thirty years, and are therefore one of the oldest houses in the West. During the busy season 600 hands are employed, who prepare for the market a large and varied class of goods in this line which are sold in various parts of the West and Northwest. The firm report this one of the most prosperous years in the history of their business. Nos. 244 and 246 Monroe street is their location.

SAFES AND SCALES.

HALL'S SAFE AND LOCK COMPANY.

PERFECT SECURITY.

The devastation of the elements and the criminal enterprise and ingenuity of the midnight thief constantly jeopardize and menace the security of capital. No desideratum, therefore, is of greater importance to the merchant and banker than knowledge of the fact that their possessions are in absolute safety. This certain assurance can be met with in the thoroughly reliable fire and burglar proof safes manufactured by the Hall Safe and Lock Company.

For thirty-six years Mr. Joseph L. Hall, the President of the company, has been earnestly engaged in studying and perfecting their safes and locks, over 300 patents having been granted to him by the United States Government. His efforts have been crowned with marked and triumphant success, and the reward of superiority has long been unanimously awarded to their products.

Among the leading and vital features of merit which place their safes so pre-eminently above those of all competitors may be mentioned their system of *dove-tailing* the *plates* around the edges of the door, superior *bolt work*, the patent *traverse* and *cam hinge*, solid steel *bent* or *angle corners*, *tight* and compact *joints*, constructing the walls of alternate plates of iron and carbonized steel, detached eccentric arbor, patent concrete filling, and many other important points of great value.

All their safes and locks are simple in construction, elegant in finish, easily operated, and combine in the highest degree beauty, utility, and strength (the hand of iron under the glove of silk).

Mr. Joseph L. Hall established the business

at Cincinnati in 1845 originally upon a capital of $50,000. The company now have $800,000 invested, and their works are the largest of their kind in the world. The vast buildings, which are built in a substantial manner of stone and brick, cover eight acres of ground, in which 1,365 skilled workmen are employed, who build sixty-five complete safes every day; 800,000 pounds of iron and 450,000 pounds of steel enter into the manufacture and are consumed each month. Their business is colossal, branch houses, each with a large stock, being located at New York, Chicago, Boston, Philadelphia, Pittsburg, Cleveland, Louisville, St. Louis, St. Paul, Kansas City, Omaha, Denver, San Francisco, and New Orleans.

The Chicago branch, at No. 67 Washington street, was established in 1867, and under the capable and energetic management of C. O. Hall and J. W. Donnell is second only to the parent house in the extent and importance of its trade. Any information desired by bankers, jewelers, merchants, and others in regard to their goods will meet with immediate and courteous attention by addressing the Chicago house.

B. F. SMITH.

BURGLAR AND FIRE-PROOF SAFES.

Mr. B. F. Smith, general agent for Mosler, Bahmann & Co.'s Fire and Burglar Proof Safes, at No. 58 Dearborn street, Chicago, Ill., represents one of the oldest and best known safe manufacturers in this country, with a reputation that has become world-wide.

Mosler, Bahmann & Co.'s goods are distributed in almost every city, town, village and hamlet from Maine to California, Manitoba to Mexico. Their product for the past ten years, placed in a continuous line, would reach from Chicago to Milwaukee, a distance of ninety miles. They have made and sold more safes than any other house in America.

Their burglar work has long borne a high reputation and has been the trusty custodian of untold wealth. Their fire and burglar proof lined safes, a new departure, made for storing bulky articles, such as jewelry, etc., are being almost universally adopted.

Important improvements, covered by valuable patents, have lately been made in their fire-proof safes, which places them many steps in advance of all others. Instead of separate pieces rivited together, forming square corners and panels, as safes have hitherto been constructed, in this the angle bars and plates are each a separate piece, cut at first to the required length, then bent to the proper shape with round corners and finished without a joint. The round corners, having the principle of the arch and being formed solid, give the utmost possible strength to the design. The smooth, unbroken surface on the top and sides allows more scope for handsome decorations, and affords no opportunity for dust to collect and lodge, as in case of panels.

The most novel feature, however, is the lock, susceptible to 100,000,000 changes, and so arranged that when locked it becomes detached from the bolts and cannot be connected without a knowledge of the combination. Should the handle be broken off and the spindle driven in, it would carry nothing with it, and its destruction would not render the lock any the less secure, thus making the the fire-proof safe substantially proof against the ordinary thief.

Their public offer to donate ten safes to any person proving a single instance where these safes had failed to preserve their contents remains unchallenged.

THE CHICAGO SCALE COMPANY.

RELIABLE AND ACCURATE.

Probably the name of no manufacturing company is more familiar to a greater number of people in all parts of the country than that of the Chicago Scale Company. Being among the pioneer manufacturers of the West, they have kept up with the demands of this rapidly growing country, and are always prepared to furnish scales upon which to weigh the immense crops of grain, the heads of cattle and hogs, and commodities of all kinds that must be weighed to carry on the operations of trade and exchange. Men in offices, women and children, by weighing packages for the mail, ingredients for cooking, or taking their first lessons in pounds and ounces, have learned to associate the name of the manufacturers with the "Little Detective." The universal popularity of these scales is not alone due to the fact that hundreds of varieties are manufactured from the very best material, but that their system of doing business enables them to supply their customers at one-half the price any other concern can who furnish articles of equal value, and, while they would in no way detract from the laurels of others, the numerous expressions of satisfaction at receiving articles so good and so cheap, from men and women in all parts of the country, might be envied by more pretentious manufacturers. Within the last four months hundreds of articles have been added to their catalogues which they either manufacture or have manufactured in large quantities for them, all of which are sold at correspondingly low prices. If a portable forge is wante,d or blacksmith's tools of any kind, a foot-power athe, a corn-sheller, a fanning-mill or a feed-cooker, the Chicago Scale Company can supply them, as well as one of the best sewing machines made, which they are now sending out by hundreds to all parts of the country. Buying material of all kinds in large quantities and selling for cash, enables them to give the lowest possible prices, and by giving customers the privilege of returning anything not perfectly satisfactory, no better warrantee could be asked from a company which is perfectly responsible.

JOHN W. NORRIS.

BURGLAR-PROOF AND FIRE-PROOF SAFES.

While as a rule all manufacturers are complaining of lack of customers and overproduction the Western manager of the Diebold Safe and Lock Company, Mr. John W. Norris, says the sales of this concern for the past year reach fully $2,000,000 or, in other words, 33 1-3 per cent more than the previous year's business, which was by far the largest ever done in the West, if not in the United States.

CHAPTER X

CHICAGO'S INDUSTRIES.

HISTORY OF HER MANUFACTURES.

AN ENORMOUS PRODUCT.

Chicago has been a continual surprise to the world, and no part of her growth is more responsible for this than that in manufacturing. This has in less than fifty years changed Chicago from a quiet village to a great roaring metropolis, where the wheels never cease to whirl and hum, and the streets are never quiet.

It has changed Chicago from a place dependent on the East for all its manufactured articles to a great workshop, sending its products to every land under the sun, and whose trademarks are known and recognized in every city and town in the world. And all this has been as easy and natural (though rapid) growth as is that of the plant when once the seed is sown in good soil.

There has been no noise or confusion about it, and never has Chicago made appeals to the outside world for help in her manufacturing enterprises, nor even to the

PUBLIC SPIRIT OF HER OWN CITIZENS.

It has gone steadily along as the march of destiny, and no financial crisis nor labor upheaval has disturbed it, although the most world-renowned of these have had their origin and extinction here in our midst. The men who engaged in manufacturing in Chicago went about it as they would to build themselves a little home, with no other appeal to the public nor the corporation than the permission to spend their money and develop the resources of the city and its surrounding country.

Millions of money have been spent here in building huge workshops and filling them with costly machinery, and comparatively few of even our own citizens were aware of the fact until all was complete and their products began to create a commotion in the business world.

The unrivaled resources of the country immediately tributary to Chicago have in a large measure been the cause of this marvelous growth, but Chicago has advanced beyond these and passed beyond their confines and almost beyond their influence. Now the raw material is brought from all over the world to here find the skill and machinery to convert it into marketable goods.

THE POINTS OF MANUFACTURE,

Professor Newberry says, will be determined mainly by economy of fuel. Chicago then stands without a rival. The broad prairies of Illinois and adjoining States not only yield rich harvests for our granaries and produce markets, but down below the soil there is a harvest of coal extending for miles and miles, stored away long ages ago, and this is inexhaustible.

In the manufacture of Bessemer steel rails, Cook County has already distanced Alleghany County, Pa. In 1878 that great center of the iron trade manufactured 72,286 tons of Bessemer steel rails. Chicago during the same time turned out 123,000 tons, and if the neighboring county of Will be counted in, the amount would be increased to 178,000 tons, or 33,608 tons more than twice the entire production of Alleghany County. In that same year the State of Illinois produced nearly one-third of all the Bessemer steel rails produced in the United States.

One of the largest "Steel Plants" in the Union, comprising seven departments, covers an area of twenty-nine acres on the south branch of the Chicago River, with blast furnaces having a daily capacity of 330 tons, or an out-put of nearly 125,000 tons of pig iron annually.

ACCORDING TO CENSUS RETURNS

made by the Census Bureau for 1880, the greatest number of hands employed in manufacturing in Chicago was 110,819. Now there are, according to statistics from the inspectors of manufactories, 132,893 people employed.

AGRICULTURAL IMPLEMENTS.

The manufacture of agricultural implements in Chicago has grown to enormous proportions.

Malt and malt liquors have advanced to an important place in the industrial field here, and new inventions and new methods have almost revolutionized the business

The manufacture of men's and boys' ready-made clothing and furnishing goods have expanded until it is represented by millions of capital.

Chicago leather is known in all markets, and ranks among the best. The product for 1880 was estimated at 5,073,000 pounds, of which a large portion was used in the make-up of boots and shoes.

The carriage and wagon making, the sash and door manufacturing, the box factories, the linseed oil, white lead, paints, lead pipes, and shot products are immense.

The box factories use up 100,000,000 feet of lumber, worth $2,000,000, annually in making boxes to ship the products of our other manufactories, and those that require such packing are only the smaller products of this great workshop.

AN IDEA OF GROWTH.

In 1860, when Chicago began to attract attention as a manufacturing center, there were 469 establishments, employing 5,593 hands, paying $1,992,257 for wages and sending out $13,555,671 worth of products. In ten years the number of establisuments had been multiplied by three.

In 1870 the census returns show there were 1,440 establishments, employing 31,105 hands, paying $13,045,286 for wages, and producing goods valued at $92,518,742. In 1880 the returns show there were 3,752 manufacturing establishments, employing 113,507 hands, paying $37,615,381 in wages and producing $253,405,695 worth of goods. And the compiler of these figures, Robert P. Porter, at the head of the Industrial Bureau of the Census Department, closes his report with the interrogation: "Was ever such a rapid rate of material progress known elsewhere in the history of the world?"

The increase since 1880 has been even more rapid than before, and Chicago now stands without a rival in the iron trade and fifth in magnitude among the manufacturing cities of the world.

THE CHICAGO METAL FELLOE CO.

INDESTRUCTIBLE VEHICLE WHEEL.

This company, at No. 212 Dearborn street, has recently created something of a sensation by introducing to the public what is aptly termed an "indestructible vehicle wheel." It can hardly be described adequately in the space at the disposal of the writer, but it undoubtedly ranks as one of the great practical inventions of the age. The Danford patent metal felloe consists of a wrought iron tube of suitable size and shape and of sufficient length to circumvent the entire wheel. This tube is filled with a continuous piece of the best thoroughly seasoned wagon timber, which is shaped to exactly fit the interior of the tube into which it is forced by powerful machinery after having been saturated with oil. The felloe thus composed is then bent in a circle of the required size, and holes for the spokes are drilled in it. Each spoke hole is counter sunk so as to admit the full size of the spoke to a depth of from three-eighths to five-eighths of an inch, according to the size of the wheel. By this simple, but effective arrangement, it is rendered the next thing to impossible for the spoke tenon to break off, while the wrought-iron casing of the felloe renders it impervious to wear and weather. A set of wheels constructed upon this principle would outlast half a dozen sets built upon the ordinary plan, and can be furnished at but a small additional cost. The company have just completed extensive works on Fifty-third street, Chicago, and are now prep red to fill all orders. Explanatory circulars will be sent upon application.

THE LATEST IMPROVEMENTS.

MILTIMORE ELASTIC STEEL CAR-WHEEL COMPANY.

The accompanying illustrations, showing in sections what is rapidly becoming a popular wheel with railroad people, give a fair idea of the construction of the Miltimore elastic steel car-wheel. The patentee and those interested with him are so well and favorably known that it would be a waste of words to further speak of them. The wheel itself, which has already become a fixed institution, is the subject matter. After many years of experimenting Mr. Miltimore has attained the success so eagerly sought for, and has a substitute for the old cast-iron wheel which must eventually supplant, to a large extent, the latter, and insure the safety in transportation by rail that will sometime in the future make accidents absolutely impossible.

Complete wheel.

THE MILTIMORE WHEEL

is the latest improvement in the rolling stock of railroad paraphernalia, and meets all arguments that have been brought to bear against "a new thing." The one item of price alone, advertised at 40 per cent less than any other steel wheel that will give equal mileage after establishing its durability and other features of excellence, is enough to recommend it in the broadest sense. Certainly, the one difficulty of devising a perfect center removes the great obstacle of expense, and the assertion that this wheel has a center that will wear out an indefinite number of tires is by no means unreasonable. The center of this wheel, possessing all the requisite strength, durability, and strength, is also recognized for its comparative l ghtness, and as above intimated, its cost is lessened by the minimum amount of labor required for its construction.

CONSTRUCTION OF THE WHEEL.

The centrifugal pressure from the axle to the rim, which gives solidity, strength, elasticity, and stability of parts, is maximum; the centripetal force of concussion from the rim to the axle, which tends to disrupt and destroy, is minimum. To illustrate by another figure of speech, the wheel is a construction in which the tire is held to its work by sufficient pressure from the axle outwardly, a large portion of this pressure being retained as reserve strength beyond immediate needs, while the spokes are so ingeniously fitted for their double work of holding the tire and distributing the ordinary

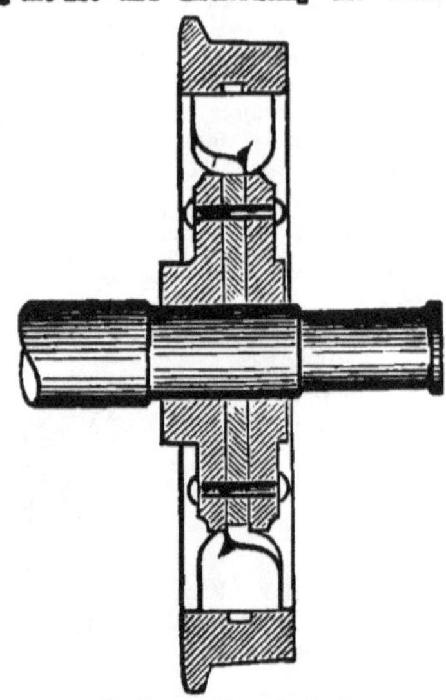

Vertical section of wheel.

destructive forces resulting from concussion that the deterioration of the strength of metal is very slight during the longest service. The tire is $2\frac{1}{2}$ inches thick, 4 inches thick on the back, and $5\frac{1}{2}$ inches wide. The spokes are 4 inches wide and 1 inch thick, and the hub plates are 19 inches in diameter. These dimensions of parts are based on the scale of the standard thirty-three-inch wheel, and gives an idea of the strength and massiveness of the construction.

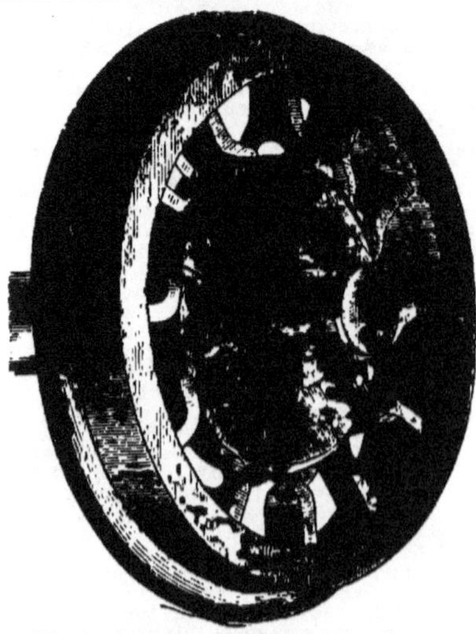

Wheel, with portion of hub-plate removed.

These wheels are in use on a large number of the best railroads in the United States, and orders are coming in too rapidly to be filled. Extensive works are now being erected at Chicago in the suburb of Pennock, and when completed will eclipse anything of the kind in the country. The general offices are at 51 and 53 Dearborn street, Chicago, and the officers are as follows: President, Homer Pennock; Vice President and General Manager, G. W. Miltimore; Secretary and Managing Director, Dwight K. Tripp.

GERTS, LUMBARD & CO.,

BRUSH MANUFACTURERS.

This old and reliable house, established over thirty years ago, have large warerooms at Nos. 204 and 206 Randolph street and their factory at the corner of Hoyne avenue and West Indiana street, where they employ a large force making all kinds of brushes, from the best painters' and varnishers' brushes to the finest solid-back hair brushes, of which they are the only manufacturers in this country.

SMOKE PREVENTION.

A PERFECT DEVICE AT LAST.

A successful smoke-consumer—one that consumed smoke and did not consume profits, directly or indirectly, at the same time—has been a much sought for blessing for many years. Innumerable smoke-consumers have been from time to time invented and patented and then laid aside in the waste heap of the impracticable or the too utterly expensive. The faults of these failures are numerous. Some of them have lacked the first essential of a smoke-consumer—failing to consume all the smoke. A large number of others, accomplishing this first essential with tolerable completeness, have failed in an essential of almost equal importance—operating them has cost too much to the users, or, in other words, has wasted the power of the engines to which they have been attached, or required the expenditure of a large extra amount of coal to counterbalance this waste. This is a defect that touches the pocket, and touches it badly, and it is a defect in every smoke-consumer that has been invented, excepting the one exhibited in the Exposition. Another objection common to all previously invented smoke-consumers is that their use soon results in the destruction or rendering unfit for service the boilers of the machines to which they are attached.

AT THE EXPOSITION.

The recently invented smoke-preventer to which reference has been made, and which has been exhibited by Mr. Charles Smith, its inventor, in the Exposition, where it daily proved its merits by the test of trial, is free from all the above named defects. This preventor, to describe it in a few words, is a furnace without steam. Its use requires the making of no holes in the boiler front, and its consequent impairment. It is, in short, a device for securing the natural combustion of smoke. It operates on the same plan as a kerosene lamp in burning smoke; that is to say, it emits the air from the flue-pipe into the furnace; there being about 800 degrees of heat when it strikes the flue pot. The advantages it possesses over other devices is that it involves the passage of no cold air over the fire, the passage of which, of course, reduces the heating power of the fire. This advantage results in a less quantity of fuel material being required than is required when other consumers are used. Another advantage of the new preventer is that it is perfectly immaterial how hard the firing is done or how the fuel is put in. Still another advantage is that the ash-pit doors being closed it shuts the air off completely from the boiler, and thus saves the boiler from the wearing influence of cold air; for when there is any cold air, even when the doors are open, the result is damage to the boiler. This furnace will last as long

as the boiler itself, for there is nothing to give out about it. Now, one of the principal defects of other consumers is the use of steam jets which injure the boiler. It is desirable, therefore, for the sake of the boiler, to avoid the use of these steam jets. A still more serious defect of these steam-jet smoke-consumers is that they have not only spoiled the boilers, but have failed to consume the smoke to any satisfactory extent. Steam jets are, in fact, impracticable, for the simple reason that steam having to be used, not only consumes the smoke, or condenses it, but consumes the fire, or, in other words, puts it out to a certain extent; while letting in the cold air, and thus lessening the degree of temperature, renders necessary the use of a proportionately extra amount of fuel to counterbalance this loss of heat.

THE USE OF WATER JETS.

Secondly, the use of water jets has resulted, in a short time, in the practical destruction of the boilers. There is another important drawback to them, and that is the noise they make by putting in live steam with cold air. Again, the cold air has a tendency to condense the steam and the fireman has to go to work again to heat up to a proper degree of complete combustion. Then, of course, the steam, if it is condensed and thrown on the boiler plate in the form of spray, will constantly injure the boiler by the successive expansion and contraction consequent upon its being covered with spray. Now, a smoke-burner, to be an advantage and not a disadvantage to the user, should create as uniform a heat as possible, and should not subject the boiler to any greater expansion or contraction than can be helped, as such alternating expansion and contraction are highly detrimental to boiler-plate. This objection is obviated in Mr. Smith's device, as no steam is used at all. Now, with other smoke-burners the fireman has to regulate his firing according to the device he uses, or the device would never work at all, and could never make it succeed when heavy firing is absolutely required. Light firing is necessary—a sine qua non—for the at all successful use of these other devices; and, together with light firing, it is necessary to fire in front. Then the valve must be opened just right, and just so much steam and no more must be let in. If too much is put on, it will blow too hard; if too little, it will do no good at all. In short, their working requires practice. Firemen must be trained for their special convenience. On this account there is great prejudice against these steam jet burners among engineers, as well as on account of the noise they create and the injury to boilers they cause. It has been asserted that the old consumers save fuel, but the assertion has been proven to be false over and over again by actual testing. The new invention makes no claim in this direction, though it probably saves a little through the burning of gas produced by combustion, which gas usually escapes through the chimney with the smoke in ordinary furnaces. The extra consumption of fuel rendered necessary by the use of the old burners has been referred to. It may here be added that this extra consumption frequently amounts to an increase of fully 25 per cent. Not being compelled to have holes in the boiler is another advantage of the new invention, as this cutting destroys the value of the boiler.

THE ENGINEERS LIKE IT.

Lastly, the engineers like it, because they cannot help but like it, for with this contrivance they can fire their boilers in any way they like to do, and thus they are saved the extra trouble and care involved in the use of the old contrivances where jet streams are used. In this connection it may be added that in the use of the new contrivance there is not the extra or special skill required in an engineer that is needed in working the jet device. It also saves the engineer the labor of keeping his flues clean, as the flues are not fouled by the smoke; while, the flues being kept free of soot, the necessary result is an increase in steam power.

To conclude, this new contrivance has been tested in all conceivable shapes, and it has stood these tests satisfactorily. It has proved a success even in the Exposition, where from twelve to thirteen tons of coal are used daily. The machine can be seen and its merits heard of at the following places, where it is in use: John Roper & Co., Nos. 37 and 39 Wabash avenue; Rand, McNally & Co., Nos. 148 and 154 Monroe street; A. G. Leonard & Co., 179 Monroe street, and at other leading establishments.

CALUMET IRON AND STEEL COMPANY.

A GREAT AND GROWING INTEREST.

This region can never be anything else but solid for a protective tariff when it sees in operation such vast work-shops as those at South Chicago (Cummings), belonging to this company, and realizes that but for that guardianship of home industry against foreign pauperized labor, one thousand pairs of willing hands—to take the specific case of this company and its pay-roll—would be thrown out of employment. The iron interest is one of the most important in this manufacturing center of the Northwest, and its prosperity or ruin are questions—it is not too strong to say—of almost vital concern to the general well being. With such convictions, not less sincerely entertained for being somewhat overlaid by wonder at the vast establishment spread out to view, The Inter Ocean man recently surveyed these works and their army of contented toilers, adding blow by blow, whether by their own arms or by machinery, to the wealth of the country. As stated, not less than 1,000 men are employed by the company, and their muscle is supplemented immeasurably by the ponderous machinery.

The works consist of a blast furnace of the first rank, yielding a molten product of 35,000 tons per annum; a splendidly equipped rolling mill, containing four trains of rolls for manufacturing merchant iron and nail plate, the ponderous machinery flattening out to the right shape not less than 40,000 tons annually of finished iron, which includes some sixty tons of nail plate a day, or rather night and day, for the mills are run constantly, the giant chimneys sustaining a dense pillar of cloud by day, like that before the itinerant Israelites, and of fire by night, so luminous that the landmark, or, rather, sky-mark, is visible for miles around, and in the immediate region supplants the moon; four open-hearth steel furnaces (Siemen's), with a capacity of 12,000 tons per annum; a nail factory, the largest in the Northwest, finishing 7,500 kegs a week, of all sizes, assorted, and yielding an annual output of 325,000 kegs of nails, or nearly 1,000 kegs a day—a great yield indeed, but needed to meet the correspondingly large pay-roll—and, be it added, needed also to compensate the ear-split visitor for the bedlam of the wonderful machinery that hammers out so lightning-like your kegful of one-penny, two-penny, three-peeny nails, up to the largest spikes that ever were driven by sledges; and last, but not least, the works embrace a new branch only just introduced, the manufacture of steel castings, a departure that promises soon to be one of the prominent features of the works.

The quality of the company's goods, like their advantages for doing business—indeed consequent thereon—is of the very best, foundry pig iron, merchant iron and nails, with the brand "Calumet" being well-known as standard. As to their prime facilities for doing business and so competing successfully in prices, to begin with, both their fuel and ore arrive by water, the latter direct from the Lake Superior region, while the Belt Line Railroad runs right into the works, and delivers cars the following day to any railroad going out of Chicago. In short, to end with as to begin, Chicago is the site of these works—Chicago, mistress of manufactures, a distributing as well as receiving point with no equal in this country.

The officers of the Calumet Iron and Steel Company are Mr. C. R. Cummings, President; Mr. D. C. Bradley, Vice President and General Manager; and Mr. J. M. Brown, Secretary and Treasurer. Office, First National Bank Building, Dearborn and Monroe streets, Chicago.

N. A. WILLIAMS,

219 WASHINGTON STREET,

manufacturer and dealer in sewer pipe, fire brick, drain tile, cement, fire clay, ground brick, chimney tops, chimney-flue linings, plaster, and fine sand, has been established in business in this city since 1869. The material he offers is superior to any that can be found in this or any other market. Akron sewer pipe is handled exclusively by him. He sold the first pipe ever manufactured by Akron pipe-makers, in 1857. It is a standard pipe, and is indorsed by the city government. He deals largely in fire brick, and his stock is composed of the best brands in this country, which have been thoroughly tested by most of the large manufacturers, and have given satisfaction. It includes the Mount Savage, manufactured in Maryland; the Scioto Star, in Portsmouth, Ohio, and others equally celebrated. He ships large quantities of sewer pipe and brick throhgh the West and Northwest, and, in fact, to all parts of the United States. His largest sales are in Akron sewer-pipe, and then comes brick, tile cement, fire clay, chimney tops, plaster, fine sand, etc. Business has prospered with him to a remarkable degree, and increased 20 per cent this year. He is the oldest firm in this line in the city, well known as a first-class business man, and is prompt, and whatever he recommends may be relied on. His stock is always large, and parties wishing to purchase should call and examine it before buying elsewhere.

THE VAN DEPOELE ELECTRIC LIGHT.

A SUPERIOR LIGHT.

The superiority of electric lighting over other methods of artificial illumination are so incontestible an patent to all that a discussion regarding its merits is superfluous.

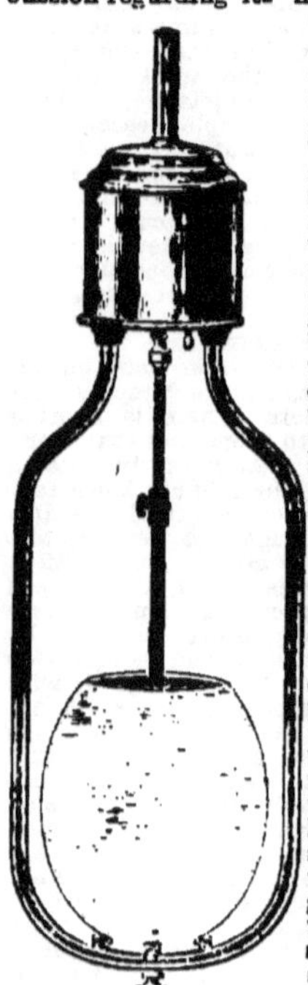

The question to be decided is which electric light or system is the best from all points of view. The writer of this article, after long examination and close observation, feels warranted in stating that the arc lamps and dynamos manufactured under the Van Depoele patents possess in the highest degree of excellence the requirements of a perfectly reliable and steady means of electric lighting. The reasons to be given for this claim are simple and decisive and consists in the extreme simplicity of construction in all parts of the system, ease of management, perfect safety, readiness of control and the incomparable perfection of the white and steady light obtained, a light so pure, soft and white that photographs have been taken thereby in nine seconds, rivalling the sun in the length of time required for exposure.

The means by which these important and vital results have been accomplished consists:

1. In the peculiar disposition of the field-magnets, and great compactness, and above

all the greatest volume of working current for the least amount of power.

2. That any number or all of the lights may be turned off or on as desired with the same ease of gas, the current regulating itself to the work to be done.

A brief description of the principle parts of the dynamo may be of interest to our readers. The *Field Magnets* consists of two large coils of copper wire wound around two soft iron cores, their north and south poles facing each other. The armature, which forms the most important part of the machine, consists of a frame made of a number of iron bars, each separated from the other. These bars are riveted to the inner and outer periphery of two metal rings, several of these rings being placed between the inner and outer layer of iron bars. And finally the rings and bars are riveted together so as to form a solid frame. The *commutator* is made of a large number of copper sections securely held together and connected to the coils of the armature. The brushes and their holders are made in a substantial manner, and are easily handled and adjusted.

The lamp has few parts, does not get out of order, is ornamental, compact, and is so insulated that it can be handled in perfect security. Even with the largest machines, any lamp or any part of the circuit may be touched with impunity, an accident having never yet been met with through the current of their machines, something which very few companies can boast of.

The Van Depoele plant is sold outright, no royalty being demanded. This system compares favorably with anything now on the market as regards cost and prices; they do not ask 30 per cent of the stock, nor make reservations of anykind; it is a bona fide outright sale of lamps and machinery.

We invite cities and towns to correspond with them, and investigate their system before purchasing elsewhere, believing that careful investigation will demonstrate that they have the most perfect system of electric lighting now offered to the public. Catalogue and prices furnished on application. The officers of the company are Norman T. Gassette, President; Theo. P Bailey, Secretary; and C. J. Van Depoele, Electrician. The main warerooms and factory are located at 203 and 205 Van Buren street, Chicago, Ill.

J. S. KIRK & CO.

"CLEANLINESS IS NEXT TO GODLINESS."

These well-known soap manufacturers have during the past year made vast strides in the extent and scope of their trade, and have placed their popular products in every city, town, village, and hamlet in the United States. Their knowledge and skill in creating a fine article has been derived from long experience, patient investigation, and a critical discrimination of the wants of the market.

Mr. J. S. Kirk, the founder of this house, began making soap at Utica, N. Y., in 1839 and has continued in the business ever since. The sons, Messrs. James A., John B., M. W., and W. F. Kirk, are ably assisting their father in the management of the business, and are constantly directing their skilled experience to the exigencies and demands of the business.

The firm began operations in Chicago in 1859, and the constant and steady growth of their business attests the genuine merit and value of their soaps, and is one of the most surprising and marvelous examples of the sudden rise to greatness which is so characteristic of Chicago, and the career of its representative business men. The factory is located at 342 to 370 North Water street, this city, and is a substantial brick edifice 120x240 feet in dimensions, and six stories in height, the motive power being furnished by a 1,400 horse power engine, the steam being supplied by twelve large steel boilers. Nearly 600 hands are constantly engaged in creating soap and perfumery in order that their fellow creatures may be clean and sweet. A saw-mill in Michigan is owned by the firm, the entire output of lumber being consumed in making the boxes required. Sixty million pounds of soap was manufactured and sold by this house during the past year, the factory running day and night in order to ship sales promptly.

The most popular brands of soaps are the Zenithia, Commonwealth, Calumet Bouquet, Palama Rosa, Fine Palm, Turtle Oil, and Windsor, in toilet products, and their laundry soaps are standard upon our market, nothing but the best tallow and oils being used in any of their goods. With the most improved and modern machinery and appliances, together with anxious and watchful attention to the details of their business, this house has built up a patronage which is second to none in this country.

Every grade of goods, from the cheapest washing to the most delicate toilet soaps, is produced. The perfumery department, though a comparatively new feature, is equipped with the utmost completeness, and the extracts which they bottle are taking the lead in popularity. The delicacy, purity, and strength of these goods have recommended them to the attention of a critical public, the Zenithia and Palestine Lily being the results of new discoveries in the compounding of essences, while their Lavender, Jockey Club, and Ylang Ylang waters are meeting with an unprecedented sale. On the whole, we know of no soap manufacturer in the country that brings a more consummate knowledge and ripened experience into the business than the gentlemen connected with this firm. They have their eyes on the wants of the American people, and seem to have fully met and satisfied their demands for a fine, honest soap at prices that compare most favorably with any other establishment of the kind in the United States.

WESTERN BRICK AND TILE COMPANY.

AN OLD INDUSTRY IN A NEW GUISE.

The manufacture of brick is one of the oldest of human industries, and from time immemorial this material has been highly popular with builders. There were reasons for this popularity; in the first place, the clay could be molded into a form convenient for handling by the workmen, or fashioned to meet any exigency of architecture, without the expense incident to carving wood, or the more lasting blocks of stone; but the chief reason remains to be assigned, the easily formed squares and oblongs of clay, when properly finished by drying or burning, were found to be more durable than anything else from which buildings could be constructed. The truth of this last statement is abundantly proved by the remains of Roman brick work which are scattered over various parts of England, and by the still more ancient ruins of brick-built structures which, in our own times, have been exhumed from the shapeless mounds that mark the sites of Babylon and Nineveh. All these relics of the almost forgotten past bear unmistakable evidence that the brick is something which is pretty nearly imperishable. There have been of course many and great improvements in the methods of manufacturing brick—since the days when the unfortunate children of Israel made them under Pharaoh's taskmasters in the land of Egypt—but these cannot be described, or even mentioned, in a trade review article for lack space. This, however, may be born in mind, the ease with which clay can be molded into any desired form, and the durability as well as the cheapness of good brick as building material, are points which have never been lost sight of by inventors, and the Patent Office at Washington will show not only a world of complicated, expensive machinery for grinding and molding the clay, but innumerable devices also in the way of kilns for burning it into a marketable condition after it had been properly fashioned. To Colonel W. L. Gregg, of Philadelphia, belongs the honor, beyond a doubt, of inventing the most perfect machinery for the manufacture of brick, and especially of pressed brick, which has ever been submitted to the inspection of the public, and of transforming a rude craft into a fine art. It is literally true that brick making—at least as practiced in Chicago in this present year of grace by the Western Brick and Tile Company—has advanced from a craft to an art, and first-class, artistic talent is in constant employ moreover by the company above referred to, to design the novelties in shape which are destined to adorn the fronts of suburban cottages and of the palatial city residences. Heretofore machine-made brick have been objected to by many leading architects for the reason that they were unequal in size, finish, and density, and very often deficient in strength. These objections have all been anticipated and obviated by Colonel Gregg's wonderful machinery, which embraces no less than ten different patents, and represent years of patient inventive toil. The brick manufactured by his processes are simply perfect. They received the highest award at the American Centennial of 1876, at the Paris International Exposition of 1878, and at various prominent State and inter-State expositions of a late date. In fine, they are conceded to be the best in quality and appearance on the market, and have been designated for use in the construction of government works afterhaving been submitted to the most severe tests by Lieutenant Colonel Gillmore, of the United States Engineers, and by the supervising architect of the new Treasury building at Washington. They were found capable of sustaining the enormous pressure of 100,000 pounds to the square inch.

The Western Brick and Tile Company, which is now manufacturing this description of building material for the Chicago market, was established in 1883, with headquarters at Galewood, about nine miles from this city, where one of the finest clay deposits in the country was discovered a few months before. The company has a capital of $500,000, and is officered as follows:

Homer Pennock, President.
D. K. Tripp, Vice President.
A. W. Penney, Secretary.
Edward Koch, Treasurer.
Colonel W. L. Gregg, General Manager.

The main works, which was built for the purpose, is a spacious two-story building, 200x100 feet in dimensions. It is capable of turning out 200,000 of the finest and most artistically perfect brick per day, and in the coming spring such additional machinery will be supplied as will double its manufacturing capabilities. It is now running night and day to fill its orders, and has already taken rank as one of the leading industries of Chicago. The office of the company is at No. 53 Dearborn street.

THE CHICAGO WIRE AND IRON WORKS,
LOCATED AT 110 LAKE STREET,

report business in their line as having been unusually good during the past season. While they have been in the business under the above name only since last April, the working organization is an old one in Chicago, formerly being the wire railing department of the Clinton Wire Cloth Company. Since the new organization their business has been largely extended. They make to order or keep in stock a full line of plain and ornamental wirework wire cloth, all kinds of wire, sheet brass, tubing and ornamental brasswork; also, stable fittings, vases, settees, crestings and finials, tower ornaments and weather vanes. They make a specialty of wrought iron fences for private residences, public buildings, parks, etc.; also, tubular fences for cemeteries, etc. They employ about 100 workmen in Chicago, and as the Western branch of the E. T. Barnum Wire and Iron Works, represent a manufacturing capacity of over 1,000 men, with the most approved machinery, distributed over a floor area of over 200,000 square feet. The illustrated catalogues of this company are the most complete ever issued, covering almost the entire list of articles made of wire and iron, and as an aid to satisfactory selection are beyond comparison.

CLEVELAND CO-OPERATIVE STOVE CO.
201 AND 203 LAKE STREET.

The Chicago branch of this well-known stove house, located at 201 and 203 Lake street, has become one of the leaders in the stove industry throughout the Northwest. The causes of their popularity lies in the fact that the class of goods manufactured by this company combine in a high degree all the essential elements that go to make a durable, elegant, and reliable stove.

The factories of the company are located at Cleveland, Ohio. We venture to say that no stove manufactory in the country brings to bear more skilled experience and judgment into their profession than the gentlemen composing this company.

The Telephone Range and Elboron Heater, two new patterns which they have recently added to their lines, possess features of novelty and excellence not often met with.

These creations, while being very popular, are at the same time the most magnificent and perfect expression of legitimate stove-plate decoration that has yet been displayed on this market.

With branch offices at Indianapolis, St. Louis, and St. Paul, this company have placed themselves and their products high in the estimation of the American public by the matchless virtues of honest dealing, low prices, and prompt delivery.

CRANE BROTHERS' MANUFACTURING COMPANY

report a largely increased business during the past year and collections satisfactory. Prices were remunerative the first part of the year, but declined the latter part, owing to the depression in the iron market, which is the more remarkable as the demand for goods has not fallen off. They manufacture steam and hydraulic elevators, which are in general use and very popular; steam engines, steam pumps, steam goods, engine trimmings, and wrought-iron pipe of all descriptions, having two mills for that purpose, the lap-weld pipe mill being very large and run to its full capacity. They make specialties of cast-iron and malleable fittings of all kinds, and brass and iron valves and cocks for steam, gas, and water. These works, covering almost a square on Jefferson and Desplaines street, give employment to 1,200 men. It is one of the largest houses in its line in the West, and occupies a very conspicuous place among the leading manufacturing industries of the West.

BURLINGTON MANUFACTURING CO.

MARBLES.

The Burlington Manufacturing Company, at the corner of Michigan avenue and Van Buren street, are extensive manufacturers and producers of marble in the form of floor tiling, mantels, wainscoting, monuments, and all kinds of interior and exterior ornamentation and decoration. They aim to secure the best grades of marble from beds of various geological formations and structure, possessing a fineness of texture and purity of shading that fit it for the choicest works of decoration and even for the sculptor; of grades held in the highest estimation by those familiar with this rock. Their experience and their determination to use none but the best material has enabled them to secure a large patronage. Their trade extends through the West and Northwest, and elsewhere to some extent.

THOMAS DOUGALL.

RECORD OF THIRTY-FIVE YEARS.

At Nos. 35 to 41 Cedar street we find the extensive establishment of Thomas Dougall. This gentleman first engaged in the manufacture of soap in Chicago thirty-five year ago, and no other laundry soap ever placed upon the market in this country has given more universal or continued satisfaction His leading brands are the "American Laundry," "German Fine Laundry," and Chemical Erasive. His soaps are sold in large quantities all over the West and at prices that defy competition. In his factory is used the latest and most improved machinery, so that his soap is manufactured at the least possible expense. Mr. Dougall reports his trade constantly on the increase and his business in a satisfactory condition.

SPIELMAN BROS.

COMPRESSED YEAST AND VINEGAR.

Among the thriving enterprises of Chicago may be mentioned that of Messrs. Spielman Bros., manufacturers of compressed yeast and vinegar. This firm, located at 103 East Erie street, has been compelled by their increase of trade to seek larger quarters, and are now located at Nos. 93 to 99 North avenue, also running their Erie street establishment. This firm was established in 1879, on a small scale, and are now the largest manufacturers of their kind of goods in America. They make white wine vinegar, and, with their increased facilities, are unable to keep up with their orders. Their yeast is known as the Chicago Compressed Yeast, and is being used by large bakers and the leading grocers of the city.

They have lately made extensive additions and improvements, which enables them in a measure to keep pace with their thriving business. We wish them merited success.

PURTELL, HANNAN & CO.

NICKEL PLATERS.

The members of this firm are practical workmen, and herein lies the secret of their success, for they have certainly been successful, and have grown in importance steadily and surely year by year, until they are now one of the most prominent firms in their line of business in Chicago. They make a specialty of fine and durable work, and pay great attention to stair and balcony railings. They also do an immense amount of work for the palace-car companies. Door plates, carriage plating, and carriage name plates are also directly in their line of business, and have recently added nickel-plating, bronzing, dipping, lacquering, polishing, and grinding to their extensive works. This firm is licensed by the United Nickel Company, of New York. They are at present located at No. 60 South Canal street, prepared to increase their business materially during 1884.

J. J. WILSON.

THE ARROW BRAND.

Mr. Wilson first engaged in the vinegar rade in Chicago in 1865 and in the pickle business in 1876, naming his pickles the "Arrow Brand," which has been registered as this trade mark. His pickles and kindred goods are well and favorably known throughout the country and give universal satisfaction to the trade. Mr. Wilson reports a steady increase of trade year by year. His office and factory are located at Nos. 12 and 14 North Clinton street, Chicago, and his salting works at Crystal Lake, Illinois.

PRUSSING VINEGAR WORKS.

STRICTLY PURE GOODS.

Among the pioneer industries of Chicago are the well-known Prussing Vinegar Works, founded by Mr. Chas. G. E. Prussing in 1848. These works occupy the block bounded by Clark, LaSalle, Twenty-fourth, and Twenty-fifth streets, and are the oldest works of the kind in America, as also the most complete and extensive in the world, their daily capacity being 400 brls. A visit to this establishment reminds one of the famous old breweries of England, as there may be seen faithful and reliable workmen grown from youth to old age in the service of the Prussings, and to this system is due much of the reliability and uniform purity of Prussing's vinegar, which has so many years brought joy to the hearts of prudent housewives, who pride themselves on the crispness and flavor of the toothsome pickle.

THE YOUNG & FARREL

DIAMOND STONE-SAWING COMPANY'S

Works on Twelfth and Lumber streets, Chicago (see cut), are most complete and admirable; it is said, indeed, they have not their equal in the world. They cover an area of about three acres, and include many wonderfully effective machines, such as overhead travelers, power and hand cranes, diamond saws, planers, rubbing beds, lathes, etc., for handling, sawing, dressing, polishing, and turning the different kinds of building stone.

The business of the company is the furnishing and erection of cut stone, whether plain, molded, or carved, for private dwellings, business blocks, churches, court houses, schools, bridges, and the like, and it makes a specialty also of planed sidewalks. It is the sole agent in the West for several of the most interesting and valuable stones, of which we may mention the red Scotch stone, known as Corsehill, so popular in the Eastern cities, and the celebrated and attractive Brinton green stone of Pennsylvania, already such a favorite in Chicago.

The company owns the patents for Young's diamond saws and for other machines used in its business, and has a branch establishment at Mott Haven, New York City, specially devoted to their manufacture and sale. By reason of abundant capital, extraordinary facilities, and long experience in every part of their business; by promptness, good work, and reasonable charges, the officers of this company feel confident of building up a magnificent business by helping to build up and embellish these magnificent cities of the great West.

The officers are Franklin Farrel, President; Hugh Young, Secretary and Treasurer; Ferdinand V. Gindele, Manager, and Robert C. Harper, Superintendent. They are exceedingly gratified with the liberal patronage of architects, builders, and the public heretofore accorded them, and are determined to deserve the continuance and increase of the same.

THE ALLEN PAPER CAR-WHEEL CO.

A WHEEL THAT IS ABSOLUTELY SAFE.

The science of railroading owes a great deal of its advancement and progress to this celebrated wheel, which has been tried and found to perform all that is claimed for it. The core of the Allen car-wheel consists of straw board compressed by hydraulic power of 5,000 tons. The centers are encircled by heavy steel tires of the most perfect and expensive manufacture. The paper, in the center of which rests the iron hub, is encased between side-plates of wrought iron, the combination of steel, paper, and iron being so securely held together as to be incapable of separation in any considerable accident. Safety and durability result as a natural consequence. As high as 200,000 miles have been obtained from these wheels without turning the tire, and 800,000 miles without renewing the tire. The economy of the wheel in every way is established. The Allen Paper Car-wheel Company, of which Mr. A. G. Darwin is President, are operating extensive works at Pullman, Morris, Ill., and Hudson, N. Y., which have an annual production of 25,000 wheels. These wheels are in use under most of the sleeping, parlor, chair, and dining cars, and many of the first-class coaches upon all the principal railways in this country.

SMOKE CONSUMPTION

A SUCCESSFUL PATENT.

Smoke consumption has at last reached a stage of development which places it among the assured successes of the age. This result has been attained only after years of experience and patient investigation and inquiry. There are numerous devices upon the market which make great claims to effectiveness and superiority, but after thorough research we have found but one device which effectually accomplishes the result sought, and in this device all the objections seem to have been met and overcome with consummate skill and completeness, and the theory that smoke cannot be consumed is exploded as is most emphatically attested by the daily operation of the

HUTCHINSON SMOKE AND SPARK BURNER.

We find about 2,200 of these machines in successful operation on locomotives, tugs, and all manner of stationary furnaces, the number exceeding all other smoke consumers combined. In no case has this device been found wanting in reliability, durability, or effectiveness.

It is simply an air-feeding device, and the fireman can supply his furnace with air in the same manner he does his boiler with water, by the use of an injector. They will attach the device to any locomotive, tug, or other furnace at their own expense, and demonstrate all they claim for them before presenting their bill for payment. Address, for particulars, 103 Adams street, Chicago.

GOSS & PHILLIPS MFG. CO.

SASH, DOORS, ETC.

In the development of the Northwest, sash, doors, and house-furnishing materials are important factors toward which the above firm has contributed very largely. Thus, in its business as a well-managed and successful lumber-manufacturing company, has done much toward the progress of the great West. Their great establishment, on the corndr of Fisk and Twenty-second streets, is one of the landmarks of the lumber district, and is equipped with the most approved machinery. Their facilities for manufacturing and shipping are unsurpassed in this great lumber market of the world. Here may be found at all times, every style of goods in their line, from the plainest to the most elaborate. Few establishments have enjoyed such extended patronage as the Goss & Phillips Manufacturing Company. While this company continues in business the consumer will always have an assurance of getting good value for their money. They are now giving particular attention to hardwood finishings. A visit to their establishment would well repay the visitor for the time thus spent.

FULLER AND WARREN COMPANY.

THE BEST STOVES.

The Clinton Stove Works, at Troy, N. Y., were established in 1831 for the manufacture of stoves, furnaces, and ranges, and by dint of careful attention to the details of their business, have extended their trade throughout the American continent and all parts of the civilized world. The establishment occupies an area of six acres of ground, with substantial buildings fully equipped with the latest modern appliances for the production of stoves, and their facilities are unquestionably without rival in the stove industry. Their goods, of all kinds, are undoubtedly superior in every minutiæ, both in construction and finish. In 1862 the Chicago branch was established, and is one of the pioneers in the Western stove trade, with sales-room at 56 Lake street; and an immense reserve stock in storage at their great warehouse in this city places them in position to meet all demands of trade promptly. Immediate attention to orders, elegant, durable, reliable goods, close prices, and prompt shipments are the causes which have placed the Chicago branch, second only in the extent of its trade to the parent house. Send for their catalogue which will be mailed free to any address upon application.

THE WESTERN LEATHER

MANUFACTURING COMPANY.

Nos. 76 and 78 Wabash avenue. This is one of the great manufacturing concerns of the West, and its goods, particularly dressing cases, sample cases, medicine cases, and leather collar and cuff boxes—many of which are protected by patents—have a high reputation the country over. Whatever is neat, tasty, and artistic in the way of fancy leather goods is made by this establishment, and cannot be excelled in quality or finish in the United States. Descriptive price-lists sent to the trade upon application.

A. H. ANDREWS & CO.,

CORNER WABASH AVENUE AND ADAMS,

report a constant increase in the volume of their business, their sales being considerably over one million in their departments of Bank Counters, Office and School Desks, Opera Chairs, Church Seating, Globes, Maps, and their specialty, the "Andrews Folding Beds." The well-known quality of their goods and the reputation of the house have combined to crowd them with orders.

BEMIS & M'AVOY, BREWERS.

The goods manufactured by this firm have a reputation co-extensive with the United States. The house does an enormous business and counts its customers by the thousand.

LUMBER.

HOLBROOK & CO.

HARDWOOD LUMBER.

One of the most extensive, and the oldest in point of continued existence, firms dealing exclusively in hardwood lumber in Chicago is Messrs. Holbrook & Co., located at the corner of Eighteenth and Grove streets. It was established there in 1853, and has occupied the same premises ever since. They deal in all kinds of hardwood lumber suitable for the use of bridge and warehouse builders, furniture manufacturers, interior and exterior finishing, and for whatever uses hardwood lumber may be wanted. They obtain their supplies mainly from Michigan, Indiana, and the South, or wherever their judgment, based on thirty years of experience, tells them the best grades of hardwood lumber can be obtained. Their business extends throughout the West, Northwest, and to some extent in the East. They have track and other facilities for shipping in and out, which are unsurpassed by any similar concern in the country. During their long and uninterruptedly fair and honorable business career they have acquired a reputation for dealing advantageously and squarely, which few firms in business as long attain and retain.

HAMILTON & MERRYMAN COMPANY,

LUMBER DEALERS.

Loomis and Twenty-second streets. The business of this company expresses exactly those methods which have made this city the greatest lumber market of the world. Beginning with the ownership of the land on which the pine tree grows, every operation in the process of preparing it for use and putting it on the market is conducted at the smallest possible expense and under one management. The mills of this company are at Marinette, Wis., where they have sawed 25,000,000 feet the past year. From the mills to the yards in Chicago the lumber is transported in their own vessels and landed at their spacious dock, where at one handling it can be placed on the cars. Thus this company is prepared to offer their customers lumber on which there is but one profit from the growing tree to the prepared article.

CHAPTER XI

CHICAGO'S SUBURBS.

THE UNION STOCK YARDS.

HISTORICAL.

The entire system of all the railways East and West center here, making the Union Stock Yards the most accessible in the country for both buyer and seller The large capacity of the yards, the facilities for unloading, feeding, and reshipping have been kept up to the requirements of the wondrous growth of this market. The elevated driveways and viaduct system have been pushed forward on such a grand scale as to render the economic handling of the stock from all divisions more convenient than at any other period in the history of the yards. These great roadways and stock drives, connecting with the city of packing-houses, are direct and wonderfully complete. Ten times as much stock can be more rapidly and conveniently handled here at present than could be done ten years ago, while the banking interest conducts the volume of two hundred millions of annual business that obtains here now with fewer complications and less red tape than was required to handle ten millions when these yards were in their infancy. Then it required the personal indorsement and assurance, at great risk, of the management and their friends to bring Eastern money here to conduct this great branch of commerce. Now it flows through in such a wave that the tide will ever be irresistible. Much has been written and said upon the subject to whom belongs the credit of concentrating in Chicago this branch of commerce, through which flows the cumulative wide Western wealth in its fullest volume. The proposition is plain and of easy solution. To those energetic spirits belongs the chief credit that gathered the nucleus and rounded into form this grand combination of united interests, and then sagaciously directed the enterprise until it has become a rock-rooted institution of Middle America, adjunctive to the civilized world. It can be said beyond a cavil or doubt that the business facilities afforded by the

UNION STOCK YARD AND TRANSIT COMPANY

to the live stock market of Chicago has been one of the chief factors in the grand agricultural development of the great West.

From the foundation of this market up to the present the same management have bent their indefatigable energy to the accomplishment of a great purpose; how well they have succeeded is known in every land and landed in every language, until the guide-book of the foreign visitor is incomplete that does not include the great Union Stock Yards and its city of packing-houses, wherein is prepared the most wholesome and richest of human food which is sent to feed the millions throughout the world. The first stock yard founded in Chicago, that attracted Eastern capitalists to this market as a live stock supply point, was managed by John B. Sherman, who was the chief spirit in organizing the present Union Stock Yards, and has been actively identified with its management ever since. These yards were constructed in the year 1865, and were opened for business Dec. 25 of the same year. The company now owns about a section of land, and over one hundred miles of railroad track, making a transit through the city, and running around and through different parts of the yards, all laid with steel rails, connecting with all the railroads centering in Chicago. Within an inclosure of 360 acres are constructed the

TRANSIT HOUSE

at a cost of $250,000, which is furnished first-class and is kept second to none in the country, charges to stockmen being only $2 per day, or 50 cents per meal. In the center of the yards is a large two-story-and-a-half building 60x380, with large wings extending south from either end, doubling the capacity of the main building. This is known as the Exchange Building, and is divided up as follows: Large Board of Trade hall, main offices for Stock Yards Company, Superintendent's, Secretary's, and Treasurer's offices, telegraph and telephone offices, postoffice, restaurant 60x80, spacious saloon, packers' offices, offices for Eastern shippers, barber shop, news stand, fruit stand, and about 150 offices for commission merchants who take charge of and sell stock consigned to them; the Union Stock Yards National Bank building, 40x60; twenty large hay barns, as many more large corn cribs, twenty scale-houses, each containing one of Fairbank's improved scales with a capacity for weighing three or four car-loads of cattle or hogs at a draft; machine shops, depot buildings, printing office, and two dozen other buildings used to transact business pertaining to the receiving and shipping live stock, including the grand new horse sales stables and the experimental fat-stock barn that is always replete with an assortment of different breeds of cattle. The water supply is furnished through the regular waterworks and a half-dozen artesian wells, a standpipe, surrounded by a tower 150 high, into which the water is forced by a powerful engine and pumps being on the spot.

Cable and telegraphic market reports from London, Liverpool, New York, Boston, Philadelphia, Baltimore, Cincinnati, Buffalo, East Liberty, Albany, and other markets both East and West are received here, and reports of this market are telegraphed each day to all Eastern cities, Europe, and through commission firms to all parts of the Western States and Territories.

Over 250 acres of land are under plank and constructed as follows: About 150 acres are in cattle yards and about 100 acres of covered hog and sheep pens; 2,000 cattle pens sufficient to yard 25,000 cattle; 1,500 hog pens sufficient to hold 200,000 hogs; 300 sheep pens that will accommodate 15,000 sheep; stabling for 2,500 horses; 2,000 car-loads of stock can be unloaded and taken care of daily; over 20 miles of macadamized streets run through different parts of the yards, and over 50 miles of water and drainage pipes, forming a perfect network, run underneath the yards. There are about 10 miles of viaducts and elevated roadway. Nearly 1,000 men are constantly employed throughout the different departments. Although the contributors to this market cover the territory from British Columbia to Old Mexico, and the intermediate country, at no single season since the foundation of the yards has there has been as many strange shippers on this market as during the past year, and the natural supposition is that with the rapid development of the West now going on this will continue. If those unacquainted with the manner of doing business here are desirous of patronizing this market, if they will address a letter of inquiry or call on the Secretary at his office in the yards, he will with pleasure give the information that will enable any stranger to become thoroughly posted respecting the market and the manner of doing business here. All stock consigned to these yards, whether in charge of man or not, will receive prompt attention and as good care as though the owner himself were along to see to it, as all the men in the employ of the Stock Yard Company are experienced in the handling and care of stock. The volume of business during the past year will exceed two hundred millions. In another place will be found the commercial report giving the business statistics of this market since its foundation.

The following-named gentlemen are the officers of the above corporation: Nathaniel Thayer, President; John B. Sherman, Vice President and General Manager; G. Titus Williams, General Superintendent; George T. Williams, Secretary and Treasurer; J. C. Denison, Assistant Secretary.

ARMOUR & CO.

AN ENORMOUS BUSINESS.

In almost every line of business there will be found men particularly suited to the undertakings in which they are engaged. They rise above and show themselves superior to the common run of business men, so that in the course of time they become leaders in their respective branches of trade. The successes of these men in some instances is marvelous, and is often attributed to circumstances and good luck. This rule, however, when the true facts in the case are taken into consideration, will be found at fault, of which the firm whose name heads this article bears ample witness. The head of the firm Philip D. Armour, as is well known, started as a poor boy, and the fact that he now superintends and controls the largest business enterprise of its kind in Chicago is due to no freaks of luck or chance, but to the fact that he was possessed with an abundance of pluck and enterprise, added to which was the gift of a keen business sense, which aided him in taking advantage of opportunities when offered. In the brief space allotted it would be impossible to give anything like a complete description of the immense business transacted by this firm during the past year. Suffice it to say that their sales in the various branches show a marked increase over all previous years. For the year 1882 they slaughtered and shipped in refrigerator cars 120,000 head of cattle; for the year ending Nov. 1, 1883, their books show an increase of 131,000, making 251,000 in all. In addition to these over 1,020,000 head of hogs were killed and dressed for the market, their sales amounting to over $30,000,000. The excellent qualities of the prepared meats turned out by this firm are so well known throughout this country and Europe that it is scarcely deemed necessary to speak of them at length in a review of this kind. No better proof as to the good quality of their meats need be given than the constantly increasing demand made for them from year to year. In addition to their great Chicago establishment the firm has branch houses at Milwaukee and Kansas City. Both of the latter have done a large business during the last year.

SOUTH BEND.

O'BRIEN VARNISH WORKS.

ELECTRIC PRIMING.

Among the most promising manufactories of South Bend is the large and perfectly arranged varnish works of Mr. P. O'Brien, the inventor of the Electric Priming, which has a popularity earned by far surpassing and completely revolutionizing all other systems. These works have just been completed, and they are the model ones in their line. A demand for the O'Brien brand of varnishes will be the result wherever these goods are known.

THE COQUILLARD WAGON.

THE FARMERS' FAVORITE.

These wagons are made of the best wood and iron to be procured, and put together by

the most experienced workmen. Every one is warranted to give satisfaction, both in regard to the quality of material and workmanship.

They are also noted for their lightness of draft and ease of running. Carriages, buggies, and sleighs of superior workmanship always on hand. Send for circular and price list to A. Coquillard, South Bend, Ind. This manufactory is one of the best conducted and most successful in the West. Its owner is not only a superior business man, but also a practical, careful, and experienced mechanic, with a rare grasp of all that is necessary to perfection in mechanics.

SISTERS OF THE HOLY CROSS.

The cut below correctly represents the very superior school conducted by the Sisters of the Holy Cross at Notre Dame, Ind. A careful examination of this institution reveals a very remarkable proficiency on the part of pupils. The course is most thorough. All of the studies that inform, refine, and mold the child into the finished woman are here given in their entirety. Graduates from St. Mary's are fitted for teachers as few can be in the more superficial seminaries. French and German are taught by native teachers, drawing and painting by artists of merit. The conservatory of music is perhaps the best in the West. The school is open to all who will conform to its very beneficial rules regarding morals and behavior. Religious studies are not required of its scholars unless prescribed by their parents. The grounds are extensive, varied, and most beautiful. The location is very healthful. The school contains a large number of excellent pianos, besides other musical instruments; a museum of minerals, fossils, and other geological curiosities rarely found in Western schools. The art rooms are profusely strewn with all the paraphernalia of the sculptors and painters' studios. Many of the productions indicate rare advance in both modern and ancient artistic work.

Special care is given to correctly teaching the practical features of decorative art, now so popular in all refined communities. The graduates of St. Mary's Academy have reflected credit upod their alma mater. Many of them are occupying high positions in society. Others, as teachers, musicians, and artists, are receiving the praise of all who know them. The fullest information will be furnished freely. Apply for a catalogue.

SAINT-MARY'S, NOTRE-DAME IND.

PORTLAND CEMENT.

AT SOUTH BEND.

Millen & Sons, Stove and Pipe Manufacturing Company, of South Bend, present the ollowing extracts from testimonials:

"Extra good quality."—Geo. C. Morgan & Co., hydraulic engineers, Chicago.

"Given entire satisfaction."—Charles Carr, Supt. B & B. Canada Southern Railway.

"Superior to stone."—Norman T. Beckley, General Manager C., W. and M. Railroad.

"The best Portland cement."—D. W. Flagler, Lieutenant Colonel commanding at Rock Island Arsenal.

"Not surpassed by any Portland cement in the world."—John Collett, State Geologist for Indiana.

The works are extensive and the business done is rapidly increasing.

DR. J. A. McGILL,

OF SOUTH BEND, IND.,

an old practitioner of medicine, and for years making female diseases a specialty with unparalleled success, will now give to the public his great specific for female diseases called Orange Blossom. The specific "Orange Blossom Absorbent" will cause a new departure in the treatment of those diseases, and will do away with nearly all surgical operations whereby so many precious lives have been lost. It has proved in more than a thousand of the worst cases to be a positive cure for female diseases. The Orange Blossom method of treatment is being used by some of the best physicians in the country, and the workings of the specific pronounced marvelous.

ROCKFORD.

THE BOSS AND ACME CHURNS.

THEIR MERITS.

The above cut represents a churn that is simplicity itself, and yet it ranks first best with experienced butter-makers all over the West. Your representative visited the factory at Rockford, and was astonished at the showing made by H. H. Palmer & Co., the owners of the patents for the Boss and Acme churns. Over forty thousand of these churns have been sold during the past year. They are made of the best white oak; and are kept sweet and clean with little care, because there are no corners in them or joints that can be opened with pressure.

These churns have taken first premiums at the Illinois State Fair. They are used by such creameries as the Madison street creamery in Chicago, where 1,000 pounds of pure cream butter are made per day. The following indorsements speak for themselves:

"OLYMPIA, W. T., Feb. 9, 1883.—Your churn takes well; every one that sees it likes it. I would not take four times what I paid for mine and do without until I could send and get another. In fact, I consider it a priceless treasure in my business. Respectfully, MRS. C. G. TYLER."

One agent writes us from Clinton, Mo., under date of Sept. 4, 1883: "J. R. Camplin, dairyman, has used the Little Boss, Rectangular, Union, and Cylinder churns, and is now using the H. H. Palmer & Co.'s Boss barrel churn, and thinks it superior to all others."

A. P. Frowlin, Cashier Henry County Bank, Clinton, Mo.; S. Jones, physician, Clinton, Mo.; D. W. Bennett, farmer, Clinton, Mo.; R. S. Hastin, farmer, Clinton, Mo., and many others, all recommend it.

R. B. PORTIS.

BUTTER COLOR.

IT TAKES THE PREMIUM.

The Bean & Perry Manufacturing Company, of Rockford, was interviewed by a Trade Review commissioner, and their extensive works carefully examined. The science of chemistry, money, and careful research has been lavishly bestowed upon perfecting a natural color for the butter made in off seasons, and the result is the June butter color made by this company. Its perfection has been admitted by numerous awarding committees, notably that of the Ohio State Fair of this year. In fact, medals, diplomas, and first premiums are familiar decorations in the company's office. The following points are claimed for this preparation, and its history more than justifies these claims of the manufacturers:

1. It does not color the buttermilk.
2. It contains no acids or alkalies, consequently works uniformly, no matter what degree of sourness the cream may possess.
3. It gives the butter a natural June color.
4. Butter colored with it brings the highest market price.
5. It is entirely harmless, saves time, labor, and returns you $20 for every $1 invested.
6. It imparts no taste to the butter.
7. Perfect keeping qualities; it does not mold or sour in any way. It has a decided tendency to preserve butter.
8. It requires no labor, as it is a liquid that is put in with the cream in the churn.

The following indorsements from the most prominent dairymen in the country speak decisively as to the superiority of the June butter color:

Gives perfect satisfaction.—John Wilhelm, Jr., Wooster, Ohio.

It is the most natural color, and you are deserving of great credit for your skill in perfecting so good and valuable an article.—D. W. Pettitt, Secretary Belvidere Butter and Cheese Manufacturing Company.

Never found one that would compare with it.—R. S. Houston, winner of the first prize for butter at Wisconsin fair.

Could not be induced to use any other.—John T. Fisk, manager Sigourney Creamery.

Prefer it to any we have used in the last six years.—J. E. Eldridge & Bro., Earlville, Iowa.

Better than any we have used before.—Parker Hildebrand & Co., Boscobel, Wis.

We find yours preferable by far.—A. Ayers & Son, Cedar Falls, Iowa.

These indorsements could be indefinitely continued, but the above extracts are sufficiently indicative.

The following announcement will be of interest to all who make butter for the market: "The Bean & Perry Manufacturing Company, of Rockford, Ill., will prepay express charges and ship securely packed to any address one of their dollar bottles of June butter color on receipt of $1."

ROCKFORD (ILL.) BUSINESS COLLEGE.

A LIVE INSTITUTION.

This is a live institution, affording a most thorough and valuable course of business training, together with instruction in the common and higher English branches, fully meeting from a common sense standpoint the educational demands of the present. Elocution, short-hand, and type-writing are among the specialties taught. Journals, circulars, etc., are sent upon application to the principals, Messrs. Winans & Stoddard.

AURORA.

THE AMERICAN WELL WORKS.

The Studebakers as wagon makers and the Olivers as plow makers occupy common ground with the Chapmans as wel makers. Each justly claims to be the best and the greatest in his line. THE INTER OCEAN'S Trade Review commissioner visited these works, located at Aurora, Ill., where they manufacture well sinking machinery and an extra strong windmill, the American Advance, which, being wrought-iron mounted, they claim has never been blown away. They are so confident in their hydraulic jetting and blowing well sinking machinery that they will sink the first well for parties buying tools and guarantee water free from the surface alkali or ask no pay. Well sinking is a science and controlled by numerous patents, the knowledge of which they give only to parties purchasing their tools. They are supplying wells for seventy steam elevators owned by Pillsbury and Hurlbut Elevating Company, of Minneapolis; are sinking wells also on the Colorado plains for the B. & M. Railway Company where water was not known. The wells sunk for the C. & N. W. Railway Company are a complete success. R. W. Hoyt, R. Q. M. at Ft. Fully, recommends the tools of this company in the strongest terms. Hundreds of feet are often made with these tools without removing them from the hole. They make a well very quickly and give large returns to the well sinker.

THE HOTEL EVANS,

AT AURORA,

Ill., has been so completely revolutionized inside and out that one would hardly recognize it. N. H. Wood, the present proprietor, is a veteran hotel-keeper, and keeps his house in a professional and not in the amateur style. No one coming to Aurora can now complain of the town as being without a first-class hotel.

WOOLEN MILLS.

THE SHIP DIRECT.

Aurora has a most excellent woolen mill, the property of J. G. Stolp & Son, well-known throughout this part of the country as practical manufacturers of a very superior line of staple and fancy all-wool cassimeres. By shipping direct from the mill commissions, enormous rents, and other expenses that are saddled upon the purchaser are saved, and the firm will prove this. Dealers are solicited to write and receive facts in detail. Samples are sent regularly to customers who desire to keep posted on the new patterns. THE INTER OCEAN can indorse the firm of J. G. Stolp & Son as being one of the oldest and best manufacturing houses in Illinois.

KENOSHA.

NORTHWESTERN WIRE MATTRESS CO.

AT KENOSHA.

Of many thriving interests in the city of Kenosha, perhaps the most notable is that of the Northwestern Wire Mattress Company. Their shops are very conveniently situated on the lake shore, so near the harbor and a track of the Chicago and Northwestern Railway as to require but little expense in handling and shipping material. Their lumber is mostly cut from the forests of Michigan, and brought here during the spring and summer months and allowed to season about one year before being put into the dry-kiln preparatory to use. Although the principal item of manufacture is woven-wire mattresses, there is an immense output of frames required by other manufacturers of mattresses throughout the country. None of the lumber goes to waste, as the remnants are made up into a variety of smaller articles. such as clothes-frames, towel-rollers, etc., making quite a catalogue. This company was established about seven years ago, and, beginning in a small way, has grown, under the direction and general oversight of the Hon. Z. G. Simmons, to be one of the largest factories of its kind. It is in contemplation by the management to erect, early in the coming year, a new factory, which will more than double its present large capacity.

MILWAUKEE.

PHOTOGRAPHS.

E. D. BANGS' ESTABLISHMENT.

One of the oldest and best established photograph galleries in Milwaukee, and the place where you can get the best pictures for the least money, is at E. D. Bangs', at 86 Wisconsin street. Parties from the country desirous of getting the best quality of cabinet photographs at prices that can't be equaled in the country towns should call at Bangs' gallery. The best grade of cabinet photographs furnished at $3.50 per dozen.

GOLDEN EAGLE CLOTHING HOUSE.

ELEGANT AND EXTENSIVE.

One of the most elegant in its appointments and extensive in the stock carried of the many clothing houses of this city is the Golden Eagle Clothing House, managed by R. T. Goodrich. There is not a citizen of Milwaukee who does not take pleasure in pointing out to visitors the Golden Eagle as the perfect clothing house. And, when it is considered that it is the handsomest and best lighted and furnished establishment of its kind in America and the largest in the Northwest, it will be seen that there is good reason for the pride taken in it. The fame of the Golden Eagle extends from the Atlantic to the Pacific, and none have done more to build up that fame than the Milwaukee branch of this immense clothing house.

JEWELRY, WATCHES, CLOCKS.

O. L. ROSENCRANS & CO.

The place to buy jewelry and watches and clocks of all the best manufacture is at O. L. Rosencrans & Co.'s, corner of Broadway and Wisconsin street, Milwaukee. The known reliability of the house is assurance enough that everything purchased is just as represented.

HARDWARE, SCROLL MATERAL, SAWS.

FRANKFURTH & CO., JOBBERS.

At Wm. Frankfurth & Co.'s, jobbers in hardware, at Milwaukee, everything in the line of scroll material, fancy wood saws, designs, etc., can be purchased. At this house a full assortment of Hobson's English choice cast steel is kept. In the stove line, Bramhell & Deener's French ranges, Monitor oil stoves, and all the other standard goods are kept. Frankfurth & Co.'s is the oldest and largest hardware jobbing house in Milwaukee, and you can find there everything that can be found in any other jobbing house in the United States, and something besides.

BUSINESS COLLEGE.

THE SPENCERIAN.

The Spencerian Business College, Milwaukee, R. C. Spencer, proprietor, is one of the oldest and best institutions of its kind, does thorough work, and is largely attended by both sexes. Circulars free to any address.

MAPS, SHOW CARDS, ETC.

SILAS CHAPMAN.

Silas Chapman, map publisher and manufacturer, 124 Grand avenue. Sectional maps of Wisconsin, Milwaukee County, city of Milwaukee, Douglas, Ashland, and Bayfield Counties, Menominee Iron Range, etc. Maps illustrated. Show cards, etc., mounted to order. Map estimates furnished free.

OSHKOSH.

CURE FOR CONSUMPTION.

OSHKOSH MEDICAL AND SURGICAL INFIRMARY.

There is located at Oshkosh, Wis., a medical institution called the Oshkosh Medical and Surgical Infirmary, chartered by the State, and owned and controlled by the London Medical Association, which is proving to be one of the most successful institutions of the kind ever established in the West. It is comparatively new, but its capital stock is $25,000, so that it has been able to supply itself with all the appliances and advantages to be found in any medical institution in the United States. The President of the institution is Dr. Kensington, and besides him five other physicians are connected with it. One of the leading features of the establishment is its laboratory for the manufacture of compound oxygen, that great remedy for consumption. The large force of physicians employed renders it possible to give home as well as office treatment. The wonderful cures effected, evidences of which can be found on file at the infirmary, prove it to be worthy of the patronage of the afflicted from all sections of this country. Patients from other States and different parts of Wisconsin can get board in private families while receiving treatment.

RACINE.

THE DICKEY FANNING MILLS,

RACINE, WIS.,

has one of the most enterprising manufacturing firms in the Northwest—Messrs. Dickey & Pease—who make a specialty of the celebrated "A. P. Dickey's" Fanning Mills, used in every part of the civilized world.

They also manufacture the "Acme" Dustless Grain Separators, bob-sleighs, and all kinds of agricultural implements. This house always turns out first-class goods.

WAUKEGAN.

POWELL & DOUGLAS.

CHAMPION WIND MILL.

One of the most enterprising manufacturers in the West is the firm of Powell & Douglas, Waukegan, Ill. They manufacture the world-renowned Champion Wind Mill. Their sales for this season has more than doubled over last. Where they have no one handling their mills they want a good agent. They also manufacture the Starwood Pumps, Boss Sickle Grinders, hunting and pleasure boats, keeping in stock the finest line of rowboats ever made in the United States. They also make to order sail and steam yachts. And any one that wishes any of these goods may write them for Catalogue A for wind mills and pumps, or Catalogue B for boats.

CHAPTER XII

CHEAPER GAS.

THE MONOPOLY BROKEN.

THE CONSUMERS' GAS, FUEL, AND LIGHT COMPANY COMMENCES BUSINESS.

Now that the Consumers' Gas, Fuel, and Light Company is an accomplished fact, demonstrated by the large amount of money invested in this commendable enterprise and also by the extensive character of the plant erected, it may not be amiss to impress upon the citizens of Chicago the necessity of supporting this company by their patronage, which, if tendered in the liberal manner characteristic of our people, must result in the future in the perpetual permanence of the price of gas now offered by the new company, thus proving another entering wedge in rending asunder the monstrous monopoly that has preyed upon the vitals of a powerless public by the systematic exaction of extortionate charges for a poor quality of gas, which has deteriorated from year to year until it has become almost valueless as a desirable illuminant.

THE INTER OCEAN, ever ready to encourage the formation of enterprises of public usefulness and benefit, and especially those that tend toward the disruption and breaking down of odious monopolies that have become enriched at the expense of the taxpayers already burdened with oppressive taxes.

TO WHOM CHICAGO OWES IT.

It is but just and proper that this journal should accord the meed of praise to the trio of gentlemen who inaugurated this grand enterprise, planning and projecting and constructing the immense buildings containing the latest improved devices and machinery for the production of pure gas, brilliant as the stars that stud the blue arched dome of heaven, manufactured by honest men with honest purposes at honest prices for honest consumers.

These gentlemen to whom we refer went to work with that becoming modesty which stamps with the sterling seal of genius all the noted men of the present age who loom up in the horizon of meritorious achievements as promoters of the public weal. They toiled and plodded without the adventitious aids of the press or the pleasing blare of trumpet-tongued commendation. Their only aim was to construct works which should benefit the citizensof a great and enterprising city, which should also in themselves attest the fact that the enterprise of furnishing cheap gas, pure gas, and luminous gas, should be indicative and prove as substantial and as permanent as the character of the plant erected under their skill, watchfulness, and direction.

The works erected are confessedly the largest and best constructed in America, not wanting in the slightest detail, and are a marvel of perfect engineering skill. They stand as a lasting monument to the energy, pluck, and genius of the construction company and will in future years be looked upon as the beacon light from which irradiated the welcome glare of a pure and cheap gas and the building of which shattered forever the deep laid schemes of a band of monopolists who endeavored to bind a free people with the shackles of an oppressive extortion.

THE OFFICERS.

The gentlemen to whom THE INTER OCEAN alludes are Messrs. M. S. Frost, Chairman; Henry Levis, Treasurer, and J. Edward Addicks, all of Philadelphia.

THE INTER OCEAN, not satisfied with its own expression of opinion and with a view to gauging the self-declared utterances of prominent business men, detailed a number of its representatives to ascertain the opinion of these gentlemen regarding the luminosity of the gas introduced by the Consumers' Gas, Fuel and Light Company, its practical value as an illuminant, the comparative merits of the old and new gas, and such other expressions as they desired to make relative to the benefits conferred upon the citizens by the new gas company in their laudable desire to furnish gas to the public at a reasonable and liberal price, and the relative attitude of the old and the new companies with reference to their status as conservators or destroyers of public tranquility, public expenditures and public happiness. We herewith append a partial list of the gentlemen interviewed, our space being too limited for the insertion of the opinions of all the gentlemen, who, taken at random, with singular unanimity heartily expressed with determined emphasis their earnest and honest convictions favorable to the new candidate for public favor and patronage.

MR. FRED EAMES.

Mr. Fred Eames, of the Commercial National Bank, was subjected to a number of queries propounded by the interviewer. In reply he said substantially that the citizens of Chicago were under deep obligations to the Consumers' Gas, Fuel and Light Company for saving to them in the aggregate millions of dollars, which, were it not for their competition, would otherwise have gone into the treasuries of the old companies to the detriment of the public. The company ought to be generously patronized, and he, as a representative of the bank, would extend to the new company his hearty support. A prompt and liberal extension of patronage would make it an utter impossibility for the old gas companies to gain any of the stock of the Consumers' Gas Company, and would insure cheap gas to the citizens perpetually. The citizens, he observed, were in duty bound to stand by the new company, which had inscribed around the halo of its light the motto of purity, brilliancy, and economy.

IRA HOLMES.

Ira Holmes, the well-known broker, No. 86 Washington street, courteously assented to the pumping process, which, having been vigorously utilized, elicited the views of the gentleman. He remarked that he was delighted with the new gas, as one burner gave as much light as three gas burners of the old company. He never saw such poor gas in his life as that furnished by the old monopoly during the past eight months. What surprised him was the fact that with competition staring the old monopolies in the face that they should have given the citizens such poor gas lately, which in his opinion was constantly deteriorating in luminosity. He understood that at present prices a fair profit could be realized by the gas companies on the capital invested, and he regarded it as a burning shame that the old monopoly should have been so devoid of conscience as to fasten its ravenous, insatiable teeth into the body of the public for so long a period in order to drain its life blood. He hailed with pleasure the advent of the Consumers' Gas, Fuel and Light Company, and should use their brilliant gas exclusively. He also said that the new gas does not freeze, which makes it invaluable to all. He had been annoyed by the freezing of the gas in the pipes of the old company connected with his premises. He had never in his experience been bothered with such poor gas as that furnished by the old concern, and in conclusion declared most emphatically that he would not take the old gas for nothing, even if he had to pay $3.75 per thousand for the gas of the Consumers' Company.

MR. WILLIS HOWE,

of the Palmer House, in response to the interrogatories of the knight of the Faber, observed that the new illuminant was in every respect a pleasing innovation and as much superior to the old gas as day is to night. The guests of his hostelry had come to him unsolicited, not knowing of the change made in the meters, and had commented favorably upon the brilliancy of the new gas light. In a number of the rooms guests were using one burner only, where formerly they had three and four burners lit. The gas was clearer whiter and of a denser illuminating power. He believed that the thanks of the community should be extended to the Consumers' Gas, Fuel, and Light Company for what they had done in bringing gas down to a reasonable figure and for affording the citizens the opportunity of supplying themselves with a better illuminant. The new company were satisfied with a fair interest upon the capital invested, had strangled an odious monopoly, ought to be liberally and earnestly supported, and had proven themselves to be in every sense of the word public benefactors. A number of citizens had come to him with the statement that their bills at $1 per thousand feet—the present price of the moribund monopoly—were larger than at the former price of $2.75 per thousand feet, charged prior to Nov. 1; or, in other words, while the gas was ostensibly $1 per thousand the bills at the end of the month showed an increase over former bills. In conclusion he said he was well pleased with the gas and its splendid illuminating power.

CHAPIN & GORE.

Mr. Carter, a member of this noted firm, was plied with pertinent queries regarding the value of the new gaslight. He fully corroborated Mr. Howe regarding the onerous increase of the monthly bills of the old monopoly. He declared that the reduction to $1 was simply a delusion and a snare, as his bill for the month of November charge for gas consumed at his residence was larger than when he paid the same company $3.25 per thousand feet, using as his family did the same quantity of gas. He was much pleased with the new light. It exceeded his expectations, and he for one was thankful that the conscienceless concern had been punctured through its peculiar vitals, viz.—its ill-gotten treasury. Mr. Bartis, the Secretary of the old company, when spoken to about the high price of gas and the Consumers' Gas, Fuel, and Light Company's intention to reduce gas to a nominal figure, laughed at the mention, saying his company had $1,000,000 as a reserve fund to fight and squelch their new competitors. The gas in his restaurant had never emitted so feeble and sickly a glare as at present, and they were anxious to get it out of their premises as soon as the Consumers' Gas Company made the connection with the new service pipe.

D. B. FISK & CO.

Mr. D. B. Fisk, of the famous wholesale millinery establishment, very courteously volunteered the information that the new gas had just been introduced, and from his slight observation regarded it as a better and much superior light. Its clearness and whiteness was particularly distinguishable. The old concern he considered, as an iron-clad monopoly which had imposed upon the public in various ways. He cited instances of gentlemen in his employment who by some oversight failed to pay their bills on the 12th of the month, and the usual discounts were not allowed to them, while others that he knew of where the bills had not been paid till a day or so following the 12th discounts were allowed. When remonstrated with the officers of the company said their rules were rigid and must be strictly adhered to, that they served one customer as they did all in a similar manner. They were clearly guilty of falsifying, and as a corporation were utterly irresponsible when their interests were at stake. The new enterprise he said, as far as he could learn, was composed of fair-dealing, reliable gentlemen, and on that account and also the further fact that they were furnishing a beautiful gas, and had made impossible the continued extortions of a selfish monopoly, that the Consumers' Gas Company had his warm encouragement.

S. W. ALLERTON,

of the firm of J. T. Lester & Co., Chamber of Commerce, and one of our leading citizens, did not desire to be interviewed. When informed that THE INTER OCEAN desired an expression of opinion relative to his impressions of the new gas, he good-naturedly responded to the interviewer that when the interests of the public were to be enhanced by a public enterprise he, as a citizen, felt in duty-bound to extend his individual encouragement and support. The new light placed in his mansion had evoked naught but praise from the members of his family and also from visitors; it was a clear, beautiful white light. He required the use of only one-half of the burners used formerly. Mr. Allerton further stated that he had intended a year ago to place a gas machine in his residence and give up the old gas because it had deteriorated in quality and luminosity constantly. The inception and opening up of the Consumers' Gas, Fuel, and Light Company had obviated the performance of this intention. The expenditure of gas was only half now under the new regime what it had formerly been. During November his gas bills had been as large at $1 per 1,000 as they were in November, 1882, when the price was $2.75. He was glad the monopoly had been so heavily sat upon by an enterprise composed of broad-gauged and public spirited citizens, and wound up his remarks by declaring with determined emphasis that the antiquated bubble now being pricked by the lash of public indignation was the damnedest robbing concern on the face of the earth.

AT THE MATSON HOUSE.

Messrs. Munger Brothers, of the Matteson House, manifested much enthusiasm in dilating upon the merits of the new light. They said it was all that it claimed to be, and certainly exceedingly satisfactory. Mr. L. J. Gage, the Vice President of the First National Bank, had been in the hotel and declared the new light a wonderful improvement. The antediluvian monopoly had so imposed upon them in furnishing so poor a gas at such extortionate prices, that they had been willing to burn tallow dips in their hotel if they could not obtain any other gas, rather than submit to the onerous exactions of a band of monopolists. Mr. Munger had spoken with the patriarchal President of the expiring monopoly some months ago with regard to the injustice of enforcing the high prices then charged. Mr. Watkins simply indulged in a boisterous fit of laughter, conveying by his conduct the impression that, like Robinson Crusoe, he was for the time being, "monarch of all he surveyed." Mr. Munger remarked that he would rather pay $2.75, the old price, to the new company than take the gas from the haughty monopolists at their present price.

MR. WARREN LELAND,

the urbane and courteous host of the famed Leland Hotel, gave his views, which are herewith presented for the edification of the readers of this journal. He proceeded to make a comparison regarding the new light and the old flicker, saying the old coal gas was a yellow glare, very trying to the eyes, smoky, and objectionable, while the new water gas was very white, clear, and had greater candle power and brilliancy. He claimed it to be brighter and better, and desirable as a perfect illuminant. As a financial enterprise he also asserted that it would prove a great success, and whenever I wish to make a profitable investment I desire nothing better than the stock of the Consumers' Gas, Fuel, and Light Company. I tried to make a contract with the old company for a number of years at their present price, but could not get their approval. The citizens must rely upon the new organization for pure, brilliant gas. He was satisfied that reliance would never be abused.

J. R. HOXIE,

one of the enterprising and wealthy citizens of Chicago was interviewed in his palatial mansion. He arose reluctantly from an afternoon siesta and graciously submitted to the wiles of the reportorial fiend. As far as his observation extended, he was satisfied that the new gas was a better illuminant by 200 per cent than the old production. The success of the Consumers' Gas, Fuel, and Light Company was now an established fact exceeding the most sanguine expectations of its projectors and stockholders. It had, he remarked, a combination of the wealthiest stockholders of any similar corporation either in Europe or America, and was already enabled to declare a dividend of 10 per cent upon its bonds and stock. He declared the old monopoly had proven faithless to the interests of the people, and he felt safe in asserting that 90 per cent of the business would ultimately be secured by the Consumers' Gas Company. The enterprise was the most beneficial to public interests ever started in Chicago, and he was glad that the public had demonstrated its unchangeable opposition to old fogyism by warmly supporting the new company.

R. P. MOULTON,

prominently identified with Chicago interests, and of the firm of Reyburn & Hunter, said that the new light was a welcome a..friendly addition to his household. He was fully conversant with its superior luminosity, having observed its workings in over sixty cities of America. In New York, Philadelphia, and Baltimore it had obtained the unstinted commendation of the citizens because of its phenomenal brilliancy and great candle power. The finest print could be read by the use of this light without blurring the eye. The use of the old yellow forky flicker dazed the eye and made reading unpleasant and undesirable.

The citizens had never had such poor gas in their lives as was furnished them by the old company. The bills were higher now than ever, because they had increased the pressure through the service pipes, forcing air into the meter, and increasing the register, which exhibited a quantity of gas that had not been consumed, but which the consumers were obliged to pay for all the same in order to satisfy the rapacious money-making desire of the monopolistic directors. In conclusion, he said the stock of the old company had gone down from 180 to 100 per share, which was the truest indication of the want of confidence manifested by the public at large.

MR. KINSLEY,

the noted restaurateur and caterer, responded to the questions propounded, which are herewith jotted down. He remarked that he noticed a perceptible difference of from 30 to 40 per cent in favor of the new light. The gas was beyond question the finest and best ever used in his restaurant. Mr. Watkins, the President of the old concern, had sent for him. He desired Mr. Kinsley to continue the use of the old gas, and was willing to make a contract for three years at $1.25 per 1,000, although they profess to furnish their gas to consumers at $1., Mr. Kinsley desired Mr. Watkins to make a contract for three years at their present price, which he refused. He was more than ever, since that interview, impressed with the belief that the old monopoly was a tricky concern, irresponsible and faithless. They would bear close watching. They had endeavored to play the freeze-out game but were themselves frozen. The citizens should compare their bills now and in the future and they would find a large-sized and ever-growing Ethiopian in the wood-pile.

MAHLER & GALES

on South Clark street, were next collared by the impetuous reporter and were asked for their opinion; as usual they confirmed what had been said by other citizens. The new gas gave splendid satisfaction, and was a welcome relief. Last month's bill of their firm had been exactly double that of November in 1882 although they were using the same quantity of gas. The old company were worse than highway robbers, because the one faced their victims boldly and demanded their purses, while this band of cormorants lifted the left hand to heaven in a prayerful and sanctimonious attitude while with the right hand they dove down deep into the pockets of their customers and took all they could legally get. Finishing his remarks Mr. Mahler said that rum-sellers are currently said to have no hearts. He was sure that the men who direct the affairs of the Shylock concern were ushered into existence without the faintest resemblance to that organ in their bodies.

W. S. EDEN,

the gentlemanly proprietor of the Palmer House and Tremont Hotel tonsorial and bathing palaces, accorded a prompt reply to the interviewer's inquisitiveness. He observed that one burner in the Tremont House had given as much light as three burners of the old company. The new gold ornamentations and frescoing of his parlors in the Palmer House had been discolored by the coal gas of the old company in ninety days, and it would prove a costly expenditure if he were obliged to use the yellow, smoky light that has disappeared from his establishment forever, thanks to the new company.

Mr. Gilman, of the Woodruff House, corner Twenty-first street and Wabash avenue, observed that the new gas is all that has been promised for it. He expressed gratification with the light, which he said was clear, steady, white, and soft to the eye. He used only one burner in the house where he had formerly used two, a saving of 100 per cent in his monthly bills. He had contemplated placing electric lights in his dining-room and other parts of the house previous to obtaining the new gas, but that was not necessary now, as the new light was a splendid illuminant, and gave him and his guests unbounded satisfaction.

Many more prominent citizens were interviewed, all of whom said in substance that the old monopoly had exhibited a grasping avariciousness and an utter disregard of public rights, which would put to blush Tweed's outrageous defiance of public opinion in his palmiest days.

CAPTAIN WILLIAM HENRY WHITE.

In according a proper share of praise for the creditable building of the plant and the seventy-five miles of main pipes THE INTER OCEAN omitted in the prefatory observations to this article to give credit to Captain William Henry White, engineer of the construction company, who was ably and efficiently assisted by his brother, Colonel C. A. White, present assistant engineer of the company. These gentlemen were indefatigable in their efforts, and may be said without doing injustice to others to have been master spirits in bringing the works to a successful completion. The officers of the company are C. E. Judson, President and Engineer; S. A. Stevens, Secretary and Treasurer; Jesse Hildrup, Vice President, and Colonel C. A. White, Assistant Engineer, all of whom are brilliant executive officers, and whose direction of the affairs of the company is a guarantee that private and public confidence will be more than realized during their administration of the Consumers' Gas, Fuel, and Light Company.

THE PRICE.

In bringing this article to a close, it may be of sufficient interest to the public to state that the price of gas of the new company is $1.25 per 1,000 feet, regardless of contracts made heretofore at an advanced figure.

The public must remember while noting the apparent difference in the price charged for gas by the two companies that the difference is fancied rather than real. The gas of the new company is much denser, and of much greater candle power than that of the old company. It is commercially much the cheapest gas.

Service pipes with meters and meter connections will be introduced free of expense.

The public may feel assured that they will be treated with politeness and due consideration in all cases from the employes of the company.

CHAPTER XIII.

THE PRODUCE TRADE.

THE PRODUCE TRADE.

NEVER IN THE HISTORY of the produce trade of the city of Chicago has the volume of business been attained as reported during the year 1883. The efforts made by our merchants to attract trade in this direction has been remarkably successful, and in the prosecution of the one object of their lives and the city's pride, they have been peculiarly surrounded, and in a great measure assisted, by very fortunate circumstances. The large emigration to the West and Northwest during the past five years has not been lost sight of, and as the great majority of the newcomers were farmers, a special effort was made to draw their attention to Chicago as a market for the products of their new farms. The acreage of land which has been developed in the country tributary to our market within the time specified has been unusually heavy, and in most instances occupied by actual settlers. The building of through lines and branches through these fertile avenues, by some of the leading railway corporations, has also been the means of increasing and enlarging the produce trade of the Northwest, and more particularly that of the Garden City. Another very fortunate circumstance was the favorable crop returns, especially of the smaller grains, which were secured in good condition, and in such quantities that producers were compelled to seek such a wholesale market as ours to dispose of their property promptly at satisfactory figures, or should the markets have been suddenly depressed, place them in our warehouses until a more favorable opportunity should be presented for disposing of it. No other city in this country is supplied with such MAGNIFICENT AND SUBSTANTIAL WAREHOUSES for the storage of grain—the capacity of which has been increased 1,000,000 bushels during the past year, and now reaches 26,200,000 bushels—and in no other market are storage rates more reasonable, and contingent expenses for handling and disposing of grain less burdensome. It may not be out of place here to state that the reliability and financial standing of the members of the produce trade has been improved in this respect—that more legitimate business has been transacted than ever before, and the "bucket-shop schemes" and "special fund swindles" are being gradually weeded out through the efforts of legitimate merchants and the enforcement of the laws by government officials. Again, the membership of the Chicago Board of Trade is virtually limited, and the transfers of membership privileges are almost exclusively from small unfortunate operators and non-traders to parties of financial standing and who have some influence in attracting trade—either in shipping or speculation—to our market. The number of firms engaged in all branches of the produce trade has been somewhat increased during the year, which was partially due to the enlarged movement of property, but more largely attributed to the growing mania for speculative investments. The recent favorable decisions of the courts—including the highest authority in the land—has had much to do with encouraging this mode of trading. The plan adopted by the Chicago Board of Trade, wherein it is declared to be the intention of the parties when the contracts are made to tender or receive such property, has also had a beneficial in checking reckless operators or small margins. The repeal of the "anti-corner" rule by that organization, too, has not led to the reckless and unscrupulous trading anticipated, and but one during the year was any unusual complaint made regarding extortionate prices, when an appeal to the courts apparently had a beneficial effect, though generally regarded as of doubtful expediency. It should be understood that deliveries on speculative contracts for produce are as freely made, proportionately as those calling for other property, and that the rules of all legitimate commercial organizations and the decisions of our courts sustain such contracts.

THE FACILITIES FOR FILLING speculative orders have been materially enlarged. Several of the leading houses have special private telegraph connections with the leading Eastern and Western markets, and others have established branch houses in the larger cities for the accommodation of their constantly growing trade. The grain markets have been very attractive to the speculative element, annd other branches of speculative trade have felt severe losses on this account—especially the stock market of Wall street. Our banking facilities are unsurpassed anywhere, and merchants in good standing experence no difficulty in obtaining financial favors, as their class of collaterals command the preference. The export trade during the year was fairly large, yet exhibited no particular increase. The orders from the foreign markets for grain have been moderate, while the inquiry from abroad for beef and hog products was somewhat increased. Our facilities for negotiating foreign exchange are equal to those of Eastern markets, and merchants meet with no inconvenience in disposing of their bills. The fluctuation in prices during the year partook of quite wide range, and in some instances resulted in temporary financial disturbances and suspension of houses engaged in speculative operations rather reckless in character. The early part of the year was apparently more favorable to holders of produce, and satisfactory prices were realized, but during the latter part of the year prices were on a declining scale. The reports of damage to the winter wheat crop early in the season led producers to believe that an unusual demand would prevail for that cereal, but while the final returns of the harvest showed quite a serious decrease in the returns, yet the spring wheat crop was an unusually good one, and this had the effect of weakening the market and

ACCUMULATING LARGE QUANTITIES OF WHEAT

in the principal markets of this country. The reports of the corn crop were favorable early, and lower prices were accepted, but the backwardness of the crop and the appearance of frost in the early autumn seriously affected the quality of the grain. The smaller grains were received in liberal quantities and in excellent condition. The supplies of live stock have been abundant and liberal numbers forwarded to our market. The production of other farm articles has been liberal.

An unfortunate misunderstanding between the representatives of the Eastern railroads and the officials of the Board of Trade caused the statistical movement of produce to be withheld from the public for about four months. This interfered greatly with compiling the returns for the year. These deficiencies have not been reported, yet sufficient data has been obtained by which an approximate idea of the movement of some of the leading articles can be had. It is sufficient, however, to say that the aggregate receipts of flour and grain—168.595,413 bushels—are

THE LARGEST ON RECORD,

while the shipments of the same articles—145,673,569 bushels—have been exceeded but once. There is little doubt, when the final returns are made, that the movement of all kinds of produce both to and from the city, will exhibit an unusually large volume.

PRODUCE STATISTICS.

AGGREGATE GRAIN MOVEMENT.

The following table exhibits the aggregate receipts and shipments of flour (reduced to bushels) and all kinds of grain at Chicago during the past ten years:

Year.	Received, bushels.	Year.	Shipped, bushels.
1874.......	95,611,713	1874.......	84,020,691
1875.......	81,087,302	1875.......	72,309,194
1876.......	97,735,482	1876.......	87,241,306
1877.......	94,416,399	1877.......	90,706,076
1878.......	134,086,595	1878.......	118,075,269
1879.......	138,154,571	1879.......	125,528,379
1880.......	165,855,370	1880.......	154,377,115
1881.......	145,020,829	1881.......	140,307,597
1882.......	126,146,483	1882.......	114,864,933
1883.......	168,595,413	1883.......	145,673,569

GRAIN CROPS.

The following are the final returns and estimates of the grain crops of the United States, with comparisons of former years, as given by the Department of Agriculture:

ARTICLE	1883.	1882.	1881.	1880.
Wheat...	420,100,000	502,789,000	380,280,090	498,549,868
Corn	*1,551,066,000	1,624,917,800	1,194,916,000	1,717,434,513
Oats.....	500,000,000	465,055,700	416,481,000	417,885,380
Barley...	44,000,000	45,000,000	41,161,330	45,165,316
Rye......	19,000,000	20,000,000	20,704,950	24,540,829
B'kwh't.	8,000,000	12,000,000	9,486,200	14,617,535

*This includes all qualities—sound and unsound corn.

MOVEMENT OF GRAIN, PROVISIONS, LIVE STOCK.

The following table exhibits the receipts and shipments of flour, grain, and live stock for two years:

ARTICLES.	RECEIPTS. 1883.	RECEIPTS. 1882.	SHIPMENTS. 1883.	SHIPMENTS. 1882.
Flour, brls.....	4,408,982	4,179,912	4,019,284	3,543,067
Wheat, bu.....	20,818,065	23,048,599	11,703,985	19,767,884
Corn, bu.......	74,459,948	49,061,775	71,198,890	49,073,609
Oats, bu.......	37,750,442	26,802,872	3[illegible],117,710	23,058,239
Rye, bu........	5,662,420	1,944,516	3,944,023	1,773,148
Barley, bu.....	10,591,619	6,488,140	7,718,508	3,298,252
Pork, brls.....	189,858,578	106,165,098	674,499,335	615,922,951
Cut meats, lbs.	53,698	78,895	400,552	435,625
Lard, lbs.......	70,921,782	49,096,384	246,720,866	235,473,520
Hogs, No.......	5,646,835	5,817,504	1,8[illegible]9,965	1,747,722
Cattle, No......	1,877,240	1,582,530	966,362	921,009
Sheep, No......	750,067	628,887	372,761	314,200

THE VISIBLE SUPPLY OF GRAIN.

The following table shows the visible supply of grain, comprising the stocks in granary at the principal points of accumulation at lake and seaboard ports, and in transit by rail and water (monthly) for the year 1883:

MONTHS.	Wheat.	Corn.	Oats.	Rye.	Barley.
January 6...	21,315,550	9,229,144	4,425,584	1,514,073	3,004,050
February 3..	22,289,[illegible]36	10,700,651	4,352,161	1,646,081	2,[illegible]57,709
March 3.....	23,8[illegible]2,271	13,645,6[illegible]	4,662,111	1,832,070	1,916,472
April 7.......	22,849,95	18,223,008	4,057,608	1,8[illegible]7,878	1,[illegible]98,[illegible]30
May 5........	20,707,249	16,168,568	1,677,1[illegible]3	1,784,097	1,020,900
June 2.......	20,[illegible]4,815	13,[illegible]93,546	3,988,577	1,741,274	[illegible]2[illegible],347
July 7........	18,598,493	1[illegible],336,529	3,70[illegible],1[illegible]7	1,712,609	398,299
August 4.....	18,750,986	10,917,788	3,[illegible]04,671	1,598,894	331,919
September 1.	21,404,798	11,337,814	4,190,[illegible]07	1,[illegible]27,831	271,102
October 6....	28,523,4[illegible]8	13,414,057	5,684,018	2,2[illegible]4,146	873,52[illegible]
November 3.	31,129,673	10,335,713	5,510,900	2,[illegible]58,881	2,366,884
December 1.	33,231,94[illegible]	8,621,995	5,912,447	2,509,808	3,503,466
December 2[illegible]	35,531,259	9,164,258	6,197,271	2,712,158	3,469,856

CASH PRICES.

THE RANGE.

The following table exhibits the opening, highest, lowest, and closing prices for the articles named (monthly) for the year 1883, compared with the highest and lowest in 1883:

NO. 2 SPRING WHEAT.

MONTHS.	1883. Opening	1883. Highest.	1883. Lowest.	1883. Closing.	1882. Highest.	1882. Lowest.
January	$ .93⅝	$1.03¾	$ .93⅝	$1.03¾	$1.36	$1.25¾
Feb'ary.	1.04½	1.11¼	1.04	1.08	1.32½	1.20¼
March..	1.08¾	1.09½	1.05	1.07½	1.32¼	1.20
April....	1.07¾	1.11⅝	1.02	1.11½	1.40	1.33
May.....	1.11½	1.13⅜	1.08	1.13	1.40	1.23
June.....	1.13½	1.13½	.98¾	1.01¼	1.35	1.25
July.....	1.00½	1.02¾	.98½	1.00⅞	1.36	1.25
August..	1.01	1.03⅜	.99¾	.99¾	1.34	.99
Sept'ber	.99¼	.99¼	.93	.95⅜	1.08	.97
October.	.96¼	.96¼	.90	.92¼	.96¾	.92¼
Nov'ber.	.93⅛	.98¾	.93⅛	.97⅝	.94½	.91¼
Dec'ber..	.96¾	.99¼	.94⅝	.94¾	.94¾	.91⅛

NO. 2 CORN.

MONTHS.	1883. Opening	1883. Highest.	1883. Lowest.	1883. Closing.	1882. Highest.	1882. Lowest.
January	.49¾	.70	.49¼	.56	.63½	.60¼
Feb'ary.	.55	.59	.54½	.50¾	.60⅝	.56¼
March..	.58	.59¼	.52⅝	.54½	.68½	.59¼
April....	.54¼	.55½	.50¾	.55½	.77¾	.69½
May.....	.55⅜	.56¾	.53¼	.56	.76⅞	.69
June....	.56	.57⅛	.50⅛	.50⅞	.75	.68½
July.....	.49⅞	.53	.47⅝	.50⅜	.81½	.74⅞
August..	.50¼	.53½	.49½	.50¼	.79¼	.74½
Sept'ber	.49	.52⅜	.47¾	.49⅜	.75	.57⅞
October.	.49¼	.49½	.46	.46⅝	.71½	.59
Nov'ber.	.47⅛	.57	.47⅛	.55¾	.72½	.64
Dec'ber..	.55	.62⅛	.54¼	.55¾	.61	.49¼

NO. 2 OATS.

MONTHS.	1883. Opening	1883. Highest.	1883. Lowest.	1883. Closing.	1882. Highest.	1882. Lowest.
January	.35¼	.38⅞	.35	.36⅞	.45⅛	.42½
Feb'ary.	.37¼	.41⅜	.37	.41	.43¼	.40¼
March..	.42	.43½	.39⅜	.40	.45½	.42
April....	.42	.43	.39½	.40	.52½	.45
May.....	.41	.42¾	.38¾	.39¼	.56⅝	.48
June....	.39½	.40⅞	.32	.32¾	.56	.48
July.....	.33¼	.36¼	.27⅛	.27½	.62	.52½
August..	.27⅞	.29	.25¾	.27	.59	.37
Sept'ber	.26	.28	.25	.27¾	.36½	.30½
October.	.27¾	.28⅜	.26¾	.27⅞	.35¾	.31⅝
Nov'ber.	.27¾	.31⅜	.27¾	.31	.39	.33⅝
Dec'ber..	.30⅝	.36⅛	.30¼	.32⅞	.41½	.34¾

NO. 2 RYE.

MONTHS.	1883. Opening	1883. Highest.	1883. Lowest.	1883. Closing.	1882. Highest.	1882. Lowest.
January	.67	.68	.57	.62	.98	.95
Feb'ary.	.63	.66	.63	.65	.95	.81
March..	.65½	.66¾	.57½	.58	.87	.81
April....	.58½	.61½	.56	.60⅛	.88½	.83
May.....	.61	.67	.61	.64½	.83	.77
June....	.64	.64	.55	.55	.76	.68
July.....	.55	.57½	.53	.56½	.75	.66
August..	.56½	.62	.56	.56	.68½	.65½
Sept'ber	.55½	.58	.54	.58	.66½	.57
October.	.56	.56	.53½	.55	.60	.57
Nov'ber.	.55	.58½	.55	.58½	.58½	.55½
Dec'ber..	.58	.60	.56½	.59	.58½	.57

NO. 2 BARLEY.

MONTHS.	1883. Open'g	1883. High't.	1883. Lowest	1883. Clos'g.	1882. High't.	1882. Lowest
January	.80	.85	.80	.82	1.08	1.03½
Feb'ary.	.82	.85	.80	.81	1.05	1.00
March..	.81	.81	.74	.76	1.05	1.00
April....	.76	.85	.75	.81	1.10	1.04
May.....	.81	.82	.78	.80	1.10	1.00
June....	....	....	....	....	1.00	.98
July.....	....	....	....	....	....	....
August..	.70	.70	.64½	.64½	.86	....
Sept'ber	.57	.65	.57	.62	.90	.79
October.	.60	.62	.59½	.60½	.87½	.81
Nov'ber.	.60	.66	.60	.66	.83½	.80
Dec'ber..	.67	.67	.63½	.65	.82	.78

MESS PORK.

MONTHS.	Open'g	High't.	Lowest	Clos'g.	High't.	Lowest
January	16.85	17.75	16.75	17.70	18.40	16.60
Feb'ary.	17.77½	18.30	17.75	18.22½	18.62½	16.75
March..	18.22½	18.35	17.90	18.30	17.37½	16.00
April....	18.27½	19.50	17.90	19.50	18.40	17.25
May.....	19.47½	20.15	19.00	19.27½	19.75	18.20
June....	19.25	19.25	15.87½	16.27½	21.75	19.45
July.....	15.87½	15.95	13.25	13.55	22.30	20.15
August..	13.25	13.37½	11.85	12.05	22.00	20.50
Sept'ber	12.05	12.10	10.20	10.50	22.35	19.12½
October.	10.62½	11.37½	10.20	10.27½	24.75	21.00
Nov'ber.	10.27½	13.10	10.25	13.10	21.50	16.75
Dec'ber.	12.75	14.87½	12.50	14.10	17.62½	17.00

LARD.

MONTHS.	Open'g	High't.	Lowest	Clos'g.	High't.	Lowest
January	10.30	10.95	10.12½	10.92½	11.30	10.90
Feb'ary.	11.07½	11.50	11.05	11.45	11.35	10.35
March..	11.45	11.45	11.00	11.42½	11.00	10.05
April....	11.40	11.72½	11.10	11.65	11.40	11.00
May.....	11.65	12.10	11.50	11.67½	11.45	11.17½
June....	11.67½	11.70	9.05	9.30	12.30	11.20
July.....	9.32½	9.32½	8.20	8.62½	12.95	12.00
August..	8.50	8.75	8.05	8.37½	12.45	12.12½
Sept'ber	8.32½	8.35	7.75	7.85	12.77½	11.15
October.	7.85	8.25	7.15	7.17½	13.10	11.30
Nov'ber.	7.22½	8.47½	7.22½	8.45	12.00	10.62½
Dec'ber..	8.22½	9.60	8.10	8.70	10.75	10.22½

SHORT RIB SIDES.

MONTHS.	Open'g	High't.	Lowest	Clos'g.	High't.	Lowest
January	8.60	8.90	8.52½	8.87½	9.20	8.45
Feb'ary.	8.95	9.75	8.95	9.75	9.40	8.90
March..	9.85	9.90	9.52½	9.87½	9.55	8.70
April....	9.87½	10.50	9.75	10.47½	10.25	9.55
May.....	10.40	10.75	9.97½	9.97½	11.20	10.15
June....	9.87½	9.90	7.95	8.15	12.60	10.90
July.....	8.20	8.20	6.75	7.20	12.95	12.20
August..	6.97½	7.12½	6.32½	6.35	13.60	13.35
Sept'ber	6.37½	6.50	5.60	5.75	14.25	13.25
October.	5.87½	7.12½	5.85	6.25	15.25	11.75
Nov'ber.	6.10	7.00	5.80	6.77½	11.75	8.75
Dec'ber.	6.50	7.40	6.50	7.10	9.15	8.60

YEARLY RANGE OF PRICES.

The following table exhibits the extreme range of cash prices for nine years of the articles named:

YEAR.	Wheat.	Corn.	Oats.	Mess pork.	Lard.
1883.....	.90 @1.13½	46 @70	25 @43½	$10.20 @20.15	$7.15 @12.10
1882.....	.91⅛@1.40	49¼@81½	30½@62	16.00 @24.75	10.05 @13.10
1881.....	.95¾@1.43¼	35¾@76⅜	29½@47¾	12.40 @20.00	8.37½@13.00
1880.....	.86½@1.32	31½@43¾	22½@35	9.37½@19.00	6.35 @ 8.75
1879.....	.81⅝@1.33½	29½@49	19½@36¾	7.30 @13.75	5.32½@ 7.85
1878.....	.77 @1.14	29⅞@43½	18 @27½	6.02½@11.45	5.32½@ 7.40
1877.....	$1.01½@1.76½	38⅛@57½	22 @45¼	11.40 @17.95	7.55 @11.55
1876.....	.83 @1.26¾	38⅝@49	27 @35	15.12½@22.72½	9.35 @13.90
1875.....	.83¼@1.31	46 @76¾	29½@63	17.70 @23.50	11.80 @15.75

ELEVATOR CAPACITY.

THE VARIOUS ELEVATORS IN CHICAGO.

The following table exhibits the grain elevator capacity of the city of Chicago at the present time:

Name of elevator.	Capacity, bu.
Central elevator A	1,000,000
Central elevator B	1,500,000
C., B. and Q. elevator A	1,250,000
C., B. and Q. elevator B	850,000
C., B. and Q. elevator C	1,750,000
C., B. and Q. elevator D	2,000,000
C., B. and Q. elevator E	1,000,000
Rock Island elevator A	1,500,000
Rock Island elevator B	1,250,000
Galena elevator	750,000
Air Line elevator	750,000
Northwestern elevator	600,000
Fulton elevator	300,000
City elevator	1,000,000
Union elevator	700,000
Iowa elevator	1,500,000
St. Paul elevator	1,000,000
Illinois River elevator	200,000
National elevator	1,000,000
Chicago and St. Louis elevator	1,000,000
Neely's elevator	600,000
Chicago and Danville elevator	350,000
Chicago and Pacific elevator	1,000,000
Wabash elevator	1,750,000
Western Indiana elevator	1,500,000
Total capacity	26,200,000

TRADE RULES.

GRAIN INSPECTION RULES.

The following are the rules adopted by the Board of Railroad and Warehouse Commissioners establishing a proper number and standard of grades for the inspection of grain, as revised by them, the same in force on and after the 1st day of September, 1883, in lieu of all rules on the same subject heretofore existing:

WINTER WHEAT.

No. 1 white winter wheat shall be pure white winter wheat, or red and white mixed, sound, plump, and well cleaned.

No. 2 white winter wheat shall be white winter wheat, or red and white mixed, sound, and reasonably clean.

No. 3 white winter wheat shall include white winter wheat, or red and white mixed, not clean and plump enough for No. 2, but weighing not less than fifty-four pounds to the measured bushel.

Rejected white winter wheat shall include white winter wheat, damp, musty, or from any cause so badly damaged as to render it unfit for No. 3.

No. 1 long red winter wheat shall be pure red winter wheat of the long-berried varieties; sound, plump, and well cleaned.

No. 2 long red winter wheat shall be of the same varieties as No. 1, sound and reasonably cleaned.

Turkish Red Winter Wheat—The grades of Nos. 1 and 2 Turkish red winter wheat shall correspond with the grades of Nos. 1 and 2 red winter wheat, except that they shall be of the Turkish variety.

No. 1 red winter wheat shall be pure red winter wheat of both light and dark colors of the shorter-berried varieties; sound, plump, and well cleaned.

No. 2 red winter wheat shall be red winter

wheat of both light and dark colors, sound, and reasonably clean.

No. 3 red winter wheat shall include red winter wheat not cleaned and plump enough for No. 2, but weighing not less than fifty-four pounds to the measured bushel.

Rejected red winter wheat shall include red winter wheat, damp, musty, or from any cause so badly damaged as to render it unfit for No. 3.

In case of the mixture of red and white winter wheat, it shall be graded according to the quality thereof and classed as white winter wheat.

SPRING WHEAT.

No. 1 hard spring wheat shall be sound, plump, and well cleaned.

No. 2 hard spring wheat shall be sound, reasonably clean, and of good milling quality.

No. 1 spring wheat shall be sound, plump, and well cleaned.

No. 2 spring wheat shall be sound, reasonably clean, and of good milling quality.

No. 3 spring wheat shall include all inferior, shrunken, or dirty spring wheat, weighing not less than fifty-three pounds to the measured bushel.

Rejected spring wheat shall include spring wheat damp, musty, grown, badly bleached, or for any other cause which renders it unfit for No. 3.

In case of the mixture of spring wheat and winter wheat, if equal or superior to No. 2, it shall be graded as mixed wheat, according to the quality thereof, and if inferior to No. 2 it shall be graded as spring wheat, according to the quality thereof.

Black sea and flinty Fife wheat shall in no case be inspected higher than No. 2, and rice wheat no higher than rejected.

CORN.

No. 1 yellow corn shall be yellow, sound, dry, plump, and well cleaned.

No. 1 white corn shall be white, sound, dry, plump, and well cleaned.

No. 1 corn shall be sound, dry, plump, and well cleaned, white and yellow, unmixed with red.

High mixed corn shall be three-quarters yellow, and equal to No. 2 in condition and quality.

No. 2 corn shall be dry, reasonably clean, but not plump enough for No. 1.

No. 2 kiln-dried corn shall be sound, plump, and well cleaned, white or yellow. All kiln-dried corn not good enough for No. 2 kiln-dried shall be graded as rejected kiln-dried corn.

New high mixed corn shall be three-fourths yellow, of any age, reasonably dry and reasonably clean, but not sufficiently dry for high mixed or No. 2.

New mixed corn may be less than three-fourths yellow, of any age, and shall be reasonably dry and reasonably clean, but not sufficiently dry for No. 2.

Rejected—All damp, dirty, or otherwise badly damaged corn shall be graded as rejected.

OATS.

No. 1 oats shall be white, sound, clean, and reasonably free from other grain.

No. 2 white oats shall be seven-eighths white and equal to No. 2 in all other respects.

No. 2 oats shall be sweet, reasonably clean, and reasonably free from other grain.

Rejected—All oats damp, unsound, dirty, or from any other cause unfit for No. 2 shall be graded as rejected.

This rule shall be in force on and after Sept. 1, 1883, but it is provided that all oats in store on said date, inspected in under the rule hereby amended, shall be inspected out in accordance with the provisions of said rule in force when inspected in.

RYE.

No. 1 rye shall be sound, plump, and well cleaned.

No. 2 rye shall be sound, reasonably clean, and reasonably free from other grain.

Rejected—All rye damp, musty, dirty, or from any cause unfit for No. 2, shall be graded as rejected.

BARLEY.

No. 1 barley shall be plump, bright, clean, and free from other grain.

No. 2 barley shall be sound, of healthy color, not plump enough for No. 1, reasonably clean, and reasonably free from other grain.

No. 3 barley shall include slightly shrunken and otherwise slightly damaged barley, not good enough for No. 2.

No. 4 barley shall include all barley fit for malting purposes, not good enough for No. 3.

No. 5 barley shall include all barley which is badly damaged, or from any cause unfit for malting purposes, except that barley which has been chemically treated shall not be graded at all.

Scotch Barley—The grades of Nos. 1, 2, and 3 Scotch barley shall correspond in all respects with the grades of Nos. 1, 2, and 3 barley, except that they shall be of the Scotch variety.

This rule shall be in force on and after Sept. 1, 1883, but it is provided that all barley in store on said date, inspected in under the rule hereby amended, shall be inspected out in accordance with the provisions of said rule.

RULE VII.

The word "new" shall be inserted in each certificate of inspection of a newly harvested crop of oats until the 15th of August, of rye until the 1st day of September, of wheat until the 1st day of November, and of barley until the 1st day of May, of each year. This change shall be construed as establishing a new grade for the time specified, to conform in every particular to the existing grades of grain, excepting the distinctions of "new" and "old."

RULE VIII.

All grain that is warm, or that is in a heating condition, or is otherwise unfit for warehousing, shall not be graded.

RULE IX.

All inspectors shall make their reasons for grading grain when necessary, fully known by notations on their books. The weight alone shall not determine the grade.

RULE X.

Each inspector is required to ascertain the weight per measured bushel of each lot of wheat inspected by him, and note the same on his book.

CHARGES FOR INSPECTION.

The said Chief Inspector is hereby authorized to collect, on and after July 1, 1883, on all grain inspected under his directions, as follows:

For In-inspection—35c per car-load, 10c per wagon or cart-load, 50c per 1,000 bushels from canalboats, ¼c per bushel from bags.

For Out-inspection—50c per 1,000 bushels to vessels, 35 cents per car-load to cars, 35c per car-load to teams, or 10c per wagon load to teams.

GRAIN INSPECTION.

RECEIVED BY RAIL.

The following table exhibits the inspection of the grain received by rail during the year 1883, compiled from the records of the Chief Inspector:

MONTHS.	WINTER WHEAT—CARS. No. 1 white.	No. 2 white.	No. 1 red.	No. 2 red.	No. 1 long red.	No. 2 long red.	No. 2 winter.	No. 3 winter.	Rejected.	No. Grade.	Total.
January	....	....	1	228	....	3	......	464	268	26	990
February	....	....	....	137	....	8	......	149	160	14	468
March	....	....	....	109	....	2	......	236	148	6	501
April	....	....	....	67	....	....	......	90	53	8	218
May	....	....	....	57	....	....	......	86	63	8	214
June	....	....	1	123	....	....	......	165	70	3	362
July	....	....	7	204	....	5	......	193	93	25	527
August	1	6	19	794	1	9	......	1,020	733	75	2,664
September	....	13	6	770	....	....	......	1,293	906	113	3,101
October	....	3	2	366	....	2	......	388	372	36	1,169
November	....	2	....	102	....	....	......	165	203	27	499
December	....	2	....	122	....	....	......	162	126	15	427
Total	1	26	36	3,079	1	29	......	4,417	3,195	356	11,140
Total, 1882	174	....	620	15,603	290	982	443	6,337	2,468	387	27,214
Total, 1881	....	....	4	536	....	12	103	974	516	54	2,098
Total, 1880	32	16	114	7,552	43	529	469	4,297	1,041	140	14,243
Total, 1879	174	554	406	5,593	17	477	1,079	3,302	682	148	12,432

MONTHS.	SPRING WHEAT—CARS. No. 1 hard.	No. 2 hard.	No. 2 mixed.	No. 3 mixed.	Rejected mixed	No. 1.	No. 2.	No. 3.	Rejected.	No. Grade.	Total.
January	....	32	....	....	....	3	607	405	98	2	1,147
February	....	4	1	....	....	1	394	354	94	5	853
March	....	37	....	....	....	....	616	510	223	13	1,401
April	....	18	9	....	....	....	470	410	100	9	1,016
May	....	1	7	....	....	....	594	360	93	5	1,060
June	....	3	8	....	....	3	1,060	651	147	18	1,890
July	....	......	....	....	....	....	547	306	94	4	952
August	....	......	4	....	....	21	879	484	158	17	1,563
September	....	15	14	....	....	39	3,721	1,429	185	46	5,4[illegible]8
October	....	59	14	....	....	21	3,915	1,342	204	20	5,577
November	....	261	8	....	....	12	3,664	1,359	247	16	5,567
December	....	907	14	....	....	3	3,918	1,442	214	20	6,518
Total	....	1,337	79	....	....	103	20,485	9,052	1,857	175	32,990
Total, 1882	31	570	36	....	....	233	9,713	7,950	2,632	254	21,419
Total, 1881	1	2,319	169	....	....	24	15,413	8,793	3,794	686	31,222
Total, 1880	1	3,442	376	138	32	81	22,842	9,294	3,224	664	40,094
Total, 1879	8	3,877	376	645	130	54	29,820	26,300	7,321	1,153	69,684

MONTHS.	RYE—CARS. No. 1.	No. 2.	Rejected.	No grade.	Total.
January	1	272	69	6	348
February	7	260	79	1	347
March	2	468	96	3	569
April	....	173	45	....	218
May	5	403	174	1	583
June	5	574	193	7	779
July	4	276	141	29	450
August	35	1,521	395	50	2,001
September	18	1,708	359	38	2,123
October	2	1,185	207	4	1,398
November	3	850	168	2	1,023
December	1	665	155	3	824
Total	83	8,355	2,081	144	10,663
Total, 1882	79	2,557	1,114	122	3,872
Total, 1881	48	1,925	531	31	2,535
Total, 1880	117	2,784	603	27	3,531
Total, 1879	352	4,280	666	90	5,358

MONTHS.	CORN—CARS. Yellow.	White.	No. 1.	High mixed.	No. 2.	New H. mixed.	New mixed.	Rejected.	No. grade.	Total.
January	1	....	....	123	1,869	628	4,317	1,876	309	9,623
February	....	....	....	97	1,311	754	3,220	2,679	731	8,792
March	1	....	....	211	3,092	771	3,703	2,409	659	10,792
April	....	....	....	196	2,107	393	1,802	806	97	6,461
May	....	....	....	590	3,435	250	1,085	1,698	151	7,209
June	1	....	2	1,413	6,723	369	884	4,439	688	13,519
July	....	....	....	897	4,464	37	261	5,476	620	11,765
August	8	....	....	2,1[illegible]9	7,638	8	10	7,822	539	11,164
September	13	....	....	2,289	7,974	......	......	9,283	103	19,663
October	9	....	....	1,584	4,739	......	1	6,368	44	12,745
November	3	....	....	1,169	2,843	3	323	4,260	157	8,758
December	....	....	....	330	2,420	114	2,094	3,037	1,192	9,187
Total	36	....	2	11,038	48,615	3,273	17,760	50,153	5,290	136,167
Total, 1882	8	....	3	11,936	32,710	1,992	9,296	33,213	1,889	91,047
Total, 1881	18	....	2	19,801	59,608	2,949	8,022	46,743	4,973	143,986
Total, 1880	68	....	16	37,149	119,738	3,416	8,646	12,510	318	181,861
Total, 1879	100	1	82	35,024	71,483	3,557	5,581	6,956	281	123,065

MONTHS.	OATS—CARS. No. 1.	No. 2 white.	No. 2.	Rejected.	No. grade.	Total.
January	....	385	535	794	16	1,730
February	....	501	453	946	28	1,928
March	8	650	635	1,245	55	2,593
April	....	558	441	1,043	46	2,088
May	1	814	563	1,441	38	2,857
June	3	1,392	1,090	1,477	60	4,022
July	....	941	733	1,271	38	2,983
August	11	1,631	1,069	1,528	100	4,339
September	11	2,099	1,387	1,099	30	4,626
October	8	1,849	1,310	1,047	19	4,233
November	5	1,374	1,204	1,253	15	3,851
December	....	680	1,268	886	15	2,849
Total	47	12,874	10,688	14,030	460	38,099
Total, 1882	24	6,736	7,522	16,620	585	31,493
Total, 1881	70	8,467	8,891	9,109	216	26,643
Total, 1880	201	10,583	6,498	6,808	144	24,194
Total, 1879	90	7,273	6,795	4,480	188	18,826

MONTHS.	BARLEY—CARS. No. 1.	No. 2.	No. 3.	No. 4.	No. 5.	No grade.	Total.	Total of all grains—Cars.
January	....	5	769	152	32	13	971	24,309
February	....	8	770	248	30	13	1,069	13,457
March	....	4	652	256	18	19	949	16,805
April	....	3	439	156	14	8	620	10,621
May	....	......	323	142	9	13	487	12,410
June	....	......	156	90	10	2	258	20,830
July	....	1	39	27	9	3	79	16,746
August	....	18	92	31	5	5	151	28,882
September	....	311	857	250	22	18	1,458	36,418
October	....	577	1,620	414	44	10	2,665	27,785
November	....	262	1,185	388	27	4	1,866	21,564
December	....	168	1,169	285	15	3	1,640	21,445
Total	....	1,357	8,071	2,439	235	111	12,213	241,272
Total, 1882	....	599	5,520	3,251	479	96	9,945	184,993
Total, 1881	7	495	3,330	2,790	462	52	7,129	212,714
Total, 1880	19	783	3,147	3,236	486	99	7,760	271,683
Total, 1879	1	806	4,357	3,059	669	80	8,972	338,337

The inspection of grain received by the Illinois and Michigan Canal and by lake during the year 1883 was as follows: Wheat—5,430 bu No. 3 spring. Corn—110,100 bu high mixed, 375,500 bu No. 2, 3,800 bu new high mixed, 1,351,000 bu rejected, 49,000 bu no grade. Oats—131,600 bu No. 2 white, 302,600 bu No. 2, 78,500 bu rejected, 9,000 bu no grade. Rye—68,200 bu No. 2, 34,000 bu rejected, 6,000 bu no grade. Barley—20,463 bu No. 2.

RATES OF COMMISSIONS.

FOR RECEIVING AND SELLING.

The following are the rates of commissions adopted by the Chicago Board of Trade for receiving and selling and accounting for consignments of the property named:

CASH PROPERTY.

For selling car-load lots of wheat and rye in store, free on board cars or vessels, on track, delivered, or to be shipped from any other point, 1c per bushel.

For selling car-load lots of corn and oats in store, ½c per bushel.

For selling corn by sample, on track, 1c per bushel.

For selling car-load lots of oats, free on cars or vessels, on track, delivered, or to be shipped from any other point, 1c per bushel.

For selling car-load lots of barley in store, 1c per bushel.

For selling car-load lots of barley, free on board cars or vessels, on track, delivered, or to be shipped from any other point, 1½c per bushel.

For selling canalboat loads of grain in store or afloat or free on board vessels, ½c per bushel.

For selling flaxseed in bulk, 1c per bushel.

For selling flaxseed in bags, 1½c per bushel.

For selling clover seed in car-load lots, 1 per cent.

For selling clover seed in less than car-load lots, 1½ per cent.

For selling timothy seed, 1½ per cent.

For selling other seeds, 2 per cent.

For selling dressed hogs in car-load lots, 1½ per cent.

For selling dressed hogs in less than car-load lots, not less than 1½ per cent nor to exceed 2½ per cent.

For selling, bran, shorts, and millstuffs, $3.50 per car.

For selling corn meal and mixed feed, $5 per car.

For selling broom corn, ½c per ℔.

For the purchase and shipment of lard, pork and other meats, ½ of 1 per cent.

SPECULATIVE TRANSACTIONS.

In cases where the transaction is made by order or for account of parties who are not members of the association:

For the purchase and sale of property in the Chicago market:

On all kinds of grain in lots of 5,000 bushels or more, ¼ of 1c per bushel.

On lard in lots of 250 tierces or more, 10c per tierce.

On mess pork in lots of 250 barrels or more, 5c per barrel.

On other meats in lots of 50,000 pounds or more, ½ of 1 per cent.

In cases where the transaction is made by order or for account of parties who are members of the association, the minimum charge shall be one-half the above rates, to wit:

For the purchase and sale of property in the Chicago market:

On all kinds of grain in lots of 5,000 bushels or more, ⅛ of 1c per bushel.

On lard in lots of 250 tierces or more, 5c per tierce.

On mess pork in lots of 250 barrels or more, 2½c per barrel.

On other meats, in lots of 50,000 ℔s or more, ¼ of 1 per cent.

For the purchase and shipment by vessel cargo:

On wheat, rye, and barley, ½ of 1c per bushel.

On other grain, ¼ of 1c per bushel.

For the purchase and shipment by rail:

On grain of all kinds, ½ of 1c per bushel.

For the purchase and shipment of lard, mess pork, and all other meats, ½ of 1 per cent.

For brokerage where the name of the principal is given the day on which the transaction is made, and the broker therefore ceases to be considered as the principal:

On all kinds of grain, 25c per 1,000 bushels.

On lard, 1c per tierce.

On mess pork, ½ of 1c per barrel.

On other meats, 3c per 1,000 ℔s.

FLOUR AND GRAIN.

FLOUR.

The flour trade in this city has not been as satisfactory in point of volume as last year, still a very fair aggregate trade has been transacted, and dealers generally feel satisfied with the year's business. Had the export demand been as general as during the year 1882, trade would have been highly satisfactory, but this has been lacking more or less throughout the entire year, and merchants have been compelled to rely upon the home trade to a considerable extent, which has been good. The Canadian trade relieved the dullness to some extent, still the market on the whole has lacked life and activity. Of course there were spasmodic spurts of activity when indications seemed favorable for continued good trade, but for some reason the market would relapse into dullness without developing any life, and while there has been more or less demand all the while, trade has been mostly of a slow and dragging nature. The reason for this has been that European markets have been well stocked with flour throughout the year. At the close of the year 1882, the foreign markets all carried pretty liberal stocks, and these instead of decreasing have increased, so that the European Continental trade has been drawing on its own supplies more than in former years. The export orders received have been mainly for special grades and brands well known to the trade in foreign markets. For instance, merchants abroad having an established trade for a certain class of choice flour possessing strength and good color, would send special orders calling for this or that grade or brand direct and such orders would occasionally comprise large lots. Russian, Mediterranean, and India wheat have been so much cheaper than formerly, owing to abundant supplies, that European millers have been able to supply the English and Continental trade during a large portion of the year with flour at lower prices than American flour could be sold at without loss to millers, thus precluding American competition for the time being. But the improved machinery for milling, and fine wheat to be had, enables American millers to produce a quality of flour which cannot be surpassed, and which commends itself to the world, even though the price may be, figuratively speaking, higher than European makes, and a certain amount always finds sale in all foreign marts. American millers have consigned a good deal of flour to European markets; in fact some of the mills have built up a regular trade by educating themselves to the wants of the Europeans, and are making flours especially adapted to their particular wants. As a rule, however, there has been less encouragement the past year to ship abroad, and yet the amount of consigned flour has been large. This mode of SHIPPING PROMISCUOUSLY TO FOREIGN MARKETS has in some instances proved rather unsatisfactory. One reason for this is that wheat in the Chicago market is kept above a shipping margin by excessive speculation, and when above its legitimate value for shipment to other points it naturally is too high for the milling interest. When wheat is held high in the Chicago market it is also generally high at all points tributary to Chicago, and so it is not alone the Chicago millers that have to suffer, but interior millers as well. The Canadian trade has been better, and promises favorable during the balance of the season. This is owing to the partial failure of the Canadian wheat crop, and notwithstanding there is an import tax of 50c on every barrel of flour imported into Canada the trade has been good. The demand has been chiefly for the lower grades, though some good stock was also taken—including choice spring wheat bakers' flours. The Southern trade has been smaller than usual, although this trade with Chicago has been on the decrease for several years, other sources evidently having developed from which to draw supplies. The local trade has been very good, a steady demand coming from this source. Jobbers have complained somewhat of doing less business, but this was only in exceptional cases, and can be attributed to an increased number of firms entering the jobbing trade, besides other channels of distribution, thus causing a more scattered business. The family trade has centered in spring wheat patents, winter wheat patents, and winter wheat straights. The difference in cost between spring wheat patents and winter wheat straights has varied from 50c to $1 per barrel, and as winter wheat straights have been the cheaper of the two, the local family trade has catered chiefly to these. The city milling interest forms a very important feature of this market. There are now two mills running in this city day and night, whose aggregate production for the past year was about 350,000 barrels. A large share of this manufacture has found a market in foreign lands, and a portion has been taken for home consumption. And while speaking of the city mills it would not be out of place to state that another mill is in course of erection, the daily capacity of which will be 500 barrels per day. This mill, like the others, will also be supplied with all the new and improved machinery, thus giving Chicago a milling capacity of about 1,800 to 2,000 barrels per day, if taxed to full capacity. The stock of flour on hand at the opening of the year 1883 was reported at 80,217 barrels, and this was the largest amount on hand at any time during the year. The smallest stock in store was in October, when it was reported at 38,074 barrels. At the close of the year the stack was about 43,000 barrels. The year opened with choice to fancy winter wheat flours selling at $4.75 to $5.40, good to choice Minnesota straights at $4.50 to $5.25, and patents at $5.75 to $7. Until June the market ruled firm, when winters sold up to $5.50 to $6.25, Minnesota to $5 to $5.75, and patents to $6.50 to $7.50, but during the last half prices eased off to $4.50 to $5.65 for winters, $4.50 to $5.25 for Minnesotas, and $5.90 to $6.50 for patents. Rye flour has ruled lower the past year under free offerings, and sold within the range of $3 to $4 per barrel, and as low as $2.65 to $2.85 a sack.

The following table exhibits the closing figures for the years named:

	1883.	1882.	1881.	1890.
Winters........	$4.75@5.65	$4.00@5.50	$6.50@7.25	$4.50@6.00
West'n spring.	4.00@5.00	2.50@5.50	4.50@7.00	4.00@5.25
Minn. spring..	4.50@5.50	4.00@6.00	4.50@7.25	4.50@6.25
Patents.........	5.80@6.50	5.75@7.00	7.00@8.50	6.00@7.25
Low grades....	2.25@3.50	2.00@3.50	3.25@4. 5	2.25@4.50

For the first time in several years flour has again been consigned from Colorado to Chicago, several shipments having been made during the last few months.

The exports from the United States for the year 1883 aggregated about 9,000,000 brls., against 7,200,000 brls. for the year 1882.

The following table shows the quantities of flour manufactured in this city during the past ten years:

Year.	Brls.	Year.	Brls.
1874	244,668	1879	285,904
1875	249,653	1880	270,000
1876	271,074	1881	250,000
1877	293,244	1882	305,000
1878	308,284	1883	358,000

The following table exhibits the receipts and shipments of flour at Chicago during the past ten years:

RECEIVED.		SHIPMENTS.	
Year.	Brls.	Year.	Brls.
1874	2,666,679	1874	2,306,576
1875	2,625,883	1875	2,285,113
1876	2,955,197	1876	2,644,838
1877	2,691,142	1877	2,482,305
1878	3,030,562	1878	2,779,640
1879	3,369,958	1879	3,090,540
1880	3,215,389	1880	2,862,737
1881	4,815,219	1881	4,499,743
1882	4,179,912	1882	3,843,067
1883	4,403,982	1883	4,019,234

WINTER WHEAT.

Early in the year trade was restricted somewhat by the very limited offerings. The demand was good and the feeling was strong, which was attributed principally to the unfavorable advices regarding the growing crop. No. 2 red sold at the opening of the year at 95c, and advanced in February to $1.13, but again eased off and in April sold down to $1.05. As crop advices continued unfavorable the market again took an upward course, and by the last of May and the 1st of June sold up to $1.15 to $1.16. The advance was stimulated largely by the active speculation which prevailed in regular No. 2 wheat, winter wheat sympathizing to a great extent. In June the market commenced to react, and take a downward course, prices declining, reaching $1.04 to $1.06 during the first half of July. This decline was due largely to the reaction in the speculative market, and also to the more general belief that the shortage of the crop had been greatly overestimated. Early in August, when the new crop commenced to move more freely, sales were being made at $1.06 to $1.07½, and from that advanced to $1.10. In September, however, prices reached 98c, and in October 96c to 97c, advancing later on to $1.03 to $1.05. During the last few months of the year sold within within 96c to $1.02 and closed quiet. Trade has, on the whole, been very good, though less than during the year 1882, which would be natural considering the large shortage of the comparative crops of the years 1882 and 1883. A steady shipping and fair milling demand has existed. The speculative demand was good about the time the new crop was beginning to move and for a while thereafter, but during the last quarter no speculation existed.

WHEAT.

That speculation has been more active in this market than during the year 1882 must certainly be admitted, and can be accounted for from several reasons. In the first place, the influences presented during the year were such as to create and stimulate a desire for speculation. Then again the trading in No. 2 wheat, which allows the delivery of either No. 2 spring or No. 2 red winter on contracts, and which was not in force until the last half of the year 1882, gave dealers more confidence to trade without so great a likelihood of becoming involved in a squeeze or being cornered. This led to free trading, so that speculation during the year has been carried on with unrestrained freedom, frequently to excess, either in buying or selling, which led to bad results. In reviewing this market for the past year, many important features and points of interest are brought to memory. From the opening to the close of the year the course of the market has been one of great uncertainty, and many operators have been badly misled, not alone by their own calculations, for such an occurrence is nothing unusual, but principally by statistical information, both of an official character and otherwise. The short crop theorists no doubt suffered severely financially. Estimates of the wheat crop as early as there was any possible chance to give them were made, setting forth a shortage of 100,000,000 bu to 125,000,000 bu, as compared with the official crop returns of the year 1882. How badly operators were misled by placing too much confidence in crop reports can best be told by those who stubbornly adhered to the short crop theory to the last. The final estimates placed the crop of 1883 at 420,000,000 bu, against the returns of 503,000,000 bu of 1882, which would give a shortage of 83,000,000 bu. While perhaps there was a large shortage of winter wheat, estimated from 75,000,000 to 100,000,000 bu, the spring wheat yielded better than anticipated. Then, again, many operators overlooked the fact of liberal stocks of old wheat remaining in the interior and at the principal markets both at home and abroad. But the various views and opinions on this subject gave ample opportunities for speculation, and the more diversified the opinions and views of operators the larger the trading. The continual disparaging tenor of advices concerning the condition of the winter wheat, caused by the thawing and alternate freezing weather last winter, and also of the backwardness of the spring wheat crop, brought out the fears of a short crop, which, together with the unfavorable nature of advices concerning the Europen crops formed the speculative basis and principal theme of speculation during the early portion of the year. But before the close of the last half of the year the condition of affairs became such as to work a

WONDERFUL CHANGE IN PRICES,

and many who had been "bulls" at over $1.15 per bushel were the strongest "bears" under $1 per bushel. This great transformation of ideas was brought about largely by the very liberal stocks of wheat and the unfavorable and unsatisfactory outlook of the condition of affairs financially. Failures of mercantile houses occurred frequently, occasionally involving prominent houses throughout the United States; also abroad. Then occurred the heavy failure of the firm which engineered the great lard corner, and which dragged down numerous other local houses. These failures were followed by a panicky feeling in stocks, until fears were really entertained of a general panic ensuing. These fears, however, were dispelled as the financial outlook appeared more encouraging. But the continued unusually heavy receipts for the last quarter of the year prevented any material or permanent advance, although the depression and almost panicky feeling, it might be said, was checked, and frequently a rally of 3c to 5c per bushel occurred. The stock of wheat in store in the Chicago elevators at the opening of the year 1883 was reported at 5,196,000 bushels, and never during the year was the stock reduced below 5,000,000 bushels, but when the new crop commenced to move freely a steady accumulation occurred, and at the close of the year the stock in store was about 12,000,000 bushels. The visible supply at the principal points of accumulation in Canada and the United States increased from 21,048,000 bushels at the opening of the year to 35,531,000 bushels at the close of the year. The shipping demand has been much less than in former years, the export demand having been unusually light. The exports for the past year were about 69,000,000 bushels, against about 108,000,000 bushels for the year 1882. This has been due in the first place to the high prices prevailing during the early months, and later to the fact that foreign wheat came in competition with American, and being sold for less of course was taken in preference, so that foreign orders were far below the average. Besides, European markets have been pretty heavily supplied with old wheat and merchants there really had not any pressing wants to supply, and they could act independently about buying. Fluctuations in prices during the year have extended through a range of 23½c, and during the year 1882 through a range of 48⅞c, in 1880 through 45½c, and 1879 through 52c. The market on the 2d day of January, 1883, ranged at 93⅝@93⅞c, and these were the lowest prices for the first half of the year. Prices advanced with frequent fluctuations to $1.13½, which figure was reached in June, and from that sold off to 90c in October, again reached 99¼c in December, but receded again and closed easier.

The following table shows the receipts and shipments of wheat in this market during the past ten years:

Year.	Received, bu	Year.	Shipped, bu.
1874	29,764,622	1874	27,634,587
1875	24,206,370	1875	23,184,349
1876	16,574,058	1876	14,361,950
1877	14,764,515	1877	14,909,160
1878	29,713,571	1878	24,211,739
1879	34,106,109	1879	31,006,789
1880	23,541,607	1880	22,796,288
1881	14,284,990	1881	17,127,540
1882	23,008,596	1882	19,797,884
1883	20,313,065	1883	11,708,385

CORN.

More interest than usual centered in the corn market during the year 1883, which may be attributed to the peculiar and in some instances unlooked for surroundings of the trade. An unusually large speculative business was transacted throughout the year, and the shipping demand was very large, especially during the season of lake navigation. The demand for export was considerably increased, the lower range of prices encouraging the movement, and increased quantities were forwarded to Great Britain and Continental Europe. The crop of 1882 was undoubtedly a heavy one—probably larger than officially reported—as the receipts at Chicago were increased about 50 per cent. The quality, however, was not quite as good as that of the preceding year—less than 50 per cent of the arrivals being suitable to deliver on special contracts. The backward and wet spring interfered somewhat with the planting of the crop of 1883, and the cool weather during the summer tended to retard its growth. The crop, however, at midsummer was regarded as two to three weeks late, but with a favorable autumn it was anticipated that the aggregate yield would reach 1,800,000,000 bushels—possibly more—and on the strength of this supposition large sales were made for future delivery. About the middle of September, the crop was reported seriously injured by frost—so much so that crop interests were reduced to 1,550,000,000 bushels. The unfavorable and changeable weather during the fall and early winter months tended to damage the quality of the crop, and while the aggregate yield may not be materially lessened, yet there is little doubt but the quantity of good merchantable corn will be proportionately less than usual. In the northern parts of Ohio, Indiana, Illinois, and Iowa, and throughout the States of Michigan, Wisconsin and Minnesota, the damage by frost and warm, wet weather has been more serious than elsewhere. The domestic demand for corn during the year 1883 was largely from the seaboard cities and the interior points of the Eastern and Middle States. The inquiry from the South was less urgent, as that section of the country was favored with a good crop last season. The demand from the distilling interests was quite brisk, but confined largely to the lower grades. The glucose manufacturers also purchased rather freely, more particularly during the early part of the year. Live stock raisers in some sections also bought moderate quantities. While prices have not fluctuated within quite as wide a range as durnig 1883, yet the fluctuations have been frequent, and in some instances were somewhat extended. The market opened rather tame with the advent of the year at $49\frac{1}{2}$c for No. 2, but under the influence of an urgent demand prices were rapidly advanced about 20c during the latter part of January, reaching the highest figure of the year—70c. The appreciation in prices was so sudden that "shorts" were dissatisfied and they appealed to the courts for an injunction, restraining certain parties from calling for excessive margins, which had the effect to greatly unsettle the market and caused a reduction of 14c to 16c in prices before the close of the month. After that period trading slackened considerably, and the fluctuations in prices were slight during the succeeding five months. In July, with warmer weather, the outlook for the growing crop was regarded more favorable, and speculative operators were more inclined to sell for future delivery. The receipts at that time were quite large, indicating that farmers had more confidence in the maturing of the crop of 1883, therefore being more willing to dispose of their surplus corn. Prices gradually receded to $47\frac{5}{8}$c during the early part of that month, but toward the close rallied again to 53c. During the month of August the receipts were unusually large—more than double those of the corresponding month in 1882. Prices ruled with considerable steadiness, especially as the shipping demand was brisk—fluctuations during that month being confined within a range of $2\frac{3}{8}$c. In September the market was very active on both shipping and speculative account, and the movement to and from the city was very large. For immediate delivery prices were moderately well maintained, but speculators were inclined to discount prices for future delivery. Fluctuations in prices were more frequent and the extreme range was $4\frac{5}{8}$c. The reports of frost in some sections of the West tended to a steadier feeling in the market, inasmuch as fears were entertained of damage to the crop owing to its backwardness. During the early part of October prices receded to 46c—the lowest of the year—but closed steadier. Speculators were now attracted to the market, and during the balance of the year an unusually heavy business was transacted, and prices gradually advanced 10c to 12c on the whole range, due in a measure to the continued unfavorable and changeable weather, which greatly interfered in securing the crop, and rendering the inspection of corn from some sections rather unsatisfactory, thereby reducing the quantity of good merchantable corn suitable for delivery on contracts.

The following table shows the receipts and shipments of corn at Chicago during the past ten years:

Year.	Received bu.	Year.	Shipped, bu
1874	35,799,638	1874	32,705,224
1875	28,341,150	1875	26,443,884
1876	48,668,640	1876	45,629,035
1877	47,915,728	1877	46,361,901
1878	63,651,518	1878	59,944,200
1879	64,339,311	1879	61,299,376
1880	97,272,844	1880	93,572,934
1881	78,393,395	1881	75,463,213
1882	49,061,755	1882	49,073,609
1883	74,459,948	1883	71,098,399

OATS.

The volume of business transacted in this market compares very favorably with that of former years. Abundant crops for two years have given this market a very large quantity of oats to care for, ann the excellent quality, together with reasonable prices, have been the means of attracting large orders, and the shipping business has grown very much. The facilities for taking care of oats, it seems, have been increased at various points, and this market has been liberally patronized by all distributing centers, and whenever prices reached a reasonable point, oats were bought in large quantities by shippers and placed where they would be available when wanted, or in other words, stocks were secured to meet the expected consumptive wants. This had the effect of keeping the market quite steady, and during the past year prices covered a range of only 18c, while the year before the range was 31½c. By this means shippers were prepared to meet any manipulation of the market, enabling them to hold off at times when prices were advanced, and bringing them to market again when a reaction occurred. The price of oats was cheaper than in 1882, probably for the reason of an ample supply, and the figures show that the market did not reach within 18½c of the highest point in 1882, and on the inside range they sold 5½c lower. A good deal of speculation was indulged in, and "longs" were not generally favored in realizing their expectations, but in several instances their disappointment was quite serious. Prices, it seems, were not destined to rule very high, one reason being the excellent arrangement made by shippers to secure and maintain their supplies, and another being the continued free receipts due to large crops. The stock of oats was very heavy during the first four months of the year, ranging from 700,000 bushels to 1,000,000 bushels more than for the same months the year before. Large purchases had been made for deferred deliveries, speculation in this direction having been encouraged by the high prices during May, June, and July in 1882. "Longs" expected an improvement, in consequence of a large outward movement, consequent to the opening of navigation. The opening of navigation did witness unusually large shipments, but the large yield during 1882 also had a telling effect. Holders in the country had been somewhat expectant of seeing prices go up during the time mentioned, and large quantities of oats were held back which came forward freely in the spring, and there were ample stocks to meet any emergency. The leading markets also became unsettled and easy, and the heavy decline occasioned by financial troubles soon caused a settling up of contracts, and the market from May to September declined steadily from 43 cents to 25 cents. Later in the year the market became more settled, the shipping business was good from the time new oats first came on the market. The quality of the new crop was in every way desirable and this exerted a good demand. Most of the business was one by sample, and the receipts were so nearly all taken that the stock rather decreased than increased, and was much smaller at the close of the year than at the same time the year before. A fair degree of speculative interest was kept up, but the feeling was quite uncertain and operators were not staying in the market with a view of seeing it go to any particular point, but a fair profit on either side seemed to be a sufficient inducement to settle contracts and prices ruled quite steady, recovering from the inside, or 25c, in September, until reaching 34@35c in December. The crop this year was about 4 per cent larger than last year and was estimated at a little over 500,000,000 bushels.

The following table exhibits the receipts and shipments of oats at Chicago for the past ten years:

Year.	Received bu.	Year.	Shipped bu.
1874	13,901,235	1874	10,561,673
1875	12,916,428	1875	10,279,134
1876	13,030,121	1876	11,271,642
1877	13,506,773	1877	12,497,612
1878	18,839,297	1878	16,464,513
1879	16,660,428	1879	13,514,020
1880	23,490,915	1880	20,619,427
1881	24,861,538	1881	23,075,177
1882	26,802,872	1882	23,658,239
1883	37,800,442	1883	33,117,706

RYE.

Two very striking features are noticed in the records of this market for the past year. The one is the heavy movement; the other the low range of prices. The highest price in 1883, which was 68c, did not come within 28c of the highest figure of the year before, which was 96c, and yet in comparing inside prices, rye this year ranged only about 2c under the inside price of the preceding year. While a smaller average price is thus shown the market ruled more steady, that is the fluctuations were not so severe, the range, in act, for the whole year was only 15c, while in 1882 prices covered a range of 40½c. Considerable more rye was carried in store than during any previous time. Stocks accumulated steadily early in the year, starting at 408,102 bu, and increasing to 835,232 bu in May. The demand for rye was very limited. Foreign orders were scarce, and the consumptive demand was very light, for distillers, with 1,500,000 brls of whisky on hand, came to an understanding that they would run only 20 per cent of their capacity. The market from January to June was a dragging one, and prices early in the year ranged at about 60 to 63c, with occasionally 68c reached, and the market early in July ranged down to 53c. About this time the foreign crop was reported badly damaged and 30 to 40 per cent less than usual. Our rye was low, and foreign buyers soon sent large orders to this country. During July and August about 1,000,000 bu of old rye was taken, and during August and September about 3,000,000 bu of new rye went for export. The price did not go up much, but remained at 55 to 62c, and the reason for it not going up more was that the stock has been enormously large and the new crop came forward with a freedom never before witnessed. The existence of a foreign demand also exerted a very large speculative trade. After September the export demand fell off entirely, for the shortage in the foreign crop was lowered to about 15 to 20 per cent, and Russia was said to be sending rye to all foreign markets. The home consumptive demand, which had amounted to but little, continued light and although this was the case, the arrivals were larger than during any previous year. Under this state of affairs stocks kept increasing, and by the close of the year the supply here exceeded that of the previous year by over 1,000,000 bushels. During the latter part of the year prices ranged at 53@58c. Speculative holders often felt rye a burden and the stock changed hands frequently. "Longs" were continually transferring their contracts from one month to another, and considerable profit was derived by holders of the actual property in the way of carrying charges.

The crop was estimated early as short. In the southern section no doubt the yield has been lighter, for rye suffered with winter wheat from the severe cold of last winter. On the other hand there has been a large gain in Wisconsin, Nebraska, Kansas, and Missouri, and this gain is said to more than make up for the loss in other sections, which are Ohio, Kentucky, Indiana, Southern Illinois, and Southern Iowa. The quality of rye this year has been exceptionally fine, nearly everything coming in grading No. 2. Kansas has been the leading State this year in the production of rye.

The following were the receipts and shipments of rye in this market for the past ten years:

Year.	Received, bu.	Year.	Shipped, bu.
1874	781,181	1874	335,077
1875	699,583	1875	310,592
1876	1,447,917	1876	1,433,976
1877	1,728,865	1877	1,553,374
1878	2,490,615	1878	2,025,654
1879	2,497,340	1879	2,234,363
1880	1,869,218	1880	1,365,162
1881	1,363,552	1881	1,104,452
1882	1,984,516	1882	1,773,148
1883	5,662,420	1883	3,944,023

BARLEY.

More barley has been handled in this market during the past year than at any previous time. Information on this point is meager, but it is safe to say that there has been a gain of fully 4,000,000 bu, the receipts and shipments both showing a heavy increase. A glance at the stock of barley in store on the first of every month reveals the fact that there was not so much carried in our elevators as during 1882, the difference is greater during the latter part of this year. This may seem inconsistent with the statement of a heavier movement, but it is a fact which will hereafter be explained. Prices have ruled lower than for two years past, on the whole range, as compared with the range of 1882. No. 2 exhibits a shrinkage of 18c to 23c per bu, and as compared with the decline is still greater, for even 1882 was considered quite a low year. The crop of barley was estimated as a trifle less than 4,000,000 bushels, the yield of 1882. The quality was not in all respects satisfactory, for the barley received here from the various States shows that barley from Nebraska, heretofore the best producing country of the West, was light, stained, and common, being affected by the rainy weather of the fall. Iowa and Wisconsin yielded the best in quality, though these are not important States when quantity is considered. Minnesota ranged next, and it must be said the barley from this State turned out better than was expected from the appearance of the first consignments received, and it finally met with considerable favor from buyers. Trade in barley was liberal. Speculative trading was, perhaps, slightly increased on the new crop on account of the grade No. 2 being changed in September. It was changed so as to admit of a little wider range in color. The reason of changing was that heretofore the grade was so high that little barley coming in would grade No. 2, and hence little was done in the grade which had always been made a basis for prices. The objections at first made to the change were soon overcome, for it was found that the barley was sound and as good for malting as could be desired. The cash business was nearly all done by sample, and this accounts for there being less barley in store than a year ago. Local brewers and maltsters took the No. 2 by sample about as fast as it arrived, and shippers bought the No. 3. After brewers had secured good stocks some No. 2 was allowed to go into store, and this brought shippers on the market, and finally, late in the year, we find speculators taking it. Prices ruled low, for late in 1882 there was an over production of malt, which had a weakening effect upon the market. Buyers preferred to buy by sample, because they could get a better selection. Selling by sample also had many advantages for receivers for a great deal of barley, owing to slight blemishes, just missed grading No. 2, and was much better than what would pass for No. 3 in store, and receivers for this reason found it to their advantage to sell by sample. Low grades were invariably dull, and had to be sold cheap. The quantity of really poor barley received was comparatively small, however, it being used presumably for feed in the country. It requires but a small space to follow prices during the year. No. 2 ranged for old barley at 76c to 85c, and closed at 80c. During June and July there was no market. New No. 2 opened at 70c, and declined to 57c in September, but later rallied again to 65c to 67c. Sample lots sold a trifle over in-store prices. In-store prices for the other grades cut no figure, trading being almost exclusively by sample and the in-store market was a good part of the time nominal. No. 3 by sample covered a range of 45c to 65c, but the heavy trading in the market was from 50c to 56c. No. 4 ranged at 38c to 50c. No. 5 sold at 32c to 38c, according to quality, and sales of screenings were frequently made at $8 to $12 per ton. The shipping business was largely increased, over former years, especially of the new crop, because prices were so low that neither Canada nor California could compete with the production of the Northwest, and the orders therefore came this way.

The following table exhibits the receipts and shipments of barley in this market during the past ten years:

Year.	Received, bu.	Year.	Shipped, bu.
1874	4,354,981	1874	2,404,538
1875	3,107,279	1875	1,868,206
1876	4,716,360	1876	2,687,932
1877	4,990,379	1877	4,213,646
1878	5,754,059	1878	3,520,983
1879	4,936,562	1879	3,566,401
1880	5,211,536	1880	3,110,985
1881	5,695,358	1881	3,113,251
1882	6,488,140	1882	3,298,252
1883	10,591,619	1883	7,718,503

PACKING AND PROVISIONS.

PORK PACKING.

This branch of trade has shown some enlargement during the past year, still it was not as large in the aggregate as during some former years. Chicago is still the largest packing point of the world, and bids fair to maintain that position in the future. Packers have improved their facilities for slaughtering hogs, and enlarged their warehouses for the curing and storage of products. About twenty of the large firms are engaged in the business during the greater portion of the year—some of them without interruption—in addition to which an equal number of smaller firms cut a fair number of hogs to supply the wants of the local retail and lake trade. The capacity of the houses is about 60,000 hogs per day. The packing during the summer months was prosecuted quite actively, and the returns show an increase of about 150,000 hogs packed. The packing for the past year aggregated about 4,350,000 hogs, or an increase of about 350,000 hogs, compared with the turns of last year. The quality of the hogs was better than usual during the summer months, but within the past three months has not been as desirable as the packers require for their trade. The supply of hogs exhibits little change from that of last year, but packers were favored with an increased supply, owing to decreased shipments to Eastern markets. Prices have ruled decidedly lower—about 20c to 30 per cent on the whole range—and the aggregate cost of hogs purchased by packers may be estimated at about $55,000,000. The aggregate amount of product made may be estimated about 785,000,000 pounds, which may be classified as follows: Sides and mess pork, 370,000,000 pounds; hams, 145,000,000 pounds; shoulders, 125,000,000 pounds, and lard, 145,000,000 pounds. The number of hands employed is about 14,000 to 18,000—the larger number when the receipts are liberal, during the winter months. Very few changes have been made in the manufacture, the preference being given to those articles required for the domestic trade. The firms which have established agencies or branch houses in foreign markets cut the larger percentage of the product required for the export trade. Mess pork attracted considerable attention during the "regular" packing season, but was neglected during the summer months. Other cuts of pork—chiefly of the lighter descriptions—were made to a fair extent, to meet the orders received. Lard was made with considerable freedom during the spring and summer months, but met with less favor during the colder weather, when a portion of the raw material could be disposed of satisfactorily to the butterine manufacturers. Hams were made chiefly into domestic cuts, and attracted considerable attention owing to the high prices obtainable. Shoulders made moderately throughout the year. Long and short clear sides met with a little more favor, yet the manufacture was not very large. Short rib sides were cut very freely throughout the year, and met with more favor than any other cut. Foreign fancy cuts of sides were made moderately, more especially by those houses which have a regular trade therefor. Bellies made in fair quantities and a new cut of shoulders for the Western trade, styled "California hams," attracted some attention.

PROVISIONS.

The provision trade of Chicago exhibited a marked degree of activity during the year 1883—in fact, during the greater portion of the time it attracted more attention from the speculative element than any other market. The supply of hog products, both from local and interior manufacturers, was larger than the previous year, consequently operators were in better position to meet the wants of all branches of the trade. The demand from the domestic markets was quite active during the greater portion of the year, yet the upward tendency of prices at times checked the trading temporarily. The foreign inquiry was moderately active, yet orders were generally for small quantities. The shipments direct to agencies and branch houses of manufactures, however, were larger than heretofore. The speculative trading was unusually heavy—the largest on record—more particularly during the first five months of the year. The unsettled feeling during the middle of June, followed by several heavy failures in the trade, caused a marked decline in the prices of the speculative articles—mess pork, lard, and short rib sides. When values had declined about 20 to 25 per cent, speculators were inclined to purchase to some extent as an investment, deeming the shrinkage in prices sufficient to place the product on a consuming basis. This attempt to check the downward tendency in prices proved inefficient, for the feeling continued nervous and unsettled and a further reduction was submitted to until only about 55 per cent of former prices were obtainable. After the severe break in the market in June, there appeared to be a general lack of confidence in the future course of the trade—not because of a disbelief in the actual value of the property, but there was a want of courage on the part of capitalists to take hold, with the remembrance of previous severe losses staring them in the face. Our trade with the South was unusually heavy, and extended over a wider extent of territory. The demand was mainly for mess pork, hams, sides, shoulders, lard, and the usual variety of smoked meats. In the winter season some of the larger distributing markets purchased rather freely of green meats. The smaller interior points bought with considerable freedom in a jobbing way. The Pacific coast markets favored our merchants with an increased number of orders, but generally for special articles. The mining districts of the Northwest purchased moderately of certain descriptions, while trade of the agricultural districts of the West and Northwest, which have been rapidly developed and traversed by new railroads, was very materially enlarged, and is now of considerable importance. Trade with Canada was somewhat light during the first half of the year, but after the shrinkage in value a marked improvement was noticed. The lumber districts appeared to favor our markets more than usual, and the lumbermen purchased larger quantities of product. Merchants in the markets of the Eastern and Middle States sought our market for large quantities of product to meet the wants of that section, and our trade in this respect was larger than heretofore. Stocks of all kinds have been quite liberal throughout the year—at times more than ample to meet the requirements of the trade. Mess pork was in good supply throughout the year, and at times was quite actively inquired for. Prices ruled somewhat irregular within the range of $10.20 to $20.15—the highest figure reached in April and the lowest in September and October. Other cuts of pork were in moderate demand, but the bulk of the trading was conducted in a quiet way. Lard attracted a great deal of attention, and trading was very large. Prices ruled irregularly within the range of $7.15 to $12.10—the highest figure reached in May and the lowest in October. Exporters purchased rather freely throughout the twelve months, and the refining demand was fully up to that of former years. Short rib sides met with more favor, both from speculators and shippers, and sold freely at an irregular range. Sales to merchants in the Southern markets were unusually heavy. Prices ranged at $5.60 to $10.75—the highest paid in May and the lowest in September. Green meats were active during the fall and winter months, and large deliveries were made on previously made contracts near the close of the year. Pickled meats—including hams, shoulders, and bellies—were in good demand throughout the year, and were apparently less affected by the depression in the trade than most other articles. Long cut hams were purchased moderately by exporters, but trade was not very satisfactory. Long and short clear sides were inquired for in fair quantities, but there was little life in the trade. Shoulders were sought for to some extent by the domestic markets, but the foreign demand was comparatively light. Other cuts of meats were in moderate request, but trading was generally conducted in a quiet way.

The following table exhibits the receipts and shipments of hog products to and from Chicago for the past ten years:

Years.	Pork, tbs.	Cut meats, tbs.	Lard, tbs.
		RECEIPTS.	
1874....	39,695	50,629,509	24,145,225
1875....	49,205	54,445,783	21,982,423
1876....	45,704	63,368,011	33,620,928
1877....	35,249	62,021,647	27,236,359
1878....	33,073	103,130,326	37,748,958
1879....	64,389	151,131,767	75,754,117
1880....	39,091	164,437,225	68,387,204
1881....	52,298	138,787,745	61,403,671
1882....	78,895	106,165,038	40,696,384
1883....	53,098	139,858,558	70,924,732
		SHIPMENTS.	
1874....	231,350	262,931,462	82,209,887
1875....	313,713	362,941,943	115,616,093
1876....	319,344	467,289,100	138,216,376
1877....	296,457	479,926,231	147,000,616
1878....	346,366	747,363,774	244,323,933
1879....	354,255	835,629,540	251,020,205
1880. ..	267,324	958,036,113	333,539,138
1881....	319,999	782,993,729	278,531,733
1882....	435,625	615,822,951	235,473,520
1883....	400,552	674,499,355	246,720,366

LIVE STOCK.

A YEAR THAT HAS NEVER BEEN EQUALED.

In many respects the year 1883 in the Chicago live stock trade has been more remarkable than its predecessor, while in some particulars the year stands out in bold relief, showing records that have never been equaled or even approached, in the memory of the pioneers in the trade.

As a live stock market Chicago eclipses anything that has been known here in the past; never was there such an extensive and varied demand for all kinds of stock as has been developed within the past twelve months. Who would have thought, even five years ago, that any market in the world could successfully and advantageously handle an average of more than 40,000 cattle per week for a period of seven or eight successive weeks? The figures seem almost incredible even now, though the performance is a matter of record.

The capacity of the Union Stock Yards has been added to considerably during the year; the chain of viaducts for handling hogs overhead, in driving to the packing houses, has been increased, and the yard room is also much greater than last year.

DECREASE IN HOGS.

The receipts of stock for the year greatly surprised everyone, both as to quantity and quality. From the reports circulated early in the year many thought that the receipts of hogs would necessarily show a falling off of several hundred thousand, whereas the decrease has been only about 160,000; and if the increased weight of the hogs this year over last be reduced to porkers the supplies for the past year would have been fully 50,000 head more than in 1882. This is estimating the weight of the hogs at 250 pounds. Despite the talk about the scarcity of cattle which was indulged in to considerable extent early in the season, the arrivals of that kind of stock were entirely unprecedented, and showed an increase of about 300,000 head over the receipts of 1882. In sheep the increase was about 125,000 head, which is a handsome gain. There certainly never was a year with so many successive banner days, weeks, and months for receipts of cattle and sheep. Nothing very extraordinary occurred in the hog department; at least there was nothing to press the largest day on record—Nov. 25, 1879—when 64,643 hogs arrived; but the quality and quantity of the arrivals all during the summer caused much astonishment.

Prices during the year have been very good on the whole, and for hogs in particular, during the past few months, have been higher than anticipated. No kind of stock sold so high as in the preceding year, but prices were more uniform and reliable.

FOR FOREIGN MARKETS.

The export demand has been good and shippers to foreign markets during the last half of the year were busy and successful. Early in the season, however, cattle exporters made large contracts for vessel room and vast sums of money were lost in April and May. In fact the first half of the year was very disastrous for exporters of live cattle. The climax came in June when the pens were flooded with the finest of cattle for weeks at a time and prices then touched the bottom. From that time to the close the prices for cattle were upward, and the closing month witnessed the highest rates of the year. In the hog and sheep export trade there were no particularly new developments. For the most part such stock is shipped drressed. Foreign mutton markets have been favorable and the only difficulty in the way of a magnificent trade in that line from this country was the inability of purchasers to get stock of good quality. Of late, however, there has been a notable improvement in the quality of the sheep coming to market, and it is evident that it will not be many years before America can hold her own with any country at producing mutton of high quality. There has been a steady demand in England for our mutton, and prices have been temptingly high, but the stock was lacking to supply the demand. The reported late action of the French Government in raising the embargo on our hog products has had a noticeable effect upon the market for hogs, but this action will probably be abandoned, or the decree only removed temporarily.

THE TOTAL VALUATION.

The total valuation of live stock received at Chicago during the year was about $200,000,000. The total valuation of live stock received since the opening of the yards is $1,889,487,051, making an average of $104,971,000 for each year since the opening. Thus it will be seen that 1883, which was $204,000,000, was about double the average for the whole time. The valuation of 1883 shows an increase of $8,000,000 over its predecessor.

During the past year the daily receipts averaged 6,000 cattle, 18,000 hogs, and 2,400 sheep. During the month of October the receipts of cattle averaged over 8,000.

The number of car-loads of all kinds of live stock received at the Union Stock Yards in 1883 reached almost 200,000, and the car-loads shipped out was 73,800.

Included in the number of cattle purchased by canners and dressed-beef operators are 140,000 slaughtered by G. H. Hammond & Co., at Hammond, Ind., which are also included in the shipments of live cattle. This must be borne in mind when deducting the live shipments and dressed beef from receipts to get the number of cattle left for local consumption. It must also be remembered that Armour & Co. have the largest local meat market in the country, and that a great deal of the beef handled by canners and refrigerator men is used for city use.

The receipts and shipments of live stock at Chicago for the past year are given below:

RECEIPTS.

MONTHS.	Cattle.	Calv's.	Hogs.	Sheep.	H'rs's.
January.....	165,546	1,056	740,674	75,939	696
February....	118,586	853	455,289	75,442	1,465
March	141,795	1,596	269,666	79,691	2,335
April.........	117,068	2,408	240,969	70,700	1,667
May..........	134,531	3,860	370,849	41,361	1,409
June..........	140,773	1,752	306,015	35,876	1,522
July...........	153,228	1,979	351,820	32,870	944
August... ...	184,678	2,476	319,225	50,268	1,146
September..	172,888	5,220	337,986	61,423	1,314
October......	217,791	4,001	516,949	77,925	1,261
November...	167,393	2,718	890,684	69,613	898
December...	165,107	2,306	750,499	78,626	486
Total....	1,878,944	30,223	5,640,625	749,734	15,143
1882	1,582,530	24,965	5,817,504	628,887	13,858

SHIPMENTS.

MONTHS.	Cattle.	Calv's.	Hogs.	Sheep.	H'rs's.
January.....	87,967	245	80,230	40,804	696
February....	68,493	148	112,639	44,623	1,425
March........	80,341	304	130,807	55,677	3,335
April..........	69,034	1,078	95,136	45,270	1,608
May..........	74,937	1,3 8	64,662	17,562	1,294
June..........	76,581	183	85,735	11,620	1,398
July...........	74,723	119	106,841	6,955	944
August	90,617	654	94,308	17,845	1,027
September..	82,900	3,530	134,822	27,271	1,281
October......	102,397	1,961	164,647	32,098	1,194
November...	80,792	1,945	108,907	31,385	898
December...	77,886	1,146	130,568	42,151	499
Total.....	966,758	12,671	1,319,192	372,761	14,599
1882.......	921,000	10,229	1,747,722	314,200	12,788

RED LETTER DAYS.

The largest day's receipts on record at the Union Stock yards were as follows:

Cattle, Nov. 15, 1882........................12,076
Calves, Sept. 28, 1881........................ 1,428
Hogs, Nov. 25, 1879.........................64,643
Sheep, Dec. 5, 1883......................... 7,982
Horses, March 21, 1881..................... 369

The largest weekly receipts were as follows:

Cattle, week ending Oct. 20, 1883........ 52,192
Calves, week ending Aug. 27, 1881 3,360
Hogs, week ending Nov. 20, 1880........300,488
Sheep, week ending Dec. 21, 1883......... 26,040
Horses, week ending March 26, 1881..... 1,125

The largest monthly receipts were as follows:

Cattle, October, 1882.......................... 217,791
Calves, August, 1881.......................... 11,604
Hogs, November, 1880....................1,111,997
Sheep, March, 1883........................... 79,691
Horses, March, 1881........................... 2,564

The largest yearly receipts were as follows:

Cattle, 1883..................................1,878,944
Calves, 1881.................................... 48,498
Hogs, 1880....................................7,059,355
Sheep, 1883.................................... 749,734
Horses, 1873.................................... 20,259

CATTLE.

THE BANNER YEAR.

The vast and unprecedented receipts of cattle for the year show that the last was a busy one in this branch of the live stock trade. The simple figures, showing an aggregate of nearly 1,900,000 head of cattle, tell a wonderful story, but figures have such a hard, matter-of-fact way of expression that we can seldom realize what they mean from the surface; we must study back of them. You see figures representing nearly 1,900,000 cattle, and are not particularly struck with their significance, because in this we deal so extensively with huge figures that we cannot appreciate the value of figures standing for a few millions only. Familiarity breeds something of contempt for large figures, but if we stop to think what a herd the last year's receipts of cattle would make altogether; how far they would reach if placed in single file; how many men and millions of money were required to handle them, then we get some idea of what the figures represent.

The year 1882 was a remarkable one in the matter of heavy receipts, but it was eclipsed in every respect by its successor. Last year stands as the banner year, and also records the banner days, weeks, and months.

HIGH AND LOW PRICES.

The highest prices for the year occurred in March and December. The lowest were recorded in June and July. Early in the year there was considerable excitement in the trade, and it looked for a time in March as if people expected a cattle famine.

The advanced rates brought unprecedented receipts of good cattle, and in fact all kinds of cattle, and the boom was followed by a serious reaction. Country shippers went wild in February, March, and April, and made contracts at current prices for June delivery, which entailed the heaviest general losses that were ever known. Vast numbers of cattle sold for $2 per hundred less than they cost in the country. Instead of fat cattle being scarce in the summer months they were more than usually abundant, and the calculations of a great many went away on that account.

The general demand for cattle was strong throughout, and the most wonderful thing in connection with the very heavy receipts was the manner in which they were disposed of. It was not an uncommon thing for the market to be strong and active throughout with 45,000 head per week on sale.

A YEAR OF SURPRISES.

Such a strong general demand was never before known, and on that account the prognostications of the most experienced dealers were more frequently wrong than otherwise. It was indeed a year of surprises, especially as there were many who, as long ago as 1881, confidently expressed the opinion that the maximum of Chicago's cattle trade had been reached.

In years gone by the supplies of fine, thoroughly mature beeves were drawn almost exclusively from nearby sections, where a few breeders and feeders had established reputations for prime stock, but this year there have been hardly any sectional limits—Nebraska, Kansas, and other Western States contributing beeves sa remarkable in quality as those for which our best Illinois breeders are renowned. It is not very long since it was possible for cattle men of experience to reckon just how many prime beeves were fattening for market, so limited was the number of men who made a practice of putting a thorough finish on their stock before consigning to the butcher. But that day is forever past. Then it was thought that fine stock, improved methods, and, in short, "book-farming," as it was called, was only for country gentlemen who raised stock and cultivated farms because they fancied it, and had no other way in which they preferred to spend their surplus. But now it is being very generally understood that the poorer the man the more he is in need of using only the best methods; that none but the wealthy can afford the questionable luxury of scrub stock.

CHICAGO FAT STOCK SHOW.

Never was there a year when there was so much activity in the fine-stock markets as during the past. The great Chicago Fat Stock Show that has now been held in the Exposition Building for six years has done much to incite breeders and feeders to better methods. Even yet, however, the common cattle are those that are rough and unfinished, but at the present rate of improvement it is evident that it cannot be very long before the cattle that are now called extra will be more common than those that are so called now.

Never was the canning and dressed-beef trade so strong and reliable. Cows and mixed stock have sold well at all times, except when in competition with Texans.

Receipts of Texas cattle were about 100,000 head less than in 1882, which fact makes all the more remarkable the enormous general gain in receipts. Range cattle were two months later than usual in coming to market. In the Southwest the drought was the cause, and in the Northwest the unprecedented rainfall made grass so rank that cattle did not fat solidly. Thus it is shown that the ranchmen must not have either too much or too little water. The high prices of the preceding year drained the herds more closely than usual, and ranchmen were not willing to part with their very young stock at the prices. Indeed, about 80,000 head of young stock cattle were sent from "the States" to Wyoming, Nebraska, Colorado, and Montana. This is something previously unknown. The result of the experiment is awaited with much interest. Ranchmen are rather confident as to the prospects for next year, and many thousand beeves that were ready to come this year, had prices been satisfactory, are being carried over for the spring market.

DISTILLERY CATTLE.

A large business was done in distillery cattle, but the trade was more concentrated; that is, the enormous profits of 1882 induced the heavy cattle feeders to go into the trade so extensively that the room for placing cattle in distilleries was soon exhausted at advanced rates, and the small fry were rather crowded out.

Distillery cattle realized handsome profits, selling at $4.50@6.50, the bulk going at $5@6; but the same kind of cattle sold in 1882 at $5@8.90, and made much more for the feeders. It is only within a year or two that it has been considered that slop-fed cattle of like weight and quality dress as much beef as corn-fed stock. Distillery bulls sold at $3.50@5.40, against $4.50@6 in 1882.

The trade in Eastern dairy calves was very light, but during the year a goodly number sold at about $10 to $18 per head to go to Western feeders. Several thousand went beyond the Missouri to ranchmen.

RANGE OF PRICES.

The extreme range of prices for shipping cattle during the past twelve months are given below, with current quotations for 1879, 1880, 1881, and 1882:

	Steers av. 1,500 to 2,200	Steers av. 1,350 to 1,500	Steers av. 1,200 to 1,350
Jan......	$5.35@6.50	$4.80@6.10	$4.55@6.00
Feb......	5.90@7.00	5.00@6.25	4.70@6.00
March...	5.90@7.30	5.35@7.05	5.15@7.00
April...	6.10@7.10	5.80@6.90	5.50@6.75
May.....	5.90@6.75	5.75@6.65	5.45@6.50
June...	5.75@6.30	5.40@6.30	5.10@6.30
July.....	5.55@6.40	5.25@6.35	4.65@6.25
Aug......	5.75@6.55	5.00@6.40	4.25@6.20
Sept....	5.90@6.50	5.15@6.50	4.10@6.15
Oct......	6.10@7.35	5.10@7.00	4.35@7.00
Nov.....	6.20@7.35	5.15@6.55	4.25@6.30
Dec.....	6.20@8.25	5.35@7.12	4.55@6.75
1883....	5.35@8.25	4.80@7.12	4.10@7.00
1882....	5.40@9.30	4.70@9.00	4.25@9.00
1881....	5.30@8.00	4.40@7.25	3.80@7.00
1880....	5.00@7.00	4.30@6.00	3.50@5.50
1879....	4.50@6.00	3.90@5.50	3.20@5.00

DISTILLERY CATTLE, STOCKERS, AND FEEDERS.

The following will be found the range of prices on distillery cattle, stockers, and feeders for the past twelve months:

Month.	Dis. Cattle.	Stockers.	Feeders.
Jan.....	$5.20@5.75	$2.90@4.15	$3.50@4.80
Feb.....	4.70@5.60	3.10@4.30	3.75@5.10
March..	5.25@6.50	3.10@4.75	4.20@5.70
April....	5.25@6.20	3.25@4.80	4.25@5.65
May....	4.50@6.40	3.00@4.90	4.40@5.80
June...	4.75@6.10	2.90@4.60	4.00@5.30
July....	5.30@6.30	3.00@4.30	3.85@4.90
Aug....	5.50@6.10	2.60@4.00	3.90@4.75
Sept....	5.40@6.15	2.70@4.05	3.85@4.60
Oct.....	....	2.50@3.90	4.45@4.65
Nov....	....	2.20@3.75	3.40@4.50
Dec.....	....	2.50@4.30	3.80@4.75

Distillery cattle ranged during 1883...4.50@6.50
Distillery cattle ranged during 1882...5.00@8.90
Distillery bulls ranged during 1883....3.50@5.40
Distillery bulls ranged during 1882...4.50@6.00

TEXANS AND FAR-WEST CATTLE.

The table given below shows the range of prices for the past season on grass Texans, wintered Texans, and Western natives:

Month.	Grass Texans.	Wintered Texans.	Far-West natives.
May......	$4.20@6.00	....	....
June....	3.50@5.50	....	....
July......	3.40@5.50	$3.75@5.25	$4.50@4.65
Aug......	3.00@5.15	3.35@5.20	3.60@5.70
Sept......	3.50@4.75	3.40@4.75	3.90@5.65
Oct......	3.25@4.55	3.35@5.00	3.65@6.00
Nov......	3.35@4.75	3.50@4.65	3.85@6.25
Dec......	4.00@5.10	4.00@4.75	4.80@5.10

The table following gives comparative figures for four years past—extreme range of prices:

Years	Grass Texans.	Wintered Texans.	Far-West natives.
1883...	$3.00@6.00	$3 35@5.25	$3.60@6.25
1882....	3.25@6.80	3.40@5.50	3.75@6.50
1881....	2.25@5.00	2.90@4.65	3.25@5.40
1880....	1.75@3.75	2.50@3.75	2.70@4.50

Below will be found receipts of grass Texans and far-West cattle for the past four years:

Year.	Grass Texans.	Far-west cattle.
1883	256,340	176,680
1882	346,300	220,700
1881	143,380	190,500
1880	88,000	109,500

Prices for range cattle were higher than in 1881, but lower than in 1882. It was a notable fact that through grass Texans sold as high or higher than wintered and double-wintered Texans from the Northwest. This, together with wire fences and railway facilities, will tend to curtail the annual drive of young Texans to the North to be wintered.

COMPARATIVE RECEIPTS AND SHIPMENTS.

The receipts and shipments of cattle at Chicago during the past ten years have been as follows:

Year.	Received No.	Shipped No.
1874	843,966	622,929
1875	920,843	696,534
1876	1,096,745	797,724
1877	1,033,151	703,402
1878	1,083,068	699,108
1879	1,215 732	726,903
1880	1,382,477	886,614
1881	1,498,550	938,712
1882	1,582,472	920,453
1883	1,878,944	966,758

It will be seen that from 1877 there has been a steady and marked increase in the volume of receipts. The arrivals for 1883 were double the receipts of 1875.

DRESSED BEEF.

PREPARING MEAT FOR EASTERN RESTAURANTS.

The most remarkable growth in the cattle trade has been the advancement of the dressed beef business. Some idea of the growth and magnitude of the canning and dressed beef business may be obtained from the fact that fully half of the total receipts of cattle for the year went into cans and refrigerator cars at Chicago to be distributed to the consumers of the East.

The following shows the principle purchases of that kind of stock:

Swift Bros. & Co.	331,550
G. H. Hammond & Co.	140,000
Libby, McNeill & Libby	113,987
Armour & Co.	253,000
Fairbank Canning Co.	120,000
Total	958,537

The increase in the number of cattle slaughtered here for that purpose was about 300,000 head, or just about the amount of the gain in receipts of cattle. The dressed beef business is expanding with remarkable rapidity, and much greater strides have been made in this trade than are generally realized.

FOR EASTERN CITIES.

A new feature, and a very important one, has been developed during the year. In former years it has been the custom for the most fastidious restaurants and hotels in New York, Boston, and other cities to have their cattle bought here, shipped East on foot, and slaughtered, but this year the bulk of the finest cattle that have come to market have been slaughtered here and forwarded in refrigerator cars to the aristocratic consumers of Eastern cities. Of course the meat reaches its destination in vastly better condition than if sent on the hoof.

When the dressed beef men invaded New York City with their trains of dressed beef every day there was a good deal of commotion in the live-stock trade. The beef on hand in the refrigerators often interfered with the sale of live stock when supplies were liberal, and as the dressed beef could be sold at a profit for considerable less than the cattle shipped on the hoof, the former had decidedly the upper hand in the fight.

The railroads endeavored to make considerable advances in freight charges to the East on dressed beef, and there was quite a lively wrangle for a time, but the shippers had to submit to a little advance. However, they can afford it, because they ship thirty-three carcasses in a car, while only about eighteen are shipped in live stock cars. Then, too, the railroads object to the refrigerator cars because they have to be hauled back empty. At the same time the railroads realize that it is useless to ignore the demands of this growing interest.

DAILY TRAINS OF DRESSED BEEF.

Regular trains are sent to the seaboard and intermediate points laden with Chicago dressed beef every day. Shipments have been made to considerable extent to the South, and a couple of car-loads of dressed beef per week were sent to St. Paul and Minneapolis this summer. This seems a little like carrying coals to Newcastle, but was profitable.

A year ago the talk about starting dressed beef establishments beyond the Mississippi was speculation and was regarded as a very long shadow of the coming event, but the talk has taken tangible shape, and meat preserving institutions on the plains are a reality. The first venture was the Continental Meat Company at Victoria, Texas. A company has been formed at Dallas, one at San Antonio, and the Fort Worth (Texas) Meat Company has its buildings and machinery thoroughly equipped for dressing and shipping meat. An establishment has been located at Cheyenne, Wyoming, and it may truly be said that a great revolution is taking place in the manner of transporting stock from the producer to the consumer.

During the year just closed there were fully twice the amount of cattle slaughtered here for the dressed beef trade that were used in the preceding year. This shows how rapid has been the growth.

SUCCESS ASSURED.

That the dressed meat business is growing in popularity and has come to stay, is evidenced by the enormous investments that are being made by shrewd business men. There can be no possible doubt as to the feasibility of the scheme, as operated here, but the success on the plains will hardly be so swift and sure as it has been here, though there is no good reason why the same care and attention to details may not be given to the business on the frontier that obtains here. At any rate there seems to be no lack of men who are willing to try their luck in the business out West.

The refrigerator men are by no means confining their attention to beef, but are handling increasing numbers of sheep. Some of the most extensive operators in the trade have been dressing some of the best sheep that have come to market, and up to the present time the demand for good sheep for that purpose has only been limited by the supply. There has been no lack in quantity of sheep, but the average quality of the offerings has been indeed miserable.

COMPETITION WITH LIVE.

When the dressed meat business first came into notice it was met with such general favor and received such a boom that it was thought the days of shipping live stock were surely numbered, but those who thought such to be the case evidently did not realize the magnitude and importance of the live stock shipping trade. It is certainly a noteworthy fact that while the growth of the dressed beef interest has been great, it has not been so much at the expense of the live stock business as many suppose. The increase of the refrigerator car business during the year is just about equal to the increase in the total receipts of cattle, which shows that what has been the gain of one has not necessarily been the loss of the other. At the same time the new way is steadily encroaching upon the ground of the old, and despite the vast amount of capital arrayed against it, there must be steady, strong growth in the dressed meat trade. The live stock shippers have not gone out of the business during the past year, and there is no prospect that they contemplate any such move during the year to come, or the year after, but it is patent to all that the refrigerator business must steadily grow in favor.

THE HOG MARKET.

CONDITION OF TRADE.

The hog trade of the year 1883 was peculiar in many respects. The receipts were larger in volume than many anticipated, and the excellent quality of the offerings was a matter of surprise to all. During the early part of the year the receipts fell far behind the corresponding periods of the preceding year, but on the last half the tide turned, and the increase was so strong that about two more weeks would have made good the deficiency. On the whole the shortage was remarkably small.

During the middle months of the year the weight of the hogs ran from ten to twenty-five pounds heavier than last year, and it was the first year in the history of the trade that thin, immature pigs outsold prime 300-pound porkers. What in ordinary times are called "skips" in many cases sold higher than prime mixed hogs. There was a raging demand for light meats, principally on foreign account, and the uncommonly large proportion of prime heavy hogs appeared to be most untimely. It is always more or less demoralizing to put a premium on half-done work, and largely owing to the discrimination in favor of unfed hogs, the average weight in November declined and was one pound less than the corresponding month in 1882. About that time, however, the demand for light meats fell off, and prime hogs, when they were beginning to get scarce, took their proper relative position at the

HEAD OF THE LIST

on the range of values. Under light receipts and strong demand prices in the early spring were unreasonably high, but from March, which was the highest month, there was a steady downward movement till the 1st of November, since when the tendency has been upward.

Many hogs were sold here in November which could have been sold in the country six months before for $2 per 100 lbs. more. All the time the reports were coming from the country that the supplies were getting short, but receipts were increasing here and the quality of the stock indicated anything but the last scrapings of a short crop.

The advance in prices during the last two months was rather unusual and unlooked for, as the first two months of the packing season are generally the lowest. Packers had to grin and bear it, however. They had their choice of paying the prices or allowing their contracts to go unfilled. For a time many of them stubbornly held off on the ground that prices were too high; but it was not very long, and for a month after the middle of November every packer was in the trade.

There has probably never been a year when the operators were so completely nonplussed, when they were so entirely in the dark as to the best policy to pursue. It is said that some of them always know how things are going, but this year the best of the packers did not seem able to tell which way the feline would bound.

RANGE OF PRICES.

The extreme range of prices for hogs during the past twelve months is given below, with current quotations for 1879, 1880, 1881, and 1882:

Months.	Rough packing.	Heavy packing and shipping.	Light bacon
Jan.....	$5.40@6.45	$6.05@7.10	$5.50@6.55
Feb.....	5.90@7.00	6.60@7.65	5.90@7.15
March...	6.15@7.65	6.95@8.15	6.10@7.75
April...	6.85@7.70	7.25@8.10	6.90@7.75
May....	6.60@7.50	7.00@7.85	6.70@7.60
June...	5.60@6.90	6.00@7.25	5.70@7.00
July....	4.85@5.90	4.90@6.25	5.00@6.55
Aug.....	4.35@5.50	4.90@5.85	5.10@6.50
Sept....	4.25@5.05	4.70@5.50	4.60@6.00
Oct.....	3.90@4.90	4.40@5.30	4.35@5.40
Nov.....	3.90@5.00	4.40@5.50	4.00@5.00
Dec	4.30@5.60	4.75@6.20	4.25@5.60
1883....	3.90@7.70	4.40@8.15	4.00@7.75
1882....	5.40@8.65	6.00@9.35	5.30@8.75
1881....	4.30@6.95	4.75@7.50	4.40@7.00
1880....	4.00@5.15	4.30@6.90	4.10@5.30
1879....	2.60@4.20	2.80@4.45	2.60@4.05

RECEIPTS AND SHIPMENTS COMPARED.

The receipts and shipments of hogs at Chicago during the past ten years were as follows:

Year.	Received, No.	Shipped, No.
1874....................	4,258,370	2,330,361
1875....................	3,912,110	1,582,643
1876....................	4,190,006	1,131,635
1877....................	4,025,970	951,221
1878....................	6,339,654	1,266,906
1879....................	6,448,330	1,692,361
1880....................	7,059,355	1,364,990
1881....................	6,474,844	1,289,679
1882....................	5,817,504	1,746,555
1883....................	5,640,625	1,319,192

There has been a general growth in volume of receipts from the opening of the yards, but 1880 was the heaviest year on record, and it will be seen that current receipts are smaller than 1878. There is one point in which the arrivals of 1882 exceeded all others, however, and that was early maturity and quality.

SHEEP.

MUTTON EATING ON THE INCREASE.

That mutton eating is on the increase is no longer a matter of doubt. There is an increasing demand for good mutton, and it is also becoming easier for the lover of "leg o' mutton" and "lamb chops" to have his taste gratified. The time was, and not very long ago, when if a person could find mutton on the bill of fare in the average restaurant he would hardly be able to tell that he was not trying to masticate a chunk of succulent sole leather, but for the said bill of fare which described it as mutton.

Receipts of sheep at Chicago were the heaviest on record, and on the whole it was the most satisfactory year's business that has been done in the sheep market.

Floods of Texas and Western stock of inferior quality kept a very wide range between good and common sheep, but the average quality of the receipts was not to be complained of when all things were taken into account. It is only lately that the shepherds of the West have deemed it necessary to pay any attention to anything but wool, and they have received but little encouragement to fit their sheep for the butcher.

The refusal of most of the Western roads to supply double-deck cars has been one of the greatest drawbacks to the trade. Sheep cannot be shipped from the West in single-decks, and make money, because the shipper is compelled to pay for a whole load, while in reality he only gets in enough weight for half a load.

The general demand for sheep has greatly improved since the last review, and

SHEEP-RAISERS FEEL ENCOURAGED.

The interest which the dressed meat folks are taking in the trade is having a good effect, and will eventually develop into something greatly to the advantage of mutton raisers. The dressed mutton operators have not been able to do much because the supplies have been insufficient, in quality if not in quantity. But the trade is growing and there is no good reason why it should not continue to grow.

Prices for sheep were not very extreme, except in the case of inferior grades, which at times glutted the market, and there were no very high prices paid for the best of the offerings. At the same time the general prices averaged well and good sheep commanded satisfactory figures.

The export demand was good and the condition of foreign markets would have justified a much heavier trade had sheep of good quality been forthcoming in greater numbers.

Fewer sheep from the far West were sent to market than in the previous year, but there was continually an oversupply of low grade native sheep.

EXTREME RANGE OF PRICES.

The extreme range of prices for sheep during the past twelve months are given below with comparisons:

Months.	Natives.	Texans.	Westerns.
Jan......	$2.00@5.87	$2.25@3.75	$3 50@4.75
Feb......	2.00@6.50	2.40@3.80	3.60@5.15
March...	2.25@7.75	2.75@4.40	4.10@6.00
April....	3.75@7.50	3.00@3.75	4.35@6.50
May.....	3.15@6.50	3.20@4.50	4.25@5.90
June....	1.90@6.00	2.00@3.80	3.25@5.50
July.....	2.25@5.10	1.70@3.75	3.20@5.25
Aug.....	2.25@5.25	2.25@3.70	3.70@4.40
Sept.....	2.25@5 10	2.20@3.60	2.55@4.30
Oct......	1.75@4.50	....	2.00@3.25
Nov......	1.75@4.65	....	2.10@3.70
Dec......	1.75@6.00	....	2.65@4.00
1883....	1.75@7.75	1.70@4.50	2.00@6.50
1882....	1.75@8.00	2.00@6.30	2.60@7.25
1881....	2.25@6.50	1.90@4.75	2.75@5.50

THE RECEIPTS AND SHIPMENTS OF SHEEP

at Chicago during the past ten years were as follows:

Year.	No. received.	No. shipp'd
1874..........................	333,655	180,555
1875..........................	418,948	243,604
1876..........................	364,095	195,925
1877..........................	310,240	155,354
1878..........................	310,420	156,727
1879..........................	325,119	159,266
1880..........................	335,810	156,510
1881..........................	493,624	253,938
1882..........................	628,769	314,200
1883..........................	749,734	372,761

Chicago was never a great sheep market previous to 1882, but the increased volume of that year and the magnificent gain of 1883 places Chicago in a position to take first place as a market for sheep, as she already has for all other kinds of food animals.

LUMBER, COAL, AND SALT.

LUMBER, SHINGLES AND LATH.

THE EXTENT OF THIS BRANCH

of industry and commerce, for which Chicago is the chief distributing center, may be inferred from the fact that the capital employed in mills, pine lands, sales yards, and vessels owned and exclusively employed in the carrying business aggregates nearly or quite $100,000,000. The territory containing this vast volume of wealth is generally known as the Northwestern Lumber District, whose limits extend as far east as Michigan, and west and northwest to the Mississippi and its tributaries. Like nearly all other leading interests the current year's operations have been less satisfactory to both manufacturers and distributors than those of the one immediately preceding. The predictions of many well-informed dealers and manufacturers, that the arrivals would show a material excess on those of 1882, were not realized. On the reverse, the receipts as returned by vessels and railroads show a reduction of 276,400,000 feet. The decrease was the more surprising as it was supposed that the profitable business in 1882 would stimulate manufacturers to increase their production. The weather was also favorable for work in the woods, and an abundance of snow greatly facilitated logging operations. In addition, the stocks piled at the mills were much heavier than at the opening of 1882. It soon became apparent, however, that there was less desire to force the production than had been supposed at the outset, and in March the efforts to curtail the cut, with a view to prevent an oversupply, culminated in the formation of

THE LUMBER MANUFACTURERS' ASSOCIATION,

for the express purpose of keeping the production of the mills within desired limits. In addition to preventing an overstock of lumber, many owners of large tracts of pine lands decided it more profitable to keep than to cut their timber at current prices for stock. The season was also a month later in opening, and closed early. The curtailment of the running time at the mills, in connection with the efforts of the Lumber Manufacturers' Association above noted, reduced the output in the Northwestern lumber regions 10 per cent. This deficiency was fully compensated for by an extra amount of lumber carried over from the previous year. Hence there was an ample supply for the requirements, which in many locations were below the estimates made at the opening of the year. The failure of the demand to meet the expectations had a tendency to weaken confidence, and although manufacturers as a rule fully comprehended the situation, and by a judicious management in sending stocks forward as the market showed an ability to absorb it, there was scarcely a time when the market was glutted. The sluggish character of the yard trade during most of the season induced the yard dealers to persistently

DEMAND CONCESSIONS ON CARGOES.

In this they were partly successful, their efforts being seconded by a number of large failures in the trade in Michigan and other sections of the country. The depression in other lines of business also contributed to render dealers conservative. Piece stuff opened in April at $10 to $10.50 per M, against $12.50 to $13 the corresponding month in 1882. In May a decline of 50c was recorded, and pieces settled to $9.50 and $10.50. During June, July, and August they ranged at $9 to $10.

The reduction on common and medium grades of boards and strips was nearly as severe. At the close of the cargo season it was generally conceded very little money had been made, and Michigan manufacturers, as a rule, claimed that they would have been richer had they left their timber standing. The Mississippi districts, while rather more fortunate, have little cause for congratulation, and the same may be said of other localities. The constant denudation of the timber lands is annually removing the supply of logs further from the mills, and necessarily increasing the cost of logging. During the past season this was equalized by lower rates of wages, and supplies, hence there was no material advance in the expenses of manufacturing, except in the enhanced value of the timber, which is steadily appreciating as the supply diminishes. The early closing of the mills, coupled with a disposition of mill-owners to restrict supplies, caused about 25 per cent of last winter's log output to be carried over. It is also conceded that the volume of lumber now piled at the mills is equal to last year. The outlook for the present winter's work in the woods is good, but there is a disposition to conservatism, and no important excess in the supply of lumber for next year is anticipated. Stocks in the country are not large, and although nothing like a boom is looked for, the best informed dealers regard the situation as healthy.

THE RANGE OF PRICES FOR CARGOES

of standard green piece stuff, boards and strips, shingles and lath at the exchange docks during the navigation season of 1883, which opened April 2 and closed about Dec. 8, and for corresponding period in 1882, were as follows:

PIECE STUFF.

	1883.	1882.
April	$10.00 to 10.50	$12.50 to 13.00
May	9.50 to 10.50	11.00 to 12.00
June	9.00 to 10.00	10.75 to 11.50
July	9.00 to 10.00	10.50 to 11.25
August	9.00 to 10.00	11.00 to 11.75
September	9.00 to 9.75	10.75 to 11.50
October	9.00 to 9.75	10.00 to 11.25
November	9.00 to 10.00	10.50 to 11.50
December	9.75 to 10.25	11.00 to 11.50

BOARDS AND STRIPS.

	1883.	1882.
April	$...... to 12.50	$12.50 to 20.00
May	12.00 to 22.00	11.50 to 22.00
June	11.00 to 22.00	11.25 to 21.00
July	11.00 to 20.00	11.25 to 21.00
August	10.50 to 20.00	12.50 to 22.00
September	10.50 to 20.00	13.00 to 22.00
October	10.50 to 16.00	13.00 to 22.00
November	10.50 to 17.00	12.25 to 22.00
December	11.50 to 17.50	12.50 to 22.50

SHINGLES.

	1883.		1882.
	Standard.	Extra "A."	Extra "A."
April	$2.60 to $2.65	$2.75 to $2.80	$2.85 to $2.95
May	2.50 to 2.65	2.55 to 2.80	2.75 to 2.95
June	2.25 to 2.55	2.40 to 2.85	2.60 to 2.95
July	2.25 to 2.40	2.40 to 2.80	2.50 to 2.95
August	2.00 to 2.40	2.40 to 2.80	2.75 to 3.00
Sept	2.00 to 2.20	2.40 to 2.60	2.80 to 3.00
October	2.00 to 2.20	2.20 to 2.60	2.70 to 2.95
Novem'r.	2.00 to 2.20	2.20 to 2.65	2.70 to 2.95
Dec	2.15 to 2.25	2.30 to 2.80	2.80 to 3.00

LATH.

	1883.	1882.
April	$.... to $2.25	None received.
May	2.10 to 2.25	$2.35 to $2.40
June	1.75 to 2.25	2.30 to 2.40
July	1.75 to 2.10	2.20 to 2.30
August	1.50 to 2.10	2.00 to 2.25
September	1.50 to 1.70	..... 2.25
October	1.50 to 1.75	..... 2.25
November	1.50 to 1.75	..... 2.25
December	1.65 to 1.80	2.25 to 2.30

THE YARD BUSINESS.

The yard trade has been exceedingly spasmodic, and the result quite different from the anticipations indulged in at the beginning of the year. The reported stocks in the yards Jan. 1, 1883, aggregated 655,013,520 feet, against 560,416,842 feet Jan. 1, 1882, showing an excess of 94,596,678 feet. As already stated the stocks piled at the mills by manufacturers who were either unwilling to sell or unable to ship ere the close of navigation were larger than customary. But the previous year's business had been profitable, and with low rates of freight to Missouri River and other Western points, buyers from those sections were willing to take liberal supplies, and the first half of January witnessed an active outward movement at well supported prices.

The free movement of grain and live stock to market and the strong upward movement in prices of such farm productions also encouraged yard dealers to suppose that farmers would be disposed to make liberal purchases of lumber for improvements. It soon became apparent that these hopes were not well founded, and after the early demand was filled, there was a decided lull, which was more marked as the month advanced, and the outlook for other branches of trade became less promising. The severity of the weather likewise proved adverse to a free distribution and the close of January and the first half of February were as remarkable for dullness as the early part of the former month had been for activity. The absence of buyers increased the desire to sell, and those who had heavy stocks bought at full prices were

NOT DISPOSED TO REFUSE AN OFFER,

providing it possessed the semblance of fairness. The pressure to realize caused considerable settlement in prices of coarse dimension stuff and boards and strips, and although there were spurts of activity, and at times signs of strength, there was no time during the year when the situation was sufficiently strong to secure and maintain any material advance on these descriptions. The vote of the Exchange at the close of November to increase card rates 50c@$1 per M on a number of grades was not fully observed, but the same list was readopted on Dec. 29, to remain in force through January.

The upper grades, being less plenty, suffered a comparatively small decline, and some are nominally a shade higher than at the close of 1882. It is generally conceded that the only dealers who have made even a fair interest on their money invested during the year were those who cut their own lumber the ordinary yard dealer simply being a sort of commercial philanthropist, who did a large business, which entailed a great deal of hard work and risk, for the benefit of the mill owners and country customers. The year closed, however, with moderate supplies in the interior, and prices down where any further depreciation would curtail production, and the best advised and most judicious dealers regard the situation as promising more profitable results during the incoming year.

In the annual review of the lumber trade for 1882 reference was made in THE INTER OCEAN to the fact that the construction of railroads into many of the chief lumber districts of the Northwest was changing the course of the trade by causing shipments to be made

DIRECT FROM THE MILLS TO CONSUMING POINTS

in the West. This branch of the business has undergone a larger development during the year under review, and has been a factor in reducing the arrivals here and at other leading distributing points, and its influence is likely to be felt in a still greater degree each succeeding year. But the position of Chicago as the great financial and trade center of the country, in connection with the large investments of its capitalists piin ne forests and mills, will ever give it direct or indirect control of the great bulk of the lumber business of the Northwest. A feature of the current year's yard transactions, and one which promises to show greater expansion in the future, has been the large increase in the receipts here of Southern yellow pine, which is rapidly growing in favor as a finishing wood in expensive residences and offices.

STOCKS ON HAND.

The stocks of lumber, lath, and shingles on Jan. 1, from 1870 to 1884, inclusive, were as follows:

	Lumber and timber.	Shingles.	Lath.
1874	328,517,742	29,542,000	28,830,150
1875	344,252,275	81,019,000	39,551,850
1876	352,587,730	83,230,750	47,058,150
1877	360,381,007	97,467,000	36,823,400
1878	385,569,024	125,640,000	43,694,000
1879	410,773,860	200,750,500	41,272,300
1880	451,282,059	190,057,000	48,630,800
1881	497,840,673	188,722,000	50,321,000
1882	560,416,842	260,906,494	48,820,438
1883	655,013,520	299,946,350	76,361,002
1884	*640,000,000	400,000,000	40,000,000

*Estimated.

YARD PRICES, WITH COMPARISONS.

The following shows the prices at the yards on Jan. 1, 1883, and for the same time last year:

	1883.	1882.
First and second clear wide, 3-inch	$49.00	$50.00
First and second clear wide, 1 and 2-inch	49.00	48.00
First and second clear wide, 1-inch	47.00	46.00
First and second clear wide, 1¼ and 1½-inch	47.00	46.00
Third clear, 1¼ to 2-inch	45.00	42.00
A select, inch	36.00	34.00
A select, 2-inch	41.00	37.00
B select, inch	25.00	25.00
B select, 1¼ to 2-inch	34.00	30.00
2x4 clear and select together	28.00	28.00
2x4 B select	23.00	23.00
2x6 clear and select	34.00	36.00
2x8 clear and select	36.00	35.00
7 and 8-inch clear base	34.00	34.00
7 and 8-inch select base	29.00	29.00
Thin clear and select, 9 inch and up	25.00	25.00
First common flooring, D. and M.	37.00	37.00
Second common flooring	34.00	34.00
Third common flooring	36.00	25.00
Fencing flooring	17.00	18.00
Clear siding	22.50	22.50
First common siding	21.50	21.50
Second common siding	18.50	19.00
Third common siding	14.00	14.00
Fencing siding	9.50	10.50
Clear ceiling, D. & M., ⅜, 4 to 6-inch	23.50	23.50
First common ceiling, ⅜, 4 or 6-inch	22.50	22.50
Second common ceiling, ⅜, 4 or 6-inch	19.50	20.00
Third common ceiling, ⅜, 4 or 6-inch	15.00	15.00
A box, 13-inch and over	47.00	47.00
B box, 13-inch and over	42.00	41.00
C box, 13-inch and over	32.00	31.00
D box, 13-inch and over	21.00	20.00
A stock, 12-inch, 12, 14, and 16 feet	41.00	39.00
B stock, 12-inch, 12, 14, and 16 feet	37.00	35.00
C stock, 12-inch, 12, 14, and 16 feet	32.00	30.00
D stock, 12-inch, 12, 14, and 16 feet	20.00	19.00
B stock, 10-inch, 13, 14, and 16 feet	31.00	31.00
C stock, 10-inch, 13, 14, and 16 feet	25.00	25.00
Common fencing, 12 to 18 feet	11.50	13.00
Common boards, 12, 14, 16, and 18 ft	12.50	14.50
Common boards, 10 and 20 ft, 12-in.	14.50	15.00
Common 4-inch fencing, 12, 14, and 16 feet	15.00	16.00
Timber, joist, and scantling, 2x4, 2x 12—14 and 16 feet	13.50	15.00
2x6, 2x8, 2x10, 12, 14, and 16 feet	12.50	15.50
Timber, 4x4 to 8x8, inclusive, 12, 14, 16 feet	13.50	15.50
2x6, 2x8, 2x10, 2x12, 18 feet	13.50	15.50
18 feet, 2x4, 4x4 to 8x8, inclusive	14.50	16.00
2x4, 4x4, and small timber, 10 and 20 feet	15.00	17.00
Common plank	9.50	11.00
Cull plank	10.00	12.00
Common pickets	8.00	9.00
Pickets, flat, rough, good	11.00	12.00
Square pickets, flat, D. & H., selected	18.00	19.00
Square pickets, dressed and pointed	21.00	21.00
Shingles, extra A	3.00	3.20
Shingles, standard	2.50	3.00
Shingles, cedar, A	2.60	2.90
Lath, dry	2.50	2.75

SALES AND SHIPMENTS.

	Lumber, ft.	Shingles, No.
1883	1,868,353,248	980,000,600
1882	2,001,107,241	905,000,000
1881	1,835,476,831	783,463,506

The comparative receipts of the articles mentioned below were as follows:

	1883.	1882.
Lumber, ft.	1,839,941,000	2,110,841,000
Shingles, No.	1,140,000,000	954,000,000
Lath, pcs.	65,477,000	59,737,000
Posts, pcs.	2,416,155	2,462,866
Ties, No.	1,714,388	3,644,711
Wood, cords	22,737	67,092
Slabs, cords	26,283	24,255
Bark, cords	26,065	22,160
Telegraph, poles	175,293	250,867

HARDWOOD LUMBER.

TRADE RATHER UNSATISFACTORY.

The trade in hardwood lumber the past year and the preceding one was on a whole rather unsatisfactory, but still the aggregate movement was large, the receipts here for the year being estimated at 280,000,000 feet, and in 1882 at 300,000,000 feet. The boom given walnut in 1880-81 has reacted, and done more harm than good, as it caused a large increase in the supply, especially of common and culls, but on choice its effect was not so marked. There was less desire manifested by furniture manufacturers and general workers in hardwood to purchase more than their wants required, and the bulk of the trade throughout the year was of a hand to mouth character. The year opened with liberal stocks and a small trade, which continued until April, with concessions constantly being made on commou in order to effect sales. During that month and the one following more life was exhibited, and as stock was continually forced on the market the feeling became weak and unsettled and prices lower, except for good cherry, which, owing to a limited supply, held up well. Orders during the late spring were better, especially for cherry, red oak, maple and other woods used chiefly in house finishing, but walnut was less in favor. The fall sales were more liberal, and the best of the year, but it lacked the spirit that characterized the trade in former seasons. Prices on Walnut declined $2 to $3 per m, but on cherry and other descriptions remaied very firm, on account of the moderate offerings, and during the closing weeks cherry advanced $5 per m, and closed firm. The supply of oak and ash in the regions where it has been obtained for a long time is becoming smaller every year. The stock of hardwood lumber here on Dec. 1 was 41,156,991 feet against 31,040,470 feet Jan. 1, and 34,214,500 feet Jan. 1, 1882.

COAL.

ILLINOIS THE SECOND STATE.

In the production of coal Illinois stands the second State in the Union, Pennsylvania being first, and Ohio third. The area of its coal fields, however, is the largest, being 45,000 square miles, as reported by the geological survey, as against 12,774 in Pennsylvania, 10,000 in Ohio, and 10,000 miles larger than any other State in the Union. Many experts, however, express the opinion that the area in Illinois is much larger than that laid down in the geological chart, and their opinions are strongly supported by numerous discoveries of coal veins outside of the territory designated by the surveys above noted. The growth of the coal mining industry in Illinois may be inferred from the fact that

THE OUT-PUT HAS RISEN

from 2,527,285 tons in 1870 to 10,508,191 tons in 1883. John S. Lord, Secretary of the Bureau of Labor Statistics, reports the progress of mining as follows:

	Mines.	Men employed.	Production.	Value.
1870	322	6,301	2,624,163	$ 6,079,432
1880	590	14,078	6,115,377	8,779,832
1882	704	19,420	9,115,653	13,696,257
1883	639	23,939	10,508,791	15,310,551

The average value per ton for what has been produced during the past three years has undergone very little change. The average for 1880 was $1.44; for 1882, $1.43, and for 1883, $1.46.

Forty-nine of the 102 counties in the State contain mines in active operation. The capacity of the mines is reported at 21,500,000 tons per annum, and the capital invested in mines worked is mentioned at $10,396,540. In addition to the capital and labor employed in mines and mining heavy sums are invested in transpsrtation facilities, and a large additioual force of employes is engaged in its distribution to consumers. The coal is

BITUMINOUS,

and although from its dry character it is not desirable for coking by any process yet discovered, it is extensively used at iron works and other manufactories. It is a fine steam coal, and the leading fuel used for heating purposes throughout the State outside of Chicago, and its popularity here is steadily on the increase, where its cheapness and free burning qualities renders it a favorite with a very large class. During the past few years the demand has exceeded the supply. Large shipments are sent to St. Louis, where it is used more than any other coal. The Indiana coalfields also furnish large supplies of block and bituminous coals for this market. These coals, from the comparatively short haul by rail and the cheapness with which they are mined, are delivered here at lower prices than any other outside coals, and as with those from the Illinois mines, the consumption responds so closely to the output as to prevent an accumulation of stock. Liberal supplies also come from Ohio, and the rapidly

INCREASING RAILROAD FACILITIES

between Chicago and the leading coal fields of that State promises to make it a far more important source of supply in the near future. The Ohio coals are noted for their high percentage of carbon, the readiness with which they burn, and freedom from sulphur. But their increased cost, which is mainly due to higher rates of freight than are paid on Illinois coals, induces a large number of consumers to prefer the latter as a matter of economy. Pennsylvania furnishes a liberal quantity of the bituminous, and all the anthracite coal consumed here or shipped to other points in the West and Northwest, for which Chicago is the chief distributing point.

Although the market has at no time developed very striking features, its general condition has been fairly satisfactory throughout the year, and the volume distributed larger than in 1882. The gain, however, was partly due to the severity of the weather during the first three months of the year, and the almost unprecedented low average of the temperature during the closing months of spring, which necessitated a continuance of fires in residences, offices, and public buildings, long beyond the customary period that artificial heat is ordinarily required. But the increased consumption during the first five months was partly compensated by the comparatively mild weather during a portion of the closing quarter of the year. There was, however, an increased population to supply. This, with an improved demand for bituminous and hard coals from interior points that drew the bulk of their stock from here, made

A LARGER BUSINESS

than in any preceding year in the history of the trade. There was also greater consumption by city and interior manufacturers and gas companies. The bituminous varieties used for the latter purpose mainly come from the Youghiogheny fields in Pennsylvania.

The year closes with a fairly satisfactory trade in both hard and soft coals. Stocks are fair, but not excessive, and the outlook for an increasing output in this State good. The total production of anthracite coal in Pennsylvania for the year just closing is reported at 30,700,000 tons, against 29,120,095 in 1882. In 1873 the production reached 21,-227,952 tons, being 1,257,596 tons greater than in 1863. Hence it will be seen that the output has increased about 208 per cent in twenty years.

RANGE OF PRICES.

The following shows the opening, highest, lowest, and closing prices from retailers' yards for the years named:

	Opening.	Highest.	Lowest.	Closing.
Lackawanna (Anthracite.)				
1883	$7.75	$7.75	$6.50	$7.50
1882	8.50	8.50	6.25	7.75
1881	7.50	9.00	7.25	8.50
1880	7.00	8.00	6.00	8.00
Illinois (Wilmington.)				
1883	$4.50	$4.50	$3.50	4.50
1882	5.00	5.00	4.00	4.50
1881	6.00	6.00	4.50	5.50
1880	4.00	6.00	4.00	6.00
Briar Hill and Erie.				
1883	$7.50	$7.50	$6.50	$6.50
1882	8.00	8.00	6.00	7.50
1881	7.50	8.50	7.00	7.50
1880	7.00	8.00	6.00	8.00

The lowest prices were in June and July, and highest in January.

RECEIPTS AND SHIPMENTS.

The following table exhibits the receipts and shipments of coal at Chicago for the past sixteen years:

Year.	Received, tons.	Shipped, tons.
1874	1,359,496	252,872
1875	1,641,488	365,811
1876	1,619,039	249,862
1877	1,749,091	271,146
1878	1,832,033	305,694
1879	2,384,974	527,844
1880	2,706,088	621,996
1881	3,399,427	843,342
1882	3,689,798	727,477
1883	3,500,000	725,000

SALT.

ABOUT THE SAME AS LAST YEAR.

The trade in salt during the year 1883 exhibited few features of interest. The sales showed no especial increase—most dealers reported their aggregate business about the same as that of the previous year, and fully as satisfactory to both themselves and the manufacturers. Prices ranged lower than in 1882, but at the close 15c per bushel higher for fine than at the opening—the range being from $1 to $1.15 on fine, and $1.35 to $1.45 on coarse. The manufacture of fine salt at Saginaw, Mich., shows a small falling from that of 1882, but an increase over any preceding year. The amount of salt made in the State of Michigan for the year ending Dec. 1, was 2,882,165 barrels, against 3,-307,317 barrels in 1882.

The production of coarse salt in New York was only about two-thirds of that of 1882, on account of the cold and rainy weather during the early part of the season, but the amount of fine made was fully up to that of former years. There was a fair amount of raw salt brought here from Louisiana for the use of packers, where large beds exist on the line of the Mobile and Ohio Railroad. Although the price realized was only $8 per ton, there was not enough handled to cut any important figure in the trade. The amount of foreign salt—Turk's Island and Mediterranean—was larger than in former years, especially of coarse, for which the consumption was larger. Prices ruled lower at $1.25 to $1.50, and for the closing five months at $1.25 to $1.35.

COUNTRY PRODUCE.

A GOOD YEAR.

Produce commission merchants, those engaged in the selling of butter, cheese, eggs, poultry, potatoes, hides, wool, etc., have transacted a large business during the past year, which, as a rule, has been profitable as well as extensive. There were seasons of temporary dullness during the year, and these periodical. Spells of quietude occur, and these can be counted upon annually. The financial standing of merchants has been good, only a few small and unimportant failures having occurred; probably in no business were the failures so few and liabilities so small as among produce commission merchants of this city. Upon this fact can our merchants be congratulated, and it is largely due to a conservative and well managed course of carrying on this particular line of trade. The arrivals of country produce have been very liberal, the continually increasing agricultural and farming interests in the West and Northwest, assuring Chicago, which is the central distributing point, an immense business, which under the favorable advantages offered and facilities at hand is yearly on the increase. The numerous railroads centering at this point traversing through the most beautiful farming lands, are extending further into the interior and thus increasing business for commission merchants.

THE DAIRYING INDUSTRY

continues to expand, new cheese and butter factories being erected throughout the West and Northwest. The capital invested in the dairy interests has been variously estimated at from $5,000,000,000 to $6,000,000,000; estimating returns of 10 per cent on the money invested would produce returns of $500,000,000 to $600,000,000. Besides the dairy interest, can be mentioned an extensive trade in poultry, which represents millions of dollars yearly, and a large trade in game, the revenue of which to commission merchants alone amounts to a great many thousands of dollars in way of commission alone. However, it might be stated here that the game trade the past year has been interfered with to some extent by adverse laws in some States which tended to prevent the sending of game outside of its boundries. The dried fruit trade is a large business of itself, and the green fruit and berry trade in season is an extraordinary large one. Potatoes have not been as renumerative as in former years, owing to an immense crop throughout the United States. The vegetable trade in season is also a good business, especially so the handling of early vegetables from far Southern points. The wool trade has been only moderately satisfactory, the numerous failures of clothing merchants having affected the wool trade very materially.

SEEDS.

As to the business done in this market there is every indication of it having been equal in volume to any previous year, but as figures are hard to obtain there is little to take as a comparison. One fact cannot be overlooked, however, as it argues a continuous growth of this trade, and that is the enlargement and improvement of the facilities for handling seeds. Besides the great distribution from this market of seeds to consumers all over the country, a great deal of speculative interest has been attracted and the various branches of the business have been well patronized. In the values of seed as compared with the previous year, we find in some instances a gain and in others a loss. Flax and clover have turned out the most favorable in this consideration, but timothy, Hungarian, and millet show in comparison a decline. At the opening of the year considerable firmness pervaded the market generally, but in order to define more clearly the market—the several descriptions having individual features of importance—it can be better understood by referring to the various departments of the trade.

FLAXSEED,

one of the most important of seeds, opened at $1.17 to $1.18½, and advanced steadily until reaching $1.60 to $1.65 in May. This great advance had hardly been looked for, and to those who placed reliance in the crop estimate of 1882 it was a most unsatisfactory realization. The crop of 1882 was estimated at 10,000,000 bu. and turned out to be but 7,500,000 bu. Because it was reported large, many crushers would not buy seed at the prices ruling during the fall and winter. The time came when they must buy to replenish their stocks, and the demand was so much increased that it gave holders a decided advantage, and when it began to look as if stocks would not hold out, prices went up with great rapidity, advancing in May to $1.60 to $1.65. The supply of old seed did finally become about exhausted, and in some cases the mills holding out the longest were hardly able to get enough seed to keep their machinery in operation. On the new crop we also find a favorable market. Futures being discounted, new seed opened a good deal lower than old closed. It opened in August at $1.35 and declined to $1.31. So much seed was sold for future delivery that it began to look as if there would be some difficulty in filling contracts, because the rainy weather of the fall checked the receipts. "Shorts" were very nervous in September and the competition for seed was so great that the market was advanced to $1.52. Ample provisions to fill contracts were finally made, however, and the market went back to $1.30 to $1.31. The receipts were not so large during the latter part of the year as the year before, and yet there was an increase in stocks. This does not exhibit well for the consumptive demand, but the seed was centered in strong hands, who were interested in future trading and could easily control the market. In October the market advanced to $1.34 to $1.35. A good deal of seed was taken for shipment during the month in order to have it forwarded before the close of navigation. During November the market reacted to $1.28, but at the close of the year it was back again to $1.40 to $1.45.

TIMOTHY

left on hand at the first of the year met with a good market. The offerings were quite liberal and the home trade only moderate, but an export demand existed which greatly relieved the market. A good many Canadian orders were received and there was a good foreign demand, for England had two short crops, the yield in 1881 and in 1882 being below the average. This outlet for our seed gave the market a very healthy tone, and during the first two months of the year prices advanced from $1.55 to $1.60 for prime to $1.90. In March trade having slacked off, the market receded to $1.55 to $1.60. The market ruled tolerably steady until after the spring trade was over, when there was a decline. In view of the large crop of both seed and hay, dealers regarded the chances for low prices on the new crop as favorable, and while in August the range was $1.45 to $1.55, after new seed came in freely the price was lowered to $1.25 to $1.30. This low range exerted a good demand both from the regular trade and for speculation. The offerings were so readily taken that the market in October improved to $1.33 to $1.35. After the fall trade was well over and when navigation closed a weaker feeling again prevailed and the market declined to $1.20 to $1.25, and did not react materially up to the close. At the close of the year we find the receipts small and the market quiet.

CLOVER

brought good prices. It was scarce the early part of the year for the crop in 1882 had been a small one. It opened at $6.40 for prime. The demand was all that could be supplied. Consignments coming on the market were wanted, and buyers had to bid up to get the seed. The market advanced steadily and in March as high as $8.40 to $8.60 was paid with choice sold at $9. Owing to so high a market dealers finally limited their purchases to actual requirements, and when the spring trade fell off the market receded to $7. It sold up again in August to $7.50 to $8, but in September fell off to $4.80 to $5. This decline was due to an expected large crop. The early frosts, however, did great damage and caused a demand from quarters where it was thought there would be seed to ship. A good trade followed with an advance late in the year to $5.75 to $6, and seller March sold at $6.50.

TRADE IN HUNGARIAN AND MILLET

was very light, and both descriptions were about the same in price. The market opened at 50c to 65c with stocks light. During the spring the market advanced to 80c and 90c. Seed was held steady on account of the rainy weather, but finally, when good cereal crops were certain, there was a desire to sell, and in July the market declined to 25c and 45c. Late in the year there was little doing. The demand and supply were both light and prices ranged at 40c to 50c, with some of the first new seed selling at 60c.

The following table shows the movement of flaxseed during the past two years:

	Received.		Shipped.	
	1883.	1882.	1883.	1882.
January....	143,455	366,353	103,839	367,204
February...	105,000	236,423	53,000	211,080
March......	116,000	134,886	104,000	151,955
April........	120,000	90,206	322,909	235,596
May..........	47,500	93,322	62,278	147,544
June.........	54,500	97,258	19,450	141,706
July.........	37,500	234,520	92,309	334,116
August......	248,500	380,500	116,739	212,074
September..	621,500	1,138,000	376,023	807,734
October.....	843,000	1,079,000	581,946	937,613
November..	581,000	859,000	425,384	687,841
December..	205,000	376,500	208,290	144,708
Total....	3,122,955	5,094,968	2,466,167	4,379,771

The stock in store is reported at 282,232 bu, against 334,630 bu one month ago, and 455,097 bu one year ago."

BUTTER.

THERE HAS BEEN A GOOD ACTIVE TRADE during the past year, that is, taking the market all in all. Of course it has required low prices to move a great deal of the stock, but there has not been that piling up and accumulation of stock that has heretofore proved so disastrous to the trade; to the contrary, however, buyers have been on the market pretty much all the time at some price, so that stocks have been moving off very fairly, and by this means the supply on sale has been kept fresh, more so than in former years. This is required to keep the market in a healthy condition, and it has been demonstrated that the sooner butter is marketed the better it is to sell it, and invariably commands a better price, even if held back on an advancing market, as experience has taught that the quality deteriorates to a greater extent than the price of held goods advances in proportion to fresh. The make has been liberal during the year, exceeding by far the make of the year 1882. According to statistics furnished the receipts for the year 1883 in the Chicago market were about 11,000,000 lbs larger than the preceding year. The stock on hand in the Chicago market on Dec. 1 was equal to about 12,000 pkgs of all kinds. In the interior the supply on hand at the close of the year was considered light, as country shippers and manufacturers have followed the plan of marketing their goods while fresh. Pasturage has been good—that is, there has been a great abundance of grass, but owing to the unusually wet season, from early in the spring to late in the fall, the milk has scarcely been as rich, therefore the make during a good share of the season lacked body and flavor, and on the whole perhaps did not average in quality as good as the year 1882. While trade has been good, it must be said that the local consumption of butter, especially during the winter season, when butterine is made, is not what it ought to be, butterine to a very great extent supplanting the genuine butter. The local retailer sells it over his counter because he can make a greater profit and yet sell it cheaper than creamery or fine dairy butter, hence the desire on the part of dealers to handle it. The export demand has been much more satisfactory; high-priced goods have not been wanted, but there has been a large amount of 10c to 15c per lb butter taken, common to good but all fresh stock, foreign buyers being as much adverse to taking stale and rancid stock as ever. Some good to choice creamery was also taken at 18c to 20c per lb, but the speculative demand that existed at these same figures interfered with the legitimate export movement, as prices were soon advanced above exports limits through this speculation. A very healthy export movement would no doubt have been established at from 18 to 20c, but exporters refused to follow any advance above these figures, and contented themselves with their home production, or else supplied their wants with oleomargarine and other manufactured goods at home. As it was, the exports have been fully three times as large for the twelve months ending Nov. 31, 1883, as compared with the same period in 1882. The low-priced butter taken for export, say at about 10c per pound, was mostly used for baking purposes, and has been preferred to oleomargarine or other manufactured goods, as the latter does not appear to work up as satisfactorily for baking purposes as butter. The butterine business has assumed gigantic proportions, and while no figures can be obtained of the amount made it can be said that the manufacture has been greatly in excess of last year; several new firms have started, and the old firms have largely increased their facilities. The butterine business will, it is feared, check the making of dairy butter to a greater or less degree every year, and dairymen may find it to their advantage to sell milk to the creameries. And why? Because the low prices at which the dairy butter sells is not remunerative enough, and good fair prices for milk will pay them better. Fine butter is always as a rule wanted. Butterine makers must have it. Without high-flavored butter butterine cannot be successfully made, and the competition for fancy fresh makes of high-flavored creamery assures the makers good paying prices pretty much the entire year round, from one source or other. Hence every year the creamery system of butter making grows in favor and increases, while the older system is gradually going out. Prices ranged at the opening of the year at 36 to 40c for creamery, and 12½ to 13½c for packing grades, but by the last of January prices declined to 32 to 35c for creamery, and advanced in March to 35 to 39c. By the first of April prices for creamery declined to 22 to 30c, and during May and June sold within 16 to 20c, and during July and August at 18 to 21c, while packing grades sold at 8 to 9½c. In September prices for creamery reacted to 18 to 22c, and from then to the last of November prices advanced to 38 to 42c, declining the last of the year to 30 to 35c. Packing grades ranged at 9 to 11c.

The following exhibits the extreme range of prices for the years named, outside prices being for fine creamery, and inside for fresh packing stock or low grades:

	Opening.	Highest.	Lowest.	Closing.
1881..	12 @30c	15 @38c	8½@19c	13 @38c
1882..	12½@38c	14 @47c	10 @21c	12½@40c
1883..	12½@40c	12½@42c	8 @20c	9 @35c

EGGS.

No regular statistics have as yet been compiled that would give any correct idea of the movement of so important a branch of the produce trade. The railroads furnish a partial report, but no figures are furnished by the express companies, which at certain seasons of the year, particularly during the spring months, furnish a large portion of our supplies. Therefore it is impossible to give even approximate figures that would in any way convey a correct idea of the magnitude of the yearly traffic in this commodity. A very satisfactory trade has existed, proving remunerative to farmers and interior shippers, prices having averaged higher than during the year 1882. This has been due largely to a good demand from parties who make a business of placing eggs in ice-houses to supply the market during the winter months. This, too, helped to keep prices firm, as whenever the market would touch a point sufficiently low in their estimation they would step in and buy, and their purchases in more than one instance during the summer checked the decline when the market appeared the weakest. So much to the advantage of the Chicago market, which has the best of cold-storage facilities. In regard to the supply of cold-storage eggs it can be stated that the supply in the country ice-houses the past year has been smaller than during the year 1882, while the city supply is believed to have been larger. Fresh eggs the first of the year ruled steady and firm at 25c to 31c. About Feb. 14 to the 15th fresh eggs commenced to arrive from St. Louis and Southern points, and the market weakened to 28c, and then off steadily from 24c to 25c, closing at these figures on the last day of February. March 1 the market opened lower, with sales at 20c to 21c, and fluctuated down in May from 14½c to 15c. In June sold up to 16c and 16½c, but sold back again to 14c and 14½c by the middle of July, which were the lowest prices reached. Then advanced steadily during the balance of the year to 25c and 28c per doz. Ice-house eggs have sold at times close to the price of fresh, and from that 4c to 5c less.

The following range of prices show the extremes for four years:

	1880.	1881.	1882.	1883.
Highest..	28@30	50@55	27@29	30@31
Lowest...	8@ 9	10@11	12@12½	14@14½

CHEESE.

Dealers expressed themselves well satisfied with the cheese trade for the year 1883. The volume of trade has been large and prices have varied widely, ruling much higher for a long period than during the year 1882, and also for a time ruled somewhat lower. During the summer receivers and dealers in general experienced a great deal of trouble with hot-weather made stock, which caused considerable dissatisfaction at the time, but otherwise the year's trade has been both profitable and satisfactory. Home consumption has been good, the Southern and Western trade having drawn well upon our supplies, and the export movement was also quite active at times when prices were within the reach of foreign buyers. The exports for the year 1883 from the United States were reported at about 110,000,000 pounds, against about 103,000,000 pounds for the year 1882. At the beginning of the year 1883 stocks were light and the market firm, full cream cheddars selling at 12½ to 13c and flats at 7 to 8c per pound. High as these prices were, an almost uninterrupted advance continued to take place during the first quarter of the year, and also during a part of April, prices reaching 15 to 15½c for prime full cream cheddars and 10½ to 12c for flats. In April prices eased off a trifle, but still maintained an unusual high range, even surprising the most sanguine bull. This state of affairs was attributed to the fact that all the large home consuming markets were almost bare of cheese, and also to the unusually late season, owing to cold and unseasonable weather. Late in April and early in May the feeling, however, changed to weakness, and by the close of the month prices had declined fully 2½c per pound. Production increased materially and consumption fell off. Supplies began to accumulate, and prices continued to decline, finally reaching 9@9½c per pound in June. Speculators evidently thought prices low, and exporters also felt as though these were bottom figures, and for a time a very sharp demand existed at 9c to 9½c and thereabouts. Speculators were the principal buyers, and the movement was so brisk that manufacturers scarcely gave cheese enough time to cure on shelves. The June make and a portion of July was taken at these prices. Operators forgetting that prices would naturally check consumption, and as production increased, all the central markets were continually crowded with fresh, uncured cheese, and the result was a further decline in prices, almost creating a panic, so much so that exporters and early buyers lost confidence in this staple, believing that we would have a repetition of the seasons of 1877 and 1878. The rapid decline in products helped the downward course in cheese. This state of affairs continued until prices reached 7½ to 8c per ℔ in August, when consumption and the shipping demand increased very rapidly, and the hot weather cheese was mostly consumed. Later on prices commenced to steadily improve, and with a light make in the fall, caused partially by early frost affecting pasturage and the corn crop, the market ruled strong, prices reaching 12½ to 13c for full cream. The year closed with light stocks in the hands of dealers and manufacturers, and indications that fall-made goods will be closed out at high prices.

The range of prices for full cream cheddars for the year 1882 was 9½ to 13½c—the lowest prices being reached in July.

HOPS.

At the date of our last annual review of the hop market, stocks were light and prices at a point never before reached. High prices were maintained during the winter, but by rigid economy in the manufacture and by drawing more freely than usual on the stocks of malt liquors by dealers, manufacturers managed to get along and the limited supply of hops proved ample, and after March prices rapidly declined to 25c per pound or 4.50 per cent from the prices of November and December. Profits of the early season were swept away and many disasters occurred among the mere speculative members of the trade.

The crop of 1883 was large in quantity but very uneven in quality. This was the condition in all the hop producing districts of the world. The result has been a wide range of prices—the better grades bearing remunerative prices and the lower being a drug at low prices.

The poor quality of the hops in the West and East was attributed to the continued cloudy and wet weather, there not being enough bright sunny weather to dry out the hops and prevent lice and mold. On the Pacific Coast it seems to have been just the reverse, too dry weather there having lessened the production of good hops.

The production of the United States is estimated at 210,000 bales of 180 pounds each; i. e., Pacific Coast, 43,000; Western States, 8,000; New York, 155,000, and New England States, 4,000.

Home consumption is estimated at 170,000 bales, leaving for export 40,000 bales, of which 27,000 have been exported, and the remainder will probably be needed by English brewers. It is generally conceded by the trade that prices for better grades will be fairly maintained during this crop year.

The condition of the trade is healthy. Chicago dealers have been conservative, and the volume of business increased with the growth of our Western territory:

The following were the figures current at the close of the years 1883 and 1882:

	1883.	1882.
Fancy New York....	@28	$....@1.00
Choice New York.......... ..	25@27	1.00@1.05
Prime New York..............	22@24	90@ 95
Low grade New York........	14@20	...@ ...
Pacific Coast, fair to good...	22@25	85@1.05
Western good.................	18@22	40@ 70
Western common............	12@17	20@ 30

BROOMCORN.

The crop of broom corn raised annually is estimated at about 24,000 tons, about 1,000 tons of which is raised in the Mohawk Valley of New York, and the rest is produced in the West. Of this amount it is estimated that nearly two-thirds is handled in the Chicago market. The crop harvested in the fall of 1882 was a large one. It was rather a poor one, though, in point of quality, the color of the corn was not good, perhaps better than usual, but there was a shortage of hurl, it running largely to a coarse and curly growth. In view of the heavy yield in 1882 dealers bought rather sparingly and only the best grades. All through the fall and winter a large portion of the crop was shipped in commission lots, and the market at times was glutted, causing prices to depreciate, so that common brush sold all through the early part of the year as low as 2c to 3c per pound. Low prices and a plentiful supply caused an increased manufacture, and while dealers sold considerably more than usual in the fall, trade was also large right through the year. There was an exception to the generally low prices of brush, in hurl and fine green self-working stock, which in spite of the large supply of low grades was found to be comparatively scarce, and advanced from 6½c to 9c per pound, it being needed to work up the coarser grades. Later in the season the accumulation of short coarse and seedy corn wore away under the inroads made upon it by large manufacturers who bought on account of cheapness, and September found the old stock pretty well cleaned up and the market was in good condition for the new crop, although a few hundred tons remained in the Illinois Central and Chicago, Burlington and Quincy Railroad districts of Illinois, and this, since the fall trade opened, has been all worked off. Planting in 1883 was smaller than the year before, partially on account of low prices consequent to a poor quality. In Kansas alone there was a falling off of about 40 per cent, according to the State reports. There was also less planting along the lines of the Illinois Central and Burlington Roads. The acreage in Nebraska was fully up to previous years. Missouri is uncertain, but is believed to have grown less than usual. As regards trade in new corn, it was good from October until along in November, but late in the year it fell off, and was mainly on orders. This year's crop was at first supposed to be better, or it might be said very good in quality, but the proportion of hurl is found to be small as compared with the lower grades, a large percentage of the crop being short, stained, and damaged. Prices until recently have ruled favorable, but have declined, although the decline has not affected choice medium and hurl, it being most severe for short and common brush. Considerable of the late brush in Kansas and Nebraska was damaged by the heavy fall rains, and growers would do well to have sheds provided before another crop, that their corn may be cured thoroughly dry, for many growers in the States named, lacking those facilities, lost heavily on account of corn being damaged. Stocks at the close of the year are ample. The depression of the market has been caused by large consignment offerings, but it is thought that these offerings will be largely taken up in a short time. The crop has been largely forwarded, for a year ago farmers held their corn and took low prices in the spring, while this year they seem to have been actuated into sending it to market about as soon as ready to ship.

HIDES.

While prices have not undergone any very serious fluctuations the trade on the whole has not been in a very satisfactory condition. Dealers have been compelled to sell on extremely small margins, and, taking into consideration the shrinkage and other disadvantages to contend with, the profits have been small and percentage of gain on the capital invested comparatively trifling. The hide trade the past few years has become entirely revolutionized. Years ago commission merchants handled the bulk of the hides coming to this market. The commission man was the first party, the hide dealer the second. But our merchants have lost the greater share of this trade by dealers establishing agencies throughout the West and Northwest, so that at one time they controlled the greater part of the hide trade. However, since Chicago has become the cattle slaughtering market of the world, dealers have lost their hold to a certain extent, and where dealers have been able to dictate prices to interior sellers on small lots picked up here and there, they are now compelled to a greater degree than before to meet the views of the city slaughterers, as the competition for large lots necessitates their buying on small margins and bidding up full prices. Thousands of cattle which have been slaughtered promiscuously throughout the West now find a market here, and hides which would find a sale through the hands of commission merchants are now lost to them. The number of tanneries in operation adjacent to and in this city are reported to be about 17. Taking green salted hides as a basis, sales have ranged from $8\frac{1}{4}$c at the opening of the year, to $8\frac{1}{2}$ to $8\frac{1}{4}$c in March, back to $7\frac{3}{4}$ to 8c in April, then up to $8\frac{1}{2}$c in June, and back again to 8c in September, ruling steady at this price during the balance of the year. Green salted calf-skins have sold at 12 to 13c. The failures which occurred in the leather houses naturally had some effect upon the hide market, and was one of the reasons for the decline during the latter half of the year.

POTATOES.

A very marked reaction from the extreme high prices current during the year 1882 has followed in the year 1883, and while in the former year prices ruled extremely high, they during the year just closed have ruled exceedingly low. Trade during the first half of the year was good, but during the last half unsatisfactory, an overabundant supply, the crop being an unusually large one, causing such low prices as to make it impossible to handle them, and shippers invariably suffered losses on their shipments. The market the first half of year was rather firm. The receipts were only fair and not more than equal to requirements, and sometimes light, so that with a moderate shipping and local trade prices ruled firm. Early in January sales ranged at 55 to 70c per bu for car lots of common to choice straight stock, advancing later in the month to 70 to 85c, and fancy stock sold to $87\frac{1}{2}$ to 90c. But in February prices receded to 60 to 75c, and in March to 40 to 65c, when mild weather influenced very free shipments from the interior. About the last of March prices again rallied to 45 to 75c, but in April sold off to 35 to 60c, and from then to the end of June, which closed the season for old potatoes, sold between 35 to 55c per bu. New potatoes made their first appearance in this market in April, the first sales of Bermuda being at $7.50 to $8 per brl and New Orleans at $5 per brl. For a few days sales were made at $4 to $5 per brl, but by the 19th of May prices had declined to $2.50 to $3.50 per brl, good to choice, and poor stock sold at $1.50. In June prices reached $1.75 to $2.25 per brl for choice, and in July, August, and September, when neighboring farmers brought potatoes to market, sales were made at 75c to $1.50 per brl. In September bulk lots commenced to arrive, and sales of these by the car ranged during the balance of the year from 25c to 30c per bu mixed to 30c to 40c for choice, and some fancy sold at 45c to 48c. In November the first severe frost caught a large number of cars of potatoes on the track not properly protected, and a great deal of the stock was so badly frosted that it was actually worthless. Peachblows during the year have not sold as well as early rose, excepting for an occasional fine car. The reason for this, it is said, is that the peachblow variety is running out, the quality being poor, the potatoes very uneven, coarse, and hollow. The early rose and Burbank varieties have been preferred.

DRIED FRUITS.

THREE MILLION DOLLARS IS THE ESTIMATE placed on the volume of business done annually in the handling of dried fruits—generally domestic—in this market. The capital invested in the prosecution of this business is approximated at about $600,000. It can hardly be said that this trade has grown much in the past year or two or has kept pace with the progress and development of other industries in this city. The reason probably is that for two seasons the fruit crop of the East has been comparatively light, and from the northern fruit belt this market has usually derived its greatest supplies, especially of apples, which form really the principal item of the list of dried fruits. And yet, while there has been no large gain in trade, this does not imply that there has been any decrease; on the contrary, business has averaged very good. The West and Northwest, the great consuming districts, hardly used so much dried fruit as in former years, for it will be remembered that in 1882 the yield of fruit of all kinds was unprecedentedly liberal all over the sections named, and while there was green fruit to use in its season there was also a little surplus left for drying and for use from time to time. This had some effect on trade, there is no doubt, for in the spring of 1883 the supply of fruit was lighter than had ever before been known, and dealers began to look for higher prices and a larger trade. They did advance prices somewhat, but they did not succeed in keeping them up because the expected demand was not realized, and probably for the reason named. As stated, the quantity of fruit on hand at the opening of the year was comparatively light, being estimated at 7,000 barrels of apples, 6,000 barr ls of peaches, 4,500 barrels blackberries, 10,000 cases evaporated apples, 2,000 barrels pared peaches, and about 800 barrels of other small fruit. Although the country demand was not up to expectations, and the order trade suffered some from the decrease, there came instead an export demand, especially for apples, which tended to stimulate the feeling when otherwise some disappointment might have followed. Before the opening of the season for handling fruit of the growth of 1883 the market was quite completely cleared of offerings. The business of the year has been quite remunerative to those engaged in it, because there has been no wild speculation. Dealers have carried about what stock they calculated they could sell at a fair profit and avoid crowding, and this act of conservatism has been beneficial in its results. Fruit of the crop of 1883 has not come forward very freely, and from September to the present time only moderate stocks have been held by dealers. There is in store at the present time about 3,000 brls apples, 2,500 brls peaches, 2,000 brls blackberries, 8,000 cases evaporated apples, 1,000 brls pared peaches, 300 brls cherries, and 150 brls raspberries. While the market is fairly well supplied, in view of current demand and prevailing business troubles, yet it is considered as an aggregate to be the smallest stock ever held in Chicago at any corresponding period. The supplies have come largely from the South and Southwest. The great Northern fruit-producing States had very small crops and have not added materially to the supply. So light has the crop been in the North for the last two seasons that in some instances evaporators of apples have changed their locations for operating to the South, where the requisite supplies could be the more readily obtained, but this move may be only temporary. The Southern and Southwestern States had fair crops of apples, but the peach crop fell off largely from former years. When it is understood that Utah and Oregon had nearly an entire failure of fruit crops, California a partial failure, and Canada almost a complete failure, it is fair to conclude that the ensuing six months will witness an active and profitable trade, as the territory ordinarily supplied from Chicago will be largely increased by a demand from the Eastern States, which in former years have sent their surplus to this market. Besides at the closing of the year prices are low enough to invite trade. Prices during the year were not subject to any violent fluctuations, for, as stated, there was not much speculation, and while there was at no time a large stock to crowd on sale, the fruit was at the same time well distributed, and there was no forced value established by concentration. Southern apples advanced from 6½c to 8c, and closed at 6½c to 7½c on fruit of the crop of 1882, while for new fruit prices have gradually receded 5½c to 6c. Michigan apples advanced in the spring from 7½c to 8½c, receded to 7¾c, and finally closed at 8c to 8½c for old fruit, and the new sold down from about 7½c to 6½c, although up to the present time few Michigan apples have come on the market. Evaporated apples have sold during the year at 9c to 15c per lb, depending on the quality. Halves peaches improved from 6c to 7¾c for old, but for new the market so far has been quiet and they have receded to about 5¾c to 6c. Blackberries opened at 7½c and sold up to 9½c. In anticipation of a good crop they sold down in August to 7c to 7½c, but new berries have not come in freely and they have reacted to 9½c to 9¾c. They are said to be largely held by speculators in the South. Raspberries sold at 32c to 36c for old and the new opened at about 25c to 26c and improved to 27c to 28c.

WOOL.

BUSINESS GOOD.

Business during the past year has been good, but not altogether satisfactory. The clip has been large and the wool of good quality, but the numerous failures in the clothing trade had an unfavorable effect upon the market for wool, and the trade during the year suffered very perceptibly in consequence. As a rule manufacturers have been loth to laying in any large stocks, but have purchased on a conservative plan, and merely bought as their wants required them to. The close margin in the clothing business on which merchants have been compelled to operate made manufacturers very cautious in their purchases, and they selected their stock more closely than in former years, being more exacting, and rejected many lots which heretofore would have passed their inspection. In fact, they were compelled to do this in order to subserve their own interests. The reduction in tariff duty, amounting to 3½c per pound on wool, created fears of foreign importations, and naturally tended to make buyers act with caution. Speculations in wool have also been restricted for the same reasons which actuated manufacturers. The quality of Western wool is said to be good, and is the result of the improvement Western sheep-raisers have made in their flocks by the introduction of new and better grades of stock. A noticeable feature in the market was that manufacturers called mostly for unwashed wool. As it is necessary for them to scour all wool before using, it is claimed they prefer to take it more in its natural state at the difference in price and clean it according to their own notions. Stocks in the hands of dealers at the close of the year were not large. In January unwashed wool sold within the range of 17 to 28c per pound, and washed within the range of 25 to 37c, but advanced in February, owing to an improved demand, to 18 to 30c per pound for unwashed, and to 25 to 41c for washed. In May, however, owing to a period of dullness, prices declined to 22 to 39c for washed and 16 to 26c for unwashed, which range was later on reduced about 1 to 2c per pound on some grades, and closed dull. The range of prices, which averages considerably lower than last year, is given below, showing the comparison with the year 1882:

	—Washed—		—Unwashed—	
	1883.	1882.	1883.	1882.
Jan......	27 to 37	30 to 42	17 to 28	16 to 27
Feb'y....	25 to 41	30 to 42	18 to 30	16 to 27
March...	25 to 41	30 to 42	18 to 30	16 to 27
April	25 to 41	30 to 40	18 to 30	16 to 30
May......	22 to 39	30 to 40	17 to 26	16 to 30
June	22 to 37	29 to 40	16 to 34	16 to 27
July......	22 to 37	29 to 40	16 to 24	16 to 27
August..	22 to 37	29 to 40	16 to 24	16 to 27
Sept.....	22 to 37	30 to 40	16 to 26	16 to 27
Oct......	24 to 37	30 to 40	16 to 26	17 to 28
Nov......	24 to 37	30 to 40	16 to 26	17 to 28
Dec......	24 to 37	26 to 38	16 to 26	17 to 28

HAY.

There was a larger trade in hay, but the movement cannot be given. The crop this year was heavy, but, owing to the wet weather, the quality of the timothy was poorer, and of prairie about the same as in 1882. There was more fine upland prairie from Western Iowa and Kansas handled than formerly. The shipping demand was fair, but not so brisk as in 1882. The local consumptive demand, however, was good the bulk of the year, and choice grades always found a ready sale, but common, which was offered freely at times, dragged. Prices ranged lower, and in comparison with those of a year ago showed a reduction of $1.50 to $2 per ton on timothy, 50c on choice upland prairie, and $1 to $2 on ordinary do.

THE MERCANTILE TRADE.

A THOROUGH CANVASS

among the manufacturing and jobbing establishments of Chicago develops, that while there has been a very fair increase in the production and distribution of nearly all leading lines of goods, and the further fact that Chicago has really suffered less in proportion to the aggregate volume of business done than any other large city in the country, the profits, as a rule, have not been commensurate with the extent of goods handled, and in most cases the returns have been little more than sufficient to allow a moderate interest on the capital invested, while in not a few cases it has been difficult to get back a new dollar for an old one. The causes that contributed to the demoralization of trade and curtailment of profits were numerous, and some of them far reaching, not the least of which was the partial failure for successive years of

THE CROPS

in a number of Western States that had previously been the most productive in the Union, the result of which was to reduce the purchasing power of a large population in the most densely settled portion of the West, from which the heaviest and most profitable business had formerly been derived. The year also opened with large stocks of nearly all lines of goods. But manufacturers had conceived the idea that the consumption would respond to the supply, and without stopping to inquire into the situation drove their establishments to their fullest capacity. It soon became apparent, however, that the consumption was not responding to the early expectations. The falling off in demand stimulated manufacturers and jobbers to greater exertions to free their factories and stores of accumulating stocks, on which a heavy shrinkage in values was inevitable. The desire to realize grew stronger as the year advanced. The weather, which is always a factor in increasing or curtailing sales as it is favorable or adverse to the consumption of goods, was exceedingly detrimental to the interests of makers and jobbers of most leading articles. The rapidity with which failures increased in nearly all parts of the country induced

STRICTER CONSERVATISM AMONG BANKERS

in granting accommodations to customers, and in many cases compelled really worthy applicants to resort to forced sales of goods as the only means of securing funds with which to meet maturing obligations. The situation of the dry goods trade, which ranks first among the jobbing interests of the country, was also further aggravated by the forced sales at auction of enormous lines of goods, for which Eastern manufacturers were unable to find buyers in the regular way. These sales occurred after Western jobbers had bought large stocks, hence they were compelled to make rates to customers to conform to those of the auction-rooms. Large failures among Eastern cloth and clothing houses also brought their stocks on the market at ruinously low prices, and Chicago dealers had to choose between meeting such competition or a loss of customers. It is scarcely necessary to say that they chose the former, feeling that they were sufficiently strong to make the sacrifice without jeopardizing their credit.

The iron trade suffered from an over-supply, coupled with a heavy decrease in consumption by railroads, the construction of which diminished 50 per cent, while the expenditures for repairs on lines in operation were greatly reduced. Heavy failures in the trade also threw large stocks on the market at prices far below the cost of production. Other classes of goods suffered from similar causes, while the lack of confidence induced greater conservatism among consumers, who, fearing a further depreciation in prices, restricted purchases to current wants, and were more than usually persistent in their demands for extreme inside prices. These unfavoring conditions compelled Chicago manufacturers and jobbers to

WORK ON THE CLOSEST POSSIBLE MARGINS,

and many lines of goods went to consumers at prices which failed to return a remuneration above cost. Nor is it surprising that failures have occurred. On the reverse, it is creditable to Chicago merchants that the percentage of suspensions were so small, compared to the volume of business done. Investigation into the affairs of the suspended firms has also discovered that their troubles were mainly traceable to causes outside of their legitimate business.

The completion during the year of the Northern Pacific Railroad through to the Pacific coast, and the extension of other Southwestern lines into Mexico, has given Chicago direct connection with a large area of country not heretofore accessible to our merchants. That a large and profitable custom will come from there in the near future is beyond question. A large additional trade has also been derived from Manitoba and other Canadian districts of the far Northwest that are rapidly settling up with a valuable population. A material increase is noted in the shipments to South and Central America, South Africa, and Australia, with which Chicago is building up a large trade in agricultural implements, vehicles, and many lines of machinery.

The rapidity with which the new Western and Northwestern States and Territories, for which Chicago is the chief financial and commercial center,

ARE UNDERGOING DEVELOPMENT,

may be inferred from the following table showing the sales of land by the General Government for the years ending June 30, from 1880 to 1883, inclusive:

	1883. Acres.	1882. Acres.	1881. Acres.	1880. Acres.
Dakota.........	6,689,595	4,355,637	253,236	2,258,493
Idaho..........	232,640	160,948	133,908	120,323
Kansas.........	808,655	904,061	169,156	1,510,469
Minnesota.....	1,202,960	1,085,737	843,968	851,027
Montana......	246,458	263,165	103,073	109,969
Nebraska......	1,315,104	884,028	643,200	1,324,718
New Mexico..	448,836	103,736	88,658	38,360
Oregon.........	499,770	304,139	204,734	239,418
Utah...........	111,914	83,909	82,702	97,461
Wyoming....	18,709	58,307	46,263	44,247
Wisconsin....	454,002	447,268	234,867	107,073
Colorado......	410,919	275,578	215,042	186,437
Total.....	12,508,371	8,850,482	5,898,818	6,897,005

It will be seen that the increase in 1883 over 1880 was nearly 100 per cent, and that the aggregate for the four years reached 34,155,678 acres. In addition it is estimated that nearly or quite 20,000,000 acres were sold by railroads and States who had land grants. These lands are being

RAPIDLY BROUGHT UNDER CULTIVATION,

and their annually increasing production will largely contribute to swell the trade of this market.

DRY GOODS.

THIS IS THE MOST IMPORTANT

branch of the mercantile trade, and embraces a greater variety of articles than are handled by any other line of business. Few, if any, other branches of merchandise have undergone such radical changes within a brief period both as regards the manner in which it is conducted, source of supply, and points of distribution. It is only a few years since the Atlantic cities had control of the entire jobbing and package trade of the United States. Goods were sold on six, nine, and twelve months' time, and, as may be inferred, the risks assumed by granting long credits by the Eastern jobbers to customers so widely scattered, and a majority of whom were only accessible by stage coach or horseback journeys, was enormous, and to cover such risks enormous profits were charged. The ease with which credit was secured and the indulgence given buyers induced tens of thousands to engage in selling goods who were as destitute of knowledge of the business as they were of capital. They bought on credit and sold on the same terms. Their customers, as a rule, were poor, and a majority destitute of ideas of business promptness. To them payment was a matter of secondary consideration. As a result of this loose system,

ONLY THE MOST JUDICIOUS

and sharpest traders succeeded. The development of the country which followed the advent of an extended railroad system in every direction caused a rapid westward movement of the center of population and agricultural production, while the increased means of transportation gave farmers a quick means of marketing their products, and made them larger and at the same time more independent buyers. The advantages of bringing dealers and consumers more closely together caused a transfer of the jobbing trade from the Atlantic cities to the West. Instead of making a journey of weeks' duration by the most tedious means of conveyance to the Eastern cities, as was the custom previous to the advent of the railroad system in the West, and selecting a six or twelve months' stock, the retailer in the Central, Western, and Southern States now steps aboard the cars, and in a few hours finds himself in Chicago or some smaller tributary point, where he buys such goods as are required for the present or near future, and takes his departure for home. This system of buying has lessened the risks of accumulating goods that fail to find buyers, and decreased the losses incurred by granting long credits. The consumption of goods has grown with the wealth and population of the country, and as it is an immutable law of trade that people will buy what they require where they find the best market for their surplus products, and as the geographical position, no less than the natural and artificial means of transportation, have given Chicago the cheaper and more direct means of communicating with all parts of the North American continent, it has necessarily

BECOME THE LEADING MARKET

in the world for the sale of farm products and the chief distributing point for dry goods to every part of the country west of the Alleghanies. Another and equally marked change as in the manner of selling and center of distribution, has been the character of goods handled. Instead of relying almost entirely on foreign markets for nearly all of the best grades of cotton and worsted dress fabrics, as was the case a quarter of a century since, the bulk of such goods now sold are from American looms. To such perfection have American makes of cotton, woolen, and worsted dress fabrics succeeded that they have almost superseded those of foreign production. This is especially the case in regard to cotton and worsted goods. Like success is also attending the manufacture of cloths and cassimeres, while domestic blankets and carpets have driven their foreign competitors from our markets. American ribbons and threads are now the standard goods at home, and their high quality is bringing them rapidly into favor in countries which have heretofore been supplied exclusively by European manufactories. New Zealand and Australia are large buyers of such goods in this country. American silk dress goods are also steadily growing in favor with those who prefer a serviceable article, but the limited extent of their production has thus far prevented them from coming largely into use. There are, however, many lines of goods, and especially plushes and velvets, that are still chiefly imported. Yet the rapid strides made in the direction of

SUPERIORITY OF OUR HOME MANUFACTURES

during the past quarter of a century, warrants the conclusion that the end of another decade will see the importion of foreign goods, which is now estimated by intelligent merchants at one-fifth of the entire consumption in this country, reduced to one-tenth. There is, in fact, no good reason why our manufacturers who have all the advantages in the shape of raw materials should not entirely supply the demand on this side of the Atlantic for cotton, woolen, and worsted goods of every description.

The year's business has been conducted under many adverse conditions; the winter was unusually severe and protracted, hence the spring trade was late in opening. The unfavorable character of the weather throughout almost the entire spring and summer checked the consumption of light fabrics suited to the ordinary season's trade. In order to reduce stocks of such lines jobbers often found it necessary to force sales at the expense of profits. The bad condition of trade in sections from which Eastern jobbers derive their largest share of custom, also induced them to make a strong invasion of territory from which they had previously been driven by Chicago jobbers, and the close competition thus created between Western and Eastern jobbers resulted in reducing prices to figures that in numerous instances failed to cover the original cost and expense of handling. In this connection it may be well to remark that while Chicago merchants recognize the unwise course of selling goods at figures that fail to yield remunerative profits, it is

FUTILE FOR NEW YORK OR OTHER JOBBERS

to suppose that they can ever hope to regain control of the trade in territory which has once been successfully canvassed by dealers in this city, and every effort to do so, while it may for the time that the contest for supremacy lasts, lessen and even destroy the profits of our jobbers, the loss will be still more severe to those who attempt to compete with them, and the sooner that Eastern dealers realize that the control of the dry goods trade west of the Alleghany Mountains has forever passed from the better for their own interest, as it is impossible to divert trade from its natural channels so long as those who are in a position to control it show the spirit of enterprise and liberalty that characterize Chicago merchants.

The heavy stocks of goods in manufactur

ers' hands, as well as in jobbers' warehouses, and the continued large production by the former during the first half of the year, added largely to the other misfortunes that beset the trade, makers found stocks accumulating, and their pressure to realize caused an almost steady shrinkage in values during the first eight months of the year. The only leading articles that did not suffer severely were prints, on which a decline of about 5 per cent is reported. The steadiness in these goods may be attributed to the fact that the almost unprecedented low prices at which they opened at the beginning of the year rendered a further large reduction in quotations an impossibility.

COTTON DRESS GOODS,

although possessing unusual merit in styles, finish, and fabrics, were in excessive supply, and were unmercifully slaughtered by manufacturers, who forced sales through auction houses regardless of prices, and thereby compelled jobbers who were carrying stocks to make corresponding reductions. The average decline on such goods is placed by experts at 20 per cent under the ruling prices in 1882, although the latter were deemed very low.

Worsted dress fabrics have attracted a large share of favor, and as stocks were more nearly adjusted to the demand prices were well maintained for all staples of popular style and quality, the only lines that suffered being those that were undesirable, and as the production of such goods was not large the losses from depreciation in values was moderate. The demand for cashmeres and similar makes of goods was about up to the demand, and prices remained steady. The same may be said of mohairs and alpacas, which have sold fairly at about last year's figures. Flannel dress goods have met a large sale, having to a great extent superseded the more common and medium grades of worsted and woolen fabrics. Such, in fact, was the call for many popular makes that the supply fell below the demand for consumption, and the year's trade was highly satisfactory to the jobber, and current stocks are lower than usual.

Colored cottons, stripes, and ticks have been in large demand, but not equal to the supply, and in their anxiety to sell makers held repeated sales at auction, which had a demoralizing influence on values and the trade generally. The ruling prices up to July showed a decline of fully 10 per cent below those of 1882. Since then the market has been comparatively steady, and as they are lower than the cost of production, and the make has been curtailed, no further shrinkage in values is anticipated.

Both brown and bleached sheetings and shirtings were largely distributed, but with heavy stocks constantly in sight, jobbers made a special effort to attract custom with them by offering "drives," and sales throughout the year were not only at lower figures than during the one immediately preceding, but below the cost of production, and such is still the case, although the output of the mills has been materially reduced.

A FEATURE IN THE TRADE

in unbleached goods has been the large increase in the volume of Southern-made goods.

The large production of underwear, and consequent pressure by manufacturers to realize, kept the trade in a most unsatisfactory condition throughout the year, and prices were lower and irregular. The consumption, however, was large in consequence.

Hoseries were active, and off grades irregular, while standard goods were fairly steady throughout, and prices showed little alteration from 1882.

The trade in white goods was comparatively quiet, and prices averaged about the same as during the three years immediately preceding.

Perhaps no other line of goods suffered so severely as woolens for men's wear. Manufacturers seemed to become utterly reckless to consequences, and instead of acquainting themselves as to the probable amount of goods required, and shaping, as they might have done, the supply to the demand, they went heedlessly to work to see how many goods they could turn out, and when they found they had accumulated enormous stocks for which there were no buyers at remunerative prices they sought relief at the auction rooms where they forced sales with as little regard to cost as they had previously shown in their efforts to produce without ascertaining how many were likely to be wanted. The constant pressure to realize by makers necessarily kept the market in a demoralized condition, and jobbers as well as manufacturers, were compelled to face losses on every hand. No matter how cheap the goods appeared when purchased they were generally dear ere they reached the store of the buyer. The severe shrinkage in values naturally caused many heavy failures in the trade; and the situation was further greatly aggravated by the forced sales of the stocks of such firms. The mild character of the weather during the closing quarter of the year likewise assisted to lessen consumption, and the year closes with the market in a most unsatisfactory condition, and the only means of restoring it to a healthy condition is by equalizing production to consumption.

FOREIGN GOODS.

The importation of foreign goods of nearly all classes has been closely gauged to the consumption, and prices have shown few changes. The small percentage of cotton dress fabrics imported have found a quick sale at remunerative prices, and the same may be said of worsted goods, although they are being steadily displaced by similar lines of American manufacture. Woolen dress goods have met a fairly satisfactory sale at well supported and remunerative quotations.

The importations of silks were on a liberal scale, the market throughout the year being glutted with low and medium qualities, which were forced on buyers at figures that entailed a loss on manufacturers, importers, and jobbers. The higher grades, although in ample supply, have met a very satisfactory demand, and remunerative profits were realized.

Linens met an unusually active sale, and although the importations were very large, the trade was seldom more satisfactory to jobbers, who say no other lines of goods were handled with such gratifying results as linens of every description, and the year closes with well-adjusted stocks.

CARPETS.

Although these goods are handled by a number of large firms who make them a specialty, they are also sold by all the regular jobbing houses. All classes of dealers in such goods report very large sales, but unsatisfactory results, due to the heavy shrinkage in values which may be said to have commenced with and continued throughout the year. The closing prices compared with the opening in January record a decline ranging from 10 to 15 per cent, as to make and quality.

AVERAGE PRICES.

The following shows the average price for the articles named in 1864, and from 1872 to 1883, inclusive:

MILLINERY AND FANCY GOODS.

AMERICAN-MADE GOODS MORE POPULAR.

New York, being the largest importing city in America, is necessarily the leading market for the sale of all classes of foreign goods in importers' packages, and especially of millinery and milliners' stock. Chicago, however, can justly claim precedence as the leading jobbing market on the continent for the same line of goods, and, in the size and elegance of the stores devoted to the distribution of such articles, it is without a peer in this country or Europe, and each year witnesses an addition to their proportions and splendor, as well as the volume of their sales, and an increase in the quality of the goods handled, the latter clearly indicating an advancement in the wealth and taste of the large and rapidly augmenting population for which this city is the trade center. Each succeeding season also witnesses an expansion of the territory that recognizes this as its most advantageous market in which to buy such goods. This is alike attributable to the rapid settlement of the country heretofore accessible to Chicago; the expanding railroad system which is yearly enlarging the facilities for reaching sections heretofore shut off from this market, and the inducements that our dealers are enabled to offer their customers in the way of new styles and attractive goods at the lowest prices and most favorable terms, the former being due to the assiduity with which they study the wants and the tastes of their customers, and the latter to their large capital, which enables them to buy at the lowest prices, and their excellent manufacturing facilities, by which they are enabled to convert raw materials into shapes best suited to the wants of customers in different sections, the styles and qualities of goods that are popular in one part of the country being unsuited to any other. The ascertainment of the wants of different localities and how to supply them most cheaply is an important factor in controlling the trade of a widely-extended country. It is, in fact, next in importance to the ability to sell goods at the lowest prices, and has in connection with the latter enabled Chicago jobbers to outstrip those of any other city in the country, and made this the center of the jobbing trade of this continent for millinery goods. The extent to which the manufacture of such goods is carried on here may be inferred from the statement that about 2,000 hands are employed by the wholesale houses, and the industry is steadily on the increase.

THE WORST SEASON FOR YEARS.

There have, of course, been periods when the trade suffered severely from the same natural causes that influenced other lines of business, and as a majority of the articles sold by the millinery trade are to a great extent classable as luxuries, whose consumption is increased or diminished in proportion to the purchasing ability of consumers, it is one ot the first lines of business to suffer from a decline in the country's prosperity, while an increased sale is regarded as unquestionable evidence of an improved condition of its leading interests. The weather also exerts a more marked influence on the millinery trade than almost any other line of goods, and seldom has its influence been more severely felt than during a considerable portion of the current year. Jobbers, with scarcely an exception, pronounced the past spring as the worst season they have had for years. Said the manager of a leading concern, "Last spring was the first one in more than a decade when the aggregate balance of our sales failed to show an increase on those of the preceding season." This, however, was partly due to the very low prices for goods, which necessitated the handling of a larger bulk to bring the aggregate value up to the preceding spring. But, as already stated, the most serious drawback to trade was the cool and unseasonable weather that prevented customers from buying goods which they were unable to utilize. The caprice of fashion is also a most powerful factor in the trade, and during the current year its influences were adverse to profits. As an example, last year there was an enormous demand for felt hats at an average of about $36 per dozen, whereas the present year the rage for hats or bonnets of the same material as the dress worn called out a demand for hat frames which were sold at $1@1.50 per dozen. In many other classes of goods the changes were decidedly unfavorable to profits, as very little is made on cheap goods. But while the aggregate value of goods distributed has not shown the increase expected, and the profits have fallen below anticipations, there has been a wider distribution of goods by the extension of the trade in new territory. The natural growth of the country by settlement and ordinary increase of population has also contributed to enlarge the consumption of such goods, and the year's footings will show that there has been an actual gain in the amount of sales, and that jobbers have not, as in some other lines of trade, worked without a moderate degree of compensation.

GROWTH OF THE TRADE.

A marked feature in connection with the trade, and one that has almost kept pace with the expansion in the business, is the steady increase in percentage of the sale of American-made goods, and a decadence of the consumption of foreign production. This is especially the case in regard to trimmings, linings, and ornaments, which constitute a liberal percentage of the goods strictly classable under the head of milliners' goods, and which a few years since were almost exclusively of foreign production.

In referring to the growth of the trade in Chicago, which, as already stated, is the largest jobbing market in the country for the sale of such goods, it may not be out of place to state that the first strictly wholesale house here, and we believe in the West, for the exclusive sale of millinery was opened in March, 1853, or a little over thirty years ago. Then Chicago was virtually unknown as a jobbing market for any class of goods. The sales during the first six months were only $9,000. At the close of the fall season the proprietor of the establishment, deeming it useless to keep his store open through the winter, packed the remainder of his goods in a single case and stored them while he visited the East to purchase a stock for the following spring, which was much larger and aggregated $40,000. At present the gentleman, whom many regarded as almost insane for making a business venture that apparently presented few chances of success, is at the head of an establishment occupying a building 144x150, six stories high, and which for the completeness of its appointments, extent and costliness of its stock, has no superior in the world, and the annual sales of millinery, which were represented by $9,000 in 1853, have reached $8,000,000 the current year. The latter figures, however, merely represent the sales by houses directly in the trade. Large amounts of such goods are also handled by houses selling notions and other lines of goods; hence a correct estimate of sales is impossible.

CLOTHING.

MANUFACTURE AND SALE.

The manufacture and sale of men's and boys' clothing has for years been a leading interest in Chicago, and each succeeding twelve months witnesses an expansion in both branches commensurate with the wealth and population of the widely extended territory for which the city has for years been the recognized trade center, and the steadily extending railroad system in all directions is annually bringing many new customers from distant sections that were previously deprived of the advantages of this market by a lack of communication. The chief acquisition during the year just closing has been Oregon, Washington Territory, and Idaho on the Northwest, and the Republic of Mexico in the Southwest. The extent of the business may be inferred from the fact that $9,000,000 is employed in the manufacturing and jobbing departments. In addition many of the leading houses have large sums invested in woolen mills where the cloths and other materials used in manufacturing clothing are woven. By making their own goods manufacturers are often enabled to secure better material adapted to special lines of goods than can at all times be found in the hands of package dealers. The large capital by which the leading houses are backed also gives them superior advantages for buying in the lowest markets. This fact, in connection with a well-directed enterprise, has given Chicago its present prestige as the leading clothing market in the United States.

Like all other branches of business, the clothing interest has felt the influence of previous over-production, and the distrust that followed "the boom" which commenced in 1879 and collapsed in 1881. It has, however, suffered less severely than many other lines of business; profits were also considerably lessened by a reckless competition which they were compelled to meet from jobbers in other cities, who early in the year laid in large stocks, which they ultimately found it necessary to work off, regardless of cost. In order to do so they invaded Chicago territory, and as a result its jobbers were not disposed to stand calmly by and see their trade wrested from them, but promptly met the issue. It is scarcely necessary to say that, although many goods sold were without profit, the contest was not altogether without compensating advantages, as those who attempted to secure the trade learned that while it was possible to sell goods in the territory occupied by Chicago dealers, it was scarcely possible to do so without loss, hence they will be less inclined to again repeat the experiment. In fact, many of them have found it necessary to retire altogether.

The unfavorable character of the weather during the greater portion of the spring and summer also operated adversely to the sale of many lines of light and medium goods adapted to these seasons. But the very liberal fall trade which was largely due to new customers from the sections of country previously referred to has partly made up for the adverse conditions already stated, and it is generally conceded that the year's sales will show an excess in volume and value over the previous one. Nearly all classes of stock have also been worked down much closer than during either of the two preceding years. The same condition is also reported by interior retailers, and as prices for all descriptions of raw materials are down to figures where any further depreciation is unlikely, if at all possible, the outlook for the incoming year is much better than at the advent of the one just closing. The prospect is further improved by the fact that the liquidation that has been going on for the past two years has driven many reckless and weak establishments in other cities from the trade and rendered the solvent ones more prudent. There are also reasons for believing that consumers as a class are in a better position to buy and pay for what they want, as there is evidently more property in the country to sell. The weeding-out process that has been going on among the retail trade for the past two years has left that branch of the business in more competent hands, and although profits are likely to be small, they will be more certain. This latter conclusion is warranted by the fact that the arrangements for the goods for the spring trade were long since made, and much of the stock is already finished at a cost that, while it renders a decline in valuation almost an impossibility, will induce a free consumption at prices that afford a fair compensation to the jobber and retailer, the loss having already been borne by the manufacturers of the cloths, who in their anxiety to keep their machinery running overstocked the markets with goods which they were in the end compelled to force on buyers at such prices as the latter were disposed to pay.

GENTLEMEN'S FURNISHING GOODS.

A GROWING TRADE.

This branch of the jobbing trade is becoming more prominent with the growth of the city and country for which it is the chief market. When the business was in its infancy all the goods sold either by the special houses or the other branches of trade were made at the East, but each succeeding year witnesses a decline in the sale of Eastern made articles and an increase in home products. All the houses whose sales are strictly confined to furnishing goods conduct large factories, where nearly every article in their line, except knit underwear, some styles of gloves and hoseries, and handkerchiefs are made. These factories employ several thousand operatives, mainly ladies and young girls. In addition to their own direct customers in the jobbing and retail business, they also supply nearly all the furnishing goods sold by the wholesale dry goods and clothing houses in Chicago and the West. Large consignments are also sent to the Eastern and Canadian cities. Manitoba is becoming an important customer, and within the past twelve months a fair number of orders were sent to Mexico and Central America, and advices from those countries justify predictions of a large increase in sales in that direction the coming year. Jobbers say that owing to the strong competition from Eastern houses who were overstocked with hoseries and knit underwear which they were compelled to work off, in addition to the low prices made by Chicago houses in other branches of trade, who, as already stated, handle such goods as collateral lines and who were inclined to supply their customers with all articles called for, the year's business, although showing a liberal increase in volume, has not been as remunerative as desired, yet there is no complaint of losses. The other branches of the trade, including all articles manufactured here, show a very liberal increase in sales and the business has also been fairly satisfactory, and the year closes with less than the customary stock to be carried over. Prices are also down where further losses from shrinkage will of necessity be very small and the general situation healthy. Retailers' stocks in most parts of the country are also low, which encourages dealers to look for a fairly active spring demand.

HATS, CAPS, AND BUCK GOODS.

NOT SATISFACTORY.

This branch of the jobbing trade has suffered to a considerable extent from the same unfavorable causes that effected nearly all leading lines of business. The slackness of demand as compared with stocks also rendered dealers anxious to sell, and houses which held more goods than they were able to carry with ease have shown a disposition to force them off. In order to do this they too frequently made sales at the expense of profits. Dealers in the same line of goods in other cities also made strong efforts to secure custom from Chicago territory, and in many instances offered goods at less than cost. As a consequence the most conservative and strongest houses in the city had to choose between losing a considerable portion of their trade or meet such competition regardless of present remuneration. It is scarcely necessary to say that they were not inclined to part with their trade, knowing as they did that the abuses practiced by weak and reckless houses would in time bring their own cure. But in spite of the many adverse conditions against which jobbers had to contend, they have, by canvassing new territory, been enabled to maintain their previous average volume of business, and, by buying close and being in a position to discount a large percentage of their purchases, conservative houses have at least made a fair interest on their capital. The anxiety to sell, as above stated, has also brought some compensatien to those who were sufficiently strong to stand the ordeal, as the liquidating process has reduced stocks to a minimum, and the new year will open with more favorable auspices to prudent houses. There is also encouragement in the fact that the retail traders are meeting their bills with more than ordinary punctuality, and many of them are availing themselves of the discounts allowed to cash buyers. The number of houses in the jobbing business is the same as at the opening of the year, the retirement of the firm that failed being replaced by a new one. During the year there was a very considerable increase in the manufacture of buck goods, which is becoming an important feature of industry, a large percentage of the skins worked up being dressed or tanned here.

BOOTS AND SHOES.

GRATIFYING RESULTS.

A canvass among manufacturers and jobbers of boots and shoes discovers that, while the business both from the general mercantile depression that affected all leading interests and failures in the leather trade, which, for a time at least, rendered buyers of manufactured goods exceedingly cautious in their purchases, the year's business shows fairly gratifying results as regards the volume of goods turned out. All the leading manufacturers report an enlargement in the output of their establishments. The increase in the variety of goods made has also been more marked than in the quantity. In the earlier days of the industry Chicago manufacturers mainly confined their products to heavy work, and nearly all the better and finer classes of boots and shoes sold here came from Eastern factories, where the class of skilled labor adapted to their production was in better supply than in the West. The past five years, however, have brought great changes in the quality of the goods made, and in no preceding year has the advance in high-grade work been so marked as during the one just closing. Not only were the factories in which they were a specialty materially enlarged, but new ones have been built, and at present Chicago contains some of the largest and best-appointed establishments of this kind in the country. The chief factors which have given, and must continue to give, this city an advantage over all others for the production and sale of boots and shoes are the low cost at which goods can be made and distributed. Being the largest tanning point on the continent, the leather can be delivered to the factories without charge for freight, and the goods shipped direct to all parts of the country. These charges, which alone constitute a fair profit, must be borne by manufacturers and jobbers in other cities. Hence it is evident that they are at a great disadvantage when brought in competition with Chicago makers and dealers. Nor is it necessary to look furthur to find the causes which have transferred the jobbing business in such goods from the East to this city, and in a little over a score of years from the date of the opening of the first factory, have made it one of the leading manufacturing centers on the continent for such goods. But rapid as has been the increase of production within the brief period mentioned, it has not been sufficient to keep pace with the expansion of the distributing trade, and Chicago jobbers are still the largest buyers at the New England factories. The leading houses report the year closing with only moderate stocks on hand; the volume of unseasonable goods to be carried over is small, and likely as all the stock now in their warehouses and factories was produced at such very low cost that a further depreciation is scarcely possible, the prospects for the incoming year are fairly encouraging. Dealers are not likely to suffer further losses from a shrinkage in prices of materials. The heavy failures that occurred in other sections of the country during the past year have also freed those who desire to do a safe and remunerative business from the competition of reckless firms who buy without judgment, and are in time compelled to force goods on customers without reference to profits. The prospective improvement in the leather trade will likewise prove beneficial to those who handle manufactured goods; and although nothing more than a fair average business is predicted, there is a fairly confident feeling that the dawn of a more prosperous period is not distant.

The sales of rubber goods, which constitute a collateral branch of the shoe trade, show a slight increase in the volume compared with 1882, the sales of some establishments showing a gain of 20 per cent, while with others it was very small. The profits, as in other lines of trade, were also close, as the competition between Eastern and Chicago houses was very sharp. On the whole, however, the year's business was not unsatisfactory.

LEATHER.

NOT A SATISFACTORY SHOWING.

Although Chicago tanners and leather dealers have suffered less than those of any other leading market in the country, the result of the year's business has been far from satisfactory. Jobbers say their patrons, who are mainly makers of custom goods, are being driven out of trade by the enlarged production and betterment of quality of factory made boots, shoes, and other articles of leather goods, in the construction of which machinery is largely used, and which are sold much cheaper than they can be produced in the small shops by hand. Hence the jobbing trade in leather is steadily on the decline, and profits suffer a diminution. The current year's business of tanners and dressers has also been severely affected by heavy failures in the leather trade in nearly every large city in the country outside of Chicago. The forcing of liquidation by such firms caused a shrinkage in values of stock on hand, and rendered it difficult for those who were not sufficiently strong financially to take every advantage of the market and buy raw materials at the lowest cash prices to make even a fair rate of interest. The unhealthy situation has also been aggravated by an increase in the cost of doing business, as it has required greater exertions to sell an equal amount of goods with previous years. The fact, however, that no failures of consequence have occurred among our leading establishments justifies the statement that although the year's business has not been as profitable as desired, it has been conducted on sound and conservative principles, and as the new year will open with moderate stocks and prices down where no further decline of any consequence is scarcely possible, the outlook for the near future is not without features of encouragement.

CHICAGO'S ADVANTAGES.

In the previous year's review of the tanning interest, THE INTER OCEAN took occasion to refer to the advantages which Chicago possessed for concentrating the hides, bark, and all other articles of raw material which enter as factors into the production of leather at lower cost than they could be brought together at any other point in this country, and in addition to its being the center of a large manufacturing and jobbing interest, gave its tanners facilities for conducting their business that were not enjoyed by those in the same line in other parts of the country. The statement then made has been strongly sustained by the fact that notwithstanding the leather trade has passed through one of the most trying periods in its history very few failures have occured here, and they were of little consequence, whereas many of the largest and heretofore strongest houses at other points have been unable to stem the adverse tide with which the tanning and jobbing interest has had to contend from the opening to the close of the year. In addition to the superiority of location a majority of Chicago tanners have been brought up to the business and know all its details, from selecting the raw hides and tanning materials ot finishing the leather and keeping their check books. They are also equally noted for their extreme conservatism. These qualifications have enabled them to keep their affairs in good shape, while those who were less favorably located or not so well drilled in the details of the business were driven to the wall.

SOME ENORMOUS FIGURES.

The extent of the business conducted here may be inferred from the fact that there are four large sole and nine upper leather tanneries here, with an aggregate annual production of 6,000,000 pounds of sole and 3,500,000 upper leather. In addition, 675,000 calf skins are tanned, about 225,000 of which are imported from France, Germany, Belgium and Holland. There are also a number of smaller tanneries, where considerable quantities of various grades of sole and other leather are made. The tanning of sheep, deer and other skins is also conducted on a very extensive sale and the product converted into goods.

Chicago capital is likewise largely interested in tanneries in Wisconsin, Michigan, and Indiana. As a large amount of the supplies for such establishments are bought in Chicago and their products sold here, they virtually constitute a portion of this city's leather industry. In point of quality Chicago leather ranks "A No. 1." This is especially the case with sole, which is almost exclusively made from hides of Texas steers, which make a firmer and in every respect finer and more durable leather than any other in the world. They also cut to excellect advantage. The most popular hides for harness leather are from domestic steers; the large number of those animals slaughtered here gives tanners their choice, and they have equal advantages in securing the best selections of cow and heifer hides from which the best upper leather used for boots and shoes is made. Chicago calf skins, like its sole leather, have a reputation second to none, being finer, more plump and uniform, and they cut to better advantage than the famous French calf. But, as there is still a certain class of customers who think there is nothing so good as a foreign article, such people must necessarily have French goods, or at least what they suppose comes from France. Such was formerly the opinion with regard to South American hides for sole leather, until, after years of hard work, tanners succeeded in convincing the most prejudiced that Texas steers furnished a better material for the purpose. The principal agent employed by Chicago tanners is hemlock bark, oak and other materials being used to a moderate extent by some establishments who turn out special lines of goods. Formerly a large amount of the upper and harness leather tanned here was sent East to be finished and again brought West for sale, but at present the leather is both tanned and finished here, and the cost of transportation to the East and back is saved to the consumer; the finishing also largely contributes to Chicago's industrial interests.

RESULTS OF THE DEPRESSION.

The general depression in the trade, as noted above, materially affected the sales of tanners, who estimate a reduction of 15 per cent in the amount of their year's transactions, about 7½ per cent of which was due to a depreciation in the price of goods, some lines being 5 per cent and others full 10 per cent below the average in 1882. The unfavorable outlook during the early part of the year induced great conservatism among a majority of Chicago tanners, and as raw hides were relatively higher than leather there was a strong tendency to reduce the amount of hides put down, which resulted in a reduction of 15 per cent in the volume of stock produced. The chief decline in product was in finished uppers. At present tanners are working with more than ordinary caution; current stocks are full 15 per cent less than at this date last year. It is conceded by those best informed that the output of the tanneries for the next six months will be much less than during the first half of 1883. The production at other leading points also promises to be correspondingly light, while the consumption promises to be as good or better than for the year just closed. Hence there are substantial reasons for predicting a fairly active and more remunerative business during the incoming year. The situation is also improved by the fact that the disastrous condition of the leather trade during the past twelve months has weeded out a majority af the imprudent concerns, and left the trade in stronger and competent hands, who will not sacrifice profits merely for the sake of swelling the volume of their transactions.

HARNESS.

HARNESS AND SADDLERY HARDWARE, ETC.

The harness business during the past year was pushed from the opening to the close, and sales were consequently heavier than in previous years. Jobbers and manufacturers carried larger and better stocks than formerly, as the call was chiefly for the best makes, but as they handled everything from the common $10 harness to the fancy $500 of American and foreign manufacture, they were able to suit all classes of buyers. Prices ranged about the same as in the previous year for standard makes, but common lower. Saddles met a larger demand than formerly, but no special change could be noted in prices. All other articles, such as whips, boots, pads, etc., met a good sale, but no particular alteration was made in values. In harness and saddlery hardware a liberal trade was enjoyed, but jobbers were more conservative, and felt satisfied with the extent of territory already covered, and preferred to keep that well in hand than to have their business scattered over a large space of country that could not be controlled as easily. Therefore they employed fewer traveling men, and sales fell about 2½ to 5 per cent under those of 1882. Good stocks were carried. Prices were steadier, and ranged a trifle higher. Profits were fair and business more satisfactory, as goods did not have to be sold on a weak and declining market as in 1882.

GROCERIES.

CAREFUL BUYING AND CLOSE SELLING.

This branch of trade has shown very few features of special interest throughout the year. Dealers in the interior were exceedingly conservative in buying, and never before in the history of the trade were goods ordered so directly in reference to immediate necessities as during the twelve months just drawing to a close. Among Chicago jobbers the disposition to move cautiously and carry stocks in conformity with current sales was equally marked. This caution was no less the outgrowth of the reserve exhibited by retailers than the recollections of the very unsatisfactory result of the previous year's business and the frequency with which large failures were reported in other lines of business. Despite, however, of the conservatism shown by both jobbers and retailers, the sales are estimated to exceed those of the year immediately preceding. The gain, however, was not the result of an increased consumption, per capita of population, but to a larger influx of emigration into the territory which draws the bulk of its supplies from here, and a material enlargement of the previous area. The extension of the railroad system has attracted buyers here that were previously debarred by an absence of transportation facilities. The profits, however, have not been commensurate to the volume of goods distributed. This was partly attributable to the close competition among dealers, many of whom were anxious to secure custom, but more largely to the steady shrinkage in values of nearly all lines of goods. This was especially severe on houses of moderate means, and it is generally conceded that the only concerns that have made money were those whose who, owing to their capital, were in a position to discount their bills, as the rebate thus secured not unfrequently exceeded the margin between the prices at which the goods were bought and sold. The adverse conditions which the jobbing trade was compelled to contend with may be inferred from the fact that the average decline on all articles, except coffee, which was dearer, is estimated at 12 to 15 per cent. But while the latter article shows a higher range than during 1882, the result of the year's sales was unsatisfactory; as the advance was due to the manipulations of speculators at the East, who attempted to "corner" the market and force quotations to a high point in the face of large stocks. As is the general rule when values are controlled by such influences, prices were very irregular, and jobbers being unwilling to carry large stocks while prices were contingent on the whims of speculators, whose operations had no other basis than their financial strength, they failed to derive any benefit from the frequent up movement in quotations. The consumption of sugar has been large, but prices lower, and goods have been handled at very small profit. The glucose trade in both sugars and sirups has been most disastrous to all who handled them. Large quantities of the latter soured in hands of jobbers and retailers, and were returned to the manufacturers. The dissatisfaction thus created is likely to result in a refusal of many dealers to handle it on any terms in the future. The rapid increase in the production of sorghum sirups, as well as the improvement in their quality, is causing them to be more generally introduced to the grocery trade than ever before. Considerable advancement has also been made in sorghum sugars, and there are reasons to hope that they will soon become an important factor in the sugar supply of the country, and many well-informed grocers venture the prediction that these goods will soon drive the fraudulent glucose from the market. The trade in teas has been large both in volume and value, and although they, like other leading lines of goods, were sold at small margins, the business has been more satisfactory. This was mainly due to the greater steadiness in prices and the conservatism of dealers, who, instead of carrying large stocks, as was the case in former years, bought more closely on the principle of supplying current wants. The establishment by the government of a system of tea inspection did much toward restoring and maintaining a healthy trade, as it checked the importation of low and worthless teas that were previously sold by unprincipled dealers in competition with those who handled genuine goods. The importation of teas direct from the source of production is steadily increasing with the other business of the city the current year's, imports being estimated at 10,000,000 pounds, or 150,000 packages, being equivalent to a little over one-seventh of the entire importations of the whole United States. The goods come overland via San Francisco, hence they are always fresher and better than those subjected to a long sea voyage, as was the case when Eastern importers had entire control of the foreign trade in such goods. All the leading Eastern importers also have agencies here, hence jobbers buy as they sell, and are not compelled to hold heavy stocks, as their supplies all come from the Atlantic cities. A majority of the Western and Northwestern jobbers also buy their teas of Chicago importers.

The sales of all classes of miscellaneous groceries to the Pacific Coast States and Territories were materially increased within the year, and jobbers say it would have been much heavier were it not for the exorbitant freight charges to California and Nevada. The late period at which the Northern Pacific Railroad was completed prevented a thorough canvass of the country which it opened up to trade from this city, but the favor with which the representatives from Chicago were received at the few points visited, justifies jobbers in predicting a large patronage from there next year, as the position of this market gives it superior advantages over all others in supplying the country traversed by or tributary to the Northern Pacific and other Oregon railroads. There has also been a material increase in the volume of goods sent to the neighboring republic of Mexico, a liberal treaty for the interchange of commodities could be effected, a heavy business might be built up with that country. Mexico produces very few articles that could not be admitted free without detriment to our own industries, while they want large lines of goods that we are only too glad to find customers for.

RANGE OF PRICES FOR COFFEES AND SUGARS.

To give a comprehensive idea of the prices, as compared with the two preceding years, we annex the following monthly range in this market for fancy Rio coffee and granulated sugars:

FANCY RIO COFFEES.

	1883.	1882.	1881.
January	10½@11½	13½@13¾	16 @16½
February	11 @12¼	13¼@13½	16 @16½
March	11½@12¼	13¼@13½	15½@16
April	11½@13	13¼@13½	15½@16
May	12½@13	12 @12½	15½@16
June	12 @13	12 @12½	15 @15½
July	12 @12½	12 @12½	15 @15½
August	12 @12⅓	12 @12½	14½@15
September	12 @12¾	12 @12½	15½@16
October	12½@13¾	11½@12	15 @15½
November	13¾@14½	11½@12	14¾@15½
December	13½@14½	11 @11½	13¾@14¼

GRANULATED SUGARS.

	1883.	1882.	1881.
January	9⅛@ 9½	9⅝@ 9¾	10⅛@10¼
February	9⅛@ 9½	....@ 9⅝	9⅞@10
March	9¼@ 9½	....@ 9⅝	9¾@ 9⅞
April	9⅛@ 9¾	...@ 9⅞	9⅞@10
May	9¼@ 9⅜	10 @10⅛	9⅞@10
June	9⅛@ 9⅜	....@10	11¼@11⅜
July	9⅛@ 9⅜	10 @10⅛	10¾@10⅞
August	9 @ 9¼	9⅞@10	10¼@10⅜
September	9⅛@ 9¼	9⅝@ 9¾	10⅛@10¼
October	9 @ 9⅛	9⅞@10	10⅜@10½
November	8⅝@ 9	....@ 9⅝	10¼@10½
December	8⅜@ 8½	....@ 9¼	....@10

FANCY GROCERIES.

The trade in all these articles has reached such proportions that it is necessary to classify them by themselves. The demand for all descriptions, such as raisins, prunes, farinaceous goods, and table delicacies was larger than for any previous year, but the aggregate volume of sales was about the same as during 1882, on account of prices ruling lower. Heavier stocks were carried by jobbers here and at all the Western river points, who have become so strong financially that they now order many of their goods direct from the East, and thereby save the profit formerly paid the Chicago jobbers and importers, and obtain about as cheap a rate of freight as they can get from here. This has greatly increased the competition for the control of the Western trade, and reduced the margin of profit to a very small figure, but Chicago merchants still manage to hold the bulk of the business, and were satisfied with their year's sales. Farinaceous goods, such as oat meal, cracked wheat, pearl barley, etc., were freely called for, and sales increased about 15 per cent over those of the previous year. Prices ranged lower, and closed at the inside, with liberal stocks. Raisins were purchased in good quantities. The crop was heavier than in 1881 and 1882, and of fine quality; less old stock was carried over, but there was no time during the year that all orders could not be filled promptly. Prices of layers ranged from $2 to $2.65 per box, opening at $2.10, and closing at $2.60. Valencia sold at 7c to 10c per pound, the opening price being 9c, and closed rather weak, with good stocks at 8c. Prunes were taken more liberally than in any former year. The crop was one of the heaviest on record and quality up to the average, but size small. The importations were unusually large and sold at 1@1½c lower than for many years. The consumption was increased to such an extent that the call for apples and peaches was reduced, as prunes were preferred at the low prices, but should an advance occur it would have a tendency to check the demand. Currants were taken in about the usual amounts. The crop this year was large, but on account of the heavy rains was badly damaged, which created a firmer market during the early part of the season. The first arrivals of new brought higher prices, but the advance was not maintained, and prices declined ½c per pound near the close. Nuts of all descriptions were taken freely, but no new features in the trade were developed. The old crop of peanuts were disposed of at good prices, but the new crop being heavy sales had to be made at reduced figures. Almonds ruled firm, as the crop was small. Filberts and Brazil nuts were stronger and higher than for years, the quality of the latter being very poor, and caused considerable dissatisfaction among dealers. Prices were forced up 4c per pound. Sales of California dried fruits were large, as the quality was fine, but on account of the high prices asked there was not as heavy an increase as there was in foreign, as they were sold cheaper.

CANNED GOODS.

THE CANNING BUSINESS

in all sections of the country has been on the increase for years, and has become a very important industry, but during the year under review the growth of the canneries was larger than the growth of the trade warranted, and the result has been a year of depression and dissatisfaction both to canners and jobbers. The over production of all except small fruits caused large lots that were held by speculators and weak jobbers to be thrown on the market, and prices were forced down to a lower figure than at any former period in the history of the trade. Goods were sold for less than it cost to produce them, and the result was that a number of small concerns were obliged to suspend operations. The low prices, however, had a very beneficial effect on the consumption, which was larger than in former years, as the poorer classes were enabled to secure them cheaper than they could the green fruit or vegetables. The quality of the canning this year was unusually good. The unsettled condition of all other branches of trade had its effect on this line, and notwithstanding the low prices realized on all goods buyers were very cautious and limited their purchases to current wants. Prices of tomatoes in 3-pound cans declined from $1.15 per dozen to 90 to 95c, and of corn in 2-pound cans from $1.15 to 85c. Very little alteration was made in the price of small fruits. In California canned goods there was not so much depression noted as in the trade of the near-by production. Sales increased 10 to 15 per cent over those of 1882, notwithstanding the fact that many of the large Western jobbers who formerly purchased their stock of dealers here have become more independent and ordered them direct from the factory, thereby cutting off considerable business that previously came here. The amount of fruit canned in California the past season was larger than that of the preceding year, and the quality very fine. Prices of apricots ranged 25 per cent lower than in 1882, and of plums the same amount higher, while peaches and pears remained steady. No strawberries were canned this year, on account of the light crop, and the little stock carried over from last year was sold early in the season. The trade in California salmon was larger; the amount canned exceded that of any former year. Prices ruled 25 per cent lower, which had the effect of putting it into markets where it was never handled before, and at such low prices that the consumption was greatly increased. Jobbers carried good stocks, but not any larger than in previous years. Sales of No. 1 goods ranged during the year at $1.27½ to $1.55 per doz, and closed at $1.40.

TOBACCO AND CIGARS.

EARLY DOUBT AND UNCERTAINTY.

The uncertainty as to the action of Congress regarding a proposed reduction of internal tax on tobacco caused an uneasy feeling among the trade at the opening of the year, as neither jobbers nor retailers were willing to buy stock while prices were likely to be instantly and largely reduced by legislation. As a consequence business during the first four months was slow and unsatisfactory, dealers merely buying in sufficient quantities to supply current wants. But the final passage of the bill, making a reduction of 8 cents per pound on tobacco, and $3 per 1,000 on cigars, which went into effect May 1, imparted confidence among all classes of dealers, and from that date to the close of the year trade in all lines of goods was brisk, and the consumption larger. Jobbers estimate an average increase of 15 per cent over the trade of the preceding year. There was also a material gain in the production of all classes of goods in Chicago, and especially of plug tobacco, the manufacture of which has undergone a large expansion. These goods are being shipped

TO ALL PARTS OF THE COUNTRY,

and meet with favor wherever introduced. There has also been a material increase in the shipments of fine cut tobacco to the Middle and Eastern Atlantic States, while all classes of goods have met with a much larger demand from Southwestern and Northwestern States and Territories, and the countries on the Pacific coast. The general result of the year's business has been more satisfactory than in 1882, and both the manufacturing and jobbing houses are regarded as in good condition.

The cigar trade was influenced by the same causes that affected tobacco, but like that article the trade shows a very considerable increase in the volume of goods sold and extent of country to which they were distributed. It is generally conceded, however, that the benefit which jobbers and manufacturers expected to derive from the reduction on the internal tax was only partly realized, the

STRONG COMPETITION AMONG DEALERS

and their anxiety to secure trade not unfrequently inducing them to give retail buyers a very large percentage, and not unfrequently the entire advantage of reduced tax

FISH AND OYSTERS.

SALT FISH.

The fish trade of Chicago is gradually growing in importance, and is now of such volume as to attract marked attention. The salt fish branch of the business is represented by six houses, who make a specialty of it. They have a combined capital of about $450,000 invested, and their aggregate sales reached $2,000,000 during the year just closed—about equal to those of the year preceding. The volume of business was not so large, as the consumption was not so heavy, on account of prices ruling higher than in many years, due to the small catch of the various descriptions. Dealers made a strong effort to extend their trade, and goods were sold over a larger territory, the gain being mainly in Minnesota, Dakota, the Canadian Provinces, and in the Southwest. More fish were sold also sold in the country previously supplied, as the population is increasing. Dealers have carried fair stocks, but the majority of the time the supply was closely adjusted to the demand. At the close, however, there was a liberal supply for the requirements until the opening of next season. About the only fault dealers had to find with the year's business was the small margin of profit on which goods had to be handled. The trade, however, was in a healthy condition, and no failure of a strictly fish dealer was recorded.

MACKEREL AND COD.

The catch of mackerel on the New England coast the past season was the smallest in fifteen years, being estimated at 250,000 barrels, against 378,863 barrels in 1882. The quality of the early catch was poor, but of the late better than the average. Prices ranged higher than for years. No. 1 opened at $15 per barrel, and in August commenced to advance, and during October reached $24, and closed firm at that price. Family mackerel was taken more freely than the higher grades on account of the extreme prices asked. No. 1 opened in January at $9.50 per barrel, declined in July to $8, but when the shortage in the catch became known, sold up to $12, which was the highest price reached in this market for many years.

The catch of cod was heavier than that of former years, and the consumption was larger. George's bank opened at $7.50 per 100 pounds, declined in June to $6.75, advanced in September to $7.25, but closed at $7, with good stocks on hand.

HERRING AND SARDINES.

Herring were caught in greater numbers than usual. The catch of Labrador is estimated at 60,000 barrels, an increase of nearly 20,000 barrels over 1882. That of Portland shore herring, however, was a failure early, but large enough lately to cover the deficiency. The quality was good, but of small size. The consumption was larger, especially among the foreign population. Prices of Labrador ranged $1 to $1.50 per barrel less than the previous year, and of Portland shore about 50 cents less. Halifax split herring were taken freely, but no particular change could be noted in prices. Scaled and smoked herring were in small supply during the summer months, as large quantities of them were used in the sardine factories, where they were put up as American sardines, and prices advanced from 25 cents to 33 cents. An increase in the stock toward the close of the year caused a reaction and prices declined to 25 cents at the close. The importations of Norway herring were 20 per cent larger than in former years, as the demand for them is continually growing. Sales were almost entirely to foreigners, who paid from $13.50 to $14.50 per barrel for them. Stockfish sold freely, and 15 per cent more was imported than in any former years.

THE LAKE FISHERIES.

The fisheries on the great lakes cut an important figure of the trade of the Northwest, as there is $1,345,975 capital invested, requiring 1,656 boats and 5,050 fishermen, with an annual catch of about 60,000,000 pounds, valued at $2,000,000.

The catch of family whitefish was increased, and prices consequently ruled lower, declining from $4.50 per half barrel to $1.50 on the arrival of the spring catch, and ranged during the season at $1.50 to $2.75, and closed with fair stocks at $2.75. While the catch of family whitefish was larger, that of No. 1 was almost a total failure on account of the stormy weather and high water, which in many instances destroyed the spawn. Very little of the catch, however, was cured, as it went into freezers for the fresh fish trade. Prices opened in January at $7.50 per half barrel, declined in July to $5.75 and $6, became firmer, and closed at $6.75, with very little stock on hand. Trout were caught in larger numbers than usual in Lake Superior and small streams in that vicinity. The quality was good, but the consumption of salted less. Sales ranged at $4 to $5.50 per half barrel, opening at the highest and closing at the lowest. Sales of salmon were 10 per cent less than in past years, on account of the catch being lighter and the bulk being taken for canning purposes. There was a large demand, however, and at times orders could not be filled promptly. Early in the season prices advanced $1 per barrel, but later the supply was larger, and a decline of $2 was the result, closing at $17.

FRESH FISH AND OYSTERS.

The fresh fish and oyster trade is as important as that in salt fish, and is steadily increasing. All varieties of fresh fish, from the little shiner to the Spanish mackerel—that can be had in any other market in this country—is purchaseable of dealers here in season. The most important branch of the fresh fish business, however, was in lake fish, chiefly whitefish and trout, which are annually caught in large numbers in Lake Michigan and Lake Superior, by fishermen in the employ of Chicago dealers, who have invested a large amount of capital in freezers, or ice houses, into which the fish are put and kept until wanted by the trade. The number of whitefish put into freezers the past season was about as large as last year. The business of keeping fish in freezers is yearly increasing, and dealers look for a diminution in then umber cured, unless there should be an unusually large catch, when an increase would be necessary. Prices ranged higher than in previous years. Whitefish and trout sold early in the season at 7½c, but advanced in the fall to 10c per pound.

The oyster business is steadily increasing. The regular season extends from Sept. 1 to May 1, and during that time more than 1,500,000 gallons were sold in this city and the Northwest, over one-third of the amount being consumed in this city. The rivalry among the different oyster houses was so great that stock was sold on a closer margin than in any former year. This has been very severe on the smaller dealers, who found it difficult to clear much more than expenses. Prices ruled about the same as in the previous season.

CHINA, CROCKERY, GLASSWARE.

DECREASE IN IMPORTATION.

The meagerness of profits in nearly all branches of commerce and industry has caused an increased economy in housekeeping and the adverse influences of such enforced economy was plainly apparent on the sales of the china and crockery houses during the year just closed. Those who import nearly all the foreign goods sold by them, as is the case with all the leading firms, also suffered severely from overimportations. Knowing that the duty on foreign ware would be very materially increased on the 1st of July, large orders were sent out for goods to arrive prior to that date, and, as the result has since shown, nearly every house in the trade overestimated the demand. Referring to the imports, the head of the largest china house in the country said: "We were all over-anxious to get the bulge on the other in the way of cheap goods, and in our efforts to do so twice as many goods were imported as were required." Finding their stores full of goods for which the demand was only fair, the desire to sell resulted in a competition which left little profit to jobbers. But a casting up of the year's transactions shows that in spite of the many adverse conditions which the trade has had to encounter, including a decline of 5 to 10 per cent in prices, the sales show an actual increase in volume over those of 1882, which was much larger than any preceding twelve months. The gain was the result of the extra exertions that were made to secure customers from new sections, and as Chicago jobbers never lose custom that is once secured, the current year's business, although done at small profit, will bring good fruit in the future.

A feature in the year's business, and one which deserves special mention, is that while the causes above mentioned have restricted the sales of common and medium grades of goods in the sections from which Chicago has for years received the bulk of its custom, the demand for expensive ware from the larger towns and cities where there is the greatest aggregation of wealth was much larger than usual. The call for costly hand-decorated china, noted in last year's report, has also materially increased, and has furnished employment to a large number of artists who make a specialty of that class of work. There have also been many changes in the patterns of the best grades of goods to suit the caprices of fashion.

In reviewing the year's trade it is a matter of sincere regret that the sales have not shown the same increase as during the previous two years. This is no doubt largely due to the fact that such goods chiefly consist of medium and common grades, the demand for which was lessened by the desire of consumers of such goods to economize, as already stated above. The excessive importations of foreign crockery and the low prices at which it was sold also prevented Chicago jobbers from giving their usual number of orders to American potteries for goods.

HOUSEHOLD FURNITURE

CHICAGO GAINING GROUND BY MANUFACTURE.

Although Chicago, from its geographical position and unequaled facilities for communicating with all parts of the country, has for many years been the center of the wholesale furniture trade west of the Alleghanies, it is only a few years since it became prominent as a manufacturing point. A quarter of a century ago fully 90 per cent of the most common articles of furniture sold here came from the Central and Eastern States. Even kitchen chairs were brought here from Ohio, and it would have been impossible to furnish a house of the most modest pretensions exclusively of furniture manufactured in Chicago. A gentleman largely identified with the trade states that as late as 1874 a very large percentage of the furniture sold here came from points further East. To-day, however, it is

THE LARGEST MANUFACTURING CITY

in the United States. Our manufacturers annually send heavy consignments to every part of the country East and West.

The most conclusive evidence that Chicago possesses superior advantages for manufacturing furniture as well as of the enterprise of its dealers is that they are the most formidable rivals in the Eastern markets of the manufacturers from whom they until recently bought the bulk of their goods. The magnitude of the city's industrial and jobbing interest in this line may be inferred from the fact that it gives employment to 17,000 workmen, and the present year's production is estimated at over $36,000,000 against $32,000,000 last year. Dealers state that while their sales in Illinois and Iowa show a decline, which is attributed to a partial failure of their corn and some other crops for three successive years, Ohio, Indiana, Kansas, Nebraska, Missouri, Wisconsin, Michigan, and the Northwestern and far Western sections, including the Pacific slope States and Territories,

BOUGHT MORE GOODS

than last year—Missouri, Kansas, Nebraska, Minnesota, and Dakota showing the largest increase. The most important shipments outside the United States were to Manitoba and Northwest Territory, whose people show a decided preference for Chicago furniture over the Canadian-made goods, and pay a heavy duty on their purchases here rather than buy from makers of the same articles in the Eastern provinces of Canada. The average cost of manufacturing, owing to a decline in prices of some articles of raw material, has been slightly below 1882. This advantage, however, has been given to the buyer, hence dealers have failed to realize any improvement in profits. On the contrary, the year's results are scarcely as satisfactory as for the preceding twelve months. There is, however, a general feeling that the shrinkage in prices that has been going on for some time has

'AT LAST BEEN CHECKED,

and that a change for the better is not distant. A gratifying feature in connection with the trade is the small percentage of losses from bad debts, the failures among the retail trade being comparatively light.

OFFICE AND SCHOOL FURNITURE.

CHICAGO THE HEAD-CENTER—IMMENSE BUSINESS.

The goods coming under the above head include all articles of bank, school, office, church, theater, opera house, and other furniture for public buildings, and its manufacture is a distinct branch of the furniture industry, and is carried on more extensively in Chicago than at any other point in the country, and there are few cities or towns where such goods are used that do not buy more or less here, including large sales to the General Government for fitting up offices in Washington City and elsewhere. Liberal shipments are also made to other countries, including Mexico, British Columbia, Manitoba, and North and South America. Unlike some other lines of manufacturing dealers say they have had an active and prosperous year. The principal establishments have increased their productive capacity 25 per cent, without being able to turn out goods as rapidly as wanted, and the year closes with more orders than can be filled during the next four months. The average prices are reported about the same as last year.

WALL PAPER, COLLATERAL GOODS.

CONSIDERABLE ACTIVITY.

This line of the jobbing trade was favorably influenced by the large degree of activity in building operations in nearly every portion of the country, which materially increased the demand for wall paper and curtain fixtures, and the leading houses handling such articles report a material gain in their sales. There was also a much larger call for better grades of goods than are usually called for by interior dealers, and especially from the more newly settled frontiers of the West and Northwest. The largest sales, however, were to the older and more wealthy States containing the largest towns and cities, the consumption of such goods in Chicago being much larger than customary for many years. Prices, however, were generally cheap, and the strong competition which jobbers here were compelled to meet from other cities which were trying to secure trade in territory that is regarded by Chicago dealers as under their especial control, often compelled them to sell goods at very small profits.

IRON AND STEEL.

A HISTORICAL REVIEW.

The iron and steel industry is the oldest not only in this country, but the oldest of which there is any record in the world's history. Hence it may strictly be regarded as the parent of all other manufacturing interests, as none could be successfully conducted without the aid of iron and steel. That the discovery of the process by which the crude ores were converted into refined metal, from which useful weapons and tools were made, was the first step toward man's civilization is beyond doubt. The date of the discovery, however, is too largely dependent on vague and unreliable traditions to admit of its location. That the discovery was old long before any system of recording events was known is certain. The first successful effort at making iron in America was by Thomas Rutter, who, in 1716, erected a blast furnace and forge on the Schuylkill River, about forty miles from Germantown, in what is now Montgomery County, Pa. Samples of this iron were sent to England and aroused such a jealousy among the English iron-makers that in 1719 a bill was introduced in the English Parliament to prohibit the importation of American iron. The bill, however, was unsuccessful, until 1750, when the increase of production in this country caused such alarm in England as to secure its passage. In 1817, just 100 years from the date of Rutter's first successful experiment, the first iron made west of Pittsburg was produced at a small forge erected by Ashbrand & Smith, about five miles southeast of Pilot Knob, Iron County, Mo. A few years later a number of small works were erected in Pope and Hardin Counties, Ill., and for years the southern part of this State, which at this time contained the bulk of the population, was largely supplied with iron and castings from the Pope and Hardin County works. But the increase in the production at Pittsburg and other points on the Ohio River, where bituminous coals and improved manufacturing facilities enabled workers there to manufacture iron so much cheaper than it could be turned out from the crude charcoal establishments in this State, caused their abandonment.

THE FIRST FOUNDRY IN CHICAGO.

In 1836 the first iron foundry was built in Chicago, on a very small scale. It was, however, many years later ere the first blast furnace was built for the production of pig iron, the development of that branch of iron-making, which is now a leading industry, being delayed by a fear that the distance from the ore and fuel supplies would prevent pig iron from being made here at a cost that would permit of an extended production. The result, however, has clearly demonstrated that nowhere outside of the coal and iron fields can pig metal be produced so successfully as in Chicago, and nowhere else out of the sections indicated is the business carried on so extensively. The total production in 1882 was returned at 360,407 tons. The exact proportion made at each point is not given, but as 13 of the 16 furnaces in the State are located in Chicago and immediate vicinity it is safe to assume that it should be credited with the great bulk of the output. The pig made here is converted into Bessemer and other steel by the establishment producing it, all of whom have extensive rolling mills.

AN UNSATISFACTORY MARKET.

The closing year's production has been materially reduced by the unsatisfactory condition of the iron and steel market, coupled with disturbances among workmen, which compelled the shutting down of the establishments during a considerable portion of the year. The Union Iron and Steel Works were also closed during almost the entire year through the failure of the company. The situation in other parts of the country was less favorable than here, and the production smaller in proportion to the capacity. Many of the furnaces located in the iron and coal fields were compelled to close from a lack of sale for their products at remunerative prices. It is stated that out of 55 charcoal furnaces in the Lake Superior district only seventeen are in blast. Of the thirty-eight now idle only six are in a condition to blow in without rebuilding. As the supply of timber for fuel where many of them are located has been so nearly exhausted as to greatly enhance the price of charcoal, there is little reason for supposing that they will ever again be put in operation. A similar condition of affairs exists in many other localities, hence it is plain that the production of charcoal iron will decline in the near future. Nor is the loss likely to be compensated by mineral coal and coke iron, as a number of the latter furnaces were unwisely built at points where pig-iron can only be made at periods when profits are extraordinary, having long been idle and will never again be blown in, hence it is plain that the productive capacity for the next two years is likely to be more nearly equalized to the demand, which argues an approach to a more healthy condition of trade in the not distant future. This assumption is strengthened by the returns gathered by James M. Swank, Esq., Secretary of the American Iron and Steel Association. Mr. Swank's report printed Nov. 1 shows that on Jan. 1, 1883, there were 417 furnaces in blast in the United States. On Nov. 1 the number had fallen to 330, showing a decrease of 87. Since then a few others have blown out, hence the reduction for the year may be placed at 100. The statistical position of the pig-iron market has also been improved by a diminished production which has fallen below the very moderate consumption. On Jan. 1 there were 383,655 gross tons of pig-iron in the hands of makers and agents. By July 1 the quantity increased to 528,590 tons. Nov. 1 there were 232,354 tons unsold. The 1st of November there were no stocks worth mentioning in the hands of speculators, nor were there at any of the ports any noteworthy stocks of foreign pig-iron. Of hypothecated stocks at that date the association heard of none worthy of notice except Marshall pig-iron at Pittsburg. This was not included in the statistics of unsold blocks July or November.

THE PIG-IRON TRADE.

A feature of the trade in pig-iron in Chicago during the current year was the large increase in sales of the products of Southern furnaces, the bulk of which came from Tennessee and Alabama, where its manufacture has more largely increased during the past few years than in any other section of the Union. The secret of the success attained by the Southern furnaces is in the low cash at which the ore fuel can be concentrated. This has enabled makers to undersell the same grades from other parts of the country.

The total production in the United States for the past eleven years, and the average price in Pennsylvania, is as follows:

	Price per 2,240 lbs.	Tons. 2,000 lbs.
1883*	$22.50	4,675,000
1882	25.75	5,178,122
1881	25.12½	4,641,564
1880	28.50	4,295,414
1879	21.50	3,070,875
1878	17.62½	2,577,361
1877	18.87½	2,314,585
1876	22.25	2,093,236
1875	25.50	2,266,581
1874	30.25	2,689,413
1873	42.75	2,868,278
1872	48.87½	2,854,558

*Estimated production.

REFINED IRON.

THE COURSE OF TRADE.

The year opened with flattering prospects for a good trade, stocks at the mills and in hands of jobbers were light, many of the former had liberal orders in advance of production, and the indications pointed to a liberal consumption at fairly remunerative prices. It soon became apparent, however, that there was trouble brewing, not only for the iron trade, but for nearly all commercial and industrial pursuits. These early admonitions of disaster were soon followed by heavy failures, including some of the largest, and, heretofore, supposed to be the strongest firms engaged in making and jobbing iron. Distrust at once succeeded confidence, many orders on file at the mills were canceled ere they had been reached, while many parties who had previously been impatiently waiting for goods were unable to receive them when ready for delivery. The reversal in the position of the market and the growing frequency of failures increased the pressure to sell, and there was a gradual settlement in values from about the opening to the end of the year. The average price in Philadelphia through January for best merchant bar was $56 per ton of 2,240 pounds. In February prices steadily settled, and averaged $53.76. As above stated, there was no reaction from the first start down and the closing price was $36. The highest price reached in forty years was in August, 1864, when it touched $170. The lowest prices previous to this year was in January, 1879, when it averaged $40.32, but closed the following December at $72.24. The depression in the trade materially interrupted the production of the Chicago rolling mills, which was further contracted by the suspension of the Union Iron and Steel Company, whose works were closed early in the year. In spite, however, of the adverse situation, the Chicago mills have done a very fair business. Their production, including bar and other classes of refined iron, was about 75,000 tons. Jobbers report a very fair distribution, including a large increase to the Northwest, far West, and other new sections not heretofore supplied from here. Profits, however, have been very light, and at the close there is less disposition to press sales, and more confidence regarding the future. The mills are also receiving a fair number of orders for delivery during the next three months. The present low prices likewise encourage dealers to think that no material decline can be possible, and that the next change of consequence is likely to be in the direction of an advance. Stocks of all classes are fair but not excessive, and the outlook justifies predictions that the production during the next few months will be more closely adjusted to the demand for consumption, and business conducted on a conservative basis.

The range of prices for common bar iron in the Chicago market each month during the past year, with comparisons, was as follows:

	1883.	1882.	1881.
January....	$2.50@2.60	$....@3.00	$....@2.50
February...	2.40@2.50	....@3.00	2.40@2.50
March.......	2.30@2.50	....@3.00	2.40@2.50
April........	2.30@2.40	....@3.00	2.40@2.50
May........	2.25@2.30	2.70@3.00	2.40@2.50
June........	2.25@2.30	....@3.00	2.40@2.50
July........	2.20@2.25	....@3.00	2.40@2.50
August.....	2.10@2.25	2.90@3.00	....@2.70
September..	2.10@2.20	2.90@3.00	....@2.80
October....	2.00@2.15	2.80@2.90	....@3.00
November..	2.00@2.10	2.60@2.80	....@3.00
December..	...@2.00	2.50@2.70	....@3.00

STEEL RAILS.

The decrease of nearly 50 per cent in railroad construction during the year, compared with the twelve months immediately preceding, and the unsettled condition of business which induced greater economy in tracks, regarding repairs by the roads already in operation, coupled with a reduction of $9 per ton in the import duty, has been severely felt by the manufacturers of steel rails, and the absence of orders at paying rates compelled many of the mills East and West to shut down, while others have only run on part time, and in a majority of instances those who continued in operation made rails without profit if not an actual loss, their object being to give work to a large number of workingmen who must otherwise have suffered for lack of employment. The cost of keeping mills idle is also an important item, as machinery suffers more from inaction than active work. This alone often induces iron and steel makers to keep their mills in operation in the face of an apparent loss on their products. The extent to which the steel-rail industry has suffered may be inferred by a comparison of the opening with closing prices of the year, the former quotation at Philadelphia $40 and the latter at $35 per ton, and even at the latter figure there are less orders than would give the Eastern mills employment for half their capacity. It is gratifying, however, to be able to state that the Chicago mills have been more fortunate in securing orders than many in other sections of the country, and, with the exception of one establishment which, owing to financial embarrassments of the corporation controlling it, was closed early in the year. The percentage of production to capacity has been larger then at other steel rail centers. The North Chicago Company, having an aggregate capacity of 325,000 tons per annum at their North Branch and South Chicago mills, have turned out 165,000 tons, and have sufficient orders booked to keep them fairly employed for some time to come; the prices at which the recent orders were taken, although not made public, supposed to be $1 to $2 over the Eastern quotations. Chicago rail mills are of the most recent construction, and are provided with every improvement calculated to save labor, and cheapen the cost of goods. Instead of casting pigs, as was formerly the custom, the molten metal runs direct from the furnaces to the convertor, where it is transformed into steel, whence it passes into a liquid state to the rollers and is shaped into rails. This is a great saving in both labor and fuel. This in connection with the lower cost of iron ores has enabled the mills here to make rails without loss in the face of the severe decline in prices since the first of the year.

The following exhibits the production of rails in this country from 1867 to 1882, and prices from 1867 to 1883, inclusive, the price for the latter year merely covering the entire range, while the average is given for the preceding years; 1867 being the first period at which they were produced in salable quantities:

Year.	Product in gross tons.	Price in currency.
1867..................	2,277	$166.00
1868..................	6,451	158.50
1869..................	8,616	132.25
1870..................	30,357	106.75
1871..................	34,152	102.50
1872..................	83,991	112.00
1873..................	115,192	120.50
1874..................	129,414	91.25
1875..................	259,699	68.75
1876..................	368,269	59.25
1877..................	385,269	45.50
1878..................	491,427	42.25
1879..................	606,397	48.33
1880..................	954,460	67.50
1881..................	1,330,302	61.12½
1882..................	1,438,155	48.50
1883..................	No report	37.50

Of the 1,438,155 tons made in 1882, Illinois produced 336,122 tons, Pennsylvania 759,524, and other States and Territories 342,509 tons.

TOOL STEELS.

There has been a liberal consumption of all grades of tools and machinists' steels, and the distribution was larger than last year, but, as with other classes of steel goods, prices were the lowest ever touched, and the margin between cash and selling figures so close that very few articles paid a profit to jobbers.

NAILS.

The trade in nails has grown to be an enormous one, especially in the West, Northwest, and Southwest. According to statistics prepared for the American Iron and Steel Association, there are seventy-four completed nail mills in the country, containing 5,008 nail machines. Five new nail works are being built and will be ready for operation about the beginning of the year 1884. At that time there will be a total of 5,999 nail machines, being an increase of 432 machines in about eighteen months. The manufacture of steel nails has commenced, there being six works engaged in making nails of steel or steel and iron combined. The annual capacity of the completed nail mills of the country, supposing them to be steadily employed, is 11,376,000 kegs of cut nails or spikes, an increase of about 25 per cent since August, 1882. This capacity will be increased about 1,000,000 kegs when the new works now being built are completed. In 1882 the product was 6,147,097 kegs of 100 pounds, and for 1883 it is estimated at 6,000,000 kegs. There are sixteen States in which nails are manufactured, but the great bulk of the trade is confined in Pennsylvania, Ohio, Massachusetts, and West Virginia. Out of the 5,008 machines in use, Pennsylvania has 1,425; Ohio, 859; Massachusetts, 616; and West Virginia, 680. The capacity of the Pennsylvania mills is 3,264,000 kegs; Ohio, 2,200,000 kegs; and West Virginia, 1,088,000 kegs. No other State reaches one million kegs. Of the new machines being added 74 are in Pennsylvania, 83 in West Virginia, 40 in Alabamba, where there are only 60 now, and 100 in Wisconsin, where there are none now. The manufacture in this city for the year was reported at 264,000 kegs of 100 lbs each, against 300,000 in 1882, the falling off being due to the destruction of the mills by fire early in the year, which required 30 days to rebuild, and by their being closed one month in the summer to limit the production, and another shut-down which occurred Dec. 20. The action of manufacturers in

LIMITING THE OUTPUT

was done to prevent the market from being overstocked and to keep prices up to as high a price as possible, but the depression in the general iron trade was too much for them and prices gradually settled from the opening to the close, which was equal to a decline of 90c per keg. The year opened with moderate stocks in the hands of Western jobbers and a liberal demand. As the season advanced, the consumption increased on account of the unusual number of buildings being erected in all parts of the West. The supply, however, was fully equal to the requirements and no difficulty to speak of was experienced in filling orders, except where round lots of sizes for which there was an unusual call, and then the delay was almost too trifling to notice. The general feeling among the trade, however, was unsettled, and purchases were more on the hand-to-mouth principle than for the past three years, as the steady settling of prices made them very timid about anticipating their wants, and the manufacturers were forced to carry the stocks, and fed the trade as it required. There was no difficulty with the employes as in 1882; and, although as many nails were sold and used as in former years, the prices were so low that manufacturers were unable to make any profit to speak of. The year closed with fair stocks and a moderate order demand, but the general feeling was that prices had reached about the lowest point, and jobbers were very conservative about naming rates for car lots unless for present delivery.

THE RANGE OF PRICES

each month during the past year, with comparisons, was as follows:

	1883.	1882.	1881.
Jan	$3.50 to 3.75	$3.50 to 3.55	$2.90 to 3.00
Feb.....	3.00 to 3.50	3.50 to 3.55	2.90 to 3.20
March ..	3.40 to 3.50	3.50 to 3.55	3 10 to 3.20
April....	3.25 to 3 50	3.40 to 3.50	3.00 to 3.25
May	3.25 to 3.50	3.40 to 3.50	..... to 3.00
June....	3.25 to	3.75 to 4.00	..... to 3.00
July	3.10 to 3.25	..... to 4.00	..... to 3.00
Aug.....	3.10 to 3.15	..... to 4 00	3.00 to 3.10
Sept....	3.00 to 3.10	4.00 to 4.25	3.10 to 3.40
Oct	2.85 to 3.00	3.75 to 4.00	3.40 to 3.50
Nov.....	2.85 to 2.95	..... to 3.75	..... to 3.50
Dec.....	2.60 to 2.80	3.60 to 3.75	..... to 3.50

METALS AND TINNERS' STOCK.

Business in everything that comes under this head, such as sheet iron, copper, tin-plate, solder, etc., was for the greater part of the year as good as in any former period. There was less desire, however, on the part of the interior jobbers and manufacturers to carry large stocks, preferring to buy more frequently than in previous years, as they regarded the outlook in many sections with considerable suspicion, which created an unsettled feeling. Jobbers here, however, kept their stocks up to what they have been, and no difficulty was experienced in filling orders. Sales were pushed in sections that they had heretofore given little attention to, and the result has been that more goods were sold, but the aggregate business was not any greater than that of 1882, as prices ruled lower on all descriptions and closed weak and unsettled for sheet iron and tin-plate at the inside of the year. Tin-plate opened in January at $7 rates for standard brands, and in February declined to $6.75, where it remained until December, when jobbers began to cut rates, and a reduction to $6.50 occurred. Sheet iron, Nos. 16 to 24, opened at $4.50 rates, and gradually settled to $3.50 at the close, with the prospect of lower prices in the near future. Copper bottoms declined from 29c to 23c per ℔ and closed at the latter figure.

HARDWARE, CUTELRY, AND TOOLS

A CONSIDERABLE INCREASE.

The demand for all classes of builders hardware has shown considerable increase over any preceding year, the gain being argely the result of the activity in building operations in nearly every portion of the country, and especially in the large cities and the newly settled sections of the West and Northwest, where the consumption was unusually heavy. There was also a wider extent of country supplied than in any former year, liberal shipments going to all the Pacific coast States and Territories. Fair bills were also sent to the Canadian provinces in the Northwest, and a few to the Republic of Mexico. The demand from the larger towns and cities also included a better line of goods, or at least a larger percentage of such articles. The augmentation in sales of fine goods was entirely due to the material increase in the number of expensive buildings erected during the year just closing. There is, however, an almost universal complaint among jobbers that while the volume of sales was much larger than in any former year, the result was not as satisfactory as could have been desired. This is attributed to the heavy production of goods, which induced more than ordinary competition among dealers who, finding that stocks were larger than required and prices steadily depreciating, made extra exertions to work them off. To quote a dealer, "prices were cut right and left, the main object being to sell." As a necessary result of the anxiety to sell, many articles reached consumers at prices that failed to cover cost of production. The steady depreciation in values also induce greater caution among jobbers, who, after their early stocks were cut down, refused to give orders in advance of current wants. This course, while relieving jobbers from losses by a decline on large stocks, was exceedingly severe on manufacturers, who, in addition to being compelled to carry goods until wanted for distribution, were required to bear almost the entire loss that occurred from depreciation between their manufacture and sale to retailers. The trade in miscellaneous lines of hardware of all other descriptions was affected by the same causes influencing builders' goods, and the result equally unsatisfactory to makers and jobbers.

The demand for cutlery was fairly active, and, with an enlarged area of territory to supply, jobbers were enabled to dispose of a large volume of goods. Unfortunately, however, they had bought excessive stocks at the close of 1882 and opening of 1883. This condition of the trade early became apparent to the trade, and was followed by a desire to sell that induced the acceptance of prices that failed to return a remuneration to the jobbers. The close of the year also finds liberal stocks in hands of manufacturers, and there is little reason to hope for a healthy improvement until the production is more nearly equalized to the consumption. It is estimated that fully 80 per cent of the cutlery consumed in this country is of American manufacture, and at the rapid rate at which its sale is increasing, compared with foreign made goods, justifies the prediction that very few years will elapse ere only a limited number of special lines of foreign goods will be imported. The exports of American cutlery to New Zealand, South and Central America, Mexico, Australia, South Africa, and Canada are also steadily increasing, the superiority of its finish, and fine temper giving it preference over any other makes where there is an approach to equality in prices.

There has been more than an ordinary activity in builders' and nearly all other lines of mechanics and miners' tools, but owing, as with all classes of goods, to the strong competition caused by over stocks in the hands of manufacturers and jobbers, business was done at prices that left little margin for profits, and the year closes with good stocks. The fact, however, that all articles of iron and steel goods are now selling at such small prices as to discourage production, and that the current cost of both raw materials and finished goods are down where no further decline is likely, if at all possible, encourages the hope that a change for the better must occur in the near future. It also argues well for the trade that, despite the many adverse conditions which jobbers of hardware, cutlery, and collateral articles have had to contend during the past twelve months, no failures have occurred among Chicago jobbers. It is also safe to assume that there are few other lines of the wholesale business that number a larger percentage of really strong houses than are to be found in this branch of trade.

WIRE GOODS.

AN ENORMOUS INCREASE.

The large increase in settlements in the West, Northwest, and Southwest, as well as its more general introduction among the farmers of the older States, has called out a very active demand for wire fencing, which is rapidly taking the place of lumber, and the product of the Chicago wire-fencing factories has been materially augmented within the year. Chicago agents of such factories in other localities have also had an increased sale for their goods. It is stated, however, that, owing to the very strong competition among producers, prices have been badly cut, the average cost being the lowest on record. The profits for handling were also light compared with the volume of business, and some firms assert that the figures at which goods were sold failed to cover the expense of making, although the prices of raw materials were lower than ever before; both materials and finished goods are now down where a further decline seems impossible.

The large increase in the demand for woven wire for screens, windows, doors, and railings, imparted an activity in the manufacture and sale of wire cloth and coarse netting, and those who manufacture and sell such goods have done more than an average business, some of the Chicago factories at times being behind with their orders. Prices of such goods have also been much lower than ever before, which, no doubt, had a tendency to enlarge the demand, especially for heavy net work, which is rapidly superseding wood for railing and similar purposes in fitting up offices.

STOVES.

CHICAGO LEADS THE TRADE.

Those who are conversant with the stove trade assert that the United States makes and uses more stoves than any other country in the world. Statistics kept by the trade also show that Chicago disposes of more stoves than any other city in the country. Hence, it may justly claim that it is the largest stove market in the world, yet while it leads in the sale of such goods it has as yet not made rapid progress in their product on compared with the volume handled. Only a moderate percentage of those sold in Chicago are made here. But it is gratifying to know the stove foundries are annually enlarging their capacity and volume of goods turned out, and this branch of manufacturing promises ere long to become a leading feature of the city's industrial interests. The facilities possessed for concentrating the iron and fuel, which are the leading factors in stove foundries, at the most reasonable cost, gives its stovemakers superior opportunities in the way of making cheap goods. Being the leading jobbing market in the United States the goods can be shipped direct from the foundry to the dealers in every part of the country, thereby saving the freight which competing establishments are compelled to pay when sending their goods here for sale. Inquiry among the leading manufacturers here regarding the materials used in stove-making develops the fact that the use of Scotch pig iron, which a few years since was regarded as absolutely requisite in the production of a strong, smooth casting, and which, from its high price, naturally enhanced the cost of the goods, has been entirely superseded by mixing different grades of American pig, which are found to make a plate of greater strength and smoothness than foundrymen were able to turn out when the foreign pig was used. Many also assert that the American castings—those made from American iron—expand more gradually under the influence of heat, and as a consequence are less likely to warp or crack while hot. Although the trade, like nearly all other leading lines of business, has had many adverse conditions with which to contend, there has been a considerable increase in the quality of goods turned out by the various stove works located here. There has also been many improvements in patterns calculated to increase their popularity with those who use them. The square heating stoves introduced last year have undergone numerous alterations that have largely added to their beauty and serviceableness. Some entirely new and novel styles have been introduced that are far more handsome than any heretofore brought out. And it is safe to assume that Chicago makers will not fall behind in the introduction of any features that are attractive and valuable. Although the year's business with Chicago makers, and the works located at other points who have agencies here has been less satisfactory than could have been desired, there is reason to believe that no serious losses have been sustained by the trade, and dealers, as a rule, feel hopeful of the future. This feeling is encouraged by the fact that prices of both the raw materials and finished goods are down to a point where a further depreciation in values is scarcely possible, hence they are not likely in the future to sustain losses from a further decline in prices of iron which would necessitate a like reduction in products.

WAGON-MAKERS' STOCK.

INCREASE OF PRODUCTION.

The articles classed under the above head includes all material used by wagon and carriage makers, much of which is manufactured in eastern and central portions of the United States. Some lines of carriage goods of the most expensive character are imported from Europe. There is, however, a steady increase in the production of both steel and iron goods in Chicago, and especially of springs for every class of vehicles requiring such articles. These latter goods are rapidly superseding those made in the Eastern States from the fact that Chicago makers can bring the new material together here as cheaply as they can be placed at the factories of their Eastern rivals, and as this is the great distributing point for such goods they have a market advantage in the way of freight over Eastern manufacturers. The great activity in the manufacture of vehicles this year has caused an active demand for all classes of heavy iron and steel goods, and those used in wagons and trucks have sold more freely than in any former year, the gain in volume as compared with 1882 being placed at 20 to 25 per cent. Owing to the decline in prices on steel and iron of about 20 per cent, the aggregate value of the goods sold shows but a small increase over 1882. Profits have also been light, as the larger stocks held during the early part of the year, in connection with the steady shrinkage in values, caused dealers and manufacturers to make extraordinary efforts to sell, and in their anxiety to work off goods prices were so badly cut that there was little margin left between the cost of manufacturing and distributing, and the prices at which they went to the retailer, or makers of wagons and carriages. During the closing months of the year the decline in values was apparently checked, and the year closes with reduced stocks of nearly all descriptions, and a more healthy feeling exists both with makers and jobbers of goods, who assert that prices are down where a further reduction in values is not likely; hence they feel that unless some unlooked-for disaster befalls the general business interests of the country, that any change that occurs will be in the direction of a more healthy trade. The production in the future is also likely to be gauged with a direct reference to current more than prospective wants.

SCALES AND WAREHOUSE TRUCKS.

LIBERAL ORDERS.

This line of business, although not exempt from the influences which have adversely affected other branches in many localities, has, on the whole, not only maintained its former large volume, but shows an increase over previous years, the losses in sales to localities where poor crops lessened trade of all kinds being more than compensated by an increase in other quarters. Business with Nebraska, Kansas, Missouri, Minnesota, and Dakota was very good. During the closing half o the year liberal orders were filled from Oregon and other sections of the Pacific slope. The establishments making such goods, especially scales and trucks, have also increased their production, but, like most other goods, prices have been close, yet the general result was not unsatisfactory. Were it not for the exorbitant freights to the Pacific coast a much larger volume of goods could have been sold in that direction, as well as to South and Central America, New Zealand and Australia, where American scales are preferred to any other, and are the recognized standard wherever they are introduced. Chicago-made trucks for stores, warehouses, and factories are also received with great favor, their lightness, combined with great strength, due to the superior materials used in their manufacture, renders them universally popular.

WAGONS AND TRUCKS.

SALE AND MANUFACTURE.

The manufacture of farm and transportation wagons, merchandise trucks, and all other classes of heavy vehicles devoted to commercial and construction purposes is an industry that had its origin almost with the birth of the city, and has grown up with it. There are very few other industrial interests whose products have had so extended a sale or enjoy such a wide degree of popularity. Chicago wagons are as well known in South and Central America, New Zealand, Australia, and South Africa as in the United States, and each year brings an increased number of orders from those countries. European dealers are also small buyers here, and, as with the first countries named, the sales in that direction are on the increase, but the prejudices of Europeans to American goods, in connection with the strong opposition of makers there of similar articles, has rendered their introduction slower, and our manufacturers have been indifferent about cultivating trade from quarters where they had to combat self-interest and prejudice, so long as they found it difficult to supply the demand from customers who were only too anxious to buy, and in most cases sent their orders considerably in advance of production. The secret of the popularity of Chicago-built vehicles is no less attributable to their skillful workmanship than to the superior stock used. Every article that enters into their construction is selected with the greatest care by intelligent experts, whose exclusive duties are to select stocks.

Each piece of timber is thoroughly seasoned before it goes to the factory, the custom being to keep several years' stock on hand, and every article that leaves the shops carries with it a guaranty of perfection as regards durability.

The current year's business shows a fairly satisfactory increase over the preceding one, and although the unsatisfactory business outlook in many quarters rendered manufacturers conservative about soliciting business, yet at times they were unable to fill large orders with promptness, and the proprietor of one of the largest works states that during a portion of the year he found it necessary to employ an extra force, and lengthened the working hours 10 per cent to enable him to respond to the calls for goods, the largest increase in the demand being for farm wagons from the newly developing sections of the Southwest, far West, and Northwest, the sales to Dakota, Montana, and the Canadian Provinces of Manitoba and Northwest Territory being very large. The increased trade from the two last-named districts was remarkable from the fact that the Canadian wagonmakers in the older provinces have secured the placing of a heavy duty on all such goods from the United States, and the fact that Chicago makers are steadily increasing their sales in that direction furnishes conclusive proof as to the superiority of their goods. The demand for wagons from Mexico for farming and mining purposes has also largely increased, and letters from that country give assurance that the present demand is merely the beginning of a trade that will develop as our railroad connections are extended and general commercial relations become more intimate by the means of reciprocal compacts. The general average prices for leading articles are slightly lower than last year, the decline being about in proportion to the reduction in the cost of some classes of materials.

CARRIAGES AND BUGGIES.

CHICAGO THE HEADQUARTERS.

Although there are no very large establishments here devoted to the manufacture of pleasure carriages and light business carriages and buggies, there are numerous factories of respectable size where their production is a specialty, and whose goods take a high rank. Their annual make amounts to a large aggregate. While Chicago cannot claim prestige in this line of manufacture, it can justly assert its supremacy as the largest market in the country for their sale. Every leading establishment in the Union has an agency here, and with some of the most extensive it is their virtual headquarters as a distributing point. A large portion of their supplies are also bought here, their factories being located at no great distance as a matter of economy in the way of securing cheaper building sites for their plant and employes' residences, lower taxes and minimum water rates, all of which are important factors in conducting a large industrial enterprise. The fact, however, that, as before stated, the supplies are largely bought and the manufactured goods sold here gives the city as substantial benefits as though the factories were within its limits. Both the local factories and the distant and nearby-establishments having agencies here have had a large trade, their shipments of fine goods being more than usually heavy and materially above any former year. Prices, however, have been a trifle lower on many lines, and profits scarcely up to the average of more prosperous periods. A feature of the trade was the very large increase in the demand for fine work of every class, those who have occasion to buy such goods no doubt feeling that there is no economy in buying cheap, rough, poorly-made articles. The increasing wealth in the older and more populous sections of the country is also proving an important factor in stimulating the demand for expensive carriages and other vehicles kept for business and pleasure.

SAFES, VAULTS, AND LOCKS.

VERY LARGE SALES.

Although the manufacture of bank and office safes, vaults, and locks is not conducted here on a scale commensurate with other industries, Chicago uses more of such goods than any other city outside of New York. In addition it is the largest distributing point on the continent. Every leading establishment making such articles has one or more large warehouses here, whose agents sell to all parts of the country, from the Alleghanies west to the Pacific slope and north to Hudson Bay and Puget Sound, south to the Mexican Gulf. Numerous export orders are also taken here, and goods are sent to Mexico, South and Central America, and other countries. Large sales of locks are made to Australia. The current year's trade, while to a considerable extent lessened by the unsatisfactory condition of business in many parts of the country, and especially in the northern portion of this and immediately adjoining States, where the crops were a partial failure, sales were materially increased by the rapid augmentation of population and building up of towns in the newly settled States and Territories and the extension of trade into sections that have not heretofore been visited by representatives of Chicago dealers. This newly derived custom swelled the aggregate sales for the year to a larger volume and valuation than those of any previous twelve months, and the general result has been very satisfactory to the houses handling such goods.

MACHINERY, ETC.

LARGER THAN EVER BEFORE.

The manufacture of all kinds of engines, boilers, and everything that is generally classed under the head of machinery has been conducted on a larger scale than in any former year in the history of this city. The majority of the largest manufactories have been running full time all the year, and the amount of goods turned out showed an increase of 10 per cent over the preceding year, which was regarded as one of the heaviest. The increase was not a surprise, as the steady growth and development of the Northwest and West is constantly requiring more machinery of all descriptions, and as the Chicago manufacturers are always on the alert for new fields in which to sell their products they have succeeded in obtaining the bulk of the business. Although more territory has been covered, the aggregate value of the sales does not show any gain over those of the preceding year, as the decline in prices at which the majority of goods were sold on account of the severe competition and the natural reaction from the extreme prices of former years balanced the gain in the sales. Manufacturers as a rule carried larger stocks of engines, boilers, and general machinery during the greater part of the season, but at the close they were not in excess of former years. In mining machinery the business during the first half of the year was lighter on account of the large number of wildcat mines being put on the market, which made legitimate mines hold off for a time, but during the closing six months the former were largely weeded out and a large summer and fall business was transacted, sales being made throughout the West and also in Mexico, as the mines in that country are being rapidly developed.

Boiler-makers as a rule enjoyed a good season, as regards the amount manufactured and sold, which was larger than in former years. Orders were filled from the far West and Southwest, where in former years nothing of consequence could be sold. The competition between manufacturers from all sections was never as severe as during the year under review, and as a natural consequence the purchasers reaped the benefit. Manufacturers were forced to pay as much for producing as formerly, but the decrease in the cost of the raw material partly recompensed them.

Wrought iron pipe was produced to a larger extent, and the sales were heavier, as they were pushed freely in all directions. One new and important feature in this line was the liberal shipments of pipe into Canada, which it has been impossible to do for five years, on account of the low price of iron, and as long as it continues at the present low rates Canadian manufacturers cannot compete with the American in any market.

AGRICULTURAL DEPARTMENTS.

CHICAGO LEADS THE WORLD.

The large increase in the acreage of land brought under cultivation in the territory which is mainly supplied by Chicago manufacturers of farm machinery and tools, in connection with an extended trade into many new section, has imparted a good degree of activity in this line of industry, and although the sales were to a considerable extent curtailed in the Central and Southern States by the partial failure of the wheat crops, the aggregate volume of business done was larger than in any preceding year.

A marked feature in the trade was the increase in shipments to Manitoba, and other British possessions in the far Northwest, and were it not for the heavy duty which the Canadian Government imposes on all classes of American farming implements, a much larger business could have been done in that direction. But the favor with which Chicago machinery has been received there justifies the hope that our trade will increase with the development of the country, which promises to be rapid.

Mexico is also increasing its purchases here, and will continue to buy more freely hereafter, as American goods are fast superseding the primitive tools so long in use there. There has also been a fair gain in the sales in Europe, South and Central America, New Zealand, Australia, and South Africa.

The largest gain in shipment, however, were to the Northwest and the States and Territories west of the Rocky Mountains, and a steady augmentation may be expected from that direction in the future. The completion of the Northern Pacific Railroad has opened an immense area of country that will find Chicago an advantageous market in which to buy farm implements, as its position as the great railroad center gives better and cheaper facilities than any other city in the country.

The superior character of a majority of the machinery and tools made here induces those who once test them to give them preference. This is especially the case in regard to all classes of plows, cultivators, harvesters, and mowers. As regards the last two species of machinery Chicago can justly claim precedence as the pioneer city, as the first successful effort to make reapers and mowers was consummated here, and it has not only maintained the lead as to the number of such articles annually produced and sold, but the machines have a reputation that is world wide, their superiority being universally recognized. The production of the different lines of farm implements here gives employment to thousands of operatives, and represents many millions of dollars in capital.

BUILDING MATERIALS.

MANUFACTURE OF PRESSED BRICK.

The manufacture of common and pressed brick in this city was the heaviest of any year on record, and aggregated 325,000,000 on the North, West, and South sides, and 20,000,000 at Pullman, making a total of 345,000,000, against 300,000,000 in 1882.

The number of fine pressed brick made was 3,446,000, against 2,266,000 in 1882, and had it not been for the destruction of the works early in the season by fire, thereby causing a loss of four months, the increase would have been larger. There was also made for use here by Chicago brick-makers, who have yards just over the boundary in Indiana, 13,500,000 common red, and 14,500,000 red pressed bricks. The stock on hand at the close of the year was larger than usual, being reported by the city yards at 30,000,000 of common on the South and West Sides, 15,000,000 on the South Side, and 1,000,000 fine pressed. In the Indiana yards the stock was 8,000,000 of pressed and common. The season for making was only a fair one, being very wet at the opening, and the average number of days worked was 120. There was considerable improvement made during the year by the largest makers, who put in more machinery and were anxious to

IMPROVE THE QUALITY

of their brick, and more fancy were made than in any former year. Patent dryers have also been put up, which will enable them to run in any kind of weather. During the fall new works were erected by Chicago brick-makers at Chester, Ill., with a daily capacity of 50,000, and at Galewood with 200,000 capacity, which they intend to sell in this city. Prices averaged lower than in 1882. Common sold at $7 to $10.40 per 1,000, and closed at $8. Pressed ranged at $18 to $28 for Indiana pressed, and $30 to $40 for other makes. The manufacture and sale of lime in this city and in the West and Northwest for the past year was the largest on record. A number of old kilns in this city that have been idle for a number of years were started about the 1st of May, and made a very satisfactory run as far as the production was concerned. The new firms, however, were anxious to push sales, and the result was that some of the old houses, who have had things for a number of years about as they wanted them, did not do so much business as expected, as they had to divide the territory. But their sales were up to those of the preceding year. Prices ranged lower at 65 to 90c per barrel in bulk, opening at the highest and closing at the lowest.

The amount of lime burned in this city for the year was reported by the manufacturers at 519,500 barrels. There were also 300,000 barrels shipped from Wisconsin and Indiana, making a total of 819,500 barrels consumed here, and shows an increase of about 15 per cent over that used in 1882. THE INTER OCEAN is indebted to the lime manufacturers along the Mississippi River, from Quincy northward, including the works in Northern Missouri, Illinois, and Southern Wisconsin, for their prompt replies to requests for their production for the year, and the aggregate is 1,800,000 barrels, an increase over 1882 of 10 per cent, due chiefly to the erection of new kilns. Many of the works in the section of country noted above are

CONTROLLED BY CHICAGO CAPITALISTS,

who have their headquarters here, but sell the greater part of their production throughout the West, and have sold more lime during the past year than in any former one, but the profits were not so large on account of prices ruling lower.

The manufacture of cements was larger than in any former year, the works being crowded to their greatest capacity and a number of new ones were erected, and some that have been idle for years started again. The amount manufactured in the West was 1,200,000 brls, which was one-third over last year.

There was also a larger amount of Portland, Me., and imported cement sold and used here than formerly. The consumption of all kinds of cement is yearly increasing, especially in this city, but more was sold all over the Northwest than ever before, and although the receipts here were unusually heavy it was rather difficult at times for some dealers to fill orders for certain brands promptly. The season closed with about the same amount of stock on hand as in previous years. Prices averaged lower, ranging from $1.25 to $1.40 per brl for common cement in a jobbing way and closed at $1.25, at which figures manufacturers as a rule have been able to make a fair profit, and generally express themselves as satisfied with their year's work.

LAND PLASTER WAS CONTROLLED

by a combination of manufacturers in Michigan, who made prices as they saw fit, but the average was lower, with sales and production larger. Plastering hair was used to a greater extent than formerly, and prices showed little variation from the preceding year. A new substitute known as vegetable fiber, which is said to be made of manilla, was put on the market, and although offered at less than half the cost of hair, plasterers were backward about purchasing, being in doubt as to how it would work, and were inclined to let some one else try the experiment to determine the lasting qualities claimed for it by the manufacturers.

SASH, DOORS, BLINDS, ETC.

THE LARGE INCREASE

in the number of buildings erected in this city and throughout the West created a good demand for all descriptions of sash, doors, blinds, etc., and sales were larger than in any former year. The manufacture was greater, on account of the gain in the sales, but dealers were able to fill orders promptly. Prices averaged about the same as in 1882. The cost of lumber suitable for such work was well maintained, and the only noticeable change was in glazed sash, which, on account of the increased cost of glass, was advanced. The year closed with fair stocks, and a moderate trade, and good prospects for a large business the incoming year.

WINES AND LIQUORS.

THE PASSAGE OF STRINGENT LAWS

regulating the traffic of liquors in a number of States has had a tendency to decrease the sales of whiskies and brandies in those sections. This disturbing element in the trade, in addition to the large stocks on hand at the opening of the year, caused a curtailment of production of whisky, and distillers say that the decrease in this and other districts in Illinois has been fully 10 per cent below 1882. There has, however, been an increased demand for native wines, which are rapidly growing in favor with consumers to the detriment of foreign goods, the sales of which are declining as the American goods increase. The manufacture and sale of beer has been large, heavy shipments having been made to all parts of the country.

DRUGS AND CHEMICALS.

THE CENTER OF THE JOBBING TRADE.

Although Chicago ranks among the most healthy cities on the continent, it is nevertheless the center of the jobbing trade of the United States for the sale of drugs, and all goods used for medical purposes. As in many other leading lines of business, however, its prestige is due to its geographical advantages, and the enterprise of those who handle such articles, rather than its near vicinity to consumers. A canvass of the situation develops the fact, that while the trade during the year just closed was not marked by the same degree of excitement, and spirited speculation, that characterized the business of the twelve months immediately preceding, the result has on the whole been more satisfactory to jobbers. Prices have shown more regularity, hence goods were handled with less risk. The average prices however, were lower than in 1882. There was also greater caution in buying stocks, which enabled jobbers to keep on a more secure basis, and rendered them conservative about granting credits. The result of the latter course was to diminish losses from bad debts, and to some extent lessen expenses, that always show a high percentage when there is a strong competition among dealers, to secure buyers for goods with which they are overstocked. But while there was less eagerness to sell goods, the general aggregate of business was fully up to that of 1882. This may be chiefly attributed to a material increase in new accounts, opened with customers in the Northwest and West, especially with Montana, Idaho, Washington and Oregon. The Southwest Territories and California, also increased their purchases to a fair extent. Some of the above noted sections were not open to Chicago jobbers until late in the year, therefore they have not been able to secure much of the custom, but during the ensuing year a strong effort will be made to obtain control of the largest part of it. Our jobbers never fail in their efforts to secure trade, and it is scarcely necessary to say that they will be successful in this venture.

BUSINESS OF SEVEN HOUSES.

There are now seven houses in the jobbing trade, with an aggregate capital of $1,500,000, and their annual sales reach $7,000,000. Although prices on nearly all articles have declined during the year, the shrinkage was less marked. Quinine opened in January at $1.85 per ounce, declined in May to $1.65, which was the lowest point ever reached in this market. In June it advanced to $1.85, and remained steady until the close of the year. During 1882 the range was $1.85 to $2.55, and closed at the inside figure. Opium sold at the opening in January at $4.50 per pound, declined in July to $4, reacted in August to $4.10 to $4.20, but afterward weakened and closed at $4. The range for 1882 was $4.15 to $4.75, and closed at $4.50. Iodide of potassium sold at $1.50 per pound in January, but on account of an increase in the manufacture the price was lowered to $1.35. Cinchonidia (sulphate), which is used as a substitute for quinine, was offered more freely than in former years, and declined from $1.05 to 85c per ounce in sympathy with quinine. Small flake manna showed about the heaviest fluctuation of anything on the list. It opened in January at 55c per pound, and advanced on account of the scarcity to $1.50 to $1.60, a heavy increase in the manufacture, brought about by the high prices, caused a decline in November to $1.25 to $1.30, and closed with a fair supply at the last named prices. Essential oils were severely effected by a reduction of the import duty. Lemon oil sold down in July from $3 per pound to $2 to $2.25, and other oils of the same class declined in about like proportion.

CASTOR OIL,

however, was an exception to the general rule, and advanced from $1.16 per gallon for No. 1, to $1.38, on account of the short crop of castor beans (from which the oil is made), and the formation of a combination of manufacturers, who took advantage of the situation to increase their profits. Norwegian cod-liver oil sold from $2.50 per gallon to $3.75, as the supply was not equal to the consumptive demand. Quassia chips, gentian root, and prairie brava, which attracted so much attention last year as a substitute for hops, were not called for to any extent, and prices showed little variation. Borax was offered more freely, and declined from 15c to 13c per pound. Gums of all description averaged a shade lower. Sulphur declined ½c per pound, as the production was increased over that of former years, and the combination which controlled the market broken. The consumption was also larger, especially on the Western sheep ranches. Chloroform and chloride of lime also showed a fair advance, especially on the latter, which was used in larger quantities than usual. Glycerine declined 3c to 4c per pound, under the influence of an increased production. All descriptions of arabic gums showed a small decline. Chemicals and all assayers' goods exhibited about the usual volume of business, and prices were comparatively steady.

THE BROKERAGE BUSINESS.

In addition to the jobbing trade in drugs and chemicals, there was a very large and steadily increasing business transacted by commission agents and drug brokers, representing Eastern importers and foreign manufacturers who were anxious to extend their trade in the West, and in order to do so were forced to keep agents in this city with good stocks of specialties that jobbers as a rule do not carry. In former years they had to order these from the East, which created considerable annoyance and delay, but now everything in the line of drugs and chemicals not ordinarily handled by jobbers can be obtained from the brokers and commission merchants here promptly. The sales of the latter reach $1,000,000—a large increase over any previous year.

PAINTS AND COLORS.

A LARGE BUSINESS.

In the manufacture of paints, colors, putty, and white lead Chicago does a very large business. Twenty-five years ago very little business in the way of making paints was done in the West, and all the stock sold at that time came from the East. Since then, however, there has been a steady growth, and now sufficient is made here annually to supply all the Western trade, and very little stock is brought from the East. The manufacture of putty was started about twenty-five years ago on a small scale, and only seven tons per week could be made, but now the works have a capacity of 100 tons per week. During the year under review the manufacture of paints, colors, etc., was larger than any of the preceding ones, and heavier stocks were carried for the bulk of the year. The volume of business was not up to their anticipations, and in fact was less than in 1882. The production was curtailed, which enabled jobbers to reduce their stocks to a better working basis, but should there be a heavy increase in the trade no difficulty would be experienced in supplying all the stock wanted, as the production could be enlarged sufficiently for all the trade. Prices of paints ruled lower than during the previous year, as much stock was forced on the market, which caused a reduction of 5@8 per cent. Caroders of white lead, of which there are two in this city, reported a liberal business, but the grinders done very little. The margins were too slight and stock could be had from the caroders cheaper than they could make it. Prices ranged from 5½ to 6c per lb. with 6c the ruling figure the greater part of the year.

OILS.

LINSEED OIL.

Linseed oil crushers did not enjoy as satisfactory a business as in 1882. The competition was greater, and the unsettled condition of the flaxseed market served to keep prices of that commodity above a point which made it impossible for crushers to purchase and produce oil at a profit. The capacity of the mills was increased 30 per cent during the year by the erection of new ones and enlarging five of the old mills. Of the new ones erected, one was in this city, one at Kansas City, and one at Sioux City, making over sixty-five mills in the States of Ohio, Indiana, Illinois, Iowa, Wisconsin, Minnesota, and Kansas. The production was the largest of any year in the history of the West, and showed an increase of 15 per cent. Although the demand was large, especially from July to November, the consumption did not keep pace with the production, and the result has been the accumulation in stocks since that time.

The range of prices for the year was narrower than in previous ones, as there was less speculation, and more desire on the part of consumers to buy only as their wants required. Raw sold in January at 49 to 50 cents per gallon, and boiled at 52 to 53 cents, which was the lowest price of the year. From that time there was a gradual advance until the last of March, when 55 cents was reached for raw, and 58 cents for boiled; in July a decline to 53 to 56 cents occurred, but in October the market became firmer, and prices advanced 1 cent, and closed at 54 cents for raw, and 57 cents for boiled. The range of raw oil in 1882 was 49 to 63 cents per gallon, and of boiled at 52 to 66 cents, and for 1881 was 50 to 63 cents for raw, and 53 to 66 cents for boiled. The consumption of oil cake in the United States and Europe was large, and is increasing very fast, as its value for fattening cattle is becoming wide-spread. The exports to Europe and Great Britain were heavier than in any former year, and more was used at home. Prices showed little change from those of 1882, but the range was not so large. Sales for the year were at $21.50 to $26 per ton, and closed at $25. In 1882 the range was $22 to $28, and closed at $22.

LARD OIL.

As Chicago leads the world in the provision trade and annually slaughters more hogs than any other point, it is natural that the business of making lard oil should be conducted on a larger scale here than at other points. The lard can be had here in greater quantities with less expense in handling; hence the Chicago lard oil presses are able to successfully compete with other points, and have succeeded in securing a very good and growing trade. This has been concentrated into a few large hands, and many of the smaller presses have been driven out of the business. The manufacture of oil the past year was heavier than in any preceding one. The capacity of the packers who have gone into this line of late years, was in a few instances nearly doubled, and enough oil is annually made here now to supply the Western trade. Prices were very unsettled on account of the rapid and severe fluctuations in the lard market and ranged lower than for the past two years. The demand was good and the aggregate sales showed a small increase over 1882. The monthly range of prices for the past four years for extra were as follows:

	1883.	1882.	1881.	1880.
January..	86 to 88	90	72 to 76	65 to 70
February..	88 to 90	88 to 90	78 to 83	65
March.....	88 to 90	86 to 88	83 to 86	65
April......	88 to 90	88 to 90	82 to 86	60 to 62
May.......	88 to 92	90	80 to 82	58 to 60
June.......	78 to 88	90 to 93	78 to 80	55
July.......	73 to 78	93 to 98	83 to 87	54
August....	67 to 73	94 to 96	86 to 88	58 to 67
September	63 to 67	94 to 96	92 to $1	65
October...	63	96 to $1	97	68 to 72
November.	63 to 65	93 to 98	93	70
December	65 to 70	88 to 93	90 to 93	70

TURPENTINE.

The market for spirits of turpentine exhibited no new feature during the year under review. The production was large and sales and consumption fully equal to the previous years. There was less speculation, as parties who have in the past manipulated the market, did not like the outlook at the time when they usually took hold. The result has been a more even set of prices, and a trade closely adjusted to the wants of consumers. The range of prices was downward, and touched the lowest point since 1880, and closed at nearly the bottom, a decline of nearly 21c per gallon. The following shows the monthly range of prices for the past four years in this market:

	1883.	1882.	1881.	1880.
January...	55 to 57	57 to 58	... to 51	47 to 48
February..	55 to 56	... to 56	47 to 49	43 to 45
March.....	52 to 55	58 to 64	48 to 50	48 to 53
April......	50 to 53	59 to 71	42 to 46	34 to 57
May.......	41 to 49	49 to 56	39 to 40	28 to 35
June......	39 to 41	49 to 50	42 to 47	28 to 32
July......	40 to 41	48 to 50	45 to 47	28 to 31
August....	40 to 45	48 to 50	48 to 55	30 to 38
Sept......	42 to 44	47 to 51	56 to 57	38 to 42
October...	42 o 43	51 to 59	55 to 57	42 to 48
November.	40 to 42	56 to 59	58 to 60	... 48
December.	36 to 38	54 to 56	58 to 59	... 50

MISCELLANEOUS OILS.

There was a liberal business transacted in machine, bank, sperm, and other descriptions of oils. Sales showed no special increase over those of the previous year. The supply was at all times sufficient to fill orders promptly, and prices remained about the same as in 1882.

COTTON SEED OIL.

Trade in cotton seed oil was not as heavy as anticipated at the opening of the year, when the price of lard was high, and the prospect for a large business very flattering. The heavy decline in lard, that started in June, caused a falling off in the home demand, as consumers who would not pay the high price for lard when cotton seed oil could be obtained at a liberal discount, refused to purchase the oil as freely when the price of lard and cotton seed became about the same, thus decreasing the consumption. The export demand was also less than anticipated, while the production showed an increase. The number of tons of cotton seed harvested the past year was 3,000,000 tons, 1,000,000 tons of which were crushed, and produced 600,000 barrels of oil. Prices ranged lower. Refined oil opened at 70c per gallon and closed at 52c, with good stocks. Liberal sales of cotton seed soap stock were made to soap-makers, and the prices declined to 2@3c per lb.

CARBON OILS.

The trade in petroleum did not attract as much attention during the year just closed as in the two immediately preceding ones. The flow of crude was large, but not up to that of 1882, as a smaller number of new wells were bored and no new oil fields discovered, as was the case in the preced ng year. Although there was a very large speculative business transacted in crude, prices were confined to a narrower range and fluctuations less frequent and severe. The sales of refined in the West and Northwest were heavier than in any year in the history of the trade in the West, as the population is increasing and a corresponding gain is expected in the consumption of oil. The territory covered was larger than formerly, more oil being sent from here into Manitoba and the Northwest Territory. Stocks of all grades were ample for the demand throughout the entire year and no difficulty was experienced in filling orders promptly. The amount of carbon oil inspected here during the year was 225,000 brls against 202,000 brls in 1882, 184,000 brls in 1881, and 119,317 brls in 1880. Prices of 150 degrees test ranged from 10c to 11½c, and closed at 10¾c. The monthly range of prices on prime white, 150 degrees test, in this market with comparisons were as follows:

	1883.	1882.	1881.	1880.
January	....@10½	10 @10¼	....@18¾	....@17¾
Febr'ry	10½@11½	10 @10¼	16¾@17¾	....@17¾
March	10½@11½	....@10	10 @13¾	12½@17
April	10 @11½	9⅞@10	10¼@10½	12 @12½
May	....@10	9½@ 9⅞	....@10	11½@12
June	10 @11¼	9 @ 9½	....@10	12¾@14
July	10¾@11	....@ 9	....@ 9¾	12 @12½
August	10¾@11	....@ 9	....@10¼	13 @15
Sept'r	10⅞@11½	9 @10½	10¾@11	15 @17
October	11 @11¼	10¾@11⅝	....@11	17½@18¾
Nov'r	10¾@11	10⅝@13⅛	10¼@10¾	....@18¾
Dec'r	10¼@....	12⅛@13⅛	....@10	....@18¾

GASOLINE AND NAPHTHA.

Sales of gasoline and naphtha were large, but showed no particular increase over those of the preceding year. The supply was good, and prices ranged lower; 87 degrees gasoline opened at 20c, declined to 18c, and closed at 19c; 74 degrees opened at 13½c, sold off to 11½c, and closed at that price. Naphtha, 63 degrees, opened at 10½c, declined to and closed at 9½c.

GLASS.

The business of Chicago jobbers in glass for the year just closed was without an exception the largest on record, and sales showed an increase of 20 per cent over those of 1882, which were 25 per cent over 1881. There were three strictly jobbing houses engaged in the business, and their sales reached $2,500,000, and, including all the glass sold by the paint, oil, and drug jobbers, would make the aggregate be over $3,000,000. During the first half of the year business was comparatively quiet, on account of the small number of buildings erected, both here and in all parts of the country which depend on this city for their supplies, but the heavy increase during the six months fully made up for the backwardness of the opening ones Dealers have no cause to complain about their sales or profits, which were unusually large. They carried about 30 per cent more stock, and secured it when prices were low, and thus reaped the advantage of the advance, which was 50 to 55 per cent on American and 40 per cent on French window. The advance was brought about by the strike of the glass-blowers in the East, which closed the bulk of the American factories from July 1 to the close of the year. The action taken by blowers enabled the manufacturers to dispose of their stock at good prices, and caused heavy importations of French to supply the deficiency in the stock here. The capacity of the American window-glass factories is large enough to meet the bulk of the requirements of the home trade, and, had it not been for the strike, the importations the past year would have cut but little figure in the trade.

The sales of plate glass were heavier, as there is a steadily growing call for it from all sections. The amount made in this country was also larger than in former years, the ncrease bei ng due to the erection of a large ew factory near Pittsburg, Pa., and a 25 per cent increase in the capacity of the largest works. The amount now made by American manufacturers equals about five-eighths of the annual sales. Prices ranged 30 per cent higher, the advance commencing about Sept. 1. The importations of French plate were larger, and more was used, but the improvements made by the American manufacturers is yearly reducing the sales of the foreign. Prices also followed the American, and advanced in about the same proportion. Mirrors were not called for as freely as during the preceding year, but no perceptible falling off could be noted in the amount of sales. The call was chiefly for la ge, square, beveled-edged plates of the best quality. Prices of fore gn were irregular, and ranged entirely different from former years, the French being 30 to 40 per cent lower, while the German were 20 per cent higher on account of the latter being under the control of a syndicate.

Fancy and colored glass, generally known as rolled cathedral and antique, met with a good call, and prices advanced during the closing three months in sympathy with other glass. The manufacture of colored glass in this country was enhanced by the starting of a large factory at Boston, but not enough is made to supply the trade. The year closes with ample stocks in the hands of jobbers and very favorable prospects for a large business next year.

SOAP.

LAUNDRY AND TOILET GOODS.

These goods have met a large sale from every part of the country and their production correspondingly increased, the leading factories having materially enlarged their capacity for producing both laundry and toilet goods. In addition, one very large establishment has been built for manufacturing the latter. The cost of production has also been lowered by the reduced cost of lard, tallow and other material that enter as factors into their manufacture. There has also been considerable improvement in the quality of all the leading lines of goods, and in this respect Chicago soaps now rank equal to the finest made in the country. Notwithstanding the fact that Chicago is among the largest, if not the largest manufacturing point in the country for such goods, large quantities are brought here from the Eastern and Middle States.

JEWELRY WATCHES, ETC.

A TEN PER CENT INCREASE.

The goods classable under the above head may be regarded more strictly as luxuries than any other line of articles, hence their sale is more entirely dependent upon the condition of the country than those handled by other lines of trade, as jewelry or watches, and ornamental goods, are about the last articles that people will buy when their income is such as to render it difficult to make both ends meet. That such has been the case with a large majority of the population during the year just closing is beyond a doubt, hence, as a necessary consequence, the demand for such goods has been lessened by the diminished ability of a majority of those who, in prosperous times, are liberal customers of those who handle such goods.

Yet in spite of the drawbacks which the business has suffered from the causes stated the leading houses in the trade place their sales at 10 per cent over those of 1882. The gain, however, as with many other branches of business, may be ascribed to the increased territory canvassed by Chicago jobbers, who have, so to speak, thoroughly worked every portion of the United States west of the Alleghanies, and sometimes have been freely sold in the Atlantic States. A considerable trade has also come from Manitoba and Mexico. The close connection now being made by railroad with the latter country also justifies the prediction that the sales in that direction will rapidly expand in the near future, as the facilities of Chicago jewelry houses for supplying dealers in that country are unequaled by those of any other city on the continent.

The manufacture of many lines of such goods in Chicago, and the immediate vicinity, has been materially increased during the year, and the aggregate volume and value of such productions is an important factor in the city's manufacturing interest, as it gives employment to a large number of operatives. Another and very important feature in connection with the trade is the large importing business in watches, diamonds, and other precious stones, which trade was formerly controlled by jewelers in Eastern cities.

MUSICAL INSTRUMENTS.

LARGE INCREASE IN SALES.

The sales of musical instruments are expected to depend very largely on the condition of other lines of trade. The present year, however, seems to have been an exception to the general rule, as dealers in such goods report an increase in their sales varying from 15 to 40 per cent over those in 1882, the average gain on pianos being full 25 per cent. The demand has also been more largely for high-grade goods, buyers evidently having become convinced that poor musical instruments, and especially poor pianos, are not things to be desired, hence those who are able to buy want good instruments or none. A majority of such goods sold here are made in the East, yet their manufacture in Chicago is steadily on the increase, and will be materially enlarged the coming year. It will, however, require time, combined with capital, courage and skill, to place Chicago on an equal footing with the old piano factories of the East, whose goods have for years held the first estimation of those who use such instruments. But the success that has heretofore attended other leading enterprises undertaken here encourages the prediction that success in this line is ultimately certain, and that it will be attained at a much earlier period than many imagine. This latter conclusion is warranted by the unparalleled expansion of organ manufacturing, which, within five years, has grown up from almost nothing to an annual production of 30,000 instruments, being one-fourth of the total made in the whole country. The superiority of finish and fine rich tone of Chicago organs recommends them wherever introduced, and instead of paying Eastern makers hundreds of thousands of dollars annually for such instruments, our manufacturers are now large sellers in the East, where they find a quick demand at remunerative prices. The most popular wood used in the construction of fine organs is black and satin walnut, both of which are yearly becoming more expensive. Hence the saving to Chicago manufacturers by having their own forests, from which they cut the lumber, saw with their own mills, and season in their own dryhouses, gives them superior advantages over Eastern makers, who have to pay exorbitant prices for materials. It is proper to state in this connection that the walnut forests above referred to are located in the most densely timbered portion of a Southern State, and were secured years since at a merely nominal price. As a result the dry lumber delivered at the factories costs very little more than a good article of Northern pine. As regards beauty of finish the satin walnut has few if any superiors among the most expensive foreign woods whose use are almost prohibited by their enormous cost, and it is surprising that American lumbermen and wood-workers were so tardy in discovering its beauty and intrinsic value.

Trade in other classes of musical goods has been irregular, the demand during the fall being fairly satisfactory, and the volume of the year's sales greater than last year.

BOOKS AND STATIONERY

STANDARD WORKS TAKE THE PLACE OF TRASH.

Trade in this line of business has shown a very satisfactory increase over any former year, and the gain in volume and value of goods sold is the more surprising from the fact that the general trade situation has not been as favorable as could be desired. A gratifying feature in the book trade has been the large increase in the demand for the highest grade of standard works, while the more trashy kinds of cheap publications show a declining sale. Buyers of the better class of books have also demanded a more expensive style of workmanship than heretofore. This demand extends to the trade in all parts of the country. The dealer on the Western frontier is no less persistent in his orders for finely and perfectly finished work than in the same line in the large towns and cities in the oldest and most populous portions of the country. The largest improvement in sales was in the West, South, and Northwest, although every part of the country has been a free buyer. Prices show little change from last year. Jobbers say they have introduced more than the usual number of new works with good success.

Stationery, which is a collateral line of the book business, has also shown a corresponding improvement, and, as with the latter, the demand has been for better goods. A leading dealer said that he had never before sold such a large percentage of high-grade articles as during the current year. "There is," he said, "a great disposition to ignore poor stock, and we have sold a line of goods to border towns that we never before supposed could be introduced there." There has also been a considerable enlargement in the number of articles called for from Western and Northwestern buyers, which indicates a growing disposition among customers in the newly developing portions of the country to gratify their tastes for finer goods, which have heretofore been sold exclusively in the more wealthy sections. This is especially the case in regard to expensive writing materials and cards, which have met an unusually large demand.

In addition to the liberal volume of sales, dealers say their business was never before so nearly on a cash basis as at present; hence they regard the outlook for the coming year as full of promise, the situation being much improved by the unusually clean and fresh character of the stocks of the leading establishments in the trade. Profits, however, were small. This, however, induces greater caution in conducting business, and induces jobbers to carry stocks commensurate with their customers' wants.

The *Western Paper Trade* makes the following estimates of the trade for the year in the articles named:

Paper	$14,000,000
Paper stock	3,465,000
Books	8,250,000
Stationery	4,200,000
Wall paper	2,750,000
Total	$32,665,000
Last year	29,610,000

TOYS.

INCREASE OF MANUFACTURE.

A canvass among the leading houses discovers that although the spring and early summer sales were but little larger than for the corresponding period in 1882, the business of the last six months showed an increase of 25 per cent, and was on the whole very satisfactory. Formerly a large majority of these goods were imported from Europe, where the cheapness of labor enabled European manufacturers to turn them out at prices that prohibited their production on this side of the Atlantic. But employment of machinery in the American toy factories within the past few years has wrought a complete change in the trade, and the imports have steadily declined until it is estimated that less than 25 per cent of such goods sold are of foreign make, and this amount promises to further decrease as American toys, aside from their cheapness, are manufactured with a better understanding of the tastes of those for whom they are intended.

WOODEN WILLOW WARE, ETC.

SATISFACTORY BUSINESS.

Under the head of wooden and willow ware a large number of articles are included, which would take up too much space to enumerate. Jobbers in this line reported a very satisfactory business throughout the year, and their sales have been larger than those of any other city in this country, and, while showing an increase of about 5 per cent in the amount of goods sold, the aggregate value was about the same as in the preceding year, on account of the prices as a rule being lower. Jobbers carried heavier stocks than formerly, and were enabled to fill all orders promptly and satisfactorily. The manufacture of wooden ware was increased, and the quality better than in former years. Prices averaged a shade higher than in 1882. The call for baskets of all descriptions showed a heavy gain, but the number turned out by manufacturers was sufficient for all requirements and no special change could be noted in prices. In the broom trade Chicago leads the entire country, being so close to the base of supplies that manufacturers can obtain their stocks readily and find a quick market for their productions. The largest broom factory in the United States is located here, and has a daily capacity of 250 to 300 dozen, and there are also a number of smaller ones whose annual make cut an important figure in the trade.

REALTY AND ROOFS.

LAST YEAR—FIFTY YEARS.

INTRODUCTORY

The history of Chicago real estate epitomizes the city's greatness; is a mirror in which is seen her gradual growth to metropolitan pre-eminence. It was the accident, or rather heaven's gift, of location, a site more commanding and imperial than the Roman terminus of all the roads in Cæsar's empire, that stamped Chicago's foundation as pure gold, and it was the uniquely, characteristic enterprise of Chicagoans themselves, ever equal to the occasion, that coined that gold for practical use. Granted that here is the gateway of all Northwestern highways, if it had not been that Titan arms drained the marsh, raised the causeway, and drove the piles to build the gate-posts—those modern pillars of Hercules—the city to-day might be merely another St. Louis.

In looking back, the semi-centennial span and the last annual arc thereof invite a wondering if cursory glance, for the arch is a perfect rainbow, splendid in itself and in its promise of what is yet to be. A faint flush back in the 30's, when the great city was born, the color intensifies forthwith, like a Norway dawn, and swiftly the deepening reds advance to glowing crimson. If now and then a sun spot of depression or panic varies the prismatic brightness, it is to remind us that Chicago real estate even is not treasure laid up in heaven; but where so remarkably as here has been asserted an innate recuperative vitality?

Now, as the gentle reader knows, approved histories are of two sorts, inductive and deductive, and, if he please, let the former, or the begin-at-the-end variety, have a brief preference, long enough for some idea of last year's doings in the Chicago land and building market, and then will come in order some resume, with anecdotal accompaniments, of the city's first half-century in these regards.

DURING 1883—NEW BUILDINGS.

And, for the immediate honoring of the dead year, let its epitaph write large that no year in all Chicago's history saw such activity and results in the building line, that inseparable strand in the cable of real estate. The figure magnifies itself and the magnificent community where such achievements are possible—86,000 feet of street and avenue frontage built up, and not less than $22,000,000 transmuted into walls of brick and stone, iron and marble. Not the year following the great fire, when practically the city had to be rebuilt, can show such footings as these; and the record looms up the bigger, considering the unexampled length of strikes last spring by the architects' other self, the bricklayer. Statistics like this—and the interesting details are tabulated further on—exhibit with a force that nothing else can the unexampled development of a community whose past, however wonderful, is only the prelude to new surprises. No particular section of the city and no particular kind of building have monopolized the activity, unless the construction of the new Chamber of Commerce, now well along toward its completion by next midsummer, should be made an exception. That office buildings are represented in the grand

PROCESSION OF NEW STUCTURES

is seen in such sky-scrapers as the "Calumet" (eleven stories) on LaSalle street, the Commercial National Bank Building (not less lofty) on Dearborn street, and half a score satellites around the Chamber of Commerce, to be equally with itself the favorites and proteges of "the cloud-compeller, Jove," whose effigy, instead of Mercury's, ought by all rights to surmount the 224-feet-high tower b y the by to be the highest pinnacle in the whole Northwest) of the bulls and bears In business and commercial blocks, the completion of the Farwell Building, which embodies more million brick than any similar headquarters of trade in America, New York not excepted, sufficiently typefies the year's progress, though mention is also merited by the $500,000 huge warehouse commenced by Mr. Sibley just over Clark street bridge. In residences, whether the cottage of the laborer, the substantial brick of the artisan, the more pretentious swell front (generally of "marble") of a social stratum more aspiring, the somewhat superabundant flat, the elegant avenue facade of pressed brick and dignity, or the millionaire's marble mansion by lake or boulevard, the upbuilding has been unprecedented. Even Wilbur F. Storey's carrara mausoleum has gone up a few inches. To particularize even a few of the splendid houses that have been added in such unexampled numbers to all the avenues, north south and west, must tax unduly the modicum of holiday leisure to peruse even THE INTER

OCEAN, and withal would be superfluous; for, behold, are they not fully recorded and described not only on Building Clerk Edgar's "stubs" of permits, but also from week to week throughout the year on the pages of the aforesaid favorite newspaper and recognized authority on all news of real estate and architecture? In one word, it may almost be said, a la Augustus and the old Chicago of Italy, that so phenomenal was the building activity in 1883 that it found this city brick and left it—pressed brick.

BIGGEST YEAR OF ALL.

The following particulars, even if somewhat detailed, will furnish enlightenment to the reader and valuable statistics to "the coming historian:"

Month.	No. of permits.	No. of build'gs.	Feet frontage.	Cost.	Sheds.
January...	55	62	1,288	$225,000	32
February..	105	134	2,466	501,720	48
March.....	272	317	5,908	1,483,650	156
April......	282	328	6,202	1,770,720	187
May.......	352	421	9,722	2,746,200	194
June......	394	543	10,935	2,577,000	164
July.......	382	493	9,699	2,317,060	144
August....	422	560	11,022	3,032,280	177
October...	314	376	8,496	2,444,640	148
November	201	276	6,424	1,398,360	125
December	110	177	4,778	1,235,700	61
Total...	3,204	4,086	85,588	21,527,610	1,602

County Hospital and City Hall.... $475,000.00
Sheds.............................. 160,000.00

Grand total.................... $22,162,610.00

Total receipts of department.... $19,190.55
Expenses of department.......... 14,455.95

Net proceeds over and above receipts........................ $4,734.60

WEST DIVISION.

Frontage........................... 48,629
Cost............................... $9,592,540

SOUTH DIVISION.

Frontage........................... 19,686
Cost............................... $7,326,610

NORTH DIVISION.

Frontage........................... 17,273
Cost............................... $5,241,460

LAND SALES IN 1883

To turn now briefly to the real estate transactions of the year, they naturally rise to the level of the grand advance just noted; for lot-selling and house-building in the normal state of communities go hand in hand. And so it is that the record of land titles transferred in 1883 by Recorder Brockway mounts up to totals so exhilarating to the broker and so worthy of Chicago as those tabulated further on. The grand total of the year's sales of real estate within seven miles of Chicago Court House was $44,164,243. An analysis of this figure in its integral parts of the individual prices realized gives equal ground for congratulation over the past and reassurance and confidence for the future. The ruling prices in the Chicago land market throughout 1883 were at once conservative and unwaveringly sustained. What else could have been expected but a strong and rising land market in a metropolis that was adding 4 000 to her roofs and a corresponding multitude of new souls to her prosperous and wide-awake population? And what else can be expected now but a continuation and augmentation of the same buoyant activity? This is Chicago, and her fulfillment has never disappointed promise. This is Chicago, and yet, throned mistress as she is and heiress of future scepters unnumbered, she to-day bestows lands within her borders at one-fourth the price of similarly situated property in Boston, and at scarcely one-tenth the New York City rate, though that settlement on Staten Island may not impossibly count but as a suburb of this commercial and manufacturing capital of the Nation almost before the century is out.

Here again, as in the case of buildings, there was no one section of the city controllingly favored above others, the sales ranging with almost equal activity from the cheap suburban lot, with small payment down, up to the transfer, only the other day, of the $500,000 McCord estate. It is

SUCH UNIVERSALITY OF INTEREST

that is the pride and hope of Chicago and her real-estate market. Equally to the capitalist who wants to net 8, 10, and 12 per cent on a down-town block (such figures are illustrated in many Chicago investments, even at current prices), and to the honest son of toil who buys on time and easy payments a lot and a modest home that he may in future escape the vile sponges that have mopped up the sweat of his brow in the past—to both and all Chicago offers the same chance—an opportunity and an investment that promises (what in the world more sure than real estate judiciously placed?) the Midas gift of gold. If any one class of sales and buyers deserved particularization as perhaps more conspicuous than another during the past year it would be the brisk investment by just the laboring people indicated in humble homes of their own, situated very often just over the limits, and so exempt from city taxes and the municipal ordinance against frame buildings. Another feature of the market, though not notably more so than in the preceding year, was the dealing in acres, the rate ruling quite steady, with commendable advances along belt and other new railway lines, as also near exceptionally solid and bustling manufacturing suburbs. Of the speculative spirit in any of its manifestations that in the past have occasionally invited criticism and cast a too general reproach, there was little or no trace whatever, and, at least in the offices of the representative brokers, land prices ruled as steady and standard as for the staples of produce along South Water street, or the "wholesale grocery row" of Michigan avenue.

To single out individual sales—impossible, and yet more repetitious, for, behold, has not this journal weekly embalmed them? and yet again, with something of even added fullness and official rank, are they not chronicled in the book of Recorder Brockway? A summary, as officially prepared by that courteous servant of the public, gives a bird's-eye view of the year, with a panoramic vista of comparison embracing its immediate predecessors:

Grand total of sales, 1872.........$ 78,183,458
Grand total of sales, 1873......... 78,427,931
Grand total of sales, 1874......... 67,871,636
Grand total of sales, 1875......... 53,149,852
Grand total of sales, 1876......... 42,153,596
Grand total of sales, 1877......... 38,123,291
Grand total of sales, 1878......... 42,126,821
Grand total of sales, 1879......... 38,123,891
Grand total of sales, 1880......... 43,082,922
Grand total of sales, 1881......... 54,859,186
Grand total of sales, 1882......... 65,735,185
Grand total of sales, 1883......... 44,164,243

Grand total for twelve years....$646,598,012

INCIDENTS OF LONG AGO.

And now, if the patient reader wants to

foreclose a mortgage on the promise—more fruitful, no doubt, of expectation than realized returns—of some incidents and outline history of the Chicago land market during fifty years—the life of the magic city—let him read on in leniency. Not that the materials, rich, rare and racy, need apology, but how to eliminate them decently to holiday compass—there's the quarter section of swamp.

And speaking of swamps (oh! oh!), Mr. S. H. Kerfoot, one of the Nestors of Chicago brokers, to this day has impressed on retina and memory the sight that met him the hour of his arrival here thirty-six years ago—a morass of mud before the then and now Sherman House, and imbedded, stalled therein—the mud, not the ancestral tavern, already a quite imposing structure—a hack up to the hubs and the horses up to their belly-bands. Property thereabouts then ruled at $100 a foot, and Chicago already possessed for fifteen years of a city charter! Yes, bargain indeed to-day to get half an inch for the money.

Another veteran agent, still in harness, is Charles Cleaver, who arrived in Chicago just fifty years ago, and within two days had cleared $650 by real estate transactions. No wonder, with such early example, that your brokers are the Vanderbilts of the community, as well as the best fellows and most perfect gentlemen in the world. [This kind two for a nickle.]

Tradition uncertainly pictures a negro, Point au Sable, as "squatting" in 1796 on the aboriginal domain and with his Indian bride inhabiting a wigwam about where the north abutment of State street bridge now stands; and that next year, or that matter, an ungallant Frenchman jumped the ranch, with nothing said as to the bride. At any rate it was this property—and here history, if somewhat previously, opens her first subdivision—that figures in the

EARLIEST AUTHENTICATED TRANSFER

of real estate in Cook County, the historic John Kinzie being the purchaser, the date not absolutely certain, but on the eve of the founding of Fort Dearborn in 1804, and the consideration paid not known either, any more than the exact property acquired, except that the good will of the Indians was considered as thrown in.

In 1817 for "a house and farm near the fort," J. H. Beaubien paid $1,000 to an army contractor, one Dean, but the day of booms was still far off, for in 1823 Major Long dried out his wrath on the bogs succeeding one another between the fort and the junction of the North and South Branches by declaring he "would not give sixpence an acre for the whole d—d region."

The year the city was chartered—just fifty years ago—William Bell sold to S. Blood for $100 a piece, two lots, 80x180 feet each, fronting north on Lake street and running through the entire block to Randolph street, west side show on LaSalle, opposite the tunnel, he himself having bought the lots three years before at canal sale for $23 and $25, respectively. But the up-grade was starting, for only eight months later Blood was not accused of taking blood money when he sold his pa r to Pearsons and Owen at $600 apiece. To-day the owners of this magnificent property would perhaps think they were giving it away to sell at $120,-000.

After a time there came an undue expansion common to the whole country, and in the financial crash of 1837 Chicago lots declined 25 per cent from the speculative value at which they had been hawked on the streets of New York and other Eastern cities. The recovery was sure, however, based on the

YOUNG CITY'S MARVELOUS GROWTH,

and in 1848 the value of real property in Chicago on a low estimate was $20,000,-000, the expanding limits now reaching to Fullerton avenue, Sedgwick street, North avenue, Western avenue, and Twenty-second street. Still the great future of the city does not seem to have been really contemplated, for prices ruled low, except along Lake and Clark streets. Thus, land at State and Washington streets, where a sale was recently made at $5,000 a front foot, was in the market at $150, with few buyers, and even in the "flush" times of 1856 Colonel George R. Clarke gave a bonus to be rid of his agreement to pay $100 per foot, all on time, for 25x195 feet on Madison street, between LaSalle and Wells (now easily worth $2,500 per front foot).

It is not incumbent to more than allude to the general financial stringency of '57, or to the similarly retarding influence of the war to the effects of the great fire and the depression following '74. Steadily the intrinsic value of Chicago real estate has developed with the influx of its 600,000 people, and no temporary weight can check the inherent buoyancy. Indeed, the great fire, in two respects, proved a benefit; first, in the consequent prohibition of wooden buildings, and again in the increased values resulting from the plan of rebuilding. The rescue, too, of the title deeds from the burning Court House was so narrow an escape as to rank as the greater benefit.

And thereby hangs a tale. Mr. John G. Shortall that night of Oct. 9, '71, grew desperate as he saw the flames draw on and no wagon at command for love or money to cart off the precious manuscripts, for "though versed in all manner of legal conveyances, he was not equal to this emergency without help from a conveyancer of a more literal or physical type." But he rose master of the situation, and

SO DID HIS REVOLVER,

and, despite obstreperousness, with this instrument kept carefully trained on the commander of an unknown craft, he coerced the fates into saving the abstracts.

On the splendidly sustained operations in the Chicago real estate market in the past few years it is not necessary to enlarge, the table above given showing the remarkable volume. In conclusion one or two instances may be cited of the wealth that has come, or might have come, from modest investments. In 1835 John S. Wright invested $4,000 in forty-four acres in the vicinity of what is now Eighteenth street, between the lake and State street; to-day the property, exclusive of improvements, is worth over $2,500,000. Again, a tract in Calumet, long owned by the late Walter L. Newberry, and descending to his heirs with the rest of his estate, brought 24,000 per cent profit—the cost price having been only $1.25, the government charge. An advance even more phenomenal occurred in the property of the William B. Ogden estate, lying west of the city, the appreciation being from the government's give-away figure to $10,000 per acre.

THE BROKERS.

DOOR PLAT.

OR BRIEF PREFACE.

With not a little satisfaction THE INTER OCEAN as the recognized organ and spokesman of the landed and rental inerests of the city, marshals in dress parade the solid corps of Chicago's chief real estate men. The ranks are long drawn out—what else would befit the city and so august a reviewal as this by our tens of thousands of holiday readers? In their own knapsacks and those of their world-wide clientage this army carries more nuggets of gold than any which marches under Board of Trade flags or the smoky pennons of manufactories; and the bayonets of integrity, good citizenship, and personal and social worth and eminence gleam as brightly as the gold.

Other sheep, too, we have, which are not of this fold, wide extended as it is; and would the reader, like Bopeep, go and hunt those sheep, they may be found browsing on the clover hilltops of the first page or chewing the cud of contentment in the equally succulent pastures of "the classified."

But with so magnificent a menu awaiting, the opening soup should be no less abbreviated than tenuous; so here goes to the next course, and the next, and let not the reader's appetite stop short of the toothpick, meanwhile considering himself and herself individually wished "a happy New Year," and—which amounts to about the same thing—the privilege of personal acquaintance and business relations with the gentlemen mentioned, it being merely premised that during 1884, as in the past, the best efforts of this journal will be directed to set forward the advantage of the Chicago real estate market and men.

E. A. CUMMINGS & CO.

SOUTHEAST CORNER MADISON AND LA SALLE.

This firm ranks as one of the older and leading real estate firms in Chicago. The magnificent business it has built up is the result of the ability, energy, and integrity that has been displayed in the management of the many interests committed to them. From an obscure rear office in 1869 it has pushed steadily forward, until to-day it occupies spacious quarters at the southeast corner of Madison and LaSalle streets, one of the most prominent locations in the city. Its corps of busy clerks, with their pleasant ways and prompt attention, make it a pleasure to do business with the house.

The firm transact a general real estate business in all its branches, and whatever they have to do they aim to at least equal any competitor. Their motto is "The best service possible for their clients," and they aim to retain their patrons by making themselves so valuable to them that there can be no inducement for a change.

They have charge of many large estates, also great properties belonging to corporations and trust companies, and their business in all departments is so perfectly systematized that from the smallest item of repair up all can be accounted for and shown in a moment.

For the purpose of keeping property in their charge in condition they have a repair shop which is under the direction of Mr. John Hatch, an experienced builder. All material needed is purchased at first hands at the lowest possible price for cash, and their clients obtain the benefit of all discounts, so that all work is done at its actual net cost. In this way Messrs. Cummings & Co. are enabled to keep the property intrusted to their charge in the best possible order at the smallest ratio of expense. In the selection of tenants great care is taken and the renting history of every applicant thoroughly examined. If there is any question the landlord is giveu the benefit of the doubt and the application refused. It is to this careful selection of tenants that a large measure of their success is owing. They endeavor to treat fairly and justly all holding leases from them, and they have many tenants who have held their leases for years. Good tenants they propose to take good care of—poor tenants they do not want at all.

Several years ago this firm established a cheap lot department to their business. This was done to enable a large class of worthy citizens of limited means to procure for the least amount of money the best possible building lot. They selected a number of available and accessible tracts of land and sub-divided the same into good-sized lots, selling them at low prices and on easy payments. The increase in this department of their business is very encouraging, as the following statistics prove:

Year.	No. lots sold.
1880	325
1881	533
1882	824
1883	1,239

Probably by far the largest business done in this line in the city.

They made Moreland quite a large town out of prairie land; Auburn also, and then Douglas Park, Lawndale, and many inside subdivisions have experienced a marked change in a few years. It requires eight branch offices, located in different parts of the city and county, to run this department. The firm have in their employ an army of agents who are constantly at work disposing of lots in their respective subdivisions, which now number thirty-seven.

The members of the firm are Edmund A. Cummings, Silas M. Moore, and Robert C. Givins, all veterans in the real estate business.

THE HOUSE AND LOT MONTHLY,

a sprightly periodical, is published by them, and is under their control. This paper, besides containing much valuable real estate information, contains their complete list of property for sale. It has a wide circulation and is itself becoming an institution of the city. This sheet contains twenty pages and will be mailed free to any address during the year 1884. Parties desirous of buying real estate will find it to their advantage to peruse *The House and Lot.*

KNIGHT & MARSHALL.

THIRTY YEARS IN BUSINESS.

No other real estate house in Chicago can point to thirty years of steady possession of one and the same office as can this well-known firm, whose specialty is the renting business. Back in 1854 they occupied, just as at present, Room 10, Larmon Block, now Reaper Block, Washington and Clark streets, and the old-time pre-eminence of the house has descended undiminished to its young and enterprising representatives of to-day—Messrs. John B. Knight and James M. Marshall—who have still further widened the scope of the firm's operations. Few renting, rent-collecting, and tax-paying agencies in any city have such extended lists of property confided to their care, both by residents and non-residents, and not one has administered the trust more to the satisfaction of patrons. At the same time, each year a large and growing aggregate of real estate is bought and sold by the firm on commission, and loans are extensively placed. All kinds of real estate papers are made to order.

Asked their ideas for THE INTER OCEAN'S New Year's prospectus on rents, building loans, and land sales, the gentlemen replied that offices and stores promised to rent as last year, or in that neighborhood, and that moderate sized dwellings, especially on the West Side, would likely rule somewhat lower. In some directions, in flats, for instance, the demand for new buildings was now fully met, and, although the firm had not a roof unrented, to go a little slow might be wisdom. For loans there was promised a steady demand at conservative rates, and the boom in cottage building would no doubt continue. As to coming purchases of city and suburban lands, the outlook betokened a marked demand, both from heavy investors and from buyers seeking homes of their own.

MEAD & COE.

REPRESENTATIVE FIRM.

For THE INTER OCEAN annual review and prospectus of real estate the well-known firm named above, officing at No. 149 La Salle street, Major Block, and who have been in continuous business since 1867 without a change of firm name—a remarkable circumstance—consented to be interviewed. Their opinions, it need scarcely be premised, embody the conservative and representative tone of the market. As to loans, the gentlemen report considerable capital now in Chicago seeking that mode of investment, the supply being more than equal to the demand, with rates fairly well sustained. Real estate secured loans continue prime favorites with trustees of estates, widows, old people—all who are pretty conservative. They only loan 50 cents on the dollar, and receive as security good improved property, on which, in event of foreclosure, they can realize unquestionably. They look for long and safe investments and only moderate rates of interest. Money for these long loans is abundant, and is largely furnished from the accumulations of Western people.

An increasingly popular substitute with capitalists for loaning money is to invest it in central business property having a steady, permanent income, and the buyer can afford to pay a fair profit to the Chicago man who has been enterprising enough to make the improvement. Thus a Philadelphia estate now seeks just such an investment in Chicago, preferring this method to loaning.

The prospect favors a sustained building activity, the cost of building having dropped in the past four months from 15 to 18 per cent—a result of the unexampled stock of material—with the probability that labor must to some extent sympathize. In previous years Chicago was unequal to supplying the material wanted here during the building season; now her facilities for manufacture and importation yield ample supplies, the quantity of brick now in stock being larger that ever before. At present prices, persons can go out, purchase real estate, and, putting a building thereon, obtain a better return for their investment than in making loans. While old buildings may in some instances suffer, new buildings will command fair rents. There has been a scarcity of stores during the last three years in the spring, but the appearances now are that the supply of stores is about equal to the demand; while there is no overbuilding. the supply is fair. Up to the present time dwellings have been well occupied on the North and South Sides of the city, and also pretty well on the West Side, yet there are more signs there of a full supply than on either of the other sides; but in favorite localities there and elsewhere rents have been well sustained, and it is inferred from the rentings made by the firm during the fall that they will continue to be well sustained. It is safe to say, however, that rents are up to their full height, or high as tenants can afford to give, the power to pay not being equal, certainly, to any new tax.

F. A. HENSHAW.

BROKERAGE AND HOUSE-RENTING.

Chicago needs many brokers, but only of the high standing and honorable record of Mr. Henshaw, whose office, room 4, National Life Building, 161 LaSalle street, is the center of a well-established and developing trade, both in general brokerage and house-renting. Non-residents find in him a faithful and prompt representative, as alive to their interests as his own, and in every client is found a referee and stanch standby. Mr. Henshaw's attention is divided about equally between renting and sales. In the new year he expects, in the land market, a sustained and enhanced activity and success. The future of Chicago real estate enfolds bargains and fortunes surpassing her past.

BAIRD & BRADLEY.

90 LASALLE STREET.

Founded in 1859, this representative firm pursue the even tenor of their way in loans, sales, and rents, in each branch of their tripartite occupation equally enterprising and conservative, as becomes a house which is at once the oldest on the street as regards continuous service, and yet as wide-awake as the newest. Kindly sparing a few moments, Mr. Lyman Baird expressed for himself and Mr. Francis Bradley the expectation, which it is reassuring to know is shared in by the other leading houses, that the year 1884 will dispel any clouds over business, and prove very active in all departments of trade and commerce, and, therefore in real estate, that great index of the public pulse. This city was Chicago, and a faith rising into confidence could be pinned to her destiny. With the steady growth of this metropolis, the value of real estate and judicious building investments must advance correspondingly, and the low figures of to-day become subjects of surprise in the near future. In short, the real estate situation and outlook were innately, inherently promising, and that fact carried with it prosperous days for building and loan investments. Indeed, in both these latter branches, scarcely less than in the firm's other prominent department of buying and selling real estate on commission, there were already to be seen evidences—as in the market generally he thought—of the quickened life of the new year.

JOHN JOHNSTON, JR.

HUMBOLDT HEADQUARTERS.

If the most pronounced feature in real estate the past year was the boom in Humboldt lots and houses, whereby the city was extended bodily and solidly across the northwestern limits, the artesian well of this flood was No. 80 LaSalle street, the office of the well-known lawyer and landed proprietor named above. A branch office on the grounds, along with a great new subdivision, was needed for the overflow, and still the tide rises. To one who has not lately visited this beautiful Humboldt Park section, the outstretching ranks of neat houses and happy homes that are so rapidly appropriating Mr. Johnston's lands, must beget a new enthusiasm over the greatness of Chicago, where suburbs are born in a day. Situated nearer the Court House than extensive portions of the city itself, and quickly and cheaply reached by steam cars and horse cars, this district of parkway and boulevard has a natural basis for the popularity which Mr. Johnston's courteous agents and reasonable terms have confirmed. Not far distant, at Milwaukee and California avenues, close to the boulevard, is another of the gentleman's subdivisions, and here too the sale of lots has been very rapid. This whole region is advancing steadily and remarkably in population, and land values must correspond. In many other directions Mr. Johnston is placing on the market property owned by him, whether city lots or acre tracts, in South Chicago and elsewhere, and as negotiations are made direct with first hands, it is easily explained how the sales of this representative house so materially swell the total of the year's transactions in the market.

J. C. MAGILL & CO.

POPULARITY AND PUSH.

It is sometimes hard to put facts, lest their adequate statement should sound to the stranger like adulation. Those, however, who know Mr. J. C. Magill and Mr. Silvanus Wilder, No. 90 Washington street, and their rank in the real-estate business of Chicago, will allow that they are entitled to all we say. With eleven and fourteen years of experience respectively, a thorough acquaintance with localities and values all over the city, with their own capital and that of numerous clients, never so many as last year, they can assist would-be house-builders as well by cash loaned as by advice as to the best spot and method to use it; with enthusiasm and dash that at once commend their energy and their pride in their business, the firm beget a like interest on the part of others in the magnificent opportunities offered to capital for investment in Chicago property. Backed, finally, by a personal equipment as fortunate as their professional, the firm ever add new friends to the old.

They have made a specialty of investments for non-residents, for whom they have made many profitable purchases.

They have also sold a large number of valuable pieces of property in other cities to parties residing there, whose local real estate agents had not succeeded in interesting them.

Therefore, it is not strange that the sales of this house the past year reached such conspicuous figures, and that their clients include the names of a large number of prominent and wealthy investors in nearly all parts of the Union, and many in Canada.

"Get as good rents as responsible tenants will pay" is their rule.

All branches of their business have more than doubled in the year 1883, the increase having been brought about largely by the disinterested efforts of their clients, to whom the firm wish to extend their sincere acknowledgments and best wishes for the new year.

PERMANENT EXHIBIT AND EXCHANGE

OF BUILDING MATERIALS AND IMPROVEMENTS.

The exhibit will be opened free to the public Feb. 1, 1884, at the northeast corner of Wabash avenue and Washington street. The enterprise is for the purpose of placing within easy reach of the building public the great variety of materials and the many inventions and improvements of building. It will give an opportunity for personal inspection of all kinds of inventions and materials, including the great variety of building stones, granites and marbles, ornamental and plain pressed bricks, specimens of terra cotta work, fire-proof materials and construction, cements, mortars, and concretes, the varied designs and inventions in sanitary appliances, heating and ventilating apparatus, tiles, roofing-tiles, slates, hardware, and specialties of hardware, plain and ornamental iron specialties, various woods, veneers, marquetry work, stucco ornamentation, ornamental glass and decorative work. Skilled attendants will be in charge of the several departments, and every facility provided for the patron seeking information regarding materials exhibited. Communication will be made by telephone and dispatch boys with every local house. Architects and their clients are cordially invited to make use of the exhibit, and every endeavor will be made to assist them where possible. Architects and others from abroad interested in building can make this institution their headquarters while remaining in the city. Communications relative to materials on exhibit will be attended to, and every endeavor made to fulfill the wants of patrons. The expenses of the institution are defrayed by a charge made to the exhibitors for space as rental, so that the public may have the full benefit of the display gratis.

The management desires to perfect the arrangements and conveniences of this institution where possible, and patrons need not hesitate to apply for any peculiar demands that may occur to them.

HENRY LORD GAY, Proprietor.

WM. D. KERFOOT & CO.

CHICAGO REAL ESTATE AGENCY.

If architecture is "frozen music," the accompanying illustration, which explains its own sharp contrast, will sing eloquently and truthfully of real estate and loan brokers *sans peur et sans reproch*—a house established twenty-one years ago, a house foremost in deals, a partnership of gentlemen—Messrs. William D. Kerfoot, William A. Merigold, George Birkhoff, Jr., No. 90 Washington street The parties, estates, and corporations represented—where are they not found? And wherever found, they are clients still or friends. Asked to name *the* real estate house of Chicago, who that is well informed would not say, "Wm. D. Kerfoot & Co.?"

OUR OFFICE THE DAY AFTER GREAT FIRE OF OCTOBER 9, 1871.

FIRST BUILDING ERECTED IN BURNT DISTRICT.

JAMES WILMOTT.

NO. 106 DEARBORN STREET.

One of the younger brokers, yet with not a little experience, having been connected with, and succeeding in business, a firm long established, Mr. Wilmott, No. 106 Dearborn street, ground floor, ranks with the veteran loan agents in point of popularity and patronage. Besides his own personal investments, he represents other large interests, and to one and all he devotes the same impartial care and attention, not forgetting either the cause of the borrower, which, after all, is that of the lender. On good security he allows no broker to underbid him in favorable terms. In building loans especially he has done a brisk trade, and negotiations already under way for the new year indicate a material activity in this direction. As to ruling rates, while the general tendency is conservative, as low as 6 per cent will no doubt be a common figure on approved collaterals. There is no question that Chicago houses and lots will always rank as the most gilt-edged of securities.

Mr. Wilmott refers to his many patrons in the E st as well as in Chicago. His record is his best reference, he never having lost a sum intrusted to his care.

GEORGE A. EMERY,

92 WASHINGTON STREET.

Geo. A. Emery says the market looks unusually bright and prosperous. Mr. Emery makes a specialty of property on the avenues and boulevards south, and is recognized as the highest authority in regard to values on the South Side. He says the tendency of this city is south, and that the city is growing more rapidly in that direction than any other. All cities have a tendency in one direction, which, when once developed, it is impossible to change. London has been growing in one direction for over 500 years, all the large cities of the world have the same tendency. On the principle that birds of a feather flock together the wealthy men of Chicago have secured homes on the South Side, and people who are not so wealthy, being desirous of locating in the same vicinity, will pay higher rents, and for that reason the land is more valuable. The city grows south about one mile every ten years. The parks, located as they are south of the city, attract people there, and the growth of the city crowds them in that direction. Each year the facilities of transportation are improving, and in a short time a person living in the vicinity of the present limits can arrive home as quickly as if he now lived at Twenty-second street. The new Board of Trade, located near the depot of the Michigan Southern and Rock Island Railroads, will, when finished, create a demand for property on the avenues and boulevards north of the parks, and our shrewdest and wealthiest men are now purchasing in that vicinity in anticipation of the rapid growth which is inevitable. The Michigan Southern Railroad now runs several trains down Clark street and across the avenues and boulevards, on Fortieth street, stopping at each one of the avenues and boulevards, to Drexel boulevard, and the Board of Trade men are buying largely for homes along on the avenues and boulevards in the vicinity. Several elegant houses are now building by Board of Trade men, and the demand seems to be increasing. Indeed, the vicinity will become a neighborhood of Board of Trade men, who, as a class, are whole-souled, genial spirits, who like to live well, make their money easy, and spend it in the same generous way. There is no doubt but what the locality will become eventually the choicest residence part of Chicago.

THOMAS E. PATTERSON.

HIS DEALS LAST YEAR.

For THE INTER OCEAN review and prospectus of the real estate situation the scribe called on the gentleman named above, office No. 188 Dearborn street, as one of the most conservative representatives of the trade, and always well posted on the market. Mr. Patterson's deals the past year, though his conspicuous modesty forebore to develop this point, helped most materially to make up the splendid volume of the year's business. Among these transactions were a number of large acre deals and others in boulevard property, besides closing out during the year three suburban subdivisions inside the city in the West Division, the gentleman handling both his own property and the interests intrusted to him by other capitalists, both in this city and the East. For the coming year the prospec s indicated a good business, both in city real estate proper and in the outlying manufacturing districts. Too much faith could not be placed in the grand destiny of this city and, therefore, in its land, the basis of all the successes to come. At rates much higher than those now ruling Chicago terra firma was the cheapest of investments.

BOGUE AND HOYT.

170 DEARBORN STREET.

The gentlemen of this representative firm, Messrs. Geo. M. Bogue, Henry W. Hoyt and Hamilton B. Bogue, have long been established in the real estate business in Chicago, and speak hopefully of the prospects of a promising business for the year 1884, a prophecy evidently founded in good measure on their extensive operations in the year just closed. They do a general real estate business, buying and selling real estate on commission, giving special attention to the care and management of property, paying taxes, collecting rents and also giving special attention to the interests of non-residents, by whom their services were more widely sought the past year than ever. Their line of property, embraced in the South Division and conveniently located to the steam cars and the Illinois Central Railroad, within and about the boulevards and parks of the South Park system, presents great attractions to people looking for the finest and most desirable location for a residence. Few people seem to have as yet appreciated the great advantage of this South Side property, in that steam communication brings the property very near to the heart of the business district. In addition to that, Michigan avenue boulevard, which affords the best carriage way in the world right down to Jackson street, must make this entire South Side property the most desirable and the most sought for of any property in or about the city.

Their South Side list of property embraces property both on the Grand and Drexel boulevards, together with finely located tracts in the choice Kenwood section. Many very costly improvements have been put up in this locality during the past season, and the indications are that the improvements during the next year will still further enhance the beauty and attractiveness of this region.

They have for sale lots in Mr. O. R. Keith's subdivision at Woodlawn, embracing the property between the right of way of the Illinois Central Railroad on the east and Woodlawn on the west, on either side of Sixty-third street. They have during the past year sold a large number of lots, on which some fifteen or twenty very cosy pleasant homes have been built and occupied by the owners, who are in most cases connected with the leading jobbing houses of the city. The Illinois Central has just completed a new brick depot at Sixty-third street, which is probably without exception the finest one along its line. The community is well supplied with school privileges. The Presbyterian denomination have secured a lot at the corner of Sheridan avenue and Sixty-fourth street on which a church building is immediately to be erected, they having already obtained a subscription of about $2,000 for that purpose. The accessibility of this property, the railroad communication, and the beautiful South Park, taken in connection with the price at which lots can be sold—$17 to $35 a foot, according to location—make it naturally a favorite and popular investment.

Among the other desirable property this firm offers they call special attention to the Illinois Central subdivision at Hyde Park, located on the east side of the tract near the lake, between Hyde Park and South Park Stations. Sewerage and water have this season been provided for this property, and it is offered at very low prices.

H. C. MOREY & CO.

85 WASHINGTON STREET.

This well-known firm, No. 85 Washington street, continues, as for years past, to do a general real-estate business, and to pay large attention to the care and management of property for non-residents and others. They have charge of the Union Mutual Life Insurance Company's varied line of property. Few brokers do as large a business; none wear their honors with more modesty. The senior member of the firm is President of the R. E. and R. A. Association, and Mr. Edgar M. Snow the junior member. The record of the house is the best explanation of the past and guarantee of the future.

E. A. WARFIELD.

99 WASHINGTON STREET.

Officing at No. 99 Washington street, this broker and genial gentleman does a real estate business without ostentation, but always on the right side of the ledger in satisfaction for his patrons, whose number has greatly increased the past year. Mr. Warfield's deals included some of the largest that went to record, particularly in the line of South Side property, while his principals and patrons are among the solidest men of the city and country. In cheap lots he did a thriving business, also, a department of the trade that promises even better results this new year. Consenting to don the prophetic robes, he foresaw for 1884 a sustained and augmented interest in the really few gilt-edged bargains now remaining in real estate property, and the same would be true, he thought, of the best located acres for manufacturing purposes.

SEARL & ZANDER.

ESTABLISHED THIRTY YEARS.

This well known real estate agency has been established on South Clinton street since 1855 and almost continuously at their present site, No. 69, just north of Madison street. This length of honorable dealing is equaled by no West Side house, and by but few in the city. The firm, consisting of George A. Searl and E. W. Zander, makes a specialty of its renting department, although transacting a general real estate business, and has on its boards a large list of stores and offices in all parts of the city. They represent Eastern and European investors, two recent deals having been for London and Paris residents. The name of the firm is synonymous with careful attention to property confided to them and courteous treatment of customers. As to the prospect of rents the coming season, Messrs. Searl & Zander consider the outlook a conservative one, with the probability that flats may rule a little dull. The marvelous and steady growth of the city, however, establishes the safety and profitableness of building investments.

HENRY C. JACOBS.

ROOM 28, 99 WASHINGTON STREET.

Making a specialty of Englewood and South Chicago property, this experienced operator deals in lots and also in acre tracts. He invites the special attention of non-residents who desire to invest in a small way, in single lots or more, he having inside advantages on price and exceptional opportunities for securing returns, as his many patrons will testify. Having subdivided ten acres in Englewood, he proposes to forward the interest of his increasing number of clients and correspondents by a somewhat novel but very advantageous way of disposing of the same to the best account.

MANN & CONGDON.

POPULAR AND ENTERPRISING.

Ex-Sheriff O. L. Mann captured when in office too many prisoners and golden opinions to let success escape him on active return to his old love, the handling of Chicago realty, especially as his enterprising young partner now is the same efficient co-operator as in the old days—Mr. E. A. Congdon. Indeed, the firm has had a continuous life since its first organization, if a partnership may be conceived of as at times playing substantially a lone hand; but General Mann is latterly once more wholly identified with the trade, as his many clients are pleased to know. Besides a wide activity in city property, the firm has extensive stakes in Dakota, where their operations are as promising as prominent. In loans, sometimes on farm securities, as also in rents, a good business has been done, and the New Year must still further pull the latch-string of these deservedly popular dealers, No. 95 Washington street.

S. E. GROSS & CO.,

CORNER MADISON AND CLARK STREETS.

This real estate house occupy the most conspicuous office in Chicago or the Northwest, the entire first floor of the building northwest corner Madison and Clark streets, those two highways of the city's commerce. Their location, made the more a landmark and a feature of Chicago by marble-white exterior walls emblazoned with uniquely beautiful ornamental signs in color and gold of the substantial, comfortable homes that the firm sells at such reasonable terms and in such vast numbers, is but a fitting index and title deed to the pre-eminent position and success of the house. S. E. Gross & Co., while not neglecting any branch of the real estate busi ness, have achieved a fame, wide as the city's, for the wholesale supply of houses and lots to the multitude. The name of S. E. Gross appears oftener on the records of Cook County in transfers of real estate than any other three men in Chicago. Great and growing as is the popularity of the house, it is yet easy of explanation, for not only are the attaches of the office gentlemanly and courteous, only less so than the chief himself, but the variety in location and style of the homes offered is only equaled by the wholesale rates and easy terms extended. If a home is your ambition, whether in city or suburb, call on S. E. Gross & Co., Madison and Clark streets.

COUNTY ABSTRACTS.

STEADILY APPRECIATING IN FAVOR.

The remarkable growth in public favor of the Cook County Abstract Department is set forth most strikingly by the logic of figures. Of course at the start such an enterprise, a new thing, would naturally not secure as many patrons as an old established business, and so for the first fifteen months after the founding of the department in August, 1875, the receipts were $4,500—not a bad beginning but still the day of small things. Look on that picture and then on this: During the past six months the department's receipts are shown by Recorder Brockway's report of Nov. 30, 1883, to have been $17,312.50—a proportion not less than ten times as great. Despite all opposition, the County Abstract Department has steadily advanced in recognition and business, and its patrons, as a glance below will demonstrate, embrace the most conservative of representative brokers and citizens. This fact is a sufficient diploma of absolute reliability and authority, while the reasonable charge for county abstracts is by no means to their disfavor; indeed, in this respect the department has held the balance of power against what had threatened to become, since the general destruction of titles in the great fire, an insupportable tyranny and a tax not to be borne. This beneficial service deserves recognition and emphasis. The perpetuation of the County Abstract Office is a constant assurance to the public that they will be enabled at all times to obtain reliable abstracts at reasonable rates. It is a sentinel, standing over the private firms, compelling them to observe reasonable and proper charges in their dealings with the public. To-day the County Abstract Office is furnishing abstracts 33 per cent less than for the same sort of work furnished by private firms. In view of such a fact, well may a department of the public service that saves to the citizen such large expense continue to receive the enlightened support of the Honorable Board of County Commissioners. As the department's earnings accrue to the public treasury, and by so much lessen the burdens of taxation, it is evidently to the common welfare that the popularity and business of the office should grow yet more rapidly. That so reasonable a support, prompted by self-interest as well as inherent merit, will be more and more generally accorded in the new year is the surer because each passing month adds yet more to the completeness and perfection of the department's unsurpassed records and facilities. On much of the success of the department the present able and polite Recorder of Deeds of Cook County is personally to be congratulated, for it has been a special protege of his care and thought, while the obliging staff of employes have efficiently re-enforced Major Brockway in popularizing the institution.

In conclusion let a very fragmentary roll call be given of the multitude of our most solid citizens, who have been quite content to patronize the unjustly maligned County Abstract Office: Elliott Anthony, A. J. Averell, Wm. Aldrich, T. S. Albright, John I. Bennet, B. I. L. & B. Co., I. K. Boyesen, Asa W. Buell, Dent & Black, Small & Moore, William Elliott Furness, William C. Seipp, Bartholomæ & Leicht, H. J. Christoph, Commercial National Bank, Clark & Silva, City National Bank, Crane Bros., Chicago and Western Indiana R. R., Cooper, Garnett & Packard, Nathan Corwith, Judge Doolittle, H. C. Durand, Lyman & Jackson, J. H. Dunham, Judge Lovell, of Elgin; L. C. Payne Freer, Home National Bank, Field & Leiter, Felsenthal & Kosminski, J. H. Follansbee, J. & J. M. Gamble, C. J. Hambleton, Van H. Higgins, Alvin Hurlbut, E. S. Hubbard, Harrison & Weeks, Hyde Park Village; Holmes, Rich & Noble, Hutchinson & Lill, Kirk Hawes, Judge Farwell, Sheriff Hanchett, Haines, English & Dunne, Heath & Milligan, Ernst & Smith, International Bank, Illinois Trust and Savings Bank, R. E. Jenkins, John Johnston, Jr., Juessen & Anderson, Jno. H. Kedzie, C. C. Kohlsaat, Wm. H. King, Keeley Brewing Company, Knauer Brothers, General Leake, Adolph Loeb & Brother, B. Loewenthal, H. B. Lewis, Englewood; H. C. Morey, Judge Adkinson, John & Walter Mattocks, Mead & Coe, B. F. Crilley, O. L. Mann, General John A. Logan, B. D. Magruder, Mechanics and Traders' Loan and Building Association, E. G. Mason, Judge Thomas Moran, J. N. Barker, Moses & Newman, S. M. Nickerson, W. C. Niehoff, X. L. Otis, Offield & Towle, H. C. Senne, Geo. Witbeck, Francis B. Peabody, Peterson & Bay, Redmond Prindville, B. L. Pease, Pierce & Ware, Frank Parmalee, M. A. Farwell, Quigg & Tuthill, Sleeper & Whiton, Snydacker & Co., Theo. Schintz, Taylor & Strong, T. J. Sudders, Jno. Sneriffs, Smith & Burgett, M. Schweisthal, Arnold Tripp, F. A. Bragg, Taggert & Cutter, H. H. Thomas, W. H. Wood, Judge Williamson, Wilson & Perry, Wasmansdorff & Heineman, Windes & Sullivan, Elbridge G. Keith, Potter Palmer.

S. H. KERFOOT & CO.

PIONEERS.

These gentlemen, especially the senior member, have too long been identified with the best life of the market to justify personal or professional encomiums.

Mr. S. H. Kerfoot, Sr., the head of this pioneer house, has resided in Chicago thirty-six years, and from the start has been foremost in advancing her landed interests, and by natural inheritance his son, Mr. S. H. Kerfoot, Jr., has succeeded to much of the same devotion and eminence. Their intimate knowledge of land values in and about Chicago, the result of close and prolonged observation, has made their professional opinion and offices greatly in demand from other capitalists proposing heavy investments, and this is a province they have occupied peculiarly alone among Chicago real-estate houses. That the requisition upon their services in this direction constantly increases is a fact not more complimentary to S. H.

Kerfoot & Co. than to the steadily developed importance and popularity of Chicago as a land market. The speculative spirit has largely retreated, and there is positive assurance of handsome rentals and other realization on capital invested. Considering her metropolitical dignity and sure destiny, Chicago is the cheapest land market in America, as S. H. Kerfoot & Co. are her most representative real-estate house.

CHICAGO ANDERSON PRESSED BRICK

IN GROWING DEMAND.

To the resident of Chicago as well as the observant visitor who has occasionally passed within her gates during the years since the fire, there is no more striking exemplification of the readiness of the people to recognize and accept that which is good among them, than has been displayed by what has assumed the form of an absolute revolution in the pressed brick business. A few years after the rebuilding of the city was begun, more than ordinary attention was attracted to pressed brick as a material for outside walls of buildings; but the fact that it was necessary to go to the East for such brick very much retarded their advance into popular favor, and, as will be observed, the large majority of the first buildings erected have outside walls of stone. The disintegrating qualities of nearly every kind of stone produced for building purposes, soon demonstrated the necessity of the introduction of a more durable, and, at the same time, cheaper material. How many busy brains wasted time, energy, and midnight oil to discover the desired substitute, will never be known. But that one of them finally brought forth the valued secret is amply evidenced by stately and ornate piles of the products of his genius which the eye encounters at every turn, in both the business and residence districts of the city. The gentleman was Mr. J. C. Anderson, and the product referred to is what is so widely and most favorably known as the Chicago Anderson pressed brick, which is manufactured by a company bearing that name. Since the establishment of the works, which was done in rather a modest way, the company's rapidly increasing business has necessitated the steady enlargement of their capacity, until to-day they have, at the corner of Asylum place and Elston avenue, a plant, the largest and most complete in the world. The superior quality of both the plain and ornamental brick manufactured by the company, has given it practically a clear field in both Chicago and the West, and as a result during the past year but two of the prominent structures erected in Chicago's center were given outer walls of stone, and with but one or two exceptions the Chicago Anderson pressed brick was used, and the same was true of the residence districts. It is now about to introduce an ornamental pressed brick that will be in every way superior, and at least 50 per cent cheaper than terra cotta, that for outside decoration of buildings will undoubtedly spring into immediate popularity. Those desiring to learn further particulars of this remarkable production, of which Chicago is so justly pround, will receive courteous consideration by application either in person or by letter, at the down-town office of the Chicago Anderson Pressed Brick Company, No. 157 LaSalle street, Chicago.

B. F. JACOBS,

99 WASHINGTON STREET.

Our long established and representative real estate dealers have in Mr. B. F. Jacobs, No. 99 Washington street, a prominent exponent, one who has been identified the past year with some of the chief transactions in the market

Of his many interests that might be named, the University Subdivision has been notably developed, this boulevard tract lying between Ashland and Western avenues, and Forty-seventh and Fifty-first streets. In that vicinity during the last two years three or four hundred buildings have been erected, and there are some manufacturing interests looking down that way because the Forty-ninth street line of the Grand Trunk Road makes the section very accessible to the city. Lake water is supplied. Lots there are increasing in value and are selling for from

$200 to $400 apiece. Churches and schools are established, and people are buying for occupation.

Just west of Hammond a tract has come into prominence, as, in addition to the occupation of the neighborhood for manufacturing purposes, a railroad is to run through the property, and eventually it is going to be built up to South Chicago. At this point Mr. Jabobs represents some large interests, and, in connection with other parties owning in the vicinity, it is proposed to put that property on the market in a manner very attractive to manufacturers and also for occupation and residence.

Mr. Jacobs has, also, a very fine subdivision near Pullman, along State street, between One Hundred and Ninth and One Hundred and Tenth streets, and has made plans favoring a rapid development and settlement. A new depot of the Western Indiana Road is to be established there at One Hundred and Eleventh street.

Early in the season this gentleman negotiated what was recognized as the leading real estate deal of the year in outside property, the location being the town of Worth, section 2. Probably important developments will be made there in the near future.

GRIFFIN & DWIGHT.

WEST SIDE HEADQUARTERS.

This well-known firm, consisting of Messrs. James F. Griffin and Walter T. Dwight, does the most extensive business of any firm located west of the river, and their spacious and convenient offices, northeast corner of Washington boulevard and Halsted street, are the recognized West Side headquarters for sales and rents, although the firm also deal extensively in the other two divisions of the city. Certainly their renting list of West Side property is not surpassed if equaled by any other agency, and it represents equally the finest class of houses, the medium, and the lower priced. Estates are managed by the firm economically and to the satisfaction of customers. Regarding rents next spring, they thought it too early to speak; at present the tone was good, scarcely one of their regular patrons lacking a tenant.

LAYTON, THAYER & CO.

REAL ESTATE AUCTIONS A SPECIALTY.

A review of the Chicago land market in 1883 would be incomplete that did not record the growing tendency to popularize land auctions, and so put this city in line with New York, Philadelphia, New Orleans, and San Francisco, where, as in all the great centers, the real estate auction is a recognized institution and benefit—not the occasional exception. That Chicago is developing upward to the right appreciation of auction land sales is shown by their greater frequency and patronage the past year, and notably so by the movement, somewhat preliminary as yet, but earnestly advocated, by which the Chicago Real Estate and Renting Agents' Association is now working upward toward this level. Indeed, a "noon call"—which is more than half way to the unreserved auction sale—will not unlikely be established by that important organization at its next meeting.

In popularizing the confessed advantages of land auctions as determining readily the selling value and in general stimulation of real estate transactions, not the least potent force has been the honorable record and experienced methods of Layton, Thayer & Co.—C. C. Thayer and R. P. Layton—the long-established land auctioneers, 182 Dearborn street, Howland Block. To their talent and energy is due not a little the growing favor of the system, which finds in them its best Northwestern exemplification, and to them personally, as to the best real estate interests of the city, congratulation is due that hereafter land auctions promise in this city to be accorded their proper place of usefulness. In addition to their specialty of real estate auction sales, Layton, Thayer & Co. pay much attention to the selling of property at private sale as well.

WINKELMAN & SIMONS.

HUMBOLDT PARK LOTS.

This firm, consisting of Frederick A. Winkelman and Charlie B. Simons, two most pleasant gentlemen to deal with, office at No. 166 East Randolph street, and operate very extensively in Humboldt Park lots, where such a boom exists. Themselves the owners, they remit to customers the commissions. Their present subdivision, close beside the park, is a resubdivision of an original subdivision by Mr. E. Simons, father of the junior member of the firm, and for forty years a resident and landowner in Chicago. The close proximity of these choice lots to the city and to great manufactories insures a continued demand for them. They range in price, with reasonable terms, from $250 to $450, according to location.

PAUL CORNELL,

69 RANDOLPH STREET.

Paul Cornell, attorney at law, rooms 1 and 2, as above, and making real estate a specialty, laid out and subdivided twenty-seven years ago the original village of Hyde Park, a part of it—section 11, on which he still re-sides—coming to him from the Canal Commissioners, or practically from the government. In 1871 he made the town plat of Cornell, now Grand Crossing, and all through his forty years of honorable residence his namehas stood for progress and improvement in our landed interests; not the least of his valuable services being in connection with the South parks. He is now closing out at the lowest possible rates some of the best residence lots and buildings in Hyde Park; also factory sites with unsurpassed railroad facilities at Grand Crossing, and in lots or tracts to suit.

J. P. WHITE & CO.,

ROOM 4, REAPER BLOCK.

These long-established real estate and loan agents, officing as above, 97 Clark street, claim to keep posted in values in all central business property. Their specialty is this intimate acquaintance with down town land quotations, an acquaintance which they keep constantly up with the times, and immediately serviceable by aid of a vast atlas in which are daily recorded all changes in ownership and purchase price. The invaluable help thus afforded in securing property at bottom figures is testified to by the increasing number of buyers who have used Mr. White's services in making purchases. With his unique facilities, all he needs is a description of property wanted in order to immediately select for inspection the most eligible property at command. Some of the best property is not advertised, or even placed in the market, yet through this agency of J. P. White & Co.'s it is often opened to negotiation and transfer, to the mutual advantage of buyer and seller.

J. E. BURCHELL.

108 DEARBORN STREET.

If a long and intimate acquaintance with Chicago land values is a desirable possession for a real estate broker, then the gentleman named above—office 108 Dearborn street—is one of the best equipped in the Chicago fraternity. His knowledge and experience are brought into requisition especially in transactions of large importance—as notably in several the past year—and few advisers so hold the confidence of capitalists. His record is his best eulogy, and every patron his reference. Handsomely established in Hyde Park, he has been identified with some of the most important transactions in that village. Speaking of the new year's prospects, Mr. Burchell said they were largely assured even by pending negotiations, and there were doubtless incubating many other developments of first magnitude. Chicago real estate at present prices was a mine for golden investment, and capitalists abroad and at home had awakened to the realization of the fact and the passing opportunity.

IRA BROWN.

"THE SUBDIVIDER."

That this title, "the subdivider," should be bestowed by THE INTER OCEAN this New Year's Day on Ira Brown, Esq., Nos. 142 and 144 LaSalle street, is a recognition demanded by the record of the past year, the most notable yet even in the long and distinguished career of this prince of cheap subdivisions for the people. Himself the originator of the $5-a-month plan on which to buy a beautiful suburban lot, he it is who has most conspicuously and beneficially developed that plan, and the result has been that the virgin prairie, in choice, eligible locations, has hardly been susceptible of swift enough partition into these popular-priced lots to meet the overwhelming demand. It is simply the record of the official documents of Cook County that Mr. Ira Brown consummates in a given space of time more deals than any other five brokers in the market, and fortunate is it for future possessors of like happy suburban homes that such is the fact. A visit to any one of the easily accessible rural spots that has had the advantage of Mr. Ira Brown's patronage will discover hundreds of pleasant cottages, each with its garden plat, its chickens, its own "vine and fig tree," and if the smiling householders rise up and call him blessed, the unique compliment is only deserved. The cottages themselves, along with the lots, Mr. Brown sells for $1,000 apiece, and lets the buyer pay for his purchase in $15 monthly installments—an offer matching the popularity of the $5-a-month lot. The past season Mr. Brown has been developing Norwood Park more especially, and with such success that he has already nearly sold out almost his entire great new subdivision, hundreds and hundreds of lots, at this point alone, being bought by the thrift and savings of their owners, who wisely determine now while they are making wages to buy themselves a home. His interests continue undiminished—because constantly supplied by new purchases—at Glencoe, LaGrange, Park Ridge, Desplaines, and South Chicago, comprising the most cheaply reached and charming environs of the metropolis. The whole number of those who have been his patrons at one or another of these points runs up into the thousands. The cheapness of the bargains offered and the rare facilities of transportation are advantages possessed by these suburban homes that will always insure them a growing popularity.

During the open weather that has characterized most of the present season Mr. Brown has gone into winter quarters as it were with regard to his suburban operations, and has been building some handsome residences in the city, an activity that he has formerly indulged in. These very desirable houses, seven in number, being two-story bricks, are at the corner of Hoyne avenue and Jackson street, and will be ready to rent by May 1. It was in this near neighborhood that last winter Mr. Brown erected that elegant block of six octagon stone-fronts. The new buildings now going up, while pleasing in architecture, will chiefly consult the pockets of tenants.

In personal traits Mr. Ira Brown is a most pleasant and honorable gentleman to deal with, and those who come as clients remain his friends. A like attention and courtesy, in large degree, characterize the attaches of the office who are only less devoted than their chief himself to the wants of customers. Certainly Mr. Brown's terms on suburban houses and lots may be denominated bargains of the first order; with land in and about Chicago rising as rapidly as it is, and with rents so high, a $100 lot and a $1,000 cottage and lot are bonanzas that are very naturally capturing the heads and hearts of the people. Considering the gentleman's record, and the inducements he offers, his sales under the auspices of the New Year must vastly outnumber those of the past, bringing to his multitude of new patrons, as may it bring to the old, a realization of the season's compliments, which he begs to extend to one and all—"a happy New Year!"

COOPER & CARSON,

180 DEARBORN STREET.

This is a newly-formed real estate firm, but its members, Messrs. Andrew J. Cooper and James D. Carson, are long experienced and heavily interested in the Chicago land market. Their recent enterprise in renting and starting to magnificently improve the vacant Brooks estate lot on Dearborn street, south of Monroe, promises one of the most handsome office and banking buildings in the city, and already it is largely rented before completed. The firm have extensive acre interests, and transactions, it being Mr. Cooper who negotiated for Mr. Pennock the purchase of Garfield. Of Hyde Park property, also, they make a feature.

O. M. WELLS & CO.

A MODEL COTTAGE.

The cut below represents the style of house that O. M. Wells & Co. have placed extensively on the market. The cottage combines great thoroughness of build and neatness of finish, along with moderate price and easy payments on the monthly plan. They are as genuine

as they are cheap. During the past season the firm have sold in their various subdivisions fully sixty of these houses, and the demand continues to grow. The office of the firm, at No. 162 LaSalle street, Room 17, is indeed the recognized headquarters for such deals, while a throng of customers is also attracted by the great variety offered in cheap lots. The gentlemen composing the firm—O. M. Wells and J. M. Secrist—confirm their customers' good will and enhance the value of bargains by strict squareness in dealing and obliging manners.

ANDREWS, BURHANS & COOPER.

A POPULAR HOUSE.

This well-known firm has remodeled its title as above, consequent on the addition of W. D. Cooper to its forces last May, but their location remains the same at 102 Washington street. No change either has come to the fair dealing and business-like methods, which have built up for the house their enviable reputation and success. Both Mr. Andrews and Mr. Cooper represent fifteen years of active real estate and financial experience in this city. The latter now devotes his wide acquaintance more particularly to the renting, loans, and general brokerage department of the house. The former has charge of all negotiations relating to money matters, the house making a specialty of real estate secured paper, and now proposing to enter upon the handling of corporate bonds. The legal business of the firm is under the supervision of J. A. Burhans, a successfully practicing lawyer, who for the past seven years has concentrated his attention to the law of real estate and taxes, especially the examination and perfecting of titles. The firm is thus equipped for a varied, as it were a triangular service, and in each field they have merited the distinction they have achieved. THE INTER OCEAN takes pleasure in testifying to the wide and growing operations and popularity of the house. They refer to leading capitalist, banking, and mercantile clients East, West, and South.

A. LOEB & BRO.

LIVELY LOANS.

As familiar as the name LaSalle street, where at Nos. 129 and 131 they have so long been located, is the title of these well-known gentlemen and real estate and loan agents. In volume of business as in length of service they are identified with the best business of the street in both these departments—no house more so. The interests of the firm embrace lands in all parts of the city and outlying suburban subdivisions, while in the line of loans the patronage of the house is very large and increasing. In both departments the marked activity of the year closed was due not a little to the firm's established name for lowest prices and business-like methods. For the new year the gentlemen see no reason for and have no expectation of a decline in the land and loan market of this capital of the Northwest. On the contrary, the prospect favors a steady appreciation of the unsurpassed securities and opportunities for investments here afforded.

HOPKINSON & SILVA.

CHICAGO'S ELIGIBLE LANDS.

To name the standard and representative houses is to sing the praises not of individuals, but of the Chicago land market, and if modesty and retiring worth are occasionally crucified, the public weal is transfigured. Mr. William Hopkinson and Mr. Chas. P. Silva, who compose this well-known firm—office, No. 123 Dearborn street—speak with cheer of the market's immediate prospects, and with assurance that Chicago's eligible lands, both urban and suburban, will continue to rise in popular appreciation and demand commensurately with the steady and splendid progress of the city. Both personally and as agents for the Blue Island Land and Building Company, the gentlemen are identified with the rare bargains offered in charming homes at Morgan Park and Washington Heights.

SHORTALL & HELMER.

110 DEARBORN STREET.

The real estate interest is sustained by no firm in a more representative and popular manner than by the well-known house of Shortall & Helmer, No. 110 Dearborn street. They deal in real estate mortgages, investment stocks, and bonds; have money in hand to loan at lowest market rates. Mr. Shortall is the same patron of music, it need hardly be said, who figures so dramatically and salutarily in the prelude to this stately procession of Chicago's real estate investors. Composing the firm are Messrs. John E. Shortall, Joseph W. Helmer, and Henry L. Frank.

TURNER & BOND.

OFFICE 102 WASHINGTON STREET.

This substantial and well-known firm transacted the past year the extensive and growing business that has placed them in the front rank of Chicago brokers. Deals the largest in the market were among those consummated through their agency. In loans the firm have placed large sums, and command any amount on security of inside real estate. Non-residents, more numerously than ever before, have confided their interests to this house, and on some of these properties —notably that of Judge David Davis—Messrs. Turner & Bond have made some of the most extensive improvements of the year, remarkable as 1883 has been for its building boom. Thus, on Hanover and Butler streets alone, the firm built over twenty houses each, and so substantial and popular were the structures that many were spoken for before completion. All over Chicago the widespread interests of the firm are found, and the yearly total of their business is representative of the vast fortunes centered here in real estate. As to the coming year the firm kindly assumed the mantle of prophecy, at the call of THE INTER OCEAN, and predicted a successor worthy to occupy the business throne of 1883; the promise, based on Chicago's present and certain future, is equally certain and assured.

EZRA L. BRAINERD,

125 DEARBORN STREET.

This well-known attorney and investor purchased property at Kenwood in 1865, and since then his operations have been extensive at that point and in Hyde Park, South Chicago, the Rock Island car shops, and South Englewood, where he is intimately posted on values. At the latter point he subdivided forty-five acres in 1873, a large part of which he still owns. Here in the past year he has sold some $15,000 worth of lots, mostly for improvement, a number of houses having already been erected. Mr. Brainerd predicts for this point a steady advance, if not an immediate boom. Values in this subdivision range from $6 to $10 per foot.

BARNES & PARISH.

RENTS AND REAL ESTATE.

This prominent house-renting and general real-estate agency, for eleven years a feature of LaSalle street, No. 157, and one of the oldest established agencies in the city, has scarcely less than 2,000 buildings under its charge, which speaks very well for the care they take of property. "How will rents be the coming year, eh?" said Mr. Barnes. "The present outlook is that they will hold their own. Offices? There are several office buildings now going up and already largely rented before completion. When the Board of Trade moves, though, there may perhaps be some decline north of Washington street. On houses I don't think there will be any advance, speaking generally. If there is any change at all, rents will be a little less, but I think they will hold their own. Expensive houses will have to show some concession, but medium-priced houses will hold their own.

"In general real estate," Mr. Parish replied, "it looks as though sales would be pretty active the coming year. Certainly at the present time the market holds its own, and the same is true of our loans, of which we are still making a good many. With the city steadily increasing in size the value of Chicago property must appreciate rapidly."

M. J. RICHARDS,

NO. 89 RANDOLPH STREET.

It is timely and fitting to note some of the strong points that belong to our land brokers themselves as well as to the lands they handle. Through a long connection with the Chicago real estate market Mr. Richards has always stood well, no man having put a finger on him, and has given good satisfaction in the business he has been connected with. He is always ready to wait on his customers, who have been numerous, and to do it to their satisfaction. His knowledge of farms in the State of Illinois and throughout the Northwest is such that any one can gain valuable information by inquiri g of him. He has made many sales for the Scotch Mortgage Company. Besides selling on commission, making extensive loans, and dealing generally in city property, the gentleman gives considerable attention to Texas and Southwestern investments, for which there is a growing demand in this metropolis, both from American and European investors, a demand which Mr Richards is largely meeting and is especially fitted to cater to through his interest in those directions. If buyers of bargains the past year in his line would duplicate their success, let them communicate with M. J. Richards, 89 Randolph street.

J. F. KEENEY.

PENNOCK, CRAGIN, ETC.

The property northwest of and adjoining the city is rapidly coming to the front as not only a great manufacturing center, but also a very desirable residence for clerks and laboring men. The property is high and dry, in easy walking distance of Humboldt Park, and only a short drive to the business center of Chicago. Its railroad facilities are the very best, with only 5-cent fare from Cragin, Garfield, and Pennock, on both the divisions of the Milwaukee and St. Paul Railroad as well as the Northwestern, the Belt Railroad, and the street railroad to Humboldt Park. There are located within two miles of Humboldt Park the Cragin Manufacturing Company, the Washburn & Moen Company, the Hibbard Spencer & Bartlett warehouse, the Foster Rotary Plow Company, the Superior Nail Company, and the extensive manufactory now being erected by Howard Pennock for the Miltimore Elastic Steel Car Wheel Company, which will give employment alone to 1,000 men.

Mr. J. F. Keeney has been largely instrumental in locating these different factories at this point and in securing the Belt Railroad for this section. C. B. Hosmer & Son and Mr. Keeney are the owners of Cragin, except ten acres sold by them to the Cragin Manufacturing Company. Mr. Keeney is owner of several acre tracts subdivided and placed as additions to Pennock. Besides he and his brothers are agents for the sale of Pennock property, and have their office and teams at Humboldt Park, at Pennock, and 94 Washington street, and are prepared at all times to show the property and make sales. Plats and prices can be obtained at either of their offices. There is no safer or better investment for a sure profit than lots at present prices in the new town of Pennock.

E. W. WESTFALL.

90 WASHINGTON STREET.

Though the veterans of the trade have largely given the Chicago real-estate market its National reputation, the young men take the cake for push. This remark is not a platitude, but exactly apt and truthfully descriptive when Mr. Westfall's name is written. With the success that crowns well-directed energy, his career compliments equally the man and the market; nor is there danger that the fame of Chicago land brokerage shall suffer demoralization in the younger generation. Doing a general real-estate business for others as well as handling his own estate, Mr. Westfall consummated some of the leading deals of the year, and his expectation of even livelier times in 1884 is a valuable index to the future.

PIERCE & WARE.

143 LA SALLE STREET.

These real estate and financial brokers have built up an enviable name and reputation, and yet one that fifteen years of honorable, business-like service has rightfully yielded them. They report a very prosperous year. Real estate is bought and sold, time loans effected, rents collected and promptly remitted. A very successful specialty is made of central business property and the care of estates for non-residents. Capitalists owning down town property have very numerously retained their services. more such property being in charge of this firm probably than of any other in Chicago, not the least popular feature of their method being the promptness and exact regularity of remittances. The outlook impresses the firm as every way encouraging.

NOAH BARNES.

HYDE PARK LANDS.

The name of this broker, who is at home at No. 85 Washington street, room 5, has long been synonymous with a successfully conservative trade, more especially in Hyde Park lands. The very prefix "Noah" suggests an ark of safety against floods of loose speculation, while the surname "Barnes" pictures truthfully in this case a secure storehouse for investments. The gentleman is one of the experienced, cautious operators, whose long acquaintance with values and men have made his ideas and services invaluable to a widening clientage, as well as in his own personal transactions. Mr. Barnes, besides his Hyde Park estate, owns extensive interests near Humboldt Park, where all property is so remarkably appreciated by the wonderful demand of late for cheap lots.

B. R. DeYOUNG & CO.,

AS PROGRESSIVE AS YOUNG.

B. R. De Young & Co., No. 85 Washington street, have won a place among the most progressive and busy young brokers in the real estate market. Their commission business in buying and selling is scarcely subordinated even to the very extensive line of down-town and residence property which they manage for non-residents. The payment of taxes and collection of rents is, at the same time, a field very extensively cultivated and with a degree of popular encouragement and success that speaks volumes for the courtesy and faithfulness of the agency. The new year, in Mr. DeYoung's estimation, promises as auspiciously as 1883.

KINNEY & KIMBALL.

86 WASHINGTON STREET.

The partners in this well-known Washington street firm of real estate and investment agents are Messrs. W. C. Kinney and J. E. Kimball. They buy and sell city and country property, negotiate loans, pay taxes and manage estates, and in all their transactions have achieved an enviable reputation and record. The firm make a specialty of property in the south division, Hyde Park and Town of Lake, handling it extensively. No firm in the city are better posted in values or have better facilities for handling property in the above sections than Messrs. Kinney & Kimball. The patronage of the house is one constantly extending, as their fidelity to clients is well known. Under such auspices and with the handsome business they transacted the past year, the firm cannot but anticipate a prosperous year in the Chicago real estate market.

WOODBURY M. TAYLOR.

FROM THE PEN TO THE ACRE.

Formerly a journalist, and always distinguished for brains and bon homme, what wonder that this genial gentleman and prudent land operator, No. 108 Dearborn street, keeps all his old friends and makes hosts of new? Returning the past year to his first love, the handling of his native land in this latitude and longitude, Mr. Taylor has at once resumed the old-time prominence and success. In Hyde Park is he not a school magnate? and where better than in the immediate circle of those townsmen who best know, respect, and honor him should be the site of his chief property and largest activity? One cannot stay to count lines in proclaiming the A 1 quality both of this man and of the rare bargains that have blessed his customers. Give him a call whether you have lands or houses to buy or sell, nor resort to oaths to make reliable the representations of a gentleman who is truth and fairness embodied.

CHARLES CLEAVER AND SON.

125 DEARBORN ST.—A VETERAN HOUSE.

The senior member of this firm commenced the purchase of real estate in Chicago as early as 1835, since which time he has dealt largely in property in all parts of the city; for the last thirty years more especially in residence property in the southern portion of the city and Hyde Park, where their sales the past year have been very extensive. Consequently his familiarity with that location renders his judgment of values second to none. Having associated with him his son, F. W. Cleaver, who is acquainted with every foot of property from Thirty-first street to the Calumet River, parties wishing either to sell or purchase may be sure of correct information as to prices, titles, etc.

JAMES M. GAMBLE,

40 DEARBORN STREET.

James M. Gamble, mortgage, loan, and real estate, financial and renting agent, late J. & J. M. Gamble, carries on a business established in 1847, his office being rooms 4, 5, 6, 7, and 8 Dickey Building, 40 Dearborn street, Chicago. This is one of the oldest houses in the West, and represents many of the very largest estates, their business in magnitude being second to none in the West. In the management of estates they represent the Dickey, the Manierre, the Hadduck, the De-Koven, the Wells, the Snow estates, and others too numerous to mention. Although this firm has upward of 1,000 tenants, in not a single case have they vacant premises, nor is this an exceptional record for them. The popular new Albany apartment building, costing $100,000, is owned by this firm.

BELDEN F. CULVER,

319 FIRST NATIONAL BANK BUILDING.

To name this well-known financial and real estate agent no words of commendation are necessary. For many years Mr. Culver has been prominently identified with the development of Chicago, and has made for himself a record for enterprise, sterling integrity, and fine business judgment. As negotiator in financial or real estate transactions he is reliable, trustworthy, intelligent, and discreet.

ERNST PRUSSING.

95 RANDOLPH STREET.

Mr. Ernst Prussing came to Chicago in 1840, and after a short time in the hardware business opened a real estate office which has continued uninterruptedly and successfully ever since, a length of service equaled by but two or three other Chicago real estate dealers. He has always been responsible for all he undertook. Mr. Prussing characterized as a wrong feature the forced depression of the more outlying sections of the city, consequent on the fire ordinance, which caused the unduly and dangerously high buildings in the center of the city. A modification of that ordinance was due to the sections so long discriminated against. The past year has seen active operations in the center of the city and in the suburbs. Mr. Prussing makes loans extensively, also has a large renting patronage. As to the business of the new year, Mr. Prussing said of course the prospect was favorable because we lived in Chicago.

H. A. HURLBUT.

THE MARKET FOR LOANS.

In order to get at the situation on loans, THE INTER OCEAN interviewed this well-known gentleman and extensive operator, No. 123 Dearborn street, being well assured of a representative answer to inquiries. "For the past year," said Mr. Hurlbut, "the tendency of my customers has been to loan rather than invest, and the amount of business has been much larger than the year previous, but more in loans than in investments. The firmness and strength with which central property has been held has been rather above what parties could consider as good bargains. Rates the past year have been firmer—6 per cent the average. The outlook for the coming year is better still, owing to the growth of the city, the actual demand for more buildings, and the building by owners of property for their own occupation."

SCHRADER BROS.,

178 DEARBORN STREET.

One of the longest-established and best-known real estate agencies in Chicago is conducted by the Schrader Bros., office as above. Since 1865 they have done a general land business, including the charge of property, tax payments, and rent collections, the business steadily growing on their hands to its present great and still developing proportions. The firm handle Lake View and Hyde Park property extensively, also advancing money for improvement purposes, and to them is due not a little of the up-building of those districts, both of which are advancing more rapidly now than ever in public favor.

J. APPLETON WILSON.

162 LA SALLE STREET.

This well-known broker has operated in lands since 1868, at which time he was the Trustee of the Ravenswood Land Company and ever since has been identified with suburban interests, more especially in Englewood, Normalville, and Lawndale. He has prominently contributed to the remarkable number of new houses that have been built and marketed the past season in the above suburbs, his houses being sold on easy payments at prices ranging from $1,200 to $5,000 and $10,000, while building lots ranged from $10 to $50 a foot. The prospect is that, with the completion of the Chamber of Commerce, just across the street from the depot, the new year will bring to these nearest and long-popular suburbs more new residents than ever. Mr. Wilson has charge of extensive estates of non-residents, besides transacting a loaning and renting business.

ALBERT WISNER.

HOMES FOR THE MANY.

Transacting a real estate business in all its branches, Mr. Wisner, No. 69 Dearborn street, Rooms 1 and 2, is now identified more particularly with the movement to furnish comfortable and moderate-priced homes, such a notable feature of the situation at this time. His subdivisions lie in all desired directions and his clients are legion. It is certainly a healthy market when such a general determination to own a home shows itself, and that dealer is a public benefactor who puts the desired boon most easily and cheaply within reach. Loans to build such homes are made by Mr. Wisner, and with the help thus afforded many of our young business men are occupying homes of their own, particularly in the south portion of the town of Lake View, adjoining the city limits. A feature of Mr. Wisner's business, also, is an extensive line of rents.

F. C. VIERLING.

YOUTH, DASH, AND SUCCESS.

No annual trade review would be thorough unless reflecting the year's record of such a representative of the youth, dash, and success that have made famous this Chicago real estate broker. In himself he epitomizes the qualities that in any vocation place their possessor at the front, and it is not strange that his spacious ground floor office, No. 110 Dearborn street, is recognized as a head-center for the trade. Besides a general real estate agency, Mr. Vierling handles as a specialty West Side business property and South Side business and residence property. The demand for lands, that surest of investments, he regards as even more auspicious for 1884 than during last year, while the call for houses, along with the rents thereof, must continue as sustained as Chicago's wonderful growth in population and importance, a growth never more notable than now.

W. H. DAVIS.

RENTS AND COMMISSIONS.

Chicago has many real estate agents, but to no one can an owner entrust property with a greater certainty that it will be carefully and faithfully looked after than to Mr. W. H. Davis, room 38, 156 Washington street. His established record and his constantly enlarging number of patrons justify this statement. Mr. Davis conducts a general real estate commission business, and has a growing line of rents. While largely on the West Side, his tracts extend over the entire city. No more affable or honorable gentleman, the remark must be interpolated, adorns his profession in this city.

JOHN H. OHLERKING.

NO. 150 DEARBORN STREET.

Both as owner and agent this active real estate broker has been established in business here for several years, and is enjoying a trade that is larger each year.

SOME SUBURBS

LA GRANGE.

A CHARMING ENVIRON.

If Chicago is the Northwestern sun, La Grange is the moon, rising queenly on the West and glowing in reflected brillance and splendor. A journey to this moon, unlike Jules Verne's, takes only thirty minutes, while no fanciful æronaut's car but a luxurious Burlington and Quincy coach cleaves the yielding space. But metaphor misleads, for this charming environ, perched on the first ridge west of the metropolis, is like unto nothing but its own unapproachable self. What other suburb has such rolling, picturesque vistas? What other such "poems" in tasteful cottage and mansioned stone, such loves of lawns, such gems of churches? Where more flourishing and abundant shade-trees, evergreens, hedges, gardens? Where more solid driveways? Where such drainage, confessedly unsurpassed. Where more pure and crystalline water, the very substratum of the village being a gravel filter? What community of 2,000 souls more cultured and refined, more steadily growing, and instinct with good neighborship? What other suburb has finer quarries of building stone at its very door? About 100 new and fine houses were added to LaGrange the past season. The markets and schools are of highest grade. There are two depots in the village, while the railway terminus in town is that headquarters of accessibility, the Union Depot, Madison street bridge. Mr. F. D. Cossitt, as the original proprietor, still owns a considerable tract of the choicest property, though the demands from purchasers and the favorable prices and terms are rapidly multiplying the lords of the manor. With the integrity of a gentleman as his basal characteristic, and with a rare superstructure of the amenities that make agreeable and pleasant, as well as profitable, the dealings of man with man, the tribute is irrepressible that Mr. Cossitt is the customers' beau ideal. Formerly for many years Mr. Cossitt was engaged with marked success in the wholesale grocery business in this city, and his reputation and standing among merchants and business men were of the best. In the general wreck at the time of the great fire, when so many obligations were compromised and notes extended, Mr. Cossitt promptly paid dollar for dollar, though, believing in home industries, home insurance, placing his policies in Chicago, he lost all. Turning his attention to the development of his landed estate, the gentleman has devoted a fortune to the enrichment and beautifying of La Grange, and it is with natural pride he now witnesses its flood-tide of prosperity and popularity. Associated with him at the LaGrange headquarters, rooms 5 and 6, 85 Washington street, are his son, Mr. F. D. Cossitt, Jr., and Mr. C. W. Richmond, and they also are ever ready with plats, maps, and a courtesy and eloquence worthy their senior to forward the quest for model suburban homes.

MAPLEWOOD.

J. WHITNEY FARLIN, OWNER.

Back in 1838 the 160 acres now embracing this flourishing suburb on the Wisconsin Division of the Northwestern Railroad, only four miles from the Court House and fifteen minutes ride, were sold for $200—no, not apiece, but in the lump. One half was sold the same year for the same total—an advance of 100 per cent—and in 1869 the same property was bought for $53,000 by Messrs. Wing & Farlin, who named their straightway subdivided estate Maplewood, in anticipation of the luxuriant maples soon to rise in umbrageous groves echoing the plash of an artesian well that flows forth in quantities of 250 gallons of pure crystal water per minute. Since then sales have been rapid, and large numbers of houses built, and still the popular interest increases. And no wonder; for are not commutation tickets but 6½ cents, with street car fare to within four blocks only 5 cents? Is not the land high and the soil rich? Are there not the best of graded schools? Does not Humboldt boulevard, that golden clasp in the city's girdle of park and drive, pass through the center of the property? While, as to the population, do not the neat, often elegant houses, bespeak its thrifty and eligible character? Indeed, there is a public spirit worthy the situation and assured future of the place. Thus, lake water is about to be supplied, via Lake View, and a rousing mass meeting the other night inaugurated still further additions to the exceptional improvements already enjoyed. Here residences of frame are lawful, being outside the fire limits; here no city tax collector lurks; here a home may be secured on easy terms and long payments. Mr. J. Whitney Farlin, No. 85 Washington street, who is still the owner of a large part of Maplewood —replenished by new purchases as often as diminished—sells lots for from $300 to $700. About four hundred lots have been sold, and Mr. Farlin has just added to his tract about forty acres more which will be at once placed on the market. Besides his Maplewood property, this gentleman, one of our well-known and long established dealers, owns other extensive tracts, as for instance near McCormick's reaper works and in Hyde Park.

WESTERN SPRINGS.

MEDICINAL WATER—CHARMING HOMES.

As the title intimates, there is no need to go into Wisconsin to find another Waukesha with waters of refreshment and health; Chicago has them at her door in Western Springs. The coming health resort—and do not folks repair there already?—is but thirty minutes removed from the Burlington and Quincy depot in the heart of the city, a nearness to business that must more and more popularize and populate the suburb. The ground is rolling and elevated, and the residents the most substantial and pleasant of people. There are excellent school privileges, with churches that are well sustained. And when it is said that an atmosphere of welcome and high public morals is abroad, and that further, specially moderate terms are made by Mr. T. C. Hill, the agent, room 1, Lake Side Building, an additional prophesy is seen for a prosperous future of the suburb. Mr. Hill is making sales at figures that make a suburban home within the reach of all, and the coming year promises a quickened activity. Any one contemplating an out-of-town establishment, where health and nature wait on the resident, should pay a visit to Western Springs and his purpose will be confirmed.

MORGAN PARK—WASHINGTON HEIGHTS

ATTRACTIVE SUBURBS.

Uplifted, an island of woodland charm rising twelve miles south of the city from the treeless expanse of the prairie, lies this favorite suburb. For six miles the sylvan ridge extends, and who that has looked down from that eyrie on the outstretching panorama can soon forget it! A natural advantage so marked would of itself have endeared such a spot to Chicagoans whose business hours are level all day with monotonous low-lands, and very naturally at the evening hour, musical as vesper bell, come the homeward summons, "Come up higher!" But hard business, as well as hygiene and sentiment, has conspired to exalt this suburb. The Blue Island Land and Building Company, by their agents, Messrs. Hopkinson & Silva, No. 123 Dearborn street, have made easily accessible, through exceptionally favorable terms, these advantages of a semi-mountainous residence. By consequence few suburbs are so populous as well as popular as "The Heights," and the new influx of fortunates and the new upbuilding of handsome residences must continue steadily. Certainly more noble sites for a home than along Prospect avenue and similar driveways cannot well be imagined, and the coming year must, if possible, surpass the past in the activity of new settlement. As the seat of a flourishing military academy, with its educational companions of equally foremost rank—the Young Ladies' School and the Theological Seminary—Morgan Park has a reputation not confined to the West.

PENNOCK.

HEAVY MANUFACTURING.

This growing manufacturing suburb of Chicago, located five miles northwest of the Court House, in the town of Jefferson, can be reached by trains of the Chicago, Milwaukee and St Paul, both main line and Pacific branch, and also by two belt roads, one already in operation and the other in contemplation, its right of way already secured. These railroad facilities put the suburb in connection with every Chicago railroad and make it second to none in accessibility and desirability for manufacturing purposes. Fare by steam cars is only 5 cents, and, furthermore, the street cars will be extended to Pennock during next summer. The Miltimore Elastic Steel Car Wheel Company is now erecting at this point their immense factory, in which will be employed about 500 men the 1st of May. Other extensive works are now in operation, notably those of the Washburn-Moen manufactory of barbed wire. The immense factory which was originally built for locomotive works is now partly occupied for manufacturing purposes, and the unoccupied part will be utilized by May 1, also for manufacturing. Other manufactories will follow soon, and altogether thousands of people will be employed in this, Chicago's nearest manufacturing suburb. Arrangements will be made to supply the thriving town with lake water, and the streets leading to Pennock will be improved, putting it in easy driving communication with the city. This town, comprising 1,200 acres, has been purchased by the millionaire, Homer Pennock, of New York, through Dwight K. Tripp, Esq., of this city, who is managing the property as agent for Mr. Pennock along with the well-known and long-established real estate firm of E. S. Dreyer & Co., who have successfully handled many sub-divisions around the city, their transactions in this line extending over nineteen years.

There is no doubt that Pennock will be the site of the largest steel works in the entire country. Twenty-five brick houses will be commenced as soon as the weather permits, and trades-people have already engaged lots on which they will locate their shops and business places next spring. Lots can be secured in Pennock at from $300 upward, according to location, and are actviely in request, as the tide of settlement is rapidly advancing in this direction. There have been fully 400 houses built northwest of the city within the last two years, being out of the fire limits and beyond the reach of city taxes, and this drift is keeping up steadily toward Pennock. An interesting sight can be had by taking the Milwaukee and North avenue street cars to their present terminus and then by walking over to Pennock, the houses being so numerous as to seem like an extension of the city. It will be a pleasant walk, as sidewalks extend along North and Armitage avenues quite to the rising works, as multitudes of seekers after homes are now proving. To accommodate the growing demand a branch office for the sale of these popular lots will be opened Jan. 15 by E. S. Dreyer & Co. right on the ground opposite the depot. For the convenience and cheapness of building, bricks are made by the company in the immediate neighborhood, and in a certain part of the town only bricks will be used, but the rest can be improved in a manner to suit the taste of settlers. The land is high, dry, beautiful of location and with facilities for perfect drainage.

CUMMINGS.

RECENT BUT BOOMING.

The town of Cummings, named for the Hon. O. R. Cummings, of Brown, Howard & Co., formerly known as Irondale, between the Calumet River and Lake Calumet and immediately west of the Calumet Iron and Steel Company's plant, and really what might be properly called a portion of South Chicago, is the highest and dryest tract of land in that vicinity, and affords railroad facilities quite equal to any portion of South Chicago. It has the Pittsburg, Fort Wayne and Chicago Railroad, the Lake Shore and Michigan Southern Railroad, the Chicago, Rock Island and Pacific Railroad, the New York, Chicago and St. Louis Railroad (Nickel-plate), the Erie Railroad, the Louisville and New Albany Railroad, the Chicago and Western Indiana Railroad, the Chicago and Eastern Illinois Railroad, and the Belt Line Railway. There is no point outside of the city of Chicago in Cook County having so many railroad connections as this tract of land. The slip for the Calumet Iron and Steel Company is made from the river, extending west to Torrence avenue. At this point, 100 feet wide of the subdivision is held in reserve for a ship canal extending west from Torrence avenue across the subdivision nearly to Lake Calumet. Mr. Dwight F. Cameron, No. 220 First National Bank Building, who has the property in charge, has been making efforts to get a ship canal between Lake Calumet and Calumet River at this point, being the shortest distance between the two bodies of water. The effect of a canal at that point would not only afford a short outlet from Lake Calumet, but it would drain and redeem several thousand acres of land which is now low and unfit for occupation. Another great benefit arising from this canal would be that in the time of spring freshets it would afford a speedy outlet for the waters of Lake Calumet. At present the waters of that lake have to run south its full length to its mouth, and then run straight north—a distance of nearly six miles. Those who best understand the topography of the country regard the canal as an absolute necessity. With a canal through this tract of land, it would be difficult to point out a more favorable place for manufacturers, where all the railroad facilities above named are present in connection with water transportation to Lake Michigan. A real-estate operator not interested in the property, and whose opinion is entitled to consideration, recently remarked that it had the brightest future of any tract of land he knew anything about. The construction of the canal would seem an improvement of the near future. It would make of Lake Calumet, with slight dredging, a harbor of refuge for vessels, and when once completed would probably be accepted by the government as part of the navigable waters in that vicinity. There are different agents of different manufacturing establishments looking at this property with a view of locating there. In close proximity to this subdivision is the grand system of docks of the South Chicago Dock Company. Nearly $500,000 has been spent in making docks, and it will soon be teeming with lumber yards. The Calumet and Chicago Canal and Dock Company own a large tract immediately northwest of this land. The peculiar situation of Cummings, situated as it is about midway between the mouth of the Calumet River at South Chicago and the plant of the Rolling Stock Company at the Forks, makes it, as it were, right in the highway of improvements.

RAVENSWOOD.

A BEAUTIFUL VILLAGE.

The growth of no suburb on the immediate rim of the city has been more remarkable than this beautiful village just over the border to the northward. Houses have sprung up of tasteful architecture the past season, and in such numbers as to show that a pleasant suburban home in a choice neighborhood and among a people notably refined and hospitable is an ambition rapidly developing in this city. The resident alights at the pretty depot within twenty minutes of taking the Northwestern train—any one of scores a day—a measure of accessibility that must continue to make the fortune of Ravenswood in a rushing community where time is money and life. The public improvements correspond with the exceptionally neat residences, the building record of the year including two additional handsome churches. Here, too, is located the High School of Lake View. It is not strange with such advantages that Ravenswood is attracting the very best people as residents and that her borders are so rapidly extending. The only wonder is that landed interests, comprising some of the best in the village, may still be obtained at such low figures.

WOODLAWN.

BETWEEN TWO PARKS.

Only thirty-four minutes out on the Illinois Central, with its multiplied trains a day, Woodlawn is at least convenient, much more so than the majority of city homes. It is very pleasantly situated between two parks, or, rather, the two divisions of South Park, and when this splendid public improvement is finished according to plans already announced, the prettiest part of it will directly face Woodlawn. This is known as "Chicago's most promising suburb," and the claim would seem a just one, since it has more than doubled in population the past year, and the improvements are all first-class, the law of the attraction of similars explaining the many arrivals of young business men with the disposition and ability to build nice residences. Literary and social features are not the least characteristic of the suburb. A purchaser receives especially easy terms, as a rule simply the advance in down payment of a year's rent on the basis of town charges, and then all his payment is annual rent, and so he just about purchases a home with lovely surroundings for what he would waste away by living in the city. Mr. F. W. Green, of 42 Borden Block, Dearborn and Randolph streets, makes a specialty of Woodlawn property, and his numerous patrons attest both the honorable dealing of the courteous broker and the substantial bargains offered.

HAMMOND.

A YOUNG PITTSBURG.

This young manufacturing suburb, with a population of some 2,500, and situated on the Grand Calumet River at the State line, has just crowned its astonishing three years growth by a city charter. That the new dignity is authorized is shown by the array of chemical works, glove factory, steel spring works, sirup factory, vinegar works, slaughter-house, lumber and coal yards, all established and affording ample employment. In railroad facilities Hammond is Chicago's port of entry, as it were, for the iron ships of commerce. The long drawn fleets sail in over the Western Indiana, the Chicago and Atlantic, the Louisville, New Albany and Chicago, the Nickel-plate, the Michigan Central, and no less than three other railroads are contemplating entering Chicago at this point, multiplying still more the number of daily trains each way and the transfer facilities, round houses, and carshops. With transportation facilities by land, thus uniquely supplementing its dock privileges so convenient to the great lakes, Hammond has rightly won its favorite rank with manufacturers, and the time is hastening when the banks of the river for miles east of Hammond will bristle with the chimneys of the manufacturers. The low taxes will speed the day and so will the low prices at which all the available river frontage is being rapidly taken up by capitalists. Near by are rising the great works of the United States Rolling Stock Company, and there is assurance that other extensive enterprises comtemplate immediate settlement. Back from the river is the very eligible residence section. Mr. James N. Young, 97 Dearborn street, is intimately identified with the landed interests and success of the suburb.

CHICAGO LAWN.

NEAT HOUSES, LOTS FREE.

The past year this thriving suburb increased 50 per cent in the number of its inhabitants and its neat and tasteful residences. Chicago Lawn is two and a half miles from the city limits on the Chicago and Grand Trunk Road, and is not thirty minutes' ride from the down-town depot, a fact which stamps it as more accessible than large portions of the city. Fare is only 6 cents. The suburb is a nice clean place, its south-westerly situation exempting it from city currents of air. Its public school-house is a gem of architecture; there is a handsome station house, and the streets are excellently improved and sidewalked. The popular proprietor of the town, Mr. John F. Eberhart, Room 81, 161 LaSalle street, has long been identified with the landed and educational interests of the city, an experience he has utilized for the advancement of this charming suburb. The residents are Americans, and the amenities of literature and music are cultivated by societies which contribute not a little to good neighborship. So uniformly neat and tasteful are the houses that it is difficult to believe they range in cost from $5,000 down to as low as $1,200, and with a lot thrown in to boot. This gift of land is made to every one who puts up a fair house; to others the price of lots being $200.

FERNWOOD.

A BABY JUMBO.

Chicago's baby Jumbo would appear to be this large-limbed young suburb which first saw the light only last May. In a span of life numbered by months a score of neat houses have dotted the virgin plateau, and an American settlement of as desirable people as could be wished now overlooks Englewood, Grand Crossing, and Pullman, the latter only a mile and a half distant. Fernwood is eleven miles due south of the metropolis, and rejoices in three railroads—the Rock Island, the Panhandle, and the Eastern Illinois. Trains even more frequent than the many which now serve the village are to be put on, while commutation tickets cost only $5.50 a month or ten rides for $1.20. In other respects, too, the inducements to buy a home here are overwhelming. It takes but $100 paid down, and after that monthly installments, some as low as $15, in whole cost of a wide lot in charming and healthful surroundings, and with a gem of a house reaching only from $1,100 to $1,400. The Superintendent of Improvements is S. Montgomery Smith, while the humanitarian godfather and patron of these homes for the many is Mr. E. L. Gillette, Fernwood's headquarters being room 9, 142 Dearborn street. A call there will meet the most favorable anticipations, while a run down to Fernwood itself will discover another "Auburn, loveliest village of the plain." A street car company has been organized to run to Pullman and South Chicago, and Fernwood must grow more and more in favor and convenience as a desirable residence.

KENSINGTON.

HOMES ON LIBERAL TERMS.

This town is favorably located at the junction of three railroads, and adjoins Pullman on two sides. The business and resident population find liberal and constant support from the Pullman Car Works and Foundry, and the other extensive industries that surround the town, while the general health of the people is universally good. C. B. Saw yer, 127 Dearborn street, Chicago, is largely interested in property here, which is offered upon liberal terms.

AN IMPORTANT DISCOVERY.

A NEW FUEL.

A company with a capital of $1,000,000 has recently been incorporated for the purpose of working and developing an invention which will doubtless prove to be among the most important of any brought out in this inventive age. Reference is made to the process of vaporizing crude petroleum and using the resulting vapor as a fuel, after the method as discovered by Mr. O. D. Orvis. It has already been demonstrated to be of far greater value than was ever hoped for or expected of by the inventor. This discovery of Mr. Orvis is something new in practical science, and, from the practical uses to which it has already been put, certainly seems destined to create a revolution in the use of fuel for steam purposes, from the fact that a superior quality of heat is produced at a reduced cost. It has been proven in addition that it produces the purest and most intense heat known, as well. From these facts it can be readily seen that the process must be invaluable for all kinds of smelting and puddling furnaces, as a much better quality of iron is produced than can possibly be made by the old process. Glass manufacturers will be able to make a superior quality of their product, equal too, if not superior, to that heretofore so largely imported from foreign countries. This process of Mr. Orvis' has the great merit of simplicity, and can be easily applied to locomotives, tugs, steamships, and stationary boiler furnaces of every description, and while in operation the chimney is absolutely smokeless.

There seems to be no limit to the variety of industries to which this invention can be applied, and with great, lasting benefit. The iron and glass industries, however, will doubtless receive the greatest financial benefit. That which the general public are most interested in lies in the fact that by this new process of generating steam the smoke problem is solved. As one of our leading contemporaries says in a recent issue: "When this new company is able to free Chicago from the pall of smoke which hangs over the city, and our railroads run smokeless engines free from soot, cinders, and noxious gases, then humanity will be benefited, and the Orvis Smokeless Hydro-carbon Furnace Company will be styled as public benefactors."

CHAPTER XVI

FOR SPECULATORS.

METROPOLITAN GRAIN AND STOCK EXCHANGE.

The speculative business of Chicago, which can hardly be computed by figures, is divided, rather through the result of caprice than upon any business principle which can be defined, between the operators on the regular Board of Trade, the Open Board, and the exchanges which hire the so-called "Board of Trade alley." These "exchanges" are not smiled upon as a rule by the Board of Trade gentlemen, perhaps because the great corporation which has its headquarters in the Chamber of Commerce is rather anxious to entirely control all the vast volume of traffic in grain and provisions, either for present or future delivery, which flows into this wonderful mart, and possibly because modern speculation does not fittingly reverence the great corporation, and propose to seek a market wherein it can be most advantageously found.

The Metropolitan Exchange claims to be able to fill whatever bill the speculatively inclined may call for at a less than a reasonable charge, and with a positive assurance, backed by a legal guarantee, that they will perform what they promise. Through their good offices people can readily avail themselves of the wonderful opportunities which Chicago offers for money-making by speculation, without any unpleasant forebodings that good money is to be sent in pursuit of bad, after the former has gone hopelessly astray.

The Metropolitan Exchange, the subject of this brief notice—and a trade review notice in a leading Chicago daily must of necessity be brief—was incorporated and organized under the strict statutes of the State of Illinois, and can boast of an entirely legal existence. It possesses a paid-up capital of $100,000 and an unblemished financial reputation. That it is really above reproach is evidenced by the fact that the First National Bank of Chicago, Preston & Co., bankers, of Detroit, Mich., and the Chatham Street National Bank of New York City, all permit their names to appear upon the list of references which is appended to its announcements. This Exchange is the Chicago trading place for the million, the bazar where the commodities of a district of country larger than some empires which have cut a figure in history are daily vended for the benefit of the general public, not for a favored few.

It is not quite easy to explain how this largest concern of the kind in Chicago, probably in the world, can offer inducements to customers which the regular or the Open Boards of Trade would find it difficult, if not impossible to duplicate, nor could an explanation be given in the space now at the writer's disposal. Some suggestions can, however, be made which must pass for what they are worth. In the first place, a membership on the regular, the Open, or the Call Boards of Chicago is an expensive luxury without which a person cannot do business, except through a broker in connection with those corporations. The operator who has to pay a high figure for the privilege of dealing can hardly (other things being equal) compete with the man who, with the best or very nearly the best facilities for speculative dealing at his disposal, has nothing or next to nothing to pay for the right to exercise his skill, ability, and knowledge of the market for the benefit of himself or his customers. It must not be supposed because these comparisons and suggestions are made that there is any disposition on the part of the writer to underrate the importance of the great mercantile organizations of Chicago, to whose wisdom, liberality, and enterprise the Garden City owes such an enormous debt, but it is nevertheless true that the Board of Trade and its auxiliaries, while possessed of almost boundless resources and a kind of knowledge which can be coined into current money, does not, because it cannot from the nature of things afford to the million an opportunity to do pro rata what those who have millions are continually doing, and accumulating other millions by their transactions. The Metropolitan Exchange makes an especial point of possessing all needful business facilities for operating in grain, seeds, and provisions, and stocks in large and small quantities. It has direct telegraphic communication with all the leading business centers, and the principles upon which it trades, and the option deals, which form such a prominent feature of its business, are substantially the same as those with which any regular Board of Trade speculator is familiar. There is this important modification, however, of Board of Trade rules at the Metropolitan Exchange: The trader at the latter place is only responsible for the amount of margin hazarded on each deal, and those who desire to limit their losses to a certain sum will in all instances be guaranteed against any loss in excess of that amount. This distinctive characteristic manner of trading on the Exchange deprives speculative business of its most objectionable and dangerous element. The "Metropolitan" is especially desirous of securing in every city, village, hamlet, and farm which contribute but a drop of the life-blood of trade to Chicago—the commercial heart of the civilized world—a live man to act as broker for his benefit and its own. For the benefit of this class it has lately made the following suggestions and statements in a circular letter:

You will please note our references herewith. With our capital and standing, direct telegraphic communication from our office to all points, enabling us to give immediate and quick replies to all messages, and by giving each and all orders our personal attention, our facilities for handling out-of-town orders cannot be equaled.

The principle of trading and the options dealt in are the same as on the regular Board of Trade, with the exception that the trader is only liable for the amount of margin placed on each deal. Those who desire to limit their losses to a certain amount are guaranteed against further loss by us, and are not subject to the sweeping changes of a wild or cornered market, with the liability of having their commission merchants draw on them for an amount that they had supposed there was no possibility of losing. We more especially call the attention of brokers sending orders to the regular board on commission or salary to our system; to those we offer superior advantages. We will allow much better terms, with no liability to them, than any other houses. Please note and write to our references.

THE PUBLIC GRAIN AND STOCK EXCHANGE

was organized under the laws of the State of Illinois in the year 1880, for the purpose of affording the best and most reliable facilities for the purchase and sale of grain, provisions, and stocks for immediate or future delivery.

Chicago has been known for years as the sepculative center of the world. It is the vast drawing depot into which is gathered the grain and meat products of the great American Northwest, and from hence these two essentials of living are distributed, not only to the cities of this continent but to the leading capitals of Europe also.

The advantage which this Exchange offers for trading, either in large or small quantities, may be briefly enumerated as follows:

It has special wires from its office to all parts of the country, both East and West, and are connected with first-class correspondents in all large cities, who have formerly been doing business through or with the Board of Trade, and who now represent the Public Grain and Stock Exchange, recognizing their superior facilities for doing business.

With these correspondents a dealer can buy or sell as low as 1,000 bushels of grain, fifty barrels of pork, fifty tierces of lard, and twenty-five shares of stock, or larger quantities if desired, on margins as low as 1 cent a bushel on grain, 25 cents a barrel on pork, 8 cents a tierce on lard, and $1 per share on stocks, and he is only responsible for the amount of money which he may order placed upon a trade, and cannot lose beyond that amount, and while the market goes his way his profits are unlimited. He can do his business with the Public Grain and Stock Exchange at the same commission and with no expense for telegraphing, or, in other words, can trade just the same as though he was on the Board of Trade in person. If he places his business with a broker on the Board of Trade, in the first place he will be obliged to put up five cents a bushel on grain, and the same proportion on provisions and stocks, and will be liable for additional margins wherever the market goes. He also cannot purchase less than 5,000 bushels of grain, or 250 packages of pork, that being the smallest quantities dealt in on the board.

The customer is always able to get more satisfactory prices in trading with this Exchange, for the reason that the order is executed the moment it is received in our office, providing it is not limited, and then it is filled providing the price is reached.

A NOTABLE PIONEER HOUSE.

The oldest ship-chandlery house in Chicago and the one best known to the marine service of our great lakes was founded in 1840 by George A. Robb, was succeeded in 1845 by Payson & Robb, and then in 1850 by Hubbard & Robb. George A. Robb died in 1857 in Havana, Cuba, and the name of the firm was changed to Gilbert Hubbard & Co., continuing under that name twenty-five years. Gilbert Hubbard died in May, 1881. Jan. 1, 1882, the firm was changed to its present name of George B. Carpenter & Co. For a whole generation it has been a representative house, distinguished for enterprise, for integrity, for financial responsibility, and for doing its full share in building up Chicago and in promoting the welfare of its citizens.

GEORGE B. CARPENTER & CO.,

as successors to Gilbert Hubbard & Co., are at present the largest house, and are enjoying a larger business in their line than any other house in this market. Their stock includes complete lines of cordage, cotton duck, tackle-blocks, twines of all kinds for any and all uses, among which may be especially mentioned twines and cords for horse-nets and hammocks, for grain-binding harvesters, gilling and seine twines for fishermen's use, etc.; asbestos materials of all kinds, asbestos paints, and asbestos roofings, packings, cotton waste, lubricating oils, and a general line of mill and railway supplies. In manufactured goods they deal extensively in tents wagon-covers, awnings, and anything that can be made of, or furnished with, cotton duck. As buyers from, and selling agents for, the manufacturers direct in their several lines, this firm are in a position to make prices at all times in competition with the lowest. Illustrated catalogues and price-lists are mailed free upon application.

THE POPULAR NEW PEORIA HOUSE.

Travelers visiting the "Second City" will find it decidedly to their advantage to make their headquarters at the popular new Peoria House, upon which $30,000 has recently been expended in improvements. This is one of the best managed hotels in the West, and one that charges reasonable rates. All the modern improvements for the comfort and convenience of guests are employed, and no hostelry in Peoria affords better facilities for reaching all parts of the city—being located just opposite the Court House, and on the street railway line that leads to all the large manufacturing institutions. The tables are as well supplied as the best Chicago hotels, and in other respects the new Peoria Hotel equals its most pretentious rivals in the great city on the lake. Messrs. J. S. Clarke & Son, the proprietors, are veterans in the business, and personally look after their patrons, with whom the Peoria House is always well filled.

www.ingramcontent.com/pod-product-compliance
Lightning Source LLC
Chambersburg PA
CBHW032226230426
43666CB00033B/1614
* 9 7 8 3 7 4 4 7 2 4 0 4 3 *